MONASTIC WISDOM SERIES: NUMBER FORTY-THREE

Thomas Merton

Medieval Cistercian History
Initiation into the Monastic Tradition 9

Edited with an Introduction by
Patrick F. O'Connell

Preface by
William R. Grimes

MONASTIC WISDOM SERIES

Marsha Dutton, Executive Editor

Advisory Board

Michael Casey, ocso   Terrence Kardong, osb
Lawrence S. Cunningham   Kathleen Norris
Patrick Hart, ocso   Miriam Pollard, ocso
Robert Heller   Bonnie Thurston

INITIATION INTO THE MONASTIC TRADITION SERIES

BY

THOMAS MERTON

Cassian and the Fathers:
Initiation into the Monastic Tradition (MW 1)

Pre-Benedictine Monasticism:
Initiation into the Monastic Tradition 2 (MW 9)

An Introduction to Christian Mysticism:
Initiation into the Monastic Tradition 3 (MW 13)

The Rule of St. Benedict:
Initiation into the Monastic Tradition 4 (MW 19)

Monastic Observances:
Initiation into the Monastic Tradition 5 (MW 25)

The Life of the Vows:
Initiation into the Monastic Tradition 6 (MW 30)

Charter, Customs, and Constitutions of the Cistercians:
Initiation into the Monastic Tradition 7 (MW 41)

The Cistercian Fathers and Their Monastic Theology:
Initiation into the Monastic Tradition 8 (MW 42)

MONASTIC WISDOM SERIES: NUMBER FORTY-THREE

Medieval Cistercian History
Initiation into the Monastic Tradition 9

by
Thomas Merton

Edited with an Introduction by
Patrick F. O'Connell

Preface by
William R. Grimes

Cistercian Publications
www.cistercianpublications.org

LITURGICAL PRESS
Collegeville, Minnesota
www.litpress.org

A Cistercian Publications title published by Liturgical Press

Cistercian Publications
Editorial Offices
161 Grosvenor Street
Athens, Ohio 45701
www.cistercianpublications.org

© 2019 by Merton Legacy Trust. All rights reserved. No part of this book may be used or reproduced in any manner whatsoever, except brief quotations in reviews, without written permission of Liturgical Press, Saint John's Abbey, PO Box 7500, Collegeville, MN 56321-7500. Printed in the United States of America.

Library of Congress Cataloging-in-Publication Data

Names: Merton, Thomas, 1915-1968, author.
Title: Medieval Cistercian history : initiation into the monastic tradition 9 / by Thomas Merton ; edited with an introduction by Patrick F. O'Connell ; preface by William R. Grimes.
Description: Collegeville : Liturgical Press, 2019. | Series: Monastic wisdom series ; no. 43.
Identifiers: LCCN 2018040641 (print) | LCCN 2018051169 (ebook) | ISBN 9780879074821 (eBook) | ISBN 9780879070434 (pbk.)
Subjects: LCSH: Cistercians—History—To 1500.
Classification: LCC BX3406.3 (ebook) | LCC BX3406.3 .M47 2019 (print) | DDC 271/.12—dc23
LC record available at https://lccn.loc.gov/2018040641

CONTENTS

Preface   vii

Introduction   xi

1. Cistercian History   1

2. The Cistercian Order from the Death of Saint Bernard to the Reform of Benedict XII (1153–1335)   139

Appendix A: Textual Notes   253

Appendix B: Table of Correspondences   259

Appendix C: For Further Reading   261

Index   263

Corrigenda for Volume 8   309

In grateful memory
of
Patrick Hart, OCSO
(1925–2019)
final secretary of Thomas Merton
founding editor of the Monastic Wisdom Series
mentor, guide and friend
to Merton scholars and readers
throughout the world
for the past half-century.

PREFACE

I was a novice at the Cistercian Monastery of Our Lady of Gethsemani from 1962 to 1964, and Thomas Merton was my novice master. I was present for the conferences published in this book, which were given to me and my fellow novices by Merton, or Father Louis, as we knew him. Though not a monastic historian, scholar or monk, I have a particular perspective on these conferences that I would like to share.

As I read these conference notes (and Dr. O'Connell's excellent Introduction) I began to recall actually being in the conference room and listening to Fr. Louis as he animatedly and logically went over the details of the early monastic life in England and then the wonderful and interesting medieval Cistercian history. In a Preface written for a previous volume in this series, Sidney H. Griffith asked, "One wonders if Gethsemani's novices in Merton's day had any inkling of the pioneering character of the journey to the early sources of the monastic heritage which their novice master provided for them."[1] My response to Griffith would be yes and no.

Yes, because we were aware that Fr. Louis was an incredible teacher, intellect, mystic, writer, poet, spiritual director, etc., with the most eclectic knowledge base of anyone that we had ever encountered. He was extraordinarily affable and pleasantly

---

1. Sidney H. Griffith, "Preface," in Thomas Merton, *Pre-Benedictine Monasticism: Initiation into the Monastic Tradition 2*, ed. Patrick F. O'Connell, Monastic Wisdom [MW] 9 (Kalamazoo, MI: Cistercian Publications, 2006), x.

gregarious and had a superlative sense of humor. He was a friend, spiritual guide, leader and mentor.

No, because in my opinion none of the novices had any concept of how deeply and ontologically Fr. Louis understood and was able to explain to us the many complex issues that constituted the early years of monasticism in general and Cistercian monasticism in particular. Nor were we aware at that time how lucky and blessed we were to be his students and members of this fantastic "school of charity."[2]

As I read the present material, many things that Merton said came back to me, and in some ways I felt as though I was sitting in that conference room and was enchanted by his logical method of explaining the various aspects of monastic life. I could see him leaning forward in his chair holding onto his small table while he told a story or went off on a tangent and had us totally engrossed in what would otherwise be a boring history lesson (or sometimes telling us a joke or making fun of an old monastic name or silly defunct rule).

I can still remember him relating the origins of Cîteaux and the founders who came from the Abbey of Molesme to establish a monastic life that was more in compliance with the original Rule of Saint Benedict. This explanation, of course, led into the many stories about the differences between the "black monks" (Benedictines) and the "white monks" (Cistercians). Fr. Louis was very clear about the differences, citing Cluny as an example of the Benedictine life lived with a certain avoidance of or misinterpretation of the Rule.

I remember him talking about the arrival of Saint Bernard with about thirty friends and relatives, a coming that may have saved the Order and certainly added new life and sanctity to the white monks. Bernard himself became a great force in the renewal

---

2. For this characteristically Cistercian term, see Thomas Merton, *The Cistercian Fathers and Their Monastic Theology: Initiation into the Monastic Tradition* 8, ed. Patrick F. O'Connell, MW 42 (Collegeville, MN: Cistercian Publications, 2016), 68 n. 192.

of the monastic life and was an intellect, great writer and great leader. He was elected abbot of Clairvaux and founded many other monasteries.

I recall when Fr. Louis spoke about the theology of Abelard[3] and his at times possibly heretical views. But what I remember most is his story about Abelard and Heloise.[4] This story prompted me to read the book by Étienne Gilson,[5] which was in the novitiate library. His stories about the irregularities committed by some of the early white monks were more than just accounts; he turned them into hilarious stories of antics and peccadilloes and made us understand that even as monks certainly seeking the heights of the spiritual life, they (and we) were also human and made errors.

When I started to write this preface, my question was whether or not I could see the relevance of these conferences for non-monastics in today's world. And my answer is a resounding YES. The Christian life is a journey into the very heart and essence of Jesus. We are called to become one with him and in concert with him to love and cherish all those that we come in contact with. We are called to realize the oneness that we have with all people (past, present and to come), as Merton himself stated: "[W]e are already one. But we imagine that we are not. And what we have to recover is our original unity. What we have to be is what we are."[6]

As Christians we need to look back at those who preceded us in whatever vocation they found themselves and ask ourselves what they did wrong and what they did right. How and where

---

3. For Merton's discussion of Abelard, see *Cistercian Fathers and Their Monastic Theology*, xc–xciii, 166–96.

4. For Merton's discussion of Abelard and Heloise, see *Cistercian Fathers and Their Monastic Theology*, 166–72, 184–86.

5. Étienne Gilson, *Héloise and Abélard*, trans. L. K. Shook (London: Hollis & Carter, 1953).

6. Thomas Merton, *The Asian Journal*, ed. Naomi Burton Stone, Br. Patrick Hart and James Laughlin (New York: New Directions, 1973), 308.

did they find God in their lives? How did the life and words of Jesus affect them, and how did they share his life and his goodness and mercy with others?

William R. Grimes
(Brother Alcuin)

INTRODUCTION

In the latter part of 1962, as part of his duties as master of novices at the Abbey of Gethsemani,[1] Thomas Merton was presenting concurrently the two sets of conferences on the early history of the Cistercian Order included in the present volume. On Fridays from September 7 through December 21 he gave fourteen classes to the novices on what was simply called "Cistercian History," which included a lengthy preliminary overview of European monasticism from the time of Saint Benedict in the sixth century until the foundation of the Abbey of Cîteaux in 1098, followed by detailed consideration of the first three abbots of the "New Monastery," as Cîteaux was originally called, and of some of the key documents of the early period of its history; the written text of this material concludes with at least one and possibly a number of other appendices on related topics. On Sunday afternoons between October 21 and December 9, eight conferences were presented under the more precise title of "The Cistercian Order from the Death of St. Bernard to the Reform of Benedict XII (1153–1335)." These talks, at close to an hour in length, twice as long as the weekday classes, were open to the

---

1. In specifying the responsibilities of the master of novices for instructing those under his care, the official *Usages* of the Cistercian Order in effect during Merton's tenure in this position (1955–1965) required that along with explaining the various documents and customs that regulate life in a Trappist monastery, "he also teaches the history of our Order" (*Regulations of the Order of Cistercians of the Strict Observance Published by the General Chapter of 1926* [Dublin: M. H. Gill & Sons, 1927], 258 [#545]).

xi

entire Gethsemani community, though only the novices were required to attend. They covered the period when the astounding success of the Order during its "Golden Age" had made it the most influential religious group in Europe before the rise of the mendicants in the early thirteenth century but also gave rise to various problems and conflicts within the Order itself and with political, economic, ecclesial and intellectual currents in the broader society, leading to efforts at renewal and reform that, as Merton tried to show, had rather mixed results and to some extent changed the focus and direction of both the institutional and spiritual dimensions of medieval Cistercianism.[2]

The reasons for this rather unusual procedure of presenting two series of conferences on successive periods of Cistercian history simultaneously rather than sequentially cannot be definitively ascertained, as Merton evidently never explained his rationale, but there are certain pieces of evidence available that provide at least a plausible hypothesis. In the initial conference for each sequence,[3] Merton mentions that he had begun a similar series the previous year but had dropped it because, as he told the novices at the first Friday class, it was "scandalizing" the postulants, those prospective candidates newly arrived at the abbey. Honest history, Merton emphasized, cannot simply be an inspiring, idealized account of heroic and holy predecessors

---

2. The intervening period is basically covered by the set of conferences focused on the life and work of Saint Bernard: Thomas Merton, *The Cistercian Fathers and Their Monastic Theology: Initiation into the Monastic Tradition* 8, ed. Patrick F. O'Connell, Monastic Wisdom [MW], vol. 42 (Collegeville, MN: Cistercian Publications, 2016).

3. These comments are found not in the written texts but in the recordings of Merton's conference presentations, which began to be taped in late April 1962; for details concerning the beginning of the recording of the conferences, so that the brothers could listen to them while at work in the abbey kitchen, see Victor A. Kramer's interviews with Matthew Kelty, OCSO, "Looking Back to Merton: Memories and Impressions," *The Merton Annual* 1 (1988): 69–70; and with Flavian Burns, OCSO, "Merton's Contributions as Teacher, Writer and Community Member," *The Merton Annual* 3 (1990): 83.

meeting all challenges with admirable and successful fidelity, but must take into account failures as well as successes, weakness as well as strength, missteps and confusion as well as progress and clarity.

In a journal entry for June 10, 1961, Merton had written, "Cistercian history: a new dimension there too. I am studying the 13th–14th centuries, about which I thought I knew at least a little and literally knew nothing. I assume I have knowledge I do not have. This for novitiate conferences on the decline of the Order."[4] It is clear, then, that at least part if not all of the previous year's history material was focused on the period following the Golden Age of the twelfth century, and that this was presumably what the newly arrived recruits would have found somewhat disturbing and what led to Merton's decision to cut the series short. When returning to this period a year later, he decided that it was more appropriate, and more useful, to make this material available to an audience that would include more experienced monks, who presumably also "knew nothing"—or relatively little—about this period. In the first of the Sunday presentations he explicitly states that this set of conferences is intended "for the professed," adding that he was doing the "rise of the Order" with the novices. Of course the novices were present at these talks as well and might still find some of the story disconcerting, but probably less so in an environment where they could see that their more experienced confreres were taking the less-than-edifying elements of the Order's early struggles and conflicts in stride.

But these considerations still do not explain why the two history courses were being given at the same time. The other relevant aspect of the situation is the fact that a significant change in the training of new members of the Order was about to take place at Gethsemani and other Cistercian monasteries. On September 21, 1962, Merton writes in his journal, "The General Chapter

---

4. Thomas Merton, *Turning Toward the World: The Pivotal Years. Journals, vol. 4: 1960–1963*, ed. Victor A. Kramer (San Francisco: HarperCollins, 1996), 125.

has taken steps to unite the brothers and the choir monks in one canonically homogeneous group—though the brothers will continue to have a different schedule and a somewhat different life. But there is to be one novitiate, and one formation. I do not know what this will involve."[5] On October 7 he notes that some of the less significant changes mandated by the recent General Chapter of the Order have now been implemented, but then adds, "The really big change, the merger of the brothers and the choir, will probably not be for another six or eight months. . . . One novitiate for choir and brothers may be a difficult thing to handle. There is no indication I will necessarily be the one to handle it."[6] But less than a week later, on October 13, he writes in the journal, "It is possible that the two novitiates may merge in January,"[7] and while he does not mention it here, the "indication" must have quickly become clear that he would indeed be the novice master of the combined novitiate, which was in fact instituted in January 1963.[8]

It is perhaps not coincidental, then, that the first of the Sunday history conferences was given a week later, on October 21. Merton may well have decided to make sure that he had completed all discussion of this rather controversial period of Cistercian history before the advent of the lay brother novices, and that the most expeditious way of accomplishing this goal was to use

   5. *Turning Toward the World*, 248.
   6. *Turning Toward the World*, 253–54.
   7. *Turning Toward the World*, 256.
   8. The other revision to the training process taking place simultaneously, the beginning of a new monastic formation program in which newly professed monks in simple vows continued their studies in monastic theology and spirituality rather than moving immediately to classes preparing them for priestly ordination, as had previously been the case, does not seem to have had any relevance to the issue of the timing of these history courses. For a detailed overview of these changes in the formation process, see the Introduction to Thomas Merton, *Pre-Benedictine Monasticism: Initiation into the Monastic Tradition* 2, ed. Patrick F. O'Connell, MW 9 (Kalamazoo, MI: Cistercian Publications, 2006), xi–xvi.

the longer Sunday conference periods to cover this material. In fact, on November 5 he was already noting in his journal that "I hope to finish conferences on Cistercian history (the Sunday ones) by the end of November"[9]—in fact he needed the first two Sundays of December to complete this set,[10] but by the end of 1962 he had ended both this and the Friday course on the earlier period of Cistercian history (before he had actually discussed all the material he had prepared, as will be seen below) and was ready to begin the new year with his new, enlarged group focused on fresh new topics in monastic and Cistercian history and spirituality.[11] While it is impossible to be sure to what extent, if any, this factor was directly responsible for Merton's decision to shuttle forward and backward in history between Fridays and Sundays for some eight weeks in late 1962, awareness of this imminent change in the formation process suggests at least a plausible explanation for what otherwise might seem to be a rather peculiar, if not inexplicable, arrangement.

* * * * * * *

The copy text for the material on the rise of the Order—the Friday conferences—on which the first part of the present edition is based consists of a separate title page with the heading "CISTERCIAN HISTORY" in two lines and the identification "FR LOUIS" made by an india-rubber-eraser ink-stamp carved

---

9. *Turning Toward the World*, 263.

10. On December 8 he writes in his journal, "In the evening finished the Cistercian History conferences" (*Turning Toward the World*, 271), presumably a reference to writing rather than delivering the final conference, since that day was a Saturday, but since it was a feast day (the Immaculate Conception) it is possible that he was following the Sunday schedule and did indeed give this final conference on December 8.

11. Friday classes would be devoted to the life and work of Saint Bernard and Sunday sessions to conferences on Pre-Benedictine, largely eastern Christian, monasticism. For this material see *Cistercian Fathers and Their Monastic Theology* and *Pre-Benedictine Monasticism*, respectively.

by a former postulant two years before,[12] followed by thirty-four pages of the conference text proper, then a separate page reading "Appendix—to Cistercian History" followed by three pages headed "Appendix—Historians in the Twelfth Century" and eighteen more pages discussing eight different topics in early Cistercian history. This manuscript has a number of anomalous characteristics. First of all, this is the sole witness to the text of this material. For most of the novitiate conferences, Merton's own personal notes, which he himself had produced and which he had in front of him as he taught, were copied onto stencils by novice typists during the course of the conferences, then reproduced and distributed to the students sometime close to the end of the sequence.[13] This is the only set of full conference notes for which only Merton's own copy but not a multigraphed reproduction exists; it is safe to assume that none was made for this material.[14]

---

12. See *Turning Toward the World*, 25 [8/5/1960].

13. Merton did distribute to the novices at this time a completely different, forty-six-page "Spirit Master" reproduction of a set of notes entitled "History of the Cistercian Order," focused on the writings of the great Cistercian Fathers of the twelfth and early thirteenth centuries. It is evident from his references to "recent" publications dating from 1951 and 1952 (23, 24, 32, 33), with no sources subsequent to that date (in particular no reference to the May 1953 Encyclical of Pius XII on Saint Bernard, *Doctor Mellifluus*, though advice from Pius XI to young religious to read Bernard's sermons is mentioned [9]), that these notes must have been originally prepared for a class during the period (1951–1955) when Merton was master of students, probably in late 1952 or early 1953; they are therefore not included in the present series of volumes of conferences presented by Merton while he was master of novices (1955–1965).

14. There are two long series of conferences, one on the Church Fathers from April through December 1962 and the other on art and poetry from 1964–1965, as well as some shorter sets such as those on monastic spirituality and on the brief treatise *The Ways to God* attributed to Saint Thomas Aquinas, both from early 1963, for which neither a multigraphed copy nor Merton's own manuscript is known to exist; their content is available only in the form of the live recordings of the actual conferences themselves.

Another unusual aspect of these notes is that the pages are completely handwritten, whereas typically Merton's personal copies of his lectures are largely typed, with frequent insertions by hand, usually in the margins or elsewhere on the page, or on the back of the previous page, occasionally including the addition of a page or two that is completely handwritten. Also, the pages are not consecutively numbered, as is generally Merton's standard practice for such material, and in fact the material consists mainly of discrete single pages of written text—in only three instances are there multi-page segments, consisting of groups of three, two, and two pages respectively.[15] Never is a new section begun other than at the top of a new page.

Occasionally successive pages overlap somewhat in content, but these are usually based on different sources. This arrangement suggests that the text was assembled by gathering together notes written, to some extent at least, at different times, a supposition that is supported by the fact that in two instances, the brief notes Merton frequently wrote to himself as reminders of preliminary announcements to be made before the beginning of a conference mention Lenten reading,[16] obviously not intended for the fall of 1962, so that at least these pages had been used previously at another time. Likewise a notation on a page devoted to the *Instituta Generalis Capituli*, the second part of the early Cistercian *Consuetudines* or Customary, reads, "*To follow Carta Caritatis*" (82); while there is extensive material in this series on the *Carta Caritatis*, the *Charter of Charity* that outlines the early institutional organization of the Order, the page on the *Instituta* is not in fact found directly after the *Carta* section but at the very

---

15. The discussion of specific provisions of the *Regularis Concordia* (10–19), the summary of Dom Symons' article on English monastic origins that immediately follows (19–21), and the consideration of the spirituality of the *Exordium Cistercii* (68–73).

16. The first reference is opposite the material on the spirit of Cluny (24); the second is on the reverse side of the page with material on John of Fécamp (33).

end of the notes proper,[17] preceding the Appendix. It seems more likely that it was originally associated with an earlier eight-page set of notes on the *Carta*, also completely handwritten, along with a much longer, typed discussion of the *Ecclesiastica Officia*, the first section of the *Consuetudines*,[18] and had been shifted to this set of conferences at a later time.[19]

It is not completely clear whether Merton intended the additional eighteen pages of notes following the three-page "Appendix to Cistercian History" to be considered as subsequent sections of the appendix. The likelihood is that he did not—it is not even certain that he himself had inserted this material into this file—but as they are connected to a greater or lesser extent with the main texts of one or the other set of conferences they have been included in the present volume as well.[20]

---

17. In this edition the material on the *Instituta* has been shifted to precede rather than follow the page on the *Usus Conversorum*, the laybrothers' customary, in order to correspond to the order found in the *Consuetudines*, the original source of both texts.

18. The edited text of this material is found in Thomas Merton, *Charter, Customs, and Constitutions of the Cistercians: Initiation into the Monastic Tradition* 7, ed. Patrick F. O'Connell, MW 41 (Collegeville, MN: Cistercian Publications, 2015), 1–14, 15–56.

19. A similar note, which reads "HISTORY OF THE ORDER—(to follow Carta Caritatis and Consuetudines)" is typed at the top of "The Life, Works and Doctrine of Saint Bernard," the first version of Merton's conferences on Saint Bernard (see *Cistercian Fathers and Their Monastic Theology*, liii).

20. This matter is further complicated by the fact that the folders containing this material, in the archives of the Thomas Merton Center at Bellarmine University, Louisville, KY, also include numerous additional pages of notes on a variety of non-Cistercian, in fact non-monastic, topics, such as Gregory of Nyssa, Julian of Norwich, John the Baptist, etc. It is uncertain whether this material was grouped together by Merton himself or subsequently by an archivist at the Center. One might initially suppose that the latter would be more likely to have assembled this miscellany, but on reflection there seems to be no reason why such disparate material would be found in a file labeled "Cistercian History" unless it was there already when Merton's papers were transferred to the Merton Center after his death.

Introduction xix

All these details might seem to suggest a lack of a tightly organized structure to this series of conferences, and such a supposition would not be completely inaccurate. But it should not be construed as evidence of carelessness or a lack of careful and detailed research on Merton's part, or as detracting from his purpose of providing for his novices a solid, reliable acquaintance with the circumstances, protagonists and central documents of the foundational period of the Cistercian Order. Merton did not claim to be an original historian, as he himself reminds his listeners in the opening conference of the series, but he was a conscientious investigator of whatever topic he was teaching, and his bilingualism gave him ready access to the Francophone conversation on Cistercian origins that was much more developed and vibrant than the relatively sparse scholarship on the subject available in English at the time, so that his students were exposed to current issues and questions to a greater extent than many longtime members of the Order. At the same time, a comparison of written text and oral presentation makes clear that the novice master did not overwhelm his charges with more information and interpretation than they could easily handle. His own extensive reading and research provided a solid resource from which he was able to draw in an appropriate way for an audience encountering this material for the first time. The somewhat casual assemblage of material, some of it with a rather tenuous connection to his main topic, might not be satisfactory for a text intended for the general audience of his published books but could still

---

Presumably at some point he had simply added them to this file, evidently kept in some form of three-hole binder, as a convenient place to store them, not much concerned that they really didn't belong there. This may well be how the "extra" pages of the Cistercian historical material also found their way, more appropriately, into this file, all of it directly following the "actual" appendix and preceding the rest of the material. Presently the material is kept in two file folders, the first containing all the Cistercian material except the final six pages on Cistercian Easter Sermons, which precede the miscellaneous material in the second folder.

be quite suitable for the purpose of acquainting his novices with key aspects of their monastic heritage and encouraging them to find their own place as part of this ongoing tradition.

* * * * * * *

One further anomaly in Merton's manuscript needs to be considered: there is no written text corresponding to the content of the first two conferences in this series. It is quite possible that Merton had never produced a written version of this introductory material. Certainly some of his opening comments on the demands of historical study have the off-the-cuff quality of spontaneous observations, and the overview of monastic history from the time of Saint Benedict through the eleventh century is general enough that Merton could simply have been calling to mind a sequence of familiar events rather than following a written outline, but a few of the details provided, a list of monasteries founded in Europe by Irish monks, for example, or the approximate date when the abbey of Luxeuil was attacked by Saracens, might seem to indicate that Merton may not have been relying completely on memory. In any case if there was a written version of this material it would have been two to three pages at most, and it is apparently no longer extant.

In the opening conference, after announcing that "the history of the Order" would be the focus of the Friday classes for the time being and stressing the need for teaching any sort of history in an accurate rather than a deliberately edifying way, as well as noting the demanding nature of historical research and the amount of reading it entails, Merton makes a quick mention of the basic early Cistercian documents and the relative paucity of studies on them, particularly in English. He then emphasizes the importance of first getting the background straight, and looks back to Saint Benedict, seeing the great monastic founder as presented in Gregory the Great's *Life* as successively passing through all the approved forms of monastic life, first the hermit life, then Pachomian cenobitic life of groups of small communities established in close proximity to one another (Subiaco), and finally his own form of community life as lived at Monte Cassino and articulated in his Rule.[21]

Merton goes on to counter the naïve conventional view that Benedict brought order to what had been a previously disorganized monastic life in Europe, when in fact the centuries between Benedict's death in the mid-sixth century and the early ninth-century Synod of Aix were marked by a plethora of different monastic rules and traditions, often coexisting in the same monasteries. The exterior disruptions during this period of various invasions, first of Germanic tribes, later of Vikings, and eventually of Saracens, led to destruction or exile for many monastic communities, bringing a shift in some instances to a more urban setting, as with Monte Cassino's move to Rome in the traditional telling, where liturgical functions largely eclipsed any extensive engagement in manual labor. Eventually a more missionary dimension moved to the fore as well, most notably with the mission to England of Augustine of Canterbury and his monks, sent by Pope Gregory at the end of the sixth century. He also points out that some issues not considered in the Rule, such as the influence of lay founders on the monasteries they established, could be threats to the integrity of monastic life.

In his second conference Merton provides an overview of monastic history from the ninth through the eleventh century, focusing on the role first of Charlemagne, then of Louis the Pious and Benedict of Aniane, in establishing the Benedictine Rule as the single governing document in the Carolingian realm, but now with a predominantly ritualistic orientation, marked by various liturgical accretions for the sake of benefactors, so that monasteries became principally centers of intercessory prayer for patrons and the broader lay society, with reduced attention to other traditional dimensions of Benedictine life. This focus

---

21. This same point is made in the brief *"Outline of Benedict's Life"* in Thomas Merton, *The Rule of Saint Benedict: Initiation into the Monastic Tradition 4*, ed. Patrick F. O'Connell, MW 19 (Collegeville, MN: Cistercian Publications, 2009), 17–18.

on the spread of Benedictine monasticism ascending from Italy into the north is complemented by a rather quick survey of Irish monasticism moving south (and a promise, never fully carried out, to investigate this movement in more depth at a later time). The sixth-century foundation of the British island monastery of Iona by Columba and subsequently of its daughter house at Lindisfarne off the Northumbrian coast marks the first phase of Irish monastic missionary expansion, followed by the even more extensive continental plantations by Columban and his followers at Luxeuil, St. Gall, and into Lombardy at Bobbio, then at other important monastic centers like Fontanelle, Jumièges, Rouen and Corbie, many of which would eventually also suffer from attacks of Danes, Hungarians and Saracens. After brief mention of the Anglo-Saxon missionary efforts of Saint Boniface in Germany and the foundation of the famous monastery of Fulda, Merton sums up this entire period between Benedict and the eleventh century, with a touch of pedagogically motivated hyperbole, as by and large a time of utter chaos, but concludes that subsequently, with the revival of English monasticism under Saint Dunstan at Glastonbury and then the coming of Norman monasticism to England in the wake of the Conquest, "things get pretty clear." It is at this point that his rather whirlwind survey of over four centuries of monastic history slows down, and that the surviving written text of his conferences, whether originally preceded by a couple of pages of preliminary material or marking the first written notes for this conference series, now becomes available.

* * * * * * *

Fifteen of the thirty-four pages of Merton's holograph manuscript (excluding the supplementary material found after the text proper) continue to focus on the historical background preceding the foundation of Cîteaux in 1098. While this proportion does not provide an accurate indication of the actual ratio of pre-Cistercian and Cistercian material, as a couple of these early pages have only a few lines of writing, and there are some extensive insertions in the later sections, it does make clear that this "history of the Order" is being situated in a broad chronological and even geographical context. The opening pages on *"Early Monasticism in England"*[22] in fact have no direct connection with the eventual rise of Cistercianism. They seem to be included for a number of converging reasons: because Merton's most important English-language source, David Knowles's magisterial volume *The Monastic Order in England*,[23] begins with the refounding of monastic life in England in the mid-tenth century after it had been virtually obliterated by the Viking raids over the previous two centuries; because an article on the relationship between the English revival and contemporary continental monastic movements had appeared at the beginning of 1962;[24] because Dom Thomas Symons, that article's author, had recently edited a bilingual text of the *Regularis Concordia*,[25] the richly detailed tenth-century synodal document of English monastic practices and regulations; and because English monasticism would have been of particular interest to Merton himself and presumably to his audience as well.

But this material is not therefore to be regarded as a digression pure and simple. The rebirth of English monastic life led by Saint Dunstan and his friends Aethelwold and Oswald, likewise saints, is an early witness to the dynamism of the monastic revival throughout Europe that would gain momentum over the course of the tenth and eleventh centuries and culminate with the founding of Cîteaux. Providing both an overview of key

22. Pages 1–21 in this edition.
23. David Knowles, *The Monastic Order in England: A History of its Development from the Times of St Dunstan to the Fourth Lateran Council—940–1216* (Cambridge: Cambridge University Press, 1940; 2nd ed. 1963); Merton will also rely on the three-volume sequel to this work, particularly in the second set of history conferences: David Knowles, *The Religious Orders in England*, 3 vols. (Cambridge: Cambridge University Press, 1948–1959).
24. Thomas Symons, "Some Notes on English Monastic Origins," *Downside Review* 80 (1962): 55–69.
25. *Regularis Concordia Anglicae Nationis Monachorum Sanctimonialiumque / The Monastic Agreement of the Monks and Nuns of the English Nation*, ed. and trans. Thomas Symons (London: Thomas Nelson and Sons, 1953).

figures and events of this movement (preceded by a brief look at the seventh-century origins of English monasticism), and a quite detailed investigation of "special points relevant to monastic spirituality" (10) in the *Regularis Concordia*, including the Divine Office and other liturgical customs, the practice of daily communion, Holy Week ceremonies, food and fasting, and care for the poor, the sick and the dead, Merton has made available a more thorough and circumstantial account of this early contribution to the medieval monastic revival than he does of any other pre-Cistercian developments, even those more directly relevant to the founding of Cîteaux.

This is evident by a comparison with the relatively brief consideration of Cluniac monasticism that immediately follows.[26] As the most significant and influential monastic reform movement of its time, founded in 910 when "{the} Church {was} at its lowest ebb" (21) and becoming "the greatest cultural, religious and civilizing force in Europe" (24) throughout the tenth and eleventh centuries, the Abbey of Cluny with its hundreds of dependent priories developed a form of monastic life mainly expressed by an elaborate liturgical routine, in contrast to which the early Cistercians would eventually propose and practice a simpler, more balanced Benedictine life. Merton's focus here is not on these future conflicts but on the major contributions of the series of great abbots of Cluny and then on the spirit of Cluny during its "Golden Age," from the mid-tenth through the mid-twelfth century, relying principally on his friend Jean Leclercq's chapter "Le Monachisme Clunisien"[27] (supplemented by the preceding, broader chapter entitled "Le Monachisme du Haut Moyen Age"[28]), in a recent

---

26. Pages 21–26 in this edition.

27. Jean Leclercq, chap. 22: "Le Monachisme Clunisien," *Théologie de la Vie Monastique: Études sur la Tradition Patristique* (Paris: Aubier, 1961), 447–57.

28. Leclercq, chap. 21: "Le Monachisme du Haut Moyen Age (viiie–xe siècles)," *Théologie de la Vie Monastique*, 437–45.

publication, *Théologie de la Vie Monastique*.[29] Merton notes the eschatological vision of the Church in general and the monastery in particular as *"an anticipation in time of the eternal Kingdom of Heaven"* (24–25), and thus the appropriateness of liturgical splendor as a reflection and anticipation of heavenly glory. The monastery is seen as the *"full realization* of {the} mystery of {the} Church—{the} *mystery of charity"* (25). This rather "triumphalist" spirituality seems to exist somewhat in tension with the themes of exile and a return to Paradise (particularly identified with solitude) that predominate in the hagiographical literature of the High Middle Ages (as Leclercq, rather surprisingly, labels the period from the eighth through the tenth centuries), themes that Merton himself found quite congenial and wrote about frequently[30] but touches on only briefly here. The context of chapter 8 of Romans, with all creation awaiting the full revelation of the children of God, is evident in Leclercq's conclusion to his first contribution to the collection, where he identifies the main spiritual emphasis of the era as "that of the freedom of the sons of God. The world groans in the pains of childbirth. The Christian participates in the cosmic suffering" (26).

29. In a journal entry for June 12, 1962, Merton writes of this volume, "Read a little of the new *Théologie Monastique*, which is perhaps in some ways slighter than I expected, but informative. It does not seem very often to reach the level of theology: a series of historical background notes for monastic theology perhaps" (*Turning Toward the World*, 227). Merton would also use this volume for his 1963–1965 conferences on Pachomius, Basil, Theodoret and Ephrem: see *Pre-Benedictine Monasticism*, 74–75, 76, 124, 126–27, 133, 145, 219–20, 227, 229, 231, 242–44.

30. See in particular the essays "From Pilgrimage to Crusade," in Thomas Merton, *Mystics and Zen Masters* (New York: Farrar, Straus and Giroux, 1967), 91–112; and "The Recovery of Paradise," in Thomas Merton, *Zen and the Birds of Appetite* (New York: New Directions, 1968), 116–33; see also Patrick F. O'Connell, "Paradise," in William H. Shannon, Christine M. Bochen and Patrick F. O'Connell, *The Thomas Merton Encyclopedia* (Maryknoll, NY: Orbis, 2002), 349–51.

The comparably brief discussion of Norman monasticism,[31] based almost completely on Knowles, is placed as a kind of alternative current to Cluny, but one that leads not to Cîteaux but back to England after the Conquest of 1066. Merton's own fascination with this strand of monastic history is evident in his reference to the Abbey of Mont-Saint-Michel, off the northern coast of Normandy, calling attention to the early pages of Henry Adams' classic study *Mont-Saint-Michel and Chartres*;[32] the attention given to the unjustly neglected eleventh-century abbot and spiritual writer John of Fécamp (many of whose writings were passed down as composed by other, more celebrated authors); and particularly the focus on the Abbey of Bec, its founder Herluin, and its two most significant representatives, Lanfranc and Anselm, both abbots and both eventually archbishops of Canterbury after the Norman invasion of England, and the last of course one of the greatest intellectual and spiritual teachers in the history of Christianity. Merton doesn't linger on this important component of medieval monastic history (at least in the written text), but he provides enough information to indicate that it deserves considerably more attention than he is able to give it in this set of conferences.

At this point Merton has reached the verge of his main topic. The short section on "The New Orders"[33] (still drawing mainly from Knowles) makes brief mention of various eleventh-century eremitical experiments, often evolving into more organized foundations and even orders, and then explicitly situates the Abbey of Molesme, the monastery from which the founders of Cîteaux would come, in the milieu of the second of the two major centers of French monastic reform of the late eleventh and early twelfth century—Burgundy (the other being Maine, site of Savigny and Tiron, the former eventually incorporated into the Cistercian Order).

31. Pages 27–33 in this edition.
32. Henry Adams, *Mont-Saint-Michel & Chartres* (1905; Garden City, NY: Doubleday Anchor, n.d.).
33. Pages 33–37 in this edition.

Introduction xxvii

The introductory survey of Cistercian origins, with its somewhat provocative title "*Cistercian History*—Piety or Objectivity?"[34] outlines the main stages of the early development of Cîteaux, from the circumstances of the foundation through the return of Robert to Molesme and the administration of Alberic to the abbacy of Stephen Harding, all of which will be considered in greater detail in subsequent pages. The foundation is considered as part of the broader movement of reform already in process in the 1075 move to Molesme of the community begun in the forest of Colan. Merton emphasizes that Molesme was by no means a corrupt or degenerate monastery: it was "fervent"—otherwise it would not have attracted the attention of Saint Bruno, who lived in its ambit before going off to the Grande Chartreuse, nor of Stephen Harding—yet as it developed it became "conventional . . . wealthy, comfortable" (39). It was a stage in the evolution of a truly renewed Benedictine vision and practice, but not, for many of its members, a satisfactory resolution of the question of how to live the monastic life authentically in their own time and place. This section poses, but does not answer, the first of three distinct but interrelated questions associated with the foundation event: who was the true originator of the idea of the "New Monastery"—Robert, Alberic or Stephen? Merton briefly mentions contemporary and recent champions (most of them French) of each position, without inclining toward one figure or another—the mutually exclusive claims made by Orderic Vitalis (for Robert) and William of Malmesbury (for Stephen) and in modern times by Gregor Müller (for Alberic) being implicitly considered rather rigid and simplistic, not allowing for the likelihood that each of these figures (along with Bernard) made a significant contribution, as proposed by Séraphin Lenssen,[35] whose perceptive comments Merton directs to be read (41).

34. Pages 38–46 in this edition.
35. Séraphin Lenssen, "Saint Robert Fondateur de Cîteaux," *Collectanea Ordinis Cisterciensium Reformatorum* 4 (1937–1938): 2–16, 81–96, 161–77, 241–53.

Merton goes on to interweave an account of Robert's life and further discussion on the foundation.[36] There is some overlap and repetition here as he summarizes various sources, principally in dealing with two further questions: was the withdrawal from Molesme legitimate, and was Robert's subsequent return to his old monastery and his position as abbot there justified? While assembling, or at least referring to, extensive evidence on both sides of both issues, Merton clearly supports strongly affirmative responses to both questions. He emphasizes that in the first instance Robert did not violate Church law by leaving Molesme: he had sought and received official approval, and strong personal support, from the highest ecclesiastical authority available, the Papal Legate Hugh, Archbishop of Lyons, who "encourages and blesses {the} project to go elsewhere and keep {the} *Rule* of St. Benedict more perfectly" (50).

As for the return to Molesme, Merton basically rejects as tendentious and unsubstantiated the claims of William of Malmesbury that Robert had secretly manipulated the process to secure his return, and the later assertions of Conrad of Eberbach in the *Exordium Magnum* that Robert's return was motivated by a failure of nerve in the face of severe hardships (in effect an effort by Conrad to bolster an affirmative answer to the second question by taking a negative stance toward the third). He emphasizes that the request by the Molesme community for the restoration of Robert was prompted by their increasingly dire economic situation in the absence of their highly respected and charismatic founder, that Robert's resumption of his previous abbacy was strongly urged by Pope Urban and in effect required by Hugh of Lyons at the Synod of Port Anselle, issuing a decree that Robert was to return (in a letter incorporated into the Order's official narrative of its early years, the *Exordium Parvum*). Merton's thorough familiarity with both the original Latin sources and the current, mainly French, research on these controversies gave his

---

36. Pages 46–58 in this edition.

Introduction   xxix

novices access to this scholarly discussion considerably beyond what was generally available in English at this time.

Discussion of the abbacy of Saint Alberic is considerably briefer[37] but recognizes his importance both in assuring the permanence of the new foundation and in initiating certain practices that would come to characterize Cistercian life. Merton's account relies almost exclusively on the *Exordium Parvum*, virtually the only reliable source for information about Alberic: chapter 9 provides a summary of his character, as "a literate man, sufficiently learned in divine and human matters . . . a lover of the *Rule* and of the brothers . . . a man of remarkable prudence" (59)—the latter displayed particularly by his securing letters of recommendation from influential Church leaders (chapters 11–13) that led to the so-called Roman Privilege (chapter 14), a declaration of papal protection of the new experiment from external interference. Chapter 15, the so-called *Instituta* of Saint Alberic, mandated a communal life of poverty and simplicity (as already mentioned by Merton in the earlier summary), with the institution of the laybrotherhood as an integral element of Cistercian life. Brief references to the legend of an apparition of Mary to Alberic as the source of the color of the Cistercian habit, to his date of death (1108 rather than 1109 as often given), and to the rather hazy (and long-delayed) process of his being accorded sainthood, round out Merton's discussion of the figure who was eventually designated the second abbot of Cîteaux (once Robert's position as founding abbot was definitively accepted).

It is not surprising that Stephen Harding's longer, more eventful, and more thoroughly documented abbacy is given considerably more space[38] than that of Alberic, with most of Merton's attention focused on the key documents traditionally (and in the main correctly) attributed to him, the *Exordium Parvum* and the *Carta Caritatis*. Merton had already given directions to read a long

---

37. Pages 58–62 in this edition.
38. Pages 63–75 in this edition.

passage from John Bernard Dalgairns' late nineteenth-century *Life of St. Stephen Harding*, about his entrance to Molesme just prior to the very beginning of his discussion of the founding of Cîteaux (37), and had mentioned key details of his administration in his preliminary outline of the early years of the New Monastery, so he adds little circumstantial detail on his life (drawn from the article in the *Dictionnaire de Spiritualité*[39]) here.

Merton turns instead to Stephen's writings, drawing substantially on recently discovered manuscripts of previously unknown texts of early Cistercian documents: the Laibach (or Ljubljana) text of the *Carta Caritatis Prior*, an earlier, significantly different version of this foundational document, and the composite text comprising the *Exordium Cistercii* (a brief version of the origins of Cîteaux textually independent of the *Exordium Parvum*), the *Summa Carta Caritatis* (an abbreviated version of the early text of that document), and the *Capitula*, a series of early decrees of the Cistercian General Chapter. He also summarizes (not completely consistently) the recent, already controversial theories about this material of J.-A. Lefèvre: he notes, without endorsing, Lefèvre's opinion that the *Exordium Parvum* was a late, tendentious account not written by Stephen at all and assumes the accuracy of Lefèvre's contention that the text presented to Pope Callistus for approval in 1119 was the *Exordium Cistercii–Summa Carta Caritatis–Capitula* composite, while the *Carta Caritatis Prior* was the version approved by Pope Eugene in 1152, and the *textus receptus*, the *Carta Caritatis Posterior*, was a later revision from the latter part of the twelfth century. (This sequence has been generally rejected by more recent scholars, notably Chrysogonus Waddell,[40] in favor of the *Carta Caritatis Prior* as the 1119 text and a slightly earlier version of the *Carta Caritatis*

---

39. Maur Standaert, "S. Étienne Harding," *Dictionnaire de Spiritualité Ascétique et Mystique* [*DS*], ed. F. Cavallera et al., 17 vols. (Paris: Beauchesne, 1932–1995), 4.1489–93.

40. *Narrative and Legislative Texts from Early Cîteaux*, ed. and trans. Chrysogonus Waddell, Studia et Documenta, vol. 9 (Cîteaux: Commentarii Cistercienses, 1999); see notes in the text below for more specific references.

Posterior, no longer extant, as that of 1152—Merton actually assigns the *Carta Caritatis Posterior*, not the *Carta Caritatis Prior*, to 1152 [66], a conclusion already held at that time by Msgr. Josip Turk, apparently not noticing its inconsistency with Lefèvre's position.)

Of more lasting value (though almost entirely in Latin in Merton's own text) is his summary of *"The Spirituality of the Exordium Cistercii"* (68–70), with its critical but largely irenic perspective on Molesme, its positive evaluation of Robert, its conventional but evocative description of the "wasteland" of Cîteaux, its praise of both Alberic and Stephen, its depiction of the crisis of the abbey's survival resolved by the arrival of Bernard and companions, followed by the foundation of twelve daughter houses, and a final endorsement of the "marvelously foresighted wisdom" of Stephen in composing "a text marked by discernment" (70), the *Carta Caritatis*. Likewise helpful are the side-by-side comparison of the two versions of the *Carta Caritatis* (70–73) and the summary (though incomplete) of the main provisions of the final text of the *Carta* (74–75) that completes his analysis of the texts associated with Stephen.

Earlier, Merton had been critical of the (suppressed or lost) chapters of the *Exordium Magnum* that had disparaged Robert and attributed base motives for his return to Molesme, but in his two successive segments on *"{The} Spirituality of {the} Exordium Magnum"*[41] (the second inadvertently referring to *"Exordium Parvum"* instead), Merton shows his appreciation for the text, recently published in a new critical edition,[42] as a whole, "not

---

41. Pages 75–82 in this edition.
42. Conrad of Eberbach, *Exordium Magnum Cisterciense*, ed. Bruno Griesser (Rome: Editiones Cistercienses, 1961); a second edition was published three decades later: *Exordium Magnum Cisterciense sive Narratio de Initio Cisterciensis Ordinis*, ed. Bruno Griesser, *Corpus Christianorum Continuatio Medievalis*, vol. 138 (Turnhout, Belgium: Brepols, 1994). It is now available in a new English translation: *The Great Beginning of Cîteaux—A Narrative of the Beginning of the Cistercian Order: The Exordium Magnum of Conrad of Eberbach*, trans. Benedicta Ward and Paul Savage, ed. E. Rozanne Elder, Cistercian Fathers [CF], vol. 42 (Collegeville, MN: Cistercian Publications, 2012).

'history' but rather 'temoignage' [testimony]" (75), its extensive series of edifying tales comparable to the great collection of Franciscan stories found in the *Fioretti*, but also serving as a spirited defense of the Order against attacks on its legitimacy by Black Benedictines in Germany. The initial overview is mainly a sort of table of contents of each of the six *Distinctiones* that make up the volume, noting the special focus on Clairvaux, including both the leaders (Saint Bernard in particular) and other distinguished members of this community, where Conrad had been a monk and evidently began writing his book before becoming abbot of Eberbach, where he completed it. The two final sections, with their "Beneficial Warnings, Supported by Examples, of the Danger of Certain Vices and their Punishment" (79), according to Watkin Williams, upon whom Merton relies for much of this summary, "constitute something of a treatise on moral theology in some of its monastic aspects" (79).[43] This more thematic perspective is further developed in the second part of Merton's discussion, focused on such virtues as trust in God (exemplified particularly by Stephen Harding), community as a kind of sacramental presence of Christ, poverty, love of the poor, commitment to manual labor, devotion to the Blessed Mother, practice of *lectio divina*, all exemplified by particular monks, to whom Merton makes reference, without actually relating their stories *in extenso* in his actual text—providing instead a kind of *aide memoire* for anticipated oral presentation (which in the event he never actually made, due to time constraints as he decided to end the conferences by the end of the year).

The two final topics included in the "Cistercian History" conferences text proper, the survey of selected sections of the *Instituta Generalis Capituli*[44] and a similar overview of the contents of the *Usus Conversorum*,[45] were likewise not presented by

---

43. Watkin Williams, *Monastic Studies* (Manchester: Manchester University Press, 1938), 56.
44. Pages 82–86 in this edition.
45. Pages 87–88 in this edition.

Merton before the Friday classes were concluded on December 21. His intention to do so was evident early in the course of the series, when he mentioned at the beginning of the September 28 conference that copies of selected texts from the *Instituta* (in the original Latin), as well as copies of the *Exordium Parvum* and the *Carta Caritatis*,[46] would be available for each of the novices.[47] As was previously noted, the *Instituta* summary may well have been originally part of a sequence that included discussion of the *Carta Caritatis* and of the *Ecclesiastica Officia*; there is no indication that the *Usus Conversorum* material had also been part of that sequence, but it is possible, since it forms the third and final section of the early *Consuetudines*, of which the *Ecclesiastica Officia* and the *Instituta* constitute the first and second parts, respectively. In any case the format of the two sets of selections is quite similar. For the *Instituta*, identified as "{a} summary of decisions of {the} General Chapter during St. Stephen's time" (82), eleven of the first twelve statutes are listed, along with numerous cross references, particularly for section 11, on relations between monasteries; the rest of the references are grouped thematically under four headings: "Poverty," "*De Forma Visitationis*" (with a single statute mentioned), "Liturgical Simplicity," and "Various" (a

---

46. This was a 24-page spirit master ditto, a copy of which is in the Merton Center archives, which included both of these texts in the original Latin and in English translation.

47. The title page of this mimeograph (Merton identifies it as being in black, whereas the *Exordium–Carta* copy was in blue) reads: "Instituta of the General Chapter; / Collection of the Earliest Statutes / of the General Chapter—those enacted / during the lifetime of St. Stephen / Harding or immediately after—found / in Book II of the Consuetudines, / Nomasticon page 212." The twenty-nine sections included in this selection do not correspond precisely to those sections mentioned in the conference text. Merton's own copy of this material, with certain chapter numbers circled, underlinings, checkmarks, and vertical marginal lines, corrections of a few typographical errors, and two marginal notations to section V ("cf XXII" followed by "LIX"—added at a different time), is included in the "Cistercian History" file, along with another, unmarked, copy.

miscellaneous group); in all, thirty-nine of the ninety-one statutes are referred to, most with brief descriptions of their contents, but with some of the cross-references simply by number. The list obviously would require expanded explication to be very useful.

The descriptions for the statutes of the brothers' usages—in addition to the prologue, eight (of twenty) are identified by number, though in fact four additional statutes are also referenced—are somewhat more extensive, particularly those for the daily schedule (II); the regulations on silence (VI), related particularly to distinctions between work situations and other parts of the day; brothers' participation in chapter and their rite of profession (XI); and regulations on food and clothing (XV—and following). These are preceded by a summary of the document's prologue that notes the danger of either exploiting or pampering the brothers, of taking a strictly utilitarian attitude toward them rather than looking to their interests, spiritual as well as temporal. As the second set of conferences shows, these potential problems would indeed develop as the Order grew in size and influence, so that there is an implicit, unintentional yet quite pertinent element of transition between this final topic in the "Cistercian History" text and a significant strand in the story of the Order's subsequent history "from the Death of St. Bernard to the Reform of Benedict XII."

****

But there remains in this set of notes the material explicitly labeled "Appendix to Cistercian History,"[48] along with the various miscellaneous pages connected loosely or more closely to topics already discussed in this series or to be considered in the next. In his December 9, 1962, journal entry, Merton writes, "Chenu's article on Theology and History in the 12th century is, like everything else of his, instructive and important."[49] The

---

48. Pages 89–99 in this edition.
49. *Turning Toward the World*, 272.

Introduction   xxxv

reference is to the third chapter of the Dominican historical theologian M.-D. Chenu's *La Théologie au Douzième Siècle*, entitled "Conscience de l'Histoire et Théologie,"[50] which along with related material from the twelfth chapter of the same work, "Moines, Clercs, Laïcs: Au carrefour de la vie évangélique,"[51] is the principal source for Merton's Appendix on twelfth-century historiography, in which the "universal history of man" is viewed "as a unity—a 'sacred history,' {the} history of salvation" (89), employing various systems of temporal periodization, some going back to patristic times, but now with a tendency to sacralize and absolutize contingent historical circumstances, exemplified by the Cistercian historian (and relative of the emperor) Otto of Freising's attribution of a providential role to the Holy Roman Empire, the incorporation of the Augustinian city of man into the city of God, with the king as a kind of icon of the glorified Christ, promoting a "*static* attachment to feudal society" (97).[52] Yet already, Chenu points out, there were indications of various countermovements, the Trinitarian eschatology of the Calabrian Cistercian Joachim of Flora that foresaw the coming of a final Age of the Holy Spirit, the distinction between sacred history and political developments made by progressive historians like Orderic Vitalis and John of Salisbury, above all the "shocks" (91) stemming from the Crusades and missionary expansion that would challenge this closed system and point toward the

---

50. Marie-Dominique Chenu, *La Théologie au Douzième Siècle* (Paris: J. Vrin, 1957), 62–89; for an English translation, see Marie-Dominique Chenu, *Nature, Man, and Society in the Twelfth Century: Essays on New Theological Perspectives in the Latin West*, ed. and trans. Jerome Taylor and Lester K. Little (Chicago: University of Chicago Press, 1968), "Theology and the New Awareness of History" (162–201).

51. *Théologie au Douzième Siècle*, 225–51; "Monks, Canons, and Laymen in Search of the Apostolic Life" (*Nature, Man, and Society*, 202–38).

52. Merton's critique of such theories and their contemporary equivalents is found in his journal comments while reading Chenu; see below, pages 95, 96, notes 534, 536, for quotations.

identification of the apostolic life not simply with clerical monasticism as a "glorification of God in cult, {a} manifestation of Christian victory" (96), but with the rise of the mendicants and itinerant preaching, and even with a growing recognition of the vocation of the laity.

Merton does not explicitly connect these historiographical theories with the rise of Cistercianism during this same period, though he does pay particular attention to Otto, and is also prompted by a passing reference to an Easter sermon by Garnier de Rochefort, ninth Abbot of Clairvaux, to examine and summarize this text, in which a passage from the Book of Numbers is used to align the seven days of creation with the seven periods of history, in the course of which the "three main languages" are juxtaposed in a kind of dialectical arrangement: "Greek {is} said with {the} lips; Hebrew {is} said in {the} throat; Latin {is} in between—*therefore* Latin {is} the language of {the} Kingdom of God, which is to *unite* Greek and Jew!!" (93)—the only material from the appendix that finds its way, as a humorous aside, into the oral presentation of these conferences. This appendix as a whole is a reminder of some of the intellectual ferment that is taking place while the earliest Cistercians were endeavoring to recover the purity of the Benedictine ideal in their personal and communal lives.

The first of the supplemental materials, entitled *"Decline of {the} Cistercian Order,"*[53] is obviously closely related to the second set of 1962 Cistercian history conferences, perhaps dating from the aborted series of the year before, though there is no direct textual relationship between this preliminary investigation of the topic and the full-scale text of "The Cistercian Order from the Death of St. Bernard to the Reform of Benedict XII." This discussion is actually a series of four distinct engagements with the topic, each based on a different main source. The first is simply a list, drawn largely from an encyclopedia article by J.-M.

---

53. Pages 99–109 in this edition.

Canivez,[54] of major factors contributing to the decline: power struggles among the principal Cistercian abbots, economic problems, dissension and decline among the brothers, unsuccessful missionary engagements, and the question of studies associated with the establishment of the College of Saint Bernard in Paris. Then Merton turns to the treatment of the decline found in the *Compendium of the History of the Cistercian Order*,[55] written anonymously by the Gethsemani monk Fr. Alberic Wulf, which cited a breakdown in the visitation process, spotty attendance at General Chapter meetings, a decline in commitment to poverty, and a spirit of dissension among "*certain major abbots*" (104), all of which Merton finds inadequate, marked by a "characteristic vagueness" (104) in contrast with the treatment of these issues by David Knowles, whose analysis of these factors is considerably more nuanced. Merton then turns to Knowles' own discussion of the decline, based principally but not exclusively on English developments, in the first volume of his *Religious Orders in England*, which emphasizes an eventual loss of spiritual fervor (though not of regularity) and economic difficulties that developed with the wool trade, the major basis of English Cistercian prosperity in its first period. Finally, depending principally on the work of Louis Lekai,[56] he considers the rivalry between the Abbot of Cîteaux and the abbots of the four earliest foundations, especially Clairvaux, as it developed in the century leading up to the promulgation of the papal document *Parvus Fons* of 1265, which tried to solve the problem by creating structures of centralization largely alien to the Cistercian tradition. All these issues are considered

---

54. J.-M. Canivez, "Cîteaux (Ordre)," *Dictionnaire d'Histoire et de Géographie Ecclésiastiques*, ed. Alfred Baudrillart et al. (Paris: Letouzey et Ané, 1912–), 12.874–997.

55. A Father of the Abbey of Gethsemani, Kentucky [Alberic Wulf, OCSO], *Compendium of the History of the Cistercian Order* (Trappist, KY: Abbey of Gethsemani, 1944).

56. Louis Lekai, *The White Monks: A History of the Cistercian Order* (Okauchee, WI: Our Lady of Spring Bank, 1953).

in much greater detail in the later examination of this period, though Merton's use of Canivez's article and his engagement with the *Compendium* are unique to this treatment of the topic.

The extensive list of "*Privileges of {the} Cistercian Order*"[57] that follows is not explicitly associated with the decline of the Order, but can certainly be considered to have contributed to this process. Merton has culled from the article of Canivez various examples of exemptions and papal privileges between the twelfth and fourteenth centuries that were both signs of the high regard in which the Order was held by Roman authorities and a means of protection from unwarranted interference by potentially hostile local officials (bishops in particular), but by fostering a situation of increasing independence from the local church, these provisions over the course of time, as Canivez shows, contributed to tensions between monks and bishops that often led to an estrangement quite different from the submissive respect toward bishops envisioned by the founders of Cîteaux and by Saint Bernard, who denounced in the strongest terms all seeking of privileges on the part of his fellow abbots. There is no indication how Merton might have intended to make use of this list in his teaching, but the supplemental notes he added to the list proper, referring to the complaints of Cluny, of the archbishop of Canterbury, and of Pope Alexander III, a strong friend of the Order, suggest that he intended to highlight the problematic aspects of accumulating these instances of special treatment.

When discussing the Abbey of Cluny in the conference text proper, Merton did not mention the conflict that developed with the Order of Cîteaux in the course of the twelfth century. This is the focus of "*Cîteaux and Cluny in {the} Twelfth Century,*"[58] preceded by a brief overview[59] of the *Dialogus inter Cluniacensem Monachum et Cisterciensem de Diversis Utriusque Ordinis Observantiis* (*Dialogue between a Cluniac Monk and a Cistercian about the*

57. Pages 109–14 in this edition.
58. Pages 114–18 in this edition.
59. Pages 113–14 in this edition.

Differing Observances of Each Order), a late twelfth-century work in which representatives of the two orders discuss their differences. This latter material was clearly intended to preface the longer discussion of Cluny and Cîteaux, since an insertion contrasting the predominant character traits of Peter the Venerable and Saint Bernard is written on the reverse side of the *Dialogus* page, with an arrow stretching across the two facing pages indicating the place for its insertion, but rather oddly there is no mention of Cluny in the brief notes, which are concerned exclusively with "{The} Account of {the} Foundation of Cîteaux in {the} Dialogus," essentially reproducing, and even quoting directly from, the relevant portion of the *Exordium Parvum*. Its original purpose and its connection with what follows thus remains quite obscure.

As for the material on the relations between the two groups, Merton first tries to keep the controversy in perspective, noting that various factors need to be taken into account: the disagreement concerning observances, political and economic conflicts, local and personal issues, even personalities (particularly those of Peter the Venerable and Saint Bernard). He warns against a partisan or simplistic attitude in which all these disparate elements are "lumped together and made a 'great issue' in which one must take sides" (115), and he notes that in the long run the controversy actually benefited both groups, leading the Black Benedictines to engage in some soul-searching about observances and the Cistercians to do the same with respect to humility. Merton refers to the critiques not just of Peter, whose "basic distinction . . . between ESSENTIALS of observance which cannot change, and ACCIDENTALS which can" (116), was not only accepted by Bernard but became the standard theological position henceforward, but those of Abelard, Rupert of Deutz and Hugh of Amiens. He then provides a detailed reading of a letter of Peter to Bernard in which the abbot of Cluny gives concrete examples of his general principle, maintaining that "the *simplex oculus* of faith and pure intention and *sincere charity*" (117) is the genuine expression of authentic Christian faith and the true criterion of mature monastic profession. While Merton later discusses the tensions between Cluniacs and Cistercians, and the complex but mutually appreciative relationship between Peter and Bernard (including this letter), at much greater length in his conferences on Bernard's life and writings,[60] this succinct look at the issues and people involved both illustrates his sympathetic appreciation of Peter and provides some basic information on the other Benedictines' criticisms, not discussed by Merton elsewhere.

Toward the conclusion of the second series of history conferences, Merton mentions among the topics not given due attention "The nuns of the Order, {including} the mystics and saints . . . where we must look for the greatest Cistercian saints of the period. . . . a real and vitally important development in the spirituality of the Order" (246). The material on "Cistercian Nuns,"[61] drawn from Jean de la Croix Bouton's history of the Order,[62] does provide at least a relatively brief overview of the somewhat obscure and erratic early history of the women's branch of the Order. He notes the foundation by Molesme of Jully, a convent where many of Bernard's relatives, including his sister Humbeline, became nuns, but which never came under Cistercian jurisdiction, and then turns to Tart, the first convent to follow Cistercian observances, founded about 1120 as a "special project of St. Stephen Harding" (119). He goes on to note the various ways in which women's foundations were made, the development of nuns' general chapters, first in Spain and subsequently in France, the "confused and irregular" (119) situations that developed in which it was not always clear, even to the nuns themselves, to what extent women's communities adhering to Cistercian observances were officially related to the Order, and finally a list of some of the great women mystics and saints, largely from the thirteenth century, who were associated in some way, official or unofficial,

---

60. See *Cistercian Fathers and Their Monastic Theology*, lx–lxii, lxxxix–xc, 125–60.

61. Pages 118–21 in this edition.

62. Jean de la Croix Bouton, *Histoire de l'Ordre de Cîteaux*, 3 vols. (Westmalle, Belgium: Notre Dame de Aiguebelle, 1959, 1964, 1968).

with the Cistercian family. While not an adequate treatment of the topic, as Merton would be the first to admit, it does indicate his awareness of its importance and the need for further research, which has significantly developed in subsequent decades.

A biographical overview of the life of Saint Stephen Harding,[63] taken from the work of Archdale King,[64] is actually more chronologically specific and complete than the comparable material in the conference text proper and also includes a concise summary of the establishment of the first four daughter houses of Cîteaux along with an enumeration of the foundations of each of these five abbeys, information not found in the "Cistercian History" notes themselves. It is apparent from a reference to the *Exordium Magnum* text as found in the *Patrologia Latina*, rather than in the critical edition that Merton consistently uses for the conferences, that these notes must have been made before the publication of the latter text in 1961. It provides a helpful supplement to the main discussion of Cîteaux's third abbot that might easily have been inserted into the conference notes proper as some of the other material found there evidently had been.

The briefest of these "supplemental" notes is the set of fragmentary biographical referents to Aelred of Rievaulx,[65] merely indicating the successive settings of his early life, his entrance into the Yorkshire monastery where he would eventually serve as abbot, his character traits of "tenderness, simplicity {and} ardent charity" (126, 128), and his major works available in Latin editions and English translation. The direction to "read from {the} life" (125–26)

---

63. Pages 121–25 in this edition.
64. Archdale A. King, *Cîteaux and Her Elder Daughters* (London: Burns & Oates, 1954), 11–22.
65. Pages 125–28 in this edition. In the "Cistercian History" file this page actually precedes that on Saint Stephen Harding; it has been transposed in this edition both to provide a proper chronological sequence and to allow it to function as a sort of preface to the discussion of Aelred's sermons to follow.

of Aelred by his friend and disciple Walter Daniel[66] the account of his initial encounter with the Cistercians of Rievaulx and his entrance into the community immediately afterward adds to this material a passage that is some twenty times longer than the handwritten note itself!

The final addition is also considerably the longest, six pages of detailed summary and analysis of four *"Cistercian Easter Sermons,"*[67] two by Aelred, one of them recently rediscovered, and two by his contemporary Isaac of Stella. The common dimension of this group of sermons is identified at the outset as presenting the *"Spiritual Sense of Scripture"* (129)—an application of the literal text to the personal spiritual development of the audience, in this context the monastic communities of the two Cistercian abbots. Thus in Aelred's first sermon the text "As newborn babes, desire the rational milk without guile, that thereby you may grow unto salvation" (1 Pet 2:2) is read as associating milk with the nourishing sweetness of Christ experienced in the resurrection but in this life kept in fruitful tension with the experience of Christ's suffering represented by the bitter wine given him on the cross and shared in the Eucharistic cup: "{the} disciples {are} nourished with {the} milk of {the} Resurrection because they could not face the Passion (!!) and {the} invisible things of His divinity. . . . The women announce it, for it is woman's role to give milk to children" (131–32). In Aelred's second sermon, "The Easter feast on earth {is the} shadow of the *perfect Paschal Supper in heaven"* (132), likened to the Passover meal of the Jews in Exodus, to the movement of Christians from desire for Christ to reception of Christ in the Eucharist, and finally to the *transitus* from mortality to immortality. (This sequence corresponds to the three-fold spiritual sense—typological: an interpretation of an Old Testament event as foreshadowing its fulfillment in the New; tropological: the personal appropriation of the text and its

---

66. Walter Daniel, *The Life of Ailred of Rievaulx*, ed. and trans. F. M. Powicke (New York: Thomas Nelson, 1950), 10, 12–15.

67. Pages 129–38 in this edition.

application to the spiritual life of the believer; and anagogical: the final eschatological fulfillment of the salvific pattern revealed in the text, experienced imperfectly in this life.)

In Isaac's first sermon, the bond between humans and God restored by the Resurrection is likened to the bond between man and wife, that between mother and child, and that of the human person with his own alienated self. In the second sermon, the three births, carnal, spiritual and immortal, are paralleled to the three levels of "Nourishment—in carnal life, . . . material food; in spiritual life, {the} sacraments; in {the} resurrection, God Himself, without sacraments" (138). These analyses, much more detailed and complex than indicated in these brief references, of course have nothing directly to do with Cistercian history per se, unlike the rest of the supplementary materials summarized here, but they do serve as a reminder that ultimately it is the spiritual and pastoral teaching of these and the other Cistercian fathers of the first generations that provides at least part of the rationale for the continued interest in studying the Cistercians and their history both inside and outside the Order, and certainly for Thomas Merton's commitment to transmitting that history accurately to young aspirants so that they might find themselves as participants in an ongoing personal and communal journey that is a part of history but that also, to be fully realized, transcends it.

* * * * * * *

The recordings of these conferences as actually presented by Merton not only serve as the only source for the background material with which the series begins but also provide the opportunity to observe how Merton actually communicates the material he has prepared to his audience. As was customary in his conferences generally, he usually begins with various announcements, sometimes matters of "housekeeping" (keeping windows open) or of community business (the expected arrival of a new postulant, a visit from Episcopalian seminarians, plans for the merger of the novitiates or for the new monastic formation program, comments on the exam he has recently given on poverty for the class on the vows—generally less good in expression than in understanding). Twice he mentions saints whose feasts are being celebrated that day: Saint Edmund Rich on November 16 and Saint Clement of Rome on November 23. Occasionally there is a sardonic comment about particular incidents—he remarks on the Christmas carols being played over the p.a. system in the farms' building while the monks are packing cheese for holiday delivery: "I came here to get away from background music!" But he also tries to keep the novices up to date on some of what is going on in the world beyond the monastery—most significantly, during the time period of these conferences, the Cuban missile crisis and the opening of the first session of the Second Vatican Council. The novices would no doubt have heard something of both these momentous events from the abbot at the daily chapter, but Merton tries to let them know of the latest developments of these and other current events, such as upcoming elections and the border war between India and China. Merton's own commitment to engaging, as monk and contemplative, with the crucial issues of the contemporary world is at least implicitly evident in many of these comments.

While the focus of the lectures, as of the written text, is primarily factual and historical, with a particular emphasis on the need for a critical engagement with the sources, Merton does indicate the spiritual relevance of the material for the novices at appropriate points. For example, he points out that the custom of beginning every act with a blessing as described in the *Regularis Concordia* should not be regarded simply as a rule but as a spiritual directive that can become a transformative practice, and he asks the students what comparable acts might be helpful today; likewise he notes that bowing to other community members should not become a merely mechanical gesture but should be a conscious expression of humility and mutual submission. In connection with liturgical and ecclesial finery, Merton stresses that while not wrong in itself it can gradually lead to the development of an overly refined taste and a habitual expectation of a "grand style" in costly or elaborate decor that can interfere with a commitment to simplicity and austerity. In the context of the various monastic experiments of the eleventh century, Merton comments that any monk worth his salt has at some point a sense that he should be living a more intense spiritual life, impossible where he now is, but adds that this doesn't mean that everyone should become a founder—what is partly grace is often partly temptation, and there is a need to be receptive to the one without succumbing to the other; plenty of people, he warns, lose everything for wanting more. "Don't get ahead of the Holy Ghost," he counsels; one may have the grace for one type of life but not for something one might consider superior. (His listeners probably have little idea to what extent this bit of advice is the fruit of Merton's own personal experience.)

Merton often leavens his presentations with pertinent anecdotes. Some are personal reminiscences, as when he comments on the English fondness for bell-ringing evident in the *Regularis Concordia* and remaining evident a millennium later in the complex change-ringing still practiced in many English churches, as he recalls from his schooldays. With reference to Stephen Harding's prohibition of the Duke of Burgundy from holding court at Cîteaux, he recalls the centenary of the founding of Gethsemani held in 1948, when the monastery was overrun with visitors, including the Kentucky governor and his entourage—his verdict: "it was terrible!" At other times he makes historical connections with events of other periods. Referring to Saint Dunstan's Abbey at Glastonbury, he notes it is still a shrine, the traditional burial place of King Arthur, supposedly founded by Joseph of Arimathaea and connected with the legend of the Holy Grail. Again in connection with bells, he notes that John Bunyan, author of *Pilgrim's Progress*, was very attracted to bell-ringing but worried it was sinful; he stopped ringing them himself but still listened to them, until on one occasion he was standing beneath the church tower when it collapsed and nearly crushed him!

In connection with ecclesial pomp, he relates a story he had recently read about the uncle of Copernicus, a high ecclesiastic, in whose household no one was allowed to cross the courtyard to the great hall for dinner until he had emerged from his private quarters, signaled by the sudden barking of his many dogs, at which point all the retainers raced after him in a disorderly rout. Speaking about the Norman Conquest, he recalls the opening scene in Sir Walter Scott's novel *Ivanhoe*, where a pair of Anglo-Saxon retainers comment on the fact that what was for them a commonplace *pig* was for the Normans the fancy *porc*; an ordinary *cow* was elevated to *veau* by the Normans. Mention in the *Regularis Concordia* of the "*Quem Quaeritis?*" trope, the brief dialogue between angel and women coming to the tomb acted out within the Holy Week liturgy that was considered to be the origin of medieval drama, leads to a short summary of the late medieval morality play *Everyman*, when the title character summoned by Death searches in vain for companions to accompany him until his good deeds are unbound by his repentance and confession of sin. (Merton's spontaneous reference to the play is slightly more hazy than this.)

Merton's trademark humor also appears throughout the talks. In the very first conference, he remarks, "Benedict comes along," and then with perfect comic timing adds, "*if* he came along," eliciting appreciative laughter from the students, who recognize an allusion to a memorable talk by Dom Leclercq on "Recent theories about St. Benedict and the Rule" a year earlier. Merton wrote at the time, "What seems to have stirred people most is the hypothesis that St. B. never existed. By this Dom L.'s visit will be most remembered."[68] Discussing the importance of blessing in connection with the *Regularis Concordia*, he tells a story from Gregory the Great's *Dialogues* of a nun who was possessed by a devil; after she was exorcised, the demon was asked how it had happened, and he replied that while he was sitting on a cabbage leaf the nun ate the leaf without blessing herself . . . so what could he do!? Possession was easier back in those days, Merton concludes.

---

68. *Turning Toward the World*, 124 [6/6/1961].

In connection with the custom of *biberes*, or taking a drink before going to work, he recalls a story told by his own novice master of the days when a keg of beer was occasionally brought out into the fields where the monks were at work, and of one of the monks who was to return to get the church ready for the next Office, as he did, but he then wandered out of the church and wasn't seen again for hours, such was the effect of the beer on a hot day. At one point Merton repeats a joke about the conservative Cardinals Ottaviani and Ruffini, who were on their way to the Council—of Trent![69] As with the other asides and anecdotes, Merton's humorous comments are intended not just to keep the novices engaged but to make connections between the events being related and a wider range of experiences, past and present.

Early in the series, Merton seems to be going at a quite leisurely pace, as if he had no established deadline for completing the course—typically his sets of conferences could continue for a year or more. Thus topics considered rather summarily in the written text might be spun out at considerable length in the conferences themselves. Cluny takes up an entire class period, beginning with a rather lengthy and not very successful attempt on the novices' part to locate its site on a map, and incorporating some new or elaborated details—brief comments on the controversy with Cîteaux, a short excursus on the distinction between Romanesque and Gothic architecture when mentioning the abbey church as an example of the former. Likewise, the next conference, on Norman monasticism, also takes up the entire period, as Merton comments on the dangers of being caught far out on the sands by incoming high tides at the foot of Mont-Saint-Michel and reads extensive excerpts from Henry Adams's *Mont-Saint-Michel & Chartres*. In discussing the early documents of the Order, he spends a good deal of time looking at the Preface to the *Exordium Parvum*, not specifically discussed in his written manuscript, comparing

---

69. He records the same joke in a journal entry for October 27, 1962 (*Turning Toward the World*, 261), and evidently liked it so much that he retold it in the initial Sunday conference.

the early text found in the Laibach codex with that provided for the novices in the multigraphed copies distributed to them.[70] Alberic gets an entire conference to himself, in which the written text receives various elaborations: mention that Alberic is briefly imprisoned by his brothers at Molesme when he is left in charge by Robert leads to discussion about monastic jails generally and their location in particular (probably under the stairs leading from the chapter room to the dormitory)—with some humorous asides about an incarcerated brother making faces at his confreres as they pass by. The institution of the laybrotherhood leads to comments about their imminent change in canonical status (to be monks in the full sense of the word, with voting rights, etc.) and Merton's sense that there is a need to be careful not to spoil their unique vocation in the process. There is even some further textual discussion in relation to variants in chapter 12 of the *Exordium Parvum*: *sanctiorem vitam* ("holier life") in the Laibach text rather than *secretiorem vitam* ("more hidden life") in the received text. The following conference considers at some length the legislation found in chapter 15 of the *Exordium Parvum*, simply mentioned in passing at this point in the written text.

But in the last couple of conferences this approach changes. Merton actually directs the novices to take notes (in their copies of the *Exordium Parvum* and *Carta Caritatis*) on the three different versions of the *Carta* (*Summa, Prior* and *Posterior*) as a way of

---

70. He is particularly interested in the phrase *ad exaltationem spiritus* ("to the elevation of the spirit") that he finds in the Laibach text and considers to be an enigmatic phrase characteristic of Stephen and having some relation to union with God, but that is actually not the authentic reading, which is *"ad exhalationem spiritus"*: see Chrysogonus Waddell, "Liturgical-Patristic Resonances on The Prologue to the Exordium Parvum," in *The New Monastery: Texts and Studies on the Earliest Cistercians*, ed. E. Rozanne Elder, CF 60 (Kalamazoo, MI: Cistercian Publications, 1998), 175: "More than one scribe has been puzzled by the expression, and has substituted *exaltationem spiritus*. I remember the joy with which Father Louis [Thomas Merton] once pounced on this variant: the early Cistercians were encouraged to toil even unto . . . ***ecstasy! mystical rapture!*** Alas, the authentic reading is about toiling, rather, to the last, the very last gasp."

quickly getting this material clearly sorted out. He follows this with a quick overview of the sections and unique elements of the *Carta Caritatis Prior* text—though apparently in his haste he himself becomes a bit muddled about at least one provision: saying first that the local bishop is involved in the deposition of an unworthy abbot in the *Summa Carta Caritatis* but not in the *Carta Caritatis Prior*, but then asking (but not concluding—correctly) whether this procedure is found rather in the *Carta Caritatis Prior* but not the *Carta Posterior*.[71] The *Exordium Cistercii* is mentioned at the conclusion of the conference, but its contents are not discussed as they are in the written text.

In the following, final conference, however, after a general statement to the effect that Cistercian spirituality is more or less monastic spirituality generally—an integral part of a much longer tradition (as laid out in these very conferences, of course), and the assertion that the best and clearest statements of the Cistercian vision are found in the composite text that includes the *Exordium Cistercii*, he turns specifically to the phrase near the outset of that text to the effect that the founders of Cîteaux preferred to focus on heavenly concerns rather than earthly business (*elegerunt potius studiis celestibus occupari quam terrenis implicari negociis* [68]). He then devotes almost the entire remainder of this last class to soliciting suggestions from the novices as to what specific means for doing so are provided by Cistercian monastic life. The discussion is casual (at one point early in the discussion a novice who mentions poverty, chastity and obedience is humorously upbraided by Merton for not leaving two of these for others to select) but elicits thoughtful responses from the students, summed up by

---

71. In the *CC Prior*, the bishop is informed and expected to summon, examine, and correct or depose the delinquent abbot; if he fails to do so the abbot of Cîteaux is to call together a small group of fellow abbots and deal with the situation as they think best; in the *Summa*, the bishop is informed but the deposition is effected by fellow abbots; in the *CC Posterior* no mention is made of the bishop in this context at all. See Waddell, *Narrative and Legislative Texts from Early Cîteaux*, 406, 447–48, 503, and especially the notes on the text: 449, 505.

Merton as representing a particularly Cistercian emphasis on poverty and solitude in community, remote from the world. He then announces that they "won't get back to this" and that next year they will turn to something different, at which point this series of Cistercian history conferences is concluded.

****

The textual situation for the second set of history conferences is exactly the reverse of that for the previous series. Once again only a single witness is extant, but in this case it is not the author's autograph but a double-sided mimeograph of fifty-seven typed, numbered pages, copied from Merton's personal notes, which are evidently no longer extant. It is not clear when they were completed and distributed, as they are not mentioned by Merton in the conferences themselves, but it must have been only around the time when the series was concluded, as in the penultimate presentation on December 2, when he discusses the letters of Stephen of Lexington, he notes that he has just come across them that week. One advantage of working with a reproduction such as this is that Merton often leaves directions for his typists to incorporate passages from his sources that he had not himself copied, so that they become part of the text proper—though there are still numerous instances where he simply writes "Read" such-and-such an excerpt—included in the notes to the present edition. The principal problem with relying on a reproduction for the copy text is that Merton's handwriting is often difficult to decipher, and while it is impossible to determine whether the original was completely handwritten or typed with handwritten additions, it is evident that there are a number of places where the typist has obviously misread Merton's handwriting.[72] Errors

---

72. See for example "Raymond" for "Raynald" (149), "1160" for "1168" (163), "Europeans" for "Emperors" (182), "William" for "Walter" (207, 208). Some errata, such as giving John Wyckliff's first name as "William" (179), are presumably slips by Merton himself.

that have been recognized are corrected and the misreadings recorded in the annotations; there may well be others that have gone undetected, but they are presumably minor and do not seriously affect the intended meaning of Merton's text.

In the brief Introduction situating the period between the death of Bernard and the papacy of Benedict XII in the context of the entire history of the Order,[73] Merton makes a couple of important preliminary points. Given the rather sketchy treatments of this crucial era that were currently available, especially in English, he emphasizes at the outset that "it is necessary to attempt a systematic study of the question, at least in outline" (141). While he makes no claim for comprehensiveness or even complete accuracy in these notes, and presents his work as a stimulus for "further personal studies" (143) on the part of his listeners, this series is certainly among the most carefully organized sets of conferences he composed during his decade as novice master. Second, he stresses the need to respect the complexity of the actual lived reality of Cistercian life during this period, to "beware of easy generalizations" (141) and avoid simplistic, one-sided conclusions that fail to incorporate both positive and negative aspects of the various topics to be considered, or that tend to support positions based on ideology or subjective, self-interested motives rather than on the full range of factual data.

He first provides a five-part chronological arrangement, which he acknowledges to be necessarily somewhat arbitrary, for Cistercian history as a whole, in which the period to be discussed is labeled "The Maturity of the Order" (139), following periods of Formation and Growth and preceding Decadence and Reform. Whereas the other periods are identified merely by dates, this one is divided into two distinct parts (139): "apogee: 1153 to 1265" (climaxing with the issuing of the papal bull *Parvus Fons*), and "centralization and decline: 1265–1335" (also climaxing with a papal document—not mentioned here—the constitution *Fulgens*

---

73. Pages 139–43 in this edition.

sicut Stella of Benedict XII, the Cistercian pope who appears in the title of this set of conferences). He then provides three preliminary observations: that this period is relatively neglected in comparison with the formative period (the subject of course of the first set of history conferences), which is usually considered through the lens of the seventeenth-century Trappist reform of the Order; that the period of "maturity" is to be understood as that of the Order's greatest influence, not of the full actualization of its ideals; and that the period also marks the beginning of the Order's *"actual decline"* that must be dealt with "prudently and humbly . . . frankly and objectively" (141).

This introductory material concludes with further consideration of this phenomenon of decline, noting that it is one manifestation of the general decline of monasticism in the Late Middle Ages, and of the wider "upheaval of Christian society" (141) that led to the Reformation and subsequent challenges of the modern world; that some subjectivity is unavoidable in such a study, but must not lead either to using this history as ammunition for current discontents or conversely to finding a complacent satisfaction in present prosperity; that the growth of the Order in size, with its inevitable concomitant diminishment of fervor, was a contributing factor to the decline but not the sole determining cause; that the arc of medieval Cistercian history shows the Order moving from being ahead of its time in its formative stages to being representative of its time in its most powerful and influential phase to becoming regressive with the rise of new religious currents in the thirteenth century; that not all developments of the period of decline were necessarily causes of that decline—the development of new patterns of education being a case in point; and finally that the tentative nature of the exploration of this little-studied period is necessarily far from definitive. It should be noted that already in this introductory material Merton is once again bedeviled by the problem of the composition and dating of the Order's foundational documents that had already caused some confusion in the first set of conferences. In referring at the very outset to what he calls "the fact that the versions of these basic texts we study belong in reality to the period after 1153" (140), he is assuming the validity of the Lefèvre chronology of the *Exordium Parvum* and *Carta Caritatis* that is accepted by some but not all of his sources, so that there is some inconsistency and inaccuracy (in the context of more recent scholarship) recurring throughout the text.

Since the *terminus a quo* for these conferences is "the Death of St. Bernard" (1153), Merton then goes on to provide a fairly detailed outline of the chronology of major events for the Order of Cîteaux in the second half of the twelfth century,[74] actually beginning with the 1147 General Chapter, in which the orders of Savigny and Obazine were incorporated into the Cistercians (under the aegis of Bernard), and progressing through the issuing in 1152 of the papal bull *Sacrosancta* by the first Cistercian pope, Eugene III, confirming a revised governance structure (again with the erroneous assumption that the *"new text"* [144] being approved was the *Carta Caritatis Prior* rather than a version of the *Carta Caritatis Posterior*); the deaths of both Bernard and Eugene the following year; the establishment of the military Order of Calatrava under Cistercian auspices, a watershed event in drawing the Cistercians into political involvements; the Order's support in the papal schism of the 1160s–1170s for Alexander III, who issued revised versions of *Sacrosancta* in 1163 and 1165 (supposedly now as confirmation of the *Carta Caritatis Posterior*, though Merton, not surprisingly perplexed, queries: "Is {the} date correct, or should it be 1190?" [146]) and who canonized Bernard in 1174; the Order's support for Thomas Becket in his conflict with King Henry II, who eventually forced the Abbey of Pontigny to expel the archbishop from his home in exile there; the confirmation of exemption from episcopal control by Pope Lucius III in 1184; and the period of Cistercian missionary activity in central Europe at the end of the century. Merton's summation of this period is that it is marked by a fundamental reorientation of the Order's purpose and direction: "The rule is the same, the life in

---

74. Pages 143–47 in this edition.

the monastery is the same, but in effect the Order of Cîteaux has become a *great active force* rather than a purely contemplative body of monks" (147).

After this detailed but rather rapid survey of later twelfth-century Cistercian history, Merton moves forward into the new century with extensive overviews of two key aspects of the Order some one hundred years after the foundation of Cîteaux: its expansion[75] and its economic situation.[76] With regard to the first, Merton documents the astounding spread of the Order geographically and the concomitant expansion of its power and influence, both largely but not exclusively due to the towering figure of Saint Bernard. But even the year before Bernard's death the Cistercian General Chapter, sensitive to the negative consequences of unchecked growth, tried to call a halt to new foundations, and subsequently to acquisition of additional property by existing abbeys, but was only partially successful.

Merton calls attention to the dangers of this "success" on a number of levels. Financially, becoming wealthy was both a source of temptation to become enmeshed in worldly concerns and an incentive to take on a burden of debt that could eventually become insupportable, for the sake of "acquiring more land and putting up larger buildings" (149). Spiritually, the huge influx of candidates, many of them not completely suited for a life of deep interior prayer, meant that a much more active orientation developed both within and beyond the monastery, as "the Order more or less consciously renounced the desire to remain purely contemplative and entered, with its eyes open, into *active participation in the contemporary struggles of the Church*" (150). Politically, the abbot became "a feudal lord . . . . very much engaged in public life" (150), not infrequently elevated to a bishopric, while the monastery cellarer was typically a key player in local and regional business life. Juridically, the spirit and even the

---

75. Pages 147–54 in this edition.
76. Pages 154–81 in this edition.

letter of early Cistercian legislation, formulated for small monasteries usually located in obscure sites, were almost inevitably transgressed on a fairly regular basis even before the end of the twelfth century.

Yet Merton is careful to point out that this does not mean that the typical monk, or the typical monastery, in the early decades of the thirteenth century was simply corrupt or degenerate; rather, "the average Cistercian monastery is a quiet, prosperous, well-ordered religious house" (151) whose members—with some egregious exceptions—were "able to lead a good strict and regular life in the cloister" but "definitely needed to be kept busy" (150). Yet while the men's communities may no longer have been marked by "contemplative fervor" (151) during this period, many convents of nuns living, officially or unofficially, according to Cistercian customs, "were centers of mystical life" (151)—another indication of the need to avoid facile generalizations about the state of Cistercian life at any given time. By the middle of the century, the period of growth had largely come to an end, and a different dynamic emerged both within the Order itself and in its interaction with the wider society.

The lengthy section on Cistercian economics that follows focuses on perhaps the most complicated topic in the entire text, and Merton's mastery of the material is evident in his impressively organized presentation, drawing on multiple sources, most but not all explicitly identified.[77] He arranges his material under

---

77. J.-M. Canivez, "Cîteaux (Ordre)"; James S. Donnelly, *The Decline of the Medieval Cistercian Laybrotherhood* (New York: Fordham University Press, 1949); Coburn V. Graves, "The Economic Activities of the Cistercians in Medieval England (1128–1307)," *Analecta Sacri Ordinis Cisterciensis* 13 (1957): 3–62; Knowles, *Monastic Order in England*; Knowles, *Religious Orders in England*; Jean Leclercq, "Épitres d'Alexandre III sur les Cisterciens," *Revue Bénédictine* 64 (1954): 68–82; Jean-Berthold Mahn, *L'Ordre Cistercien et son Gouvernement des Origines au Milieu du XIIIe Siècle (1095–1265)* (Paris: E. de Boccard, 1945); C. H. Talbot, "Cîteaux and Scarborough," *Studia Monastica* 2 (1960): 95–158.

five subheads, beginning with a brief summary of the provisions of the so-called *Instituta* of Saint Alberic, chapter 15 of the *Exordium Parvum*, which lists all the various sources of income renounced by the early Cistercians: churches, Mass stipends, burial privileges, tithes, manorial bakeries, mills, villages and serfs (154). This is the basic standard against which Merton evaluates the subsequent economic development of the Order.

Then Merton presents what he calls his "thesis," which is basically that the "peak of phenomenal economic prosperity" (154) reached by the Order by the end of its first century of existence was due to its highly efficient exploitation of resources, largely through the "epoch-making" (155) institution of the laybrotherhood, and that the respect in which the Order came to be held contributed substantially to its material growth, but that its very success eventually led to widespread criticism of a greed for land, real or apparent, and to breaches of its original commitment not only to personal but to communal austerity, which the General Chapter tried ineffectually to keep under control.

Merton then considers the efficiency of the system: opening up new land to cultivation and expanding territory through the development of the grange system, staffed by the brothers, under the management of a single overseer, the cellarer. According to David Knowles, whom Merton quotes to summarize this section, the commitment to manual labor on the part of all the monks was a return to fidelity to the vision of the Benedictine Rule, initially motivated by a desire for balance and simplicity, with the leading role of the brothers as crucial to the model's success. But eventually the economies of scale that made the abbeys so efficient aroused the enmity of neighbors with more modest plots, those who had difficulty keeping up with these powerful producers, and when the workforce of the brothers eventually diminished substantially, the resulting shift to hired laborers and rented lands, according to Knowles, made the monks "capitalists in the full sense of the word" (156). Knowles highlights the irony of this evolution: "The wheel had come full circle, and the expedient {originally devised to isolate the monastery from the life of the world} was now something which affected at least indirectly the lives of all around. From being a small Christian household, exhibiting the dignity of toil and of direct production in the midst of a feudal society, the great Cistercian abbeys had become ranches, *latifundia*, the enemies of their small neighbours" (156).

Merton then focuses on the "irregularities" that developed, systemic violations of the stipulations of the *Instituta* listed earlier, almost all of which (Mass stipends and bakeries excepted) he explicitly considers. Churches, villages, and even serfs, already possessed by the Savigniac abbeys that are incorporated into the Order in 1147, are now acquired almost routinely through donations; fees are collected from burials of patrons and from services provided by mills owned by the monasteries. Merton provides numerous specific examples of infractions of the rules related to all these matters.

But the most contentious issue is that of tithes, connected to the acquisition of all sorts of property. Since the Cistercians had renounced all acceptance of tithes (the motive for rejecting ownership of churches, villages, etc.), they were quickly exempted from paying tithes as well, but as time went on this matter became quite complex: Merton skillfully traces the shifting stages of distinguishing between exemptions on donated land cultivated by the monks themselves (*sane laborum*) and the more restrictive provision of exemption based on land newly brought into cultivation (*sane novalium*)—and thus not previously subject to tithes—with the Cistercians generally managing to win papal support for the widest possible exemption, though often with the popes themselves counseling the monks voluntarily to moderate too rigid a demand for their legal rights. The situation became further clouded when monasteries regularly began to collect tithes themselves on properties donated to them, in blatant contradiction to the regulations of the *Exordium Parvum*.

Merton concludes this section of the conferences by providing a generous sampling of the criticisms of the avarice of the Order, of varying degrees of fairness and accuracy, by contemporary witnesses, including Pope Alexander III, King Richard I of England, an archbishop and a Benedictine abbot, but most extensively by clerical literary figures, Gerald of Wales, Walter Map, Nigel Wireker, and an anonymous poet who is himself a Cistercian. The pope's criticisms, in particular, were intended to appeal to the monks' own ideals in order to preserve both their reputation and their integrity; the other authority figures seem to have a good deal of self-interest and a good deal less objectivity. The writers, having a satiric bent, are even less-trustworthy reporters, motivated to one degree or another by personal pique and a sense of injury with regard to their own professional lives as aspiring ecclesiastics thwarted, or at least feeling thwarted, in their ambitions by Cistercian opponents—or in the case of the Cistercian poet, perhaps nursing a grudge due to some intra-monastic dispute. Their critique of the Order's supposedly insatiable hunger for land is marked by colorful but wildly improbable tales of moving boundary markers (including a tree!) to gain possession of adjacent property, repeatedly sowing a neighbor's field with salt until he decides to sell it (to the monks of course), and the like.

In Merton's judgment, these negative appraisals may "have a foundation in fact, but prompted by literary and political motives, based on personal spite, they are simply a rehashing of familiar satirical themes popular among the clerics of the court at the time" (177). These authors are forerunners of the more virulent critics of monasticism in particular and of the Church generally, who would become active in the fourteenth and fifteenth centuries and prepare the way for the Reformation, and they continued to provide ammunition for "more modern historians hostile to Catholicism and the monastic order" (177). Yet, Merton suggests, Gerald, and the others as well, did "offer sufficiently interesting and valuable indications of the state of the Order at the end of the twelfth century" (175) and in the decades that followed. They need to be read judiciously, but they should not simply be dismissed out of hand, at least as one indicator of current public attitudes toward the monasteries then at the height of their power and influence.

Introduction lix

Following a brief transitional passage on thirteenth-century Europe generally, its gradual shift to a more *"urban, commercial society"* (181), its emerging nationalism, the rise of universities and their new methodologies—all of which adversely affected Cistercian life to some degree and tended toward diminishing its impact on the broader society of the time—Merton turns his attention to the major internal issue besetting the Order in the first half of the thirteenth century: "THE STRUGGLE OF CÎTEAUX *with the Four First Foundations,"*[78] the earliest daughter houses of La Ferté, Pontigny, Morimond, and above all Clairvaux, the most celebrated of Cistercian abbeys due to the renown of its first abbot, Saint Bernard. A legitimate concern for the traditional autonomy of individual Cistercian houses, as the abbot of Cîteaux began to assert a monarchical "right to intervene in the affairs of any monastery" (183) at the expense of the more communal authority of the Cistercian General Chapter, became entwined with the power struggles between Cîteaux and Clairvaux, leading to various interventions, mostly ineffectual, of pope and king, and climaxing with the formal issuing of the papal bull *Parvus Fons* in 1265.

Merton states that a "clear understanding" (183) of the controversy depends on an awareness of the various iterations of the *Carta Caritatis*, once again presented in what is in fact a muddled chronology, but one that does show the increased role of the "First Fathers" in serving as a balancing counterweight to the power of the abbot of Cîteaux in the *Carta Caritatis Posterior* as compared with the *Carta Caritatis Prior*. Merton traces the shifting state of the conflict through four phases, beginning with the other primary abbots' strenuous objections to the abbot of Cîteaux's unilateral deposition of one of these abbots in 1212, temporarily quelled by Pope Innocent's threat to raise the issue at the Fourth Lateran Council three years later. Then a council in 1222 reached a provisional resolution to limit the power and oversight of the abbot of Cîteaux while at the same time calling

---

78. Pages 182–91 in this edition.

on the abbot of Clairvaux to surrender the papal privileges accrued to that monastery, an unacceptable demand that resulted in the arrangement's collapse when he refused to do so. After a period of relative calm, the conflict broke out anew in 1262 with the irregular election of a new abbot of Cîteaux in the absence of the First Fathers, the failed attempt two years later to remove the abbot of Clairvaux from the scene by making him a bishop (in far-off Brittany no less!), an unsuccessful intervention by King Louis later that year, and a virtual declaration of independence by Clairvaux, which then hosted its own General Chapter for its daughter houses. Finally a new pope, Clement IV, took decisive action in issuing the bull *Parvus Fons* in June 1265, which both affirmed the provisions of the *Carta Caritatis* (*Posterior*), circumscribing the power of the abbot of Cîteaux, and also heightened the influence of what had been a consultative body, the *definitorium*, now a council modeled more closely on Dominican governance structures, of twenty-five abbots from the five major filiations, which eventually largely marginalized the legislative role of the General Chapter. In Merton's view, it resulted in "a very serious compromise, which destroys the original, traditional framework of {the} Cistercian Order": in effect "it destroys the autonomy of the individual house" and "destroys the originality of Cistercian law in its guarantee of a balance between the Abbot of Cîteaux and the General Chapter" (190).

Having examined the Order's internal conflicts, Merton then turns once again to Cistercian involvement in the world beyond the cloister, considering in turn its activities in the economic, ecclesial, military and political, and intellectual spheres, all of which seriously compromised the fundamental commitment of the Order to the contemplative life, detached "from the business, the litigations, the conflicts and the ambitions of 'the world,' not only in the sense of the profane world, but in the sense of the powerful ecclesiastical world of prelates and great abbeys" (192). Merton points out that the basically intramural activities related to the founding, building, growth and regular functioning of a monastery were of course necessary and compatible with Cistercian principles, and that much of the external participation of the Order in the ecclesial and even the secular life of the time was in obedience to papal wishes, marked by largely frustrated efforts of the General Chapter to keep such involvements to a minimum.

But these mandatory activities soon led to further, less justifiable types of employment, while military roles, extending even to taking up arms, that seem antithetical to the monastic vocation, were not considered by many as inherently problematic, given the ethos of the time. Resistance to these outside commitments was strong through the latter part of the twelfth century, but largely dissipated in the thirteenth, when "*general acceptance of activity* of every sort (except parish work)" came to be regarded "as normal for a Cistercian" (193).

Merton then examines in detail four broad areas of activity, beginning with the "BUSINESS OF THE ORDER,"[79] its economic interactions with the outside world. This section overlaps to some extent with the previous discussion of Cistercian economics, but here the focus is less on issues of property, of donations and their effects on religious life, etc., and more on the dynamics of doing business and the equivocal consequences of unexpected affluence—full-scale involvement in trade, attending, even sponsoring, fairs and markets, owning ships and urban warehouses, controlling mines, dealing with litigation. Skillful monastic builders eventually were employed in non-monastic projects, while large-scale expansion of the monastic plant could and often did lead to crippling debt. He presents the English wool trade as a prime example of monastic integration into the economic life of the era: well suited to the Cistercian grange system, particularly in areas not conducive to extensive agricultural development, like Yorkshire, and initially very successful, a model for other producers both religious and secular, the trade eventually led to risky speculative practices like selling wool a year or more in advance—in effect borrowing on future production—that in

---

79. Pages 193–204 in this edition.

combination with various natural disasters, royal exactions and slipshod management frequently resulted in massive indebtedness that even threatened the continued existence of some monastic houses. According to Coburn Graves, Merton's principal source for this topic, "In the end the ideal gave way completely before the facts of trade" (201).

Merton then turns his attention to the involvement of the Order in ecclesial business,[80] beginning with the impressive number of Cistercian bishops (and even two popes), at once a sign of the Order's vitality and both effect and cause of its growing power (with one final glance at the evolution of the issue of episcopal oversight of monasteries in the fuzzy context of the successive versions of the *Carta Caritatis*). Permission for small groups of monks and brothers to accompany and assist a Cistercian bishop in his duties was eventually extended to non-Cistercian bishops as well, and led in turn to monks, and particularly brothers, joining the households of kings and nobles, becoming officials, or simply workers, at the papal court, filling civil offices, financial or even military, and becoming employed in various charitable efforts. Abbots and other monastic officials were regularly dispatched by popes to institute reform measures in other orders, to engage in diplomatic missions, to serve as mediators and arbitrators in both religious and secular disputes, duties that the General Chapters tried with little success to limit. While some of these assignments may have made a positive contribution to a smoothly functioning Church and society, they hardly represented the ideal of more faithfully living the Rule of Benedict, which brought the first monks to Cîteaux.

This was even more the case with the military responsibilities assumed by Cistercians, which Merton considers next.[81] He traces this involvement from the direct engagement in the defense of Calatrava from the Moors, through the Third Crusade,

---

80. Pages 204–9 in this edition.
81. Pages 209–12 in this edition.

"largely a Cistercian operation" (209), to the complex, inconclusive campaign against the Albigensians, and the infamous Fourth Crusade, diverted to the conquest of Constantinople and the establishment of the Latin Empire there, in which Cistercians played a significant part, founding monasteries in Greece that did not outlive the bitterly resented Latin rule. Merton gives the most detailed attention to Cistercians' participation in the Albigensian Crusade, initially as papal legates and preachers sent to bring the Cathars back to orthodox faith, but eventually involving military action, particularly after the assassination of the Cistercian legate Peter of Castelnau in early 1208, spurring the "punitive crusade" (211) that eventually ended with no clear resolution. Merton points out that this was "an ineffective and hopeless task, contrary to {the} spirit of {the} Order . . . imposed on members of the Order, contrary to their own judgement and conscience" (211), yet notes as well a fundamental ambivalence within the Order, as some of the Cistercian participants "voiced no objections" (211) while others pleaded with the pope to release them from their mission and allow them to return to their monasteries.

Studies, the final topic discussed in this section,[82] might seem awkwardly connected to the preceding items, but Merton emphasizes that a primary motive for educating Cistercians at Paris and other new universities, in addition to the need for learned abbots, was to increase the monks' suitability for the various extra-monastic responsibilities they were increasingly called upon to assume: "studies outside regular monasteries of the Order, in colleges . . . went hand-in-hand with the activities and missions of the Order . . . evidently approved and encouraged by Rome" (212). In this regard, "One of the effects of the Albigensian crusade," Merton has earlier stated, "was to show that the Cistercians had *insufficient knowledge of theology*" (212).

This acceptance, by no means universal, of a need for formal education for monastics represents a decisive shift in attitude from

---

82. Pages 212–25 in this edition.

the time of Saint Bernard, who was suspicious of the new trends of early scholasticism represented above all by Abelard, and while not anti-intellectual was certainly anti-rationalist. The major figure in this new concern for education was the mid-thirteenth-century successor of Bernard as abbot of Clairvaux, the Englishman Stephen of Lexington, controversial founder of the College of Saint Bernard (!) in Paris, established with the approval of the Holy See but undertaken independently of the Cistercian General Chapter, arousing opposition that eventually led to his deposition as abbot despite papal support. Merton quotes extensively from two recently discovered letters of Stephen, written before his abbacy at Clairvaux, that indicate the basis for his passionate commitment to studies. One concerns what he saw as the chaotic situation of Irish Cistercian houses, leading him to insist that *"monks are not to be received unless they have some education in {the} humanities . . . even at Paris or Oxford"* (222); the other is addressed to the abbot of Pontigny concerning that abbey's daughter house of Cadouin, where openly heretical views were held by some monks, again making evident the crucial need for better intellectual formation. "Stephen believed that the Order was trying to solve its problems by temporal and political means, whereas the root of the trouble was spiritual, and this in turn came from {the} lack of sound theology in the Order" (223), due to inadequate education and isolation from vital currents of thought: "The members of the Order are ignorant and easily seduced by error. In silence and solitude, with no communication, the error grows unchecked" (224). In Merton's judgment, Stephen "was a great man, very gifted, {an} intelligent, prudent, firm and realistic superior with a great love for the Order, but not understood by many good men in the Order" (220). But by the early fourteenth century, the Order as a whole had come to recognize the necessity of formal study, the governance of the Paris college had been entrusted to the General Chapter, and a graduate of the school had become the second Cistercian pope, whose efforts to reform the Order included the regulation of studies.

It is this figure, the Avignon Pope Benedict XII, and his 1335 Constitution *Fulgens sicut Stella*, that are the focus of the final main section of these conference notes,[83] marking in Merton's view "the close of the great period of the Order. . . . the state of the Order as a *great active force in the Medieval Church*, and yet in decline" (225–26). His careful reading of the opening paragraph of Benedict's text reveals how even the use of traditional terminology can take on a "completely different emphasis, representing a whole new mentality" (227), probably without any conscious intent to do so. The pope praises both action and contemplation, but the activity is much more outwardly directed than in the foundational Cistercian documents, and there is little sense of contemplation being regarded as the summit of Benedictine life; "the three essential occupations of the monk" (227) are included in *Fulgens*, but equating manual labor with "*works of charity*" (226) represents a shift of focus to exterior practices more characteristic of active orders, and there are subtle changes of emphasis as well in references to the liturgy and to *lectio* (seen as a way of learning "the science of perfection") (226). Compared to Pope Paschal's "Roman Privilege," or even to the verse prologue of the *Exordium Magnum* a century later (briefly considered here in a somewhat awkward insertion), *Fulgens* according to Merton represented an effort "to organize a life that has adapted itself. . . . a stabilization of the life at a level which is in fact far from that of the early Cîteaux, yet not completely alien to its spirit" (228).

Pope Benedict himself, as characterized in Merton's principal source, the work of Jean-Berthold Mahn,[84] is presented as epitomizing the outlook of the era: intellectually well-trained, with an activist mentality, rapidly advancing in the power structure of the Order and in the hierarchy of the Church, a reformer focused more on altering institutional structures than renewing the contemplative spirit, primarily "an organizer, an administrator, 'without profound sense of religious problems'"[85] (230).

---

83. Pages 225–46 in this edition.
84. Jean-Berthold Mahn, *Le Pape Benoît XII et les Cisterciens* (Paris: Librairie Ancienne Honoré Champion, 1949).
85. Mahn, *Benoît XII*, 11.

Dealing with laxity in morals, observance and doctrine in religious orders generally, he made strenuous efforts to revitalize religious life by regulating it more strictly. With regard to specific problems of economics, regularity and studies in his own Cistercian Order, he moved decisively to establish ordinances that would minimize if not eliminate "irresponsible, independent and arbitrary disposition of monastery property by abbots, or imprudent business deals, entered into independently and irresponsibly by abbots and cellarers" (231); to tighten up criteria for admission of candidates and to restore discipline with regard to poverty and abstinence; and to require abbots to send carefully vetted monks to study, either at Paris or—for smaller, less wealthy monasteries—at other institutions of higher learning.

The results, not unexpectedly, were mixed. There was careful oversight of particularly troubled monasteries, but various loopholes in implementing the provisions of *Fulgens* were sought and found by recalcitrant abbots. The net result of the enforcement of studies was not impressive: "there is no serious theology written, and apparently what was taught was very conventional and perhaps tending in the direction of the times, towards the decadence of scholasticism. What is written is concerned with practical organizational problems, if not legal questions" (240). Not until the seventeenth century did the Order produce a significant—but highly controversial—theologian, the moralist Caramuel, whose notoriously flexible judgments on ethical questions won him the title "prince of laxists" (241) but who Merton cautions "must not simply be derided—he was a brilliant mind and an energetic worker for the good of the Order and the Church" (241–42). As for life in the colleges, particularly at Paris, nonstudent monks regularly took advantage of the lodgings in the city for their own purposes, abbots often used their students in Paris as agents for various business deals, and a considerable proportion of the students, let loose in the big city, behaved as students typically will; as Merton mordantly comments, "The atmosphere of the university was not conducive to regular life or to monastic discipline" (243).

Summing up the state of the Order at the time of Pope Benedict, Merton notes that the level of outside activity of the Cistercians actually diminished somewhat as the pope relied more and more on mendicants for various missions of diplomacy and reform. Flagrant abuses were curbed, but there was never full endorsement or cooperation on the part of Cistercian authorities, despite the fact that the pope was one of their own. It was largely a case of too little, too late, too superficial for an age when "the whole edifice of medieval religious society [was] falling apart" (245), too focused on structural and institutional issues when what was most lacking was "the deep religious insight and creative fervor that would have been necessary for a genuine and deep reform" (244). Enforcement of the program of studies "contributed little or nothing to the reform of the Order" (245) and may have ended up doing more harm than good in exposing future monastic leaders to a quite unmonastic environment, but the main problem in Merton's view was not the academic program itself, and the equivocal results of Benedict's attempts at reorganization must not be taken, Merton warns, as evidence that somehow "proves the 'danger of studies'" (246) as some would have it. "If the studies could have been carried out in regular monasteries of the Order, the program might have been of much greater value" (245).

On this note Merton concludes the final major section of the conference text, but goes on to list "Omissions,"[86] a few "important items" not given due attention in "these too brief notes" (246): the monastic missions in eastern Europe, the complicated question of the status of the Cistercian nuns, and the crisis of the laybrotherhood, though in the case of this last topic he then proceeds to set forth a five-part overview as detailed as that provided for a number of topics in the main body of the text. After a reminder of the economic benefits due to the brothers and a comment about a large contingent of brothers being a sign of the spiritual fervor

---

86. Pages 246–49 in this edition.

of a community, he points out problems that surfaced early in the Order's history: the danger of exploiting their labor, the poor or sometimes non-existent formation program for brothers, and the tendency to relax discipline as compensation for hard work. The numbers of brothers had radically diminished in the fourteenth century, and they had almost completely disappeared by the beginning of the fifteenth. Even in the early thirteenth century, the brothers were apparently coming to be considered more a liability than an advantage as secular help and rental of property became more economically advantageous, or even necessary, and many of the brothers grew increasingly dissatisfied and rebellious at perceived discriminatory attitudes and practices. Often inadequately formed, living at isolated granges apart from the religious atmosphere of the monastery, increasingly estranged from the choir monks, resenting rigid rules or taking advantage of questionable relaxations, the brothers declined precipitously in both quality and quantity, and what had been one of the signal components of early Cistercian success had now become both effect and cause of the more general decline of the Order.

This negative focus carries over into the brief Epilogue[87] that concludes the text, as Merton notes the disastrous consequences for the Order of the triple calamity of the fourteenth century: the Black Death affected religious communities, living in such close proximity, particularly heavily, with some 60% of Cistercians in northern Europe falling victim to the plague; during the Hundred Years War (1337–1453), monasteries were pillaged, abandoned, even destroyed, regular visitation became impossible, and communities grew isolated from one another; the Great Schism split the Order between communities, mainly French, supporting the Avignon papacy, and much of the rest of the Order loyal to Rome. Add to these catastrophes the widespread practice in the following century of installing commendatory abbots, non-monastics appointed by political or religious authorities for

---

87. Pages 249–52 in this edition.

Introduction lxix

services rendered, "interested only in collecting revenues and without concern for the community" (251), and the prospects for genuine monastic life were dire indeed. Attempts at reform often concentrated on the peripheral or superficial—new devotions or elaborate regalia—or were alien to Cistercian tradition, and of course the Reformation dealt a crippling blow to monasticism through much of the historic territory of the Order of Cîteaux. "It is difficult to see how the Order survived at all" (252), Merton comments, but of course it did, and in his final sentence he points to the powerful effects of the Council of Trent in bringing renewal to the Cistercian Order as to the Church at large, and thus is able to bring his text to a close on a positive note.

* * * * * * *

The series of eight oral conference presentations of this material is comparably well organized, but does not simply follow the sequence of the written text. Merton has already decided as he begins these talks on October 21 to finish them before the arrival of the new year, so his time is quite limited. Consequently he does some drastic compressing and reorganizing. He begins the first conference with a quick comment on the paucity of sources—the *Compendium* is "basically useless," the only comprehensive history in English (Lekai's *The White Monks*) is anti-Trappist (a rather overstated claim), the chief French source (Willems[88]) is a "messy job"—two chapters listed in the table of contents are simply missing: this section of Willems' manuscript was lost in a flood and never replaced! He then presents his summary of the major periods of Cistercian history and immediately jumps ahead to a discussion of the controversy between Cîteaux and the First Fathers and the promulgation of *Parvus Fons* in 1265, skipping over more than a third of the written text, much of which he does not discuss at all.

88. Eugène Willems, *Esquisse Historique de l'Ordre de Cîteaux*, d'après le Père Grégoire Muller, 2 vols. (Aubel: Notre-Dame du Val-Dieu, 1957–1958).

The next conference begins similarly by providing a framework, drawn from his introduction, of the evolution of the Order from being ahead of its time from its foundation until about 1130, to being reflective of its time, no longer "inspired," through the rest of the twelfth century, to falling behind the time, living on its reputation and getting involved in matters it was incapable of handling, from 1200 on. He then once again moves ahead to a discussion of Cistercian economic life, principally taken from the segment on the "BUSINESS OF THE ORDER" in the "ACTIVITIES OF THE CISTERCIANS" section immediately following the analysis of *Parvus Fons*, supplemented by a few details on serfs, ownership of churches, and burial fees from the earlier "ECONOMIC SITUATION OF THE ORDER" material. The third lecture finishes up his extensive discussion of the wool trade, focusing on the financial difficulties it eventually caused, and then flips back to the material on the critics of the order, particularly the satirists, that comes just before the consideration of *Parvus Fons* in the written text. The rest of the earlier sections, the survey of major events from 1147 through the end of the century, the material on the Order's expansion, and most of the details about the economic situation that follow, are simply omitted, though the abridgement is handled so smoothly that it would be completely imperceptible without the written text as a basis for comparison.

The other five sessions adhere more closely to the sequence found in the text. Conference four focuses on the various ecclesiastical and temporal positions assumed by Cistercians in the thirteenth century, from bishops to arsenal doorkeepers to preachers of and participants in crusades. Then Merton turns in the following week to the problem of studies and the founding of the Paris College of St. Bernard. The sixth talk discusses the career of Benedict XII and his issuing of *Fulgens sicut Stella*, noting that the Cistercians of the Common Observance tend to have a better sense of the developments of this period than do the members of the Strict Observance, who tend to jump from the *Exordium Parvum* and the "Golden Age" to the Trappist reform of de Rancé in the seventeenth century to the reunion of the various Strict Observance congregations in 1892. The penultimate conference turns back to Stephen of Lexington, because during the week since the previous conference Merton has become aware of the collection of Stephen's letters that provide some background for his sense of the urgent need for better intellectual training (material that he was able to insert in the written text as an appendix to his discussion of Stephen). His commentary on this material fits in smoothly here because it leads into the material in *Fulgens* on studies and the problematic results of the constitution generally, and on abuses in the colleges, concluding with a brief look at the reputation and career of Caramuel and the admonition "to put somebody like this in context" (and even more so a Stephen of Lexington) rather than simply pinning a label on them—the need to find the right questions to raise in order to get relevant answers.

The final presentation provides a summary of the post-Benedict period, adhering closely to the written text, judging that the reforms of *Fulgens* were largely organizational rather than spiritual and therefore didn't go deep enough but were better than nothing, even though largely temporary in their effect. The material on the brothers adds a few details—the fact that they were forbidden even to learn how to read, that once tithes were imposed on land worked by the community a big economic advantage to having brothers was lost and the incentive to keep them diminished significantly. Mention of the fourteenth- and fifteenth-century blows to the Order leads to the observation that it was "a miracle after this that the Order functioned at all," but also to a bit more attention, under the heading of the "Commendam," to the transformation of the Abbey of La Trappe after the conversion of its commendatory abbot, Armand de Rancé, that would move a substantial segment of the Order of Cîteaux in a new direction.

With an audience not composed exclusively of novices, there is considerably less "house business" mentioned in Merton's preliminary comments for this set of conferences—though on November 4 he does instruct his charges to keep away from the hallway outside the novice master's office during times of direction. During the previous week he had mentioned that Cistercian nuns from Belgium had stopped at the abbey on their way to California to found the Monastery of the Redwoods[89] (which Merton would visit in his trips to California in 1968[90]), and he called the group the most authentic he'd seen, with no false piety, and the mother abbess (Myriam Dardenne) the smartest Cistercian he'd ever met. On November 18 he asks for prayers for Étienne Gilson, who was sick, and reports on December 2 that Gilson is better and going to Africa. References to Vatican II are frequent: Pope John's opening speech to the council fathers is the very first thing he mentions in the opening conference, the joke about cardinals heading to Trent is told again the following week, and on November 25 he calls the previous week's events in Rome "fabulous—historic" in the critique made of triumphalism—"a key issue with the Protestants."

Once again the presentations are occasionally punctuated with personal anecdotes, recalling in connection with Henry de Marcy's conquest of Lavaur during the Albigensian Crusade that his town (St. Antonin) played Lavaur in rugby when Merton was a boy in southern France, in a game marked by lots of fighting among players and spectators, including attacks on referees, adding that only a team of New Zealand Maoris was able to subdue Toulouse (the onetime Albigensian stronghold). In connection with incidents of misbehavior at the University of Paris, Merton recalls a particularly wild party at Cambridge where those attending began to destroy the building, adding that a student who had been "kicked out" hired a hearse to take him to the railroad station; he also mentions as a particular "triumph" an occasion when he returned to Cambridge after having withdrawn from

---

89. See the journal entry for October 27, 1962 (*Turning Toward the World*, 261).

90. See Merton's journal entries for May 7–14 and October 11–13, 1968, in Thomas Merton, *The Other Side of the Mountain: The End of the Journey. Journals, vol. 7, 1967–1968*, ed. Patrick Hart (San Francisco: HarperCollins, 1998), 96–100, 200–201.

the university and was confronted by a "bulldog," a proctor's assistant in charge of discipline, who asked if he was a member of the university since he wasn't wearing a gown, and he was able to say that he wasn't, that he had been "sent down" (not strictly true) and therefore was no longer subject to the bulldog's authority. On December 2 he mentions that in a Festschrift for his friend the Argentine writer and editor Victoria Ocampo he was identified as Thomas Merton, SJ[91]—a source of great amusement for himself and his listeners.

This was only one of many occasions for laughter throughout these conferences, many of them prompted simply by the droll way Merton recounted incidents that didn't seem particularly humorous on the page—as when Cistercian brothers are entrusted with keys to arsenals, or the Abbot of Waverly is forced to escape creditors by sneaking out of the monastery by night, or King Henry III requires the Cistercians to pay huge sums for "privileges." Other incidents, like the tall tales of moving the boundary markers and sowing salt in a neighbor's field, or the story—not included in the written text—of Arnulf of Villers,[92] who ecstatically jumped up and down in choir until he had to be housed in a hut, are ready-made for laughter. At one point Merton had to remind himself and his audience of the danger of "just joking around" with some of these stories—the need to look at historical events in the context of their times. The final conference, in the midst of recounting the various catastrophes, nevertheless provokes repeated laughter, as with mention that in one monastic house devastated by the plague only an invalid and a simpleton survived, that moving out of Cîteaux to Dijon to escape the Black Death "had its effects on regularity," that one of the consequences of the Great Schism was obtaining the

---

91. See Merton's journal entry for December 4, 1962 (*Turning Toward the World*, 271).

92. For a brief biography see Thomas Merton, *In the Valley of Wormwood: Cistercian Blessed and Saints of the Golden Age*, ed. Patrick Hart, CS 233 (Collegeville, MN: Cistercian Publications, 2013), 236–44.

privilege of being "irremovable in office," that the refectory at La Trappe before the time of Rancé had been turned into a bowling alley, and finally a reminder that no one should be reduced to an image—even de Rancé (not a Merton favorite)—reinforced by a pertinent tag line from Orwell's *Animal Farm*—"four legs good"[93]—that brings a last laugh as the series comes to an end.

* * * * * * *

This overview of Merton's second set of history conferences prompts three observations. First, in the past half century there have been tremendous advances in the study of Cistercian history by scholars both within and outside the Order, so that some of Merton's information and analysis, as is evident in the matter of the sequence and significance of early Cistercian documents, no longer represents the consensus position of historians. But Merton has put together a coherently organized synthesis of the best of the studies available at the time, many of them not in English, and made the results of this research available to his monastic audience in a clear and accessible form, in both its written text and its oral presentation. Second, his approach is objective but not detached. Contemporary historians of the Order tend to be uncomfortable with the notion of a normative era against which other eras can be evaluated, signaling decline or renewal; they prefer to stress a process of adaptation to new circumstances as the broader culture in which monastic life is situated evolves.[94] Such a perspective is a valuable corrective to a simplistic binary of an idealized formative period of authentic religious life and subsequent eras that either succeed or more often fail to reach that ideal.

---

93. George Orwell, *Animal Farm: A Fairy Story* (1946; New York: Signet Classic, 1956), 40.

94. See Janet Burton and Julie Kerr, *The Cistercians in the Middle Ages* (Woodbridge, UK: Boydell & Brewer, 2011); Emilia Jamroziak, *The Cistercian Order in Medieval Europe, 1090–1500* (New York: Routledge, 2013).

But from a monastic standpoint, awareness of and fidelity to the charism of an order's founder(s) is an essential element in fulfilling one's own religious vocation, as *Perfectae Caritatis*, the Decree on the Renewal of Religious Life of Vatican II, just beginning when these conferences were being presented, made clear.[95] This is Merton's approach as instructor and guide for those who have made or are preparing to make a commitment to monastic life, for whom this history is, or should be, not of simply academic interest. Despite the preponderance of information, the ultimate goal of these and all of Merton's conferences is transformation, a deepening of commitment to a chosen way of life.

Finally, if a balanced Benedictine life of prayer, work and reflective reading oriented toward contemplative union with God and unity with all humanity and all creation is the foundational charism of the Cistercian life, detailed study of this particular period is useful in demonstrating how historical circumstances can clarify or obscure awareness of that charism and consequently assist or hinder a commitment to actualize it in one's own life. As the complex circumstances surrounding the founding of Cîteaux and the early expansion of the Order discussed in the other set of history conferences make clear, it is not simply a matter of an initial period of prevailing sanctity giving way to an ethos of compromise and mediocrity, but of a vision and articulation of a way of Christian discipleship that remains an invitation and a challenge to be actualized in the concrete circumstances of each unique time and place. This ultimately is Merton's main lesson for his readers and listeners here.

There are no further sets of Cistercian history conferences in the remaining two and a half years of Merton's mastership. The specifically Cistercian component of his teaching for the next year and a half is concerned with the life and work of the Order's most influential figure, Saint Bernard. At the very end

---

95. *Perfectae Caritatis*, 2, in *The Documents of Vatican II*, ed. Walter M. Abbott (New York: America Press, 1966), 468.

of these notes he says of the period preceding and encompassing the Reformation that it is "an important period and should be studied" (252), but he never returns to it, nor does he ever focus on the Trappist reform of the seventeenth century,[96] which had such an influence on Cistercians of the Strict Observance up to his own day. Whether he would have turned to these later periods if he had not withdrawn to the hermitage in August 1965 is unknown, but it can be safely said that he felt no obligation simply to make sure each successive period of Cistercian history would be given due attention. Much of his interest in the era from Bernard to Benedict was evidently prompted by the reciprocal illumination that the period of "The Maturity of the Order" and that of "The Formation of the Order" (139) could cast on one another, so that the alternation from one to the other in the last months of 1962 may well have provided a stimulus for reflection to both presenter and audience beyond what a more conventional sequential arrangement would have produced.

* * * * * * *

Since each set of Cistercian history conferences has only a single written version, Merton's handwritten notes for "Cistercian History" and the mimeographed typescript for "The Cistercian Order from the Death of St. Bernard to the Reform of Benedict XII," the task of establishing a critical text is simplified. All substantive additions made to the text, in order to turn elliptical or fragmentary statements into complete sentences, are included in braces, as are the few emendations incorporated directly into the text of the first set, so that the reader can always determine exactly what Merton himself wrote; those emendations in the second set that are judged to be the result of typists' misreadings are not put in braces, since the latter do not represent Merton's own

---

96. For Merton's early perspective on the Trappist reform, see chapter 2 of Thomas Merton, *The Waters of Siloe* (New York: Harcourt, Brace, 1949), 32–49.

wording, but are identified in the notes. No effort is made to reproduce Merton's rather inconsistent punctuation, paragraphing, abbreviations and typographical features; a standardized format for these features is established that in the judgment of the editor best represents a synthesis of Merton's own practice and contemporary usage: e.g., all Latin passages are italicized unless specific parts of a longer passage are underlined by Merton, in which case the underlined section of the passage is in Roman type; all other passages underlined by Merton are italicized; words in upper case in the text are printed in small caps; periods and commas are uniformly included within quotation marks; patterns of abbreviation and capitalization, very inconsistent in the copy texts, are regularized. All references to primary and secondary sources are cited in the notes. Untranslated Latin passages in the original text are left in Latin but translated in the notes; unless otherwise noted, the translations are by the editor. Scripture passages are quoted from the Douay-Rheims version customarily used by Merton at the time these conferences were given.

Appendix A records all alterations made by Merton in his holograph manuscript of the "Cistercian History" notes, both those made on-line as he was writing and those added subsequently. Since there are no authorial changes made to the mimeograph of the second set of conferences, there are no entries from this material in this appendix. Appendix B provides a table correlating the written texts and the taped lectures of both sets of talks, including indications of those conference recordings that have been made available commercially, in order to facilitate comparison of Merton's written version of the material as published in this edition with the conferences as actually delivered to the novices and young monks in his class. Appendix C lists Merton's other works in which the history of the Cistercian Order is discussed, followed by a selected list of important recent studies on this subject, which will provide helpful updating on material discussed by Merton.

* * * * * * *

In conclusion I would like to express my gratitude to all those who have made this volume possible:

- the Trustees of the Merton Legacy Trust, Peggy Fox, Anne McCormick and Mary Somerville, for permission to publish the *Medieval Cistercian History* conferences and for their consistent support in this and other projects;

- the late Robert E. Daggy, former director of the Thomas Merton Center, Bellarmine College (now University), Louisville, KY, for first alerting me to the project of editing Merton's monastic conferences, and for his encouragement in this and other efforts in Merton studies;

- the late Brother Patrick Hart, OCSO, the founding editor of the Monastic Wisdom series, for his friendship and guidance in the publication of this series of volumes of Thomas Merton's monastic conferences;

- Deacon William R. Grimes, former novice at the Abbey of Gethsemani, who was present for the conferences in this volume, for the lovely preface in which he shares his memories of Merton as teacher and spiritual guide;

- Paul M. Pearson, director and archivist of the Merton Center, and Mark C. Meade, assistant archivist, for their gracious hospitality and valued assistance during my research visits to the Center;

- Brother Gaetan Blanchette, OCSO, librarian at the Abbey of Gethsemani, and Father Lawrence Morey, OCSO, monastery archivist, for their deeply appreciated aid and support in locating and making available relevant materials in the abbey's collections;

- publisher Hans Christoffersen, series editor Marsha Dutton and production manager Colleen Stiller at Liturgical Press, for guiding this and previous volumes of

Merton's conferences through the publication process with grace and efficiency;

- The Gannon University Research Committee, which has awarded a generous grant that allowed me to pursue research on this project at the Abbey of Gethsemani, at the Merton Center, and at various libraries;

- Mary Beth Earll of the interlibrary loan department of the Nash Library, Gannon University, for once again providing invaluable assistance by locating and procuring various obscure volumes;

- library staff of the Hesburgh Library of the University of Notre Dame, the Latimer Family Library of St. Vincent College, and the Institute of Cistercian Studies Collection at the Waldo Library of Western Michigan University, for assistance in locating important materials in their collections;

- again and always to my wife Suzanne and our children for their continual love, support and encouragement in this and other projects.

CISTERCIAN HISTORY

Early Monasticism in England

While Roman monks settled in {the} south, Celtic monks settled in {the} north. St. Columba {founded} *Iona*.[1] Lindisfarne {was the see of} St. Cuthbert.[2] (Whitby {is associated with} St. Hilda {and} Caedmon.[3]) St. Benedict's influence penetrates to {the} north through *St. Wilfrid*, {associated with} Lindisfarne and Ripon,[4] who went to Rome and brought back {the} *Rule* of

1. For the foundation in 565 of the monastery of Iona, off the west coast of Scotland, by the Irish abbot Columba (d. 597), see Bede, *A History of the English Church and People*, trans. Leo Sherley-Price (New York: Penguin, 1955; rev. ed. 1968), 146–47 (bk. 3, chap. 4); Iona became the great center of missionary activity by Celtic monks in northern Britain.

2. The monastery of Lindisfarne, off the coast of Northumberland, was founded from Iona in 635 by Aidan (d. 651) (see Bede, *History*, 144–45, 148–49 [bk. 3, chaps. 3, 5]); the great hermit and contemplative Cuthbert became Bishop of Lindisfarne in 685, serving for two years before returning to solitude and dying soon afterward (see Bede, *History*, 259–69 [bk. 4, chaps. 27–32]).

3. Hilda (d. 680), of royal blood, was the founding abbess of the double monastery of Whitby, site of the famous synod in 664 to settle the controversy between the Celtic and Roman dating of Easter and other disputed matters (for the life of Hilda, see Bede, *History*, 245–50 [bk. 4, chap. 23]; for the synod, see 185–92 [bk. 3, chap. 25]). Caedmon was a retainer at Whitby who became the first known vernacular poet in English; his brief hymn on creation is still extant (see Bede, *History*, 250–53 [bk. 4, chap. 24]).

4. Wilfrid (d. 709), an influential proponent of Roman customs at the Synod of Whitby and eventually archbishop of York, began his monastic life at Lindisfarne and was founding abbot of the monastery of Ripon (for his life see Bede, *History*, 305–13 [bk. 5, chap. 19]).

St. Benedict.⁵ *St. Benedict Biscop* accompanied Wilfrid to Rome; {he} stayed two years at Lérins, returned and was {for} two years abbot at Canterbury. Then {he} took {the} *Rule* and Roman customs to the north: {the} *Rule* {was the main} spiritual influence; {to introduce the} Roman liturgy, Benedict Biscop brings John, archcantor of St. Peter's.⁶ *Glastonbury*, {in} Somerset, {was} originally Celtic, {but} became Benedictine. *Wearmouth and Jarrow* {were} founded by St. Benedict Biscop {in} 674 {and} 685, {respectively}. Bede entered at Jarrow. {The} life {there was} very close to {that lived at the} original Monte Cassino. The *Rule* here {was} a directory and inspiration; {the} houses {were ordered} with {their} own customs. {At the} end of {the} eighth century, an Anglo-Saxon, *Willibald, helps revive Monte Cassino*. {The} *Danish invasions*⁷ wreak havoc on Anglo-Saxon monasteries—{there is a} *complete collapse*: monasteries practically disappear, except {the} community of Lindisfarne, which migrates to Durham ({a} stronghold).

{A} *monastic revival* {takes place} under Dunstan and King Edgar {in the} tenth century.⁸ {In} 934,⁹ St. Dunstan becomes Abbot

---

5. See David Knowles, *The Monastic Order in England: A History of its Development from the Times of St Dunstan to the Fourth Lateran Council—940–1216* (Cambridge: Cambridge University Press, 1940; 2ⁿᵈ ed. 1963), 21–22; Knowles actually writes that Wilfrid had brought the Rule from Gaul rather than from Rome. Subsequent details in this paragraph are taken from Knowles, *Monastic Order*, 22–23, 32.

6. For Benedict Biscop and John the Archcantor, see Bede, *History*, 236–38 (bk. 4, chap. 18).

7. The Viking raids began with an attack on the (Celtic) monastery of Lindisfarne in 793 and led to large-scale Danish settlements in extensive areas of east-central England throughout the following century, with continuing conflict until Alfred of Wessex (d. 899) defeated the Danes and established peace.

8. Merton relies in this paragraph on Knowles, *Monastic Order*, 31–38.

9. This is the approximate date of his reception of the monastic habit from his kinsman Aelfheah, rather than of his becoming abbot (see below); it is perhaps the result of a quick scan of Knowles, *Monastic Order*, 38, which mentions that around this date Aelfheah, who urged him to become a monk, was consecrated Bishop of Winchester. For the correct date of ca. 940, see below.

of Glastonbury. He had grown up at Glastonbury—it was still a famous shrine but {had} no monks (?); probably clerics served {at the} shrine; a library existed there. Dunstan {was} educated by {the} Irish {and} became {a} monk by private vow, then {a} priest. King Edmund took Dunstan as {a} counselor, then revived {the} Abbey of Glastonbury with Dunstan as abbot in gratitude for the fact that his life was saved in Cheddar Gorge.[10] {In} 956, Dunstan {is} in Flanders, especially {at} Ghent; {he} returns {in} 961[11] {to} Worcester and {subsequently becomes} Archbishop of Canterbury. Monasteries {are} restored, {and} monks replace (decadent) clerics in big churches. Monastic bishops reform {the} Church.

{In} 970, the *Regularis Concordia* {is} drawn up at {a} meeting of bishops and abbots at Winchester. {This document} concerns {the} monastic liturgy—{the} ceremonial, {the} prayers for {the} dead. {It is a} compendium of customs then in force in England (read D. Knowles, p. 44, bottom[12]); {it was} influenced by FLEURY

---

10. Shortly after deciding to send Dunstan, who had many detractors because of his piety, into exile, Edmund almost died on this crag while hunting; repenting his decision, he brought Dunstan to Glastonbury and seated him in the abbot's chair (see Knowles, *Monastic Order*, 38).

11. This date is also erroneous: Dunstan was recalled from exile and became bishop of Worcester in 957 and archbishop of Canterbury two or three years later (see Knowles, *Monastic Order*, 39).

12. "But though the *Concordia* differs little from other European customaries of the epoch there are a few provisions in which allusion is made to English practice. Thus a fire is allowed in a special room in winter, and the monks may work in shelter instead of in the cloister when the weather is cold; the pealing of bells is to be prolonged in the national fashion on Christmas and certain other feasts; processions are assumed as taking place not in the monastic buildings only, as came to be the custom abroad, but in the streets that lay between the monastic church and one of the town churches, and (a practice still more peculiar to England) it is assumed that the people will assist at the chief Mass on Sundays and feasts. Equally peculiar to the *Concordia* is the exhortation to daily Communion; it is difficult to say whether this was inspired by English custom or was directly due to the initiative of Dunstan and Ethelwold, perhaps recollecting the celebrated letter of Bede the Venerable."

also (Abbo of Fleury {was} exiled at Ramsey[13])—{there was also} Cluniac influence. The monastery, with {a strong} social orientation, stabilizes {the} kingdom. Missionaries go out to Scandinavia. Monastic centers of art {develop}; chant (also {the} organ and {the} beginning {of} polyphony) {is nurtured} (read D. K. 60[14]). {The} great monastic centers {of} Abingdon, Winchester, Ely, Peterbor-

---

13. Knowles notes (*Monastic Order*, 46, n. 3) that this exile occurred later, in 986–988, at which point Abbo was elected abbot of Fleury, but that he had been in England ca. 970 and may have been present at the Winchester council.

14. "From the first the leaders of the revival, in full agreement with the monastic tradition of recent centuries, had set the solemn performance of the liturgy in the forefront of their design. One of the chief motives for the expulsion of the secular clerks from the Old and New Minsters was that the offices might be more worthily accomplished. There is clear evidence that at the two great centres, Winchester and Ramsey, the elaborate rendering of ceremony and chant was a feature of the life at least during the generation of Aelfric and Byrhtferth. From Winchester, besides the service books that have survived, we have the two 'tropers' which show that in addition to the full body of plain chant the English monasteries made use not only of the elaborate additional modulations which interpolated and prolonged the important parts of the chant of the Mass and Office, but also a system of *organa* or polyphony which indeed shows a greater development in England than anywhere abroad. In addition, the English monasteries, as is clear from several indications, made much of organ music and of the treble voices of the children of the cloister, both in contrast to the voices of the monks and in polyphonic combination. In all this, it must be remembered, there was nothing uncouth or embryonic; the plain chant was a developed art-form of extreme flexibility, subtlety and beauty, and the music of Winchester in the days of Aelfric was in all essentials identical with that of the Vatican gradual and antiphoner of the present day. From the descriptions in which the Ramsey monk, the anonymous author of the life of Oswald, takes especial pleasure we can see that equal richness of liturgical life prevailed in the houses which derived from Fleury. English treble voices have ever been celebrated for their purity and sweetness of tone, and all who took part in the choral service had been trained from their earliest years in the Gregorian chant. The Mass and Office on high festivals must have provided a musical feast of great richness, and we can readily understand the admiration with which Cnut, in the well-known story, heard across the water the singing of the monks of Ely" (Knowles, *Monastic Order*, 60–61).

ough {and} Ramsey {flourish}. (Read D. K. p. 54 {for a} portrait of Dunstan;[15] the death of Dunstan {occurs in} 988.) {The} *Danish conquest* {takes place} after Dunstan's death, {in} 1015, {leading to the} reign of Canute[16] {and the} reign of St. Edward.[17]

The *Regularis Concordia* (Dunstan—Ethelwold—Oswald[18]) and the Benedictine revival of the tenth century ({the} reign of Edgar: 959–975).[19]

---

15. "Dunstan died . . . in 988. His last years had been given almost wholly to the pastoral care of his diocese and to the direct service of God. From the many living touches of his earliest biographer a very real portrait of this great and eminently holy man emerges, though the traits are so many and so minute that a reader can scarcely analyse the whole for himself, still less transmit the impression to others. The sympathetic, receptive nature which in his early manhood made him the friend and guide of so many varied characters, the unshakable strength of his later years which made him to the end the master even of Ethelwold, the wisdom and statesmanship which enabled him to be the counsellor and friend of successive kings and one of the creators of a united England, the gift of artistic creation of the highest order which is perhaps the most remarkable of all his gifts, and, finally, the mature sanctity which in his later years transcended and superseded his other activities and characteristics—all these, revealed to us in this way or that, make of Dunstan a figure of singular attractiveness, whose final and lasting impression is one, not of brilliance and fire, but of a calm and mellow light."

16. The Danish King Canute (Cnut) (ca. 995–1035) became king of England in 1016 and ruled until his death.

17. Edward the Confessor (b. 1003) ruled England from 1042 until his death in 1066.

18. The three great monastic reformers and ecclesial leaders of tenth-century England who presumably were largely responsible for drawing up the *Regularis Concordia*: Dunstan (d. 988) was abbot of Glastonbury, bishop of Worcester, and archbishop of Canterbury; Ethelwold (Aethelwold) (d. 984) was abbot of Abingdon and bishop of Winchester; Oswald (d. 992) was reformer of the Abbey of Ramsey, bishop of Worcester, and archbishop of York.

19. The material in this section is based on "The English Monastic Revival of the Tenth Century," the first section of the Introduction to *Regularis Concordia Anglicae Nationis Monachorum Sanctimonialiumque / The Monastic Agreement of the Monks and Nuns of the English Nation*, ed. and trans. Thomas Symons, OSB (London: Thomas Nelson and Sons, 1953), ix–xxviii.

{This} revival {came} after {the} Viking raids, {with the} new unity built by Alfred (ninth century):

1) {the} necessity of education: few were left who could read Latin;

2) {the} need to rebuild monasteries: monasticism {was} almost wiped out by {the} Danish raids; St. Augustine's Canterbury had survived, {but} other monasteries remained without regular life; Alfred built new monasteries rather than try to reform the old ones—especially Winchester ({founded} by his successor Edward {the} Elder [899–924]); {the} growth of great monasteries of {the} tenth century {included} Milton Abbas, Crediton, Worcester, Bath, Abingdon, etc.;

3) *St. Dunstan*, born {in} 909 in Glastonbury, entered {there} about 923 to study {but} retained contact with {the} court; {he} received {the} monastic habit {in} 934 (about), {was} ordained about 939 {and became} abbot about 940 (appointed by King Edmund);

4) {the} reorganization of Glastonbury {took place} under Dunstan, {who} also {had} influence at court;

5) Ethelwold, {a} disciple of Dunstan, takes over Abingdon {in} 954 {and} reorganizes {it} on Glastonbury principles, and with monks from Corbie (to teach chant);

6) {in} 955, Dunstan has to flee to Ghent, then being reformed by Gerard of Brogne; {he was} recalled to be Bishop of Worcester, {and in} 960, Archbishop of Canterbury—{the} most active and general reform {was} now undertaken;

7) Oswald left Winchester to be {a} monk at Fleury {but was subsequently} recalled as Bishop of Worcester {and} took part in {the} monastic movement, especially {in relation to} Ramsey, {in} Huntingdonshire, as {a} center of reform, founded by him; later {he became} Archbishop of York;

8) {the} Council of Winchester, {in} 970 (?), unifies monastic observance: {the} *Regularis Concordia* {is} drawn up, mainly to organize reform, as against irresponsible innovations—{it was} inspired from abroad, {introducing} new devotions, etc.

9) {in} 988, Dunstan dies after years of retirement and semi-disgrace, on {the} nineteenth {of} May, {the} Saturday after {the}

Cistercian History

Ascension; {he had} consecrated {Ethelwold's new church at} Ely in 983 (?).

{The} *Regularis Concordia* {provides a} picture of tenth-century monasticism.[20] {The} *officers* {included: the} *abbot*, elected among the members of {the} community (usually), with {the} consent of the king; {he is} aided by {the} provost and one dean, generally—or {the} dean (= {the} prior) (or {the} prior = any superior or officer); {the} cellarer ({who is} not mentioned in {the} *Regularis Concordia*); {the} sacristan or *secretarius*; {the} *magister* or *custos*—in charge of the children; {the} cantor; {the} *circa*—in charge of claustral discipline (cf. {the} subprior).

Regular life: in addition to {the} canonical office (these directions {were} not innovations {but the} customary practice of the day), {this included the} little office of all saints (lauds—vespers); {the} office of the dead (omitted from Palm Sunday to {the} octave of Pentecost); {the} *trina oratio* (three times a day); psalms etc. for {the} king after each office, except prime; gradual and penitential psalms; litanies (one after prime, one before {the} major Mass); two conventual Masses daily, {with} DAILY communion ({which was} unusual {for the time}): tierce, {followed by} {the} morrow Mass,[21] {then} chapter, *work*, sext, {the} major Mass, {then} none; {there were also} private Masses; {a} *daily mandatum*[22] of {the} poor ({a} special devotion of *St. Oswald*)—special care of poor guests {was} emphasized—and three {of the} regular poor got maundy and food from {the} monks' table; {there was a} *Saturday maundy of monks*. {The} result of this {was that} the *lectio*[23] after matins

---

20. The material in this section is based on "Organisation and Life," part II of Symons' Introduction (xxxi–xl).
21. I.e. the matutinal or morning Mass, celebrated each day at an earlier time than the principal conventual Mass.
22. I.e. footwashing ("maundy").
23. "[Spiritual] reading"; for an extensive discussion of this essential part of Benedictine monastic life, see Thomas Merton, *Monastic Observances: Initiation into the Monastic Tradition* 5, ed. Patrick F. O'Connell, Monastic Wisdom [MW], vol. 25 (Collegeville, MN: Cistercian Publications, 2010), 149–58, 166–84.

{was} taken up with prayers for {the} king, etc.; other *lectio*, and work, {were} affected by extra prayers and observances; intellectual work—copying manuscripts—{was this done} in *lectio* time? more probably {during} work time. {With regard to} work—had manual labor become non-existent? Certainly {there was} necessary work around {the} house, including cooking and baking, etc. Did {the} monks build? {At} Abingdon, they helped. {According to the} *Vita Oswaldi*,[24] at Westbury {the} building {was} done by *contemptibiles personae*[25] while the brethren prayed. {As for} *meals*, {there were} two outside {of the periods of} monastic fast, and on all Sundays and Feasts of Twelve Lessons; {there was} one after none in winter, after vespers in Lent. {Was there} meat?—eaten by the children? *Silence* {was} *absolute* during {the} great silence and times of *lectio*. Probably {there was} no regular recreation. Confession {took place} *weekly or* {was} *more frequent*.

Sources of {the} Regularis Concordia: {it was} "substantially a mosaic,"[26] yet {its} sources {are} hard to account for, apart from St. Benedict, St. Ambrose (*De Sacramentis*),[27] {the synodal} Council of Winchester,[28] the *Ordo Qualiter*,[29] {the} *Ordo Romanus*:[30]

---

24. *Vita Oswaldi Auctore Anonymo, Historians of the Church of York*, ed. James Raine, Rolls Series 71, 3 vols. (London: Longman, 1879–1894), 1.424, cited by Symons (xxxv).

25. "insignificant persons."

26. Symons, *Regularis Concordia*, xlv; the material in this section is based on "Sources of the Regularis Concordia," part III of Symons' Introduction (xlv–lii).

27. *De Sacramentis* 5.4.25 is quoted in #23 (*Regularis Concordia*, 19).

28. The decisions of the council, at which the *Regularis Concordia* was drawn up, are incorporated into the document's Proem, ##8–12 (*Regularis Concordia*, 5–9).

29. Symons identifies this document as "a Benedictine writing of the eighth century" (xvi) and "the only document which we can affirm to have been extensively used in the Concordia" (xlviii).

30. According to Symons, "the principal services of Holy Week and Easter are based on, and some half dozen rubrical directions are cited verbally from, *Ordo Romanus Primus* . . . or some form of that document" (xlix).

1) *Anglo-Saxon customs*, especially prayers for {the} Royal House,[31] daily communion,[32] ringing all bells (see p. 30[33]);

1a) *Early Benedictine customs*: *biberes post nonam*;[34] psalmody at labor;[35]

1b) *Reform of Benedict of Aniane*: *trina oratio*;[36] gradual psalms before nocturns;[37]

2) *Cluny reforms*, from Fleury, reformed by St. Odo in 930: offices of all saints, office of {the} dead,[38] silence on feast days;[39]

3) *Lorraine reform* ({from} Ghent, restored by Gerard of Brogne in 937): Holy Week rites (substantially Roman, not monastic—see #50;[40] v.g. the *Easter Trope*: #51[41]).

---

31. #18 (*Regularis Concordia*, 13–14).

32. #23 (*Regularis Concordia*, 19).

33. "On these days between the feast of the Innocents and the Octave of Christmas, since the *Gloria in excelsis Deo* is said at Mass on account of the solemnity of such a feast, all the bells shall ring at Nocturns and Vespers as at Mass, as is the custom among the people of this country" (#32 [*Regularis Concordia*, 29–30]).

34. "Drink after None" (*Regularis Concordia*, xlviii) (#30 [*Regularis Concordia*, 13–14]).

35. #25 (*Regularis Concordia*, 21).

36. #16 (*Regularis Concordia*, 12). "The psalms and collects given here went by the name of *Trina oratio*, a form of threefold prayer (in honour of the Blessed Trinity: 27, 12). It was performed three times daily: before Nocturns . . . before Tierce . . . or Prime . . . and after Compline" (*Regularis Concordia*, 12, n. 3).

37. #17 (*Regularis Concordia*, 13).

38. ##19, 25, 29, 31, 56, 59, 60, 66-68 (*Regularis Concordia*, 15, 22, 26, 29, 55, 58, 59, 65–67).

39. #24 (*Regularis Concordia*, 20).

40. *Regularis Concordia*, 49: "On the holy day of Easter the seven canonical hours are to be celebrated by monks in the Church of God after the manner of Canons, out of regard for the authority of the blessed Gregory, Pope of the Apostolic See, as set forth in his Antiphonar" ("the Antiphonar in question being that of the Office, that is, the Roman or Secular as distinct from the Monastic" [49, n. 3]).

41. *Regularis Concordia*, 49–50: "While the third lesson is being read, four of the brethren shall vest, one of whom, wearing an alb as though for

{In the} *Regularis Concordia*, special points relevant to monastic spirituality {include the following}:

I. *Blessing*; II. {*The*} *Night Office*: #14: "All things {are} to begin with a blessing" (p. 11[42])—*omnia sive corporalia sive spiritualia;*[43] *maximi muniminis mos pernecessarius, tam in modicis rebus quam magnis.*[44] Warnefrid says[45] {the} custom was to begin all things with {saying} three times {the} *Deus in adjutorium*[46] (cf. Cassian:

---

some different purpose, shall enter and go stealthily to the place of the 'sepulchre' and sit there quietly, holding a palm in his hand. Then, while the third respond is being sung, the other three brethren, vested in copes and holding thuribles in their hands, shall enter in their turn and go to the place of the 'sepulchre', step by step, as though searching for something. Now these things are done in imitation of the angel seated on the tomb and of the women coming with perfumes to anoint the body of Jesus. When, therefore, he that is seated shall see these three draw nigh, wandering about as it were and seeking something, he shall begin to sing softly and sweetly, *Quem quaeritis*. As soon as this has been sung right through, the three shall answer together, *Ihesum Nazarenum*. Then he that is seated shall say *Non est hic. Surrexit sicut praedixerat. Ite, nuntiate quia surrexit a mortuis*. At this command the three shall turn to the choir saying *Alleluia. Resurrexit Dominus*. When this has been sung he that is seated, as though calling them back, shall say the antiphon *Venite et videte locum*, and then, rising and lifting up the veil, he shall show them the place void of the Cross and with only the linen in which the Cross had been wrapped. Seeing this the three shall lay down their thuribles in that same 'sepulchre' and, taking the linen, shall hold it up before the clergy; and, as though showing that the Lord was risen and was no longer wrapped in it, they shall sing this antiphon: *Surrexit Dominus de sepulchro*. They shall then lay the linen on the altar."

42. Text reads: "every action . . . should be begun with a blessing."

43. *Regularis Concordia*, 11, which reads: "*omnia . . . spiritualia siue corporalia*" ("every action, spiritual or temporal").

44. *Regularis Concordia*, 11 ("This is a most necessary custom and a very great safeguard in small things as in great").

45. *Pauli Warnefridi, Diaconi Casinensis, In Sanctam Regulam Commentarium* (Monte Cassino: Typis Abbatiae Montis Casini, 1880), 335, cited by Symons (11, n. 4).

46. "God, [come to] my assistance" (Ps 69 [70]:2).

*Conferences*⁴⁷). *"Legitime a cunctis iugo regulae deditis iugi teneatur custodia."*⁴⁸ "For nothing can stand firm and strong which lacks the blessing of Christ Who created all things and Who rules justly that which He has created."⁴⁹

#15: What is done and said on arising: {the} sign of {the} cross and three *Domine labia mea*,⁵⁰ then {the} whole {of} Psalm 69 (*Deus in adjutorium*—read⁵¹)—a short psalm {of} special beauty (comment); after {taking care of the} needs of nature etc. {they process} to {the} oratory saying Psalm 24. {Upon} *entering church*, etc., *cum summa reverentia et cautela* {. . .} *ut alios orantes non impediat* {. . .} *flexis genibus in loco congruo ac consueto"*;⁵² praying in his heart with compunction, *and {each} begins the trina oratio* privately (see p. 12)—and again for {the} king and {the} royal family after

---

47. John Cassian, *Collationes*, 10.10 (J.-P. Migne, ed., Patrologiae Cursus Completus, Series Latina [PL], 221 vols. [Paris: Garnier, 1844–1865], 49:832B); for a discussion (which includes mention of both Warnefrid and the *Regularis Concordia*), see Thomas Merton, *Cassian and the Fathers: Initiation into the Monastic Tradition*, ed. Patrick F. O'Connell, MW 1 (Kalamazoo, MI: Cistercian Publications, 2005), 53–54.

48. *Regularis Concordia*, 11 ("wherefore it should ever be kept as law by all those who live under the yoke of the Rule").

49. *Regularis Concordia*, 11, which reads: "For it is beyond doubt that nothing."

50. "Lord [open] my lips" (Ps 50 [51]:17) (*Regularis Concordia*, 11).

51. "Unto the end, a psalm for David, to bring to remembrance that the Lord saved him. O God, come to my assistance; O Lord, make haste to help me. Let them be confounded and ashamed that seek my soul: Let them be turned backward, and blush for shame that desire evils to me: Let them be presently turned away blushing for shame that say to me: Tis well, tis well. Let all that seek thee rejoice and be glad in thee; and let such as love thy salvation say always: The Lord be magnified. But I am needy and poor; O God, help me. Thou art my helper and my deliverer: O Lord, make no delay."

52. *Regularis Concordia*, 12, which reads, "*cautela intrans ut . . . impediat: at tunc flexis . . . congruo et consueto*" ("entering with the most profound reverence and taking the greatest care lest he disturb others at their prayers. Then, kneeling down in his proper and accustomed place").

nocturns; *trina oratio* {consists in} groups of psalms with orations: note the second[53] is *pro devotis amicis* in our missal;[54] the third[55] {is} a postcommunion in {the} Mass *pro defuncto*;[56] then the gradual psalms (presumably the *pueri*[57] are saying their *trina oratio* at this time); {then} nocturns,[58] {followed by} *prayers for* {the} *king*,[59] {then a} brief interval (given to prayers usually); *lauds* {and} after {the} *Miserere*[60] two psalms for {the} royal family (Ps. 31; Ps. 85), {then} antiphons,[61] lauds of all saints and of {the} dead; *prime* (p. 15)—

53. *"Deus qui caritatis dona per gratiam Sancti Spiritus tuorum cordibus fidelium infudisti; da famulis et famulabus tuis, pro quibus tuam deprecamur clementiam, salutem mentis et corporis ut te tota uirtute diligent et quae tibi placita sunt tota dilectione perficiant. Per Dominum"* (*"O God Who hast poured forth the gifts of love into the hearts of Thy faithful through the grace of the Holy Ghost, grant to Thy servants, for whom we beseech Thy clemency, health of mind and body that they may love Thee with all their strength, and with all their love do those things which are pleasing to Thee. Through our Lord"*) (#16 [*Regularis Concordia*, 12]).

54. "for faithful friends" (*Missale Cisterciense: Reformatum juxta Decretum Sacrorum Rituum Congregationis Diei 3 Julii 1869* [Westmalle: Ex Typographia Ordinis Cist. Strict. Obs., 1951], 78*).

55. *"Inueniant quaesumus Domine animae famulorum famularumque tuarum lucis aeternae consortium, qui in hac luce positi tuum consecuti sunt sacramentum. Per Dominum"* (*"We beseech Thee O Lord that the souls of Thy servants may attain to the fellowship of eternal light who in the light of this life have followed after holiness. Through our Lord"*) (#16 [*Regularis Concordia*, 13]).

56. See *Regularis Concordia*, 13, n. 1, which notes the use of this prayer as a postcommunion for the *"Missa in agenda mortuorum plurimorum"* ("Mass offered for more than one deceased") in the Gelasian, Gregorian and Leofric sacramentaries (with the addition of the words *"omnium in Christo quiescentium"* ["all resting in Christ"] following *"famulorum famularumque tuorum"*); it is not found in the *Missale Cisterciense*.

57. I.e. the children (students and oblates) of the monastery, who arise somewhat later than the monks.

58. #17 (*Regularis Concordia*, 13).

59. #18 (*Regularis Concordia*, 13–14).

60. Ps 50 [51].

61. Specified as "of the Cross, of St Mary and of the saint whose name is honoured in that church or, if there be none such, of the dedication of that church" (*Regularis Concordia*, 14).

note {the} quantity of extra psalms and finally {the} litany, {said} prostrate on {the} ground.[62]

#21 {discusses the daily} chapter: *versa facie ad orientem salutent crucem*;[63] *se vultu inclinato humilient*;[64] {the} prayers {were} exactly as today; {there was the} reading of {the} *Rule, or of {the} gospel on a feast day*; {the} chapter of faults {responded to the} "need to be judged in {the} present life" etc.;[65] {this} "*spiritualis pergaminis negotium*"[66] {was} connected also with *confessionis salubre remedium*,[67] which replaces {the} chapter of faults on Sundays and feasts, {and with the} *evening "Confiteor" to neighbors* (#27 [p. 23]);[68] *everybody* {recites the} *Confiteor* in chapter {on} Holy Thursday (p. 29).[69] After chapter *five* psalms {were said}.

#23,[70] re: communion, {notes that} in {the} Lord's Prayer we ask for our daily bread, not our annual bread. {In} #24,[71] note {the} major Mass on Friday {was the} votive of {the} Holy Cross, {and on} Saturday {the} votive of {the} Blessed Virgin Mary; {the}

---

62. #19 (*Regularis Concordia*, 14–15).

63. "Turning to the east they shall salute the Cross" (*Regularis Concordia*, 17).

64. "With bared heads abase themselves [before one another]" (*Regularis Concordia*, 17).

65. "For it is meet that in all our negligences, whether of thought, word or deed, we should be judged in this present life by sincere confession and humble penance lest, when this life is over, our sins declare us guilty before the judgment-seat of Christ" (*Regularis Concordia*, 18).

66. "duty of spiritual purgation" (*Regularis Concordia*, 18, which reads: "*negotio*").

67. "the healing remedy of confession" (#22 [*Regularis Concordia*, 18]).

68. The use of this same phrase here is identified "as meaning the *Confiteor* at Compline" on the basis of a reference to a life of Dunstan (*Regularis Concordia*, 13, n. 5).

69. "the brethren shall all, with lowly devotion, beg pardon of the abbot, who takes the place of Christ, and ask forgiveness of their many failings, saying the *Confiteor*" (#31 [*Regularis Concordia*, 29]).

70. *Regularis Concordia*, 19.

71. *Regularis Concordia*, 20.

minor Mass on Sundays {was that} of {the} Trinity.[72] #27[73] {calls for the} *trina oratio in {the} evening*, {after which, when} retiring, holy water {was} given {the brethren} by {the} hebdomadary,[74] *"et sic pergant ad requiem suam cum summae tranquillitatis reverentia"*;[75] one can stay in church for private prayer until a first bell is rung by the sacristan; sprinkling of {the} dormitory {takes place} after all are in bed. #29[76] {is a} beautiful chapter on {the} calefactory, etc. #34[77] {discusses} Lent: *pinguedo* (cooking in lard—*adeps, sagina*[78]) {is} dropped from Septuagesima {onward}; milk and eggs {are} dropped after Quinquagesima—also {the} fast {continues} until vespers, according to {the} *Rule;*[79] {a} procession *as on Ash Wednesday* {is held} on all Wednesdays and Fridays during Lent, after none, before Mass—from one church to another—then Mass and vespers {follow}.[80] #37[81] {considers} Holy Week: *"Tenebrae"* (see pp. 36–37, with explanation and excuse[82]); the candle in the mouth of the

---

72. "the Morrow Mass . . . on Sundays, if no feast day falls thereon, should be of the Trinity" (#23 [*Regularis Concordia*, 19]).

73. *Regularis Concordia*, 23–24.

74. I.e. the monk assigned to particular liturgical duties for that week.

75. "[they] shall then go to their rest with reverence and the utmost quiet" (*Regularis Concordia*, 24).

76. *Regularis Concordia*, 25–26.

77. *Regularis Concordia*, 32–33.

78. These are the corresponding terms in the Cluniac customs (*Regularis Concordia*, 27, n. 3).

79. *The Rule of St. Benedict in Latin and English*, ed. and trans. Justin McCann, OSB (London: Burns, Oates, 1952), 98/99 (chap. 41).

80. #35 (*Regularis Concordia*, 33).

81. *Regularis Concordia*, 36–37.

82. "On Thursday, which is called *Cena Domini*, the night Office shall be performed according as is set down in the Antiphonar. We have also heard that, in churches of certain religious men, a practice has grown up whereby compunction of soul is aroused by means of the outward representation of that which is spiritual, namely, that when the singing for the night is over, the antiphon of the gospel finished and all the lights put out, two children should be appointed who shall stand on the right hand side of the choir and

Cistercian History 15

serpent;[83] maundy;[84] {the} abbot serving in {the} refectory.[85] #44:[86]

---

shall sing *Kyrie eleison* with clear voice; two more on the left hand side who shall answer *Christe eleison*; and, to the west of the choir, another two who shall say *Domine miserere nobis*; after which the whole choir shall respond together *Christus Dominus factus est oboediens usque ad mortem*. The children of the right-hand choir shall then repeat what they sang above exactly as before and, the choir having finished their response, they shall repeat the same thing once again in the same way. When this has been sung the third time the brethren shall say the *preces* on their knees and in silence as usual. The same order of singing shall be observed for three nights by the brethren. This manner of arousing religious compunction was, I think, devised by Catholic men for the purpose of setting forth clearly both the terror of that darkness which, at our Lord's Passion, struck the tripartite world with unwonted fear, and the consolation of that apostolic preaching which revealed to the whole world Christ obedient to His Father even unto death for the salvation of the human race. Therefore it seemed good to us to insert these things so that if there be any to whose devotion they are pleasing, they may find therein the means of instructing those who are ignorant of this matter; no one, however, shall be forced to carry out this practice against his will."

83. #41 (*Regularis Concordia*, 39) ("this was a candlestick shaped like a serpent and attached to the end of a pole or staff" [39, n. 5]).

84. "Afterwards, when these [poor men] have been gathered together in a suitable place, the brethren shall proceed to carry out the Maundy at which, singing the antiphons proper to this ceremony, they shall wash, dry and kiss the feet of the poor men. And when water has been offered for their hands, food also shall be given to the poor men and money, according to the abbot's discretion, distributed among them" (#40 [*Regularis Concordia*, 39]).

85. "When the ministers of the week, preceding the abbot as is their wont, come to the Maundy, they shall perform their part in it, and after them the abbot shall wash the feet of all in his own basin, drying and kissing them, being assisted by those whom he has chosen for this service. When he has done this, the abbot shall sit in his own place and the seniors shall minister to him in like manner, then, rising, he shall offer water for the hands of the brethren and again the like service shall be rendered to him. . . . Meanwhile the abbot shall go round among the brethren drinking the health and kissing the hand of each. Having ministered to all, the abbot shall sit down and *Tu autem Domine* shall be said" (#42 [*Regularis Concordia*, 40–41]).

86. "When these prayers have all been said, the Cross shall straightway be set up before the altar, a space being left between it and the altar; and it

Good Friday {is arranged} like our Ritual.[87] {#45[88]} {provides texts of the} *prayers for {the} adoration of {the} Holy Cross*—another *trina oratio.* {In} #46, note the "sepulchre" where the cross is laid away until Easter Sunday—with {an} explanation "for the unlearned"[89]

---

shall be held up by two deacons, one on either side. Then the deacons shall sing *Popule meus,* two subdeacons standing before the Cross and responding in Greek, *Agios o Theos, Agios Yschiros, Agios Athanatos eleison ymas,* and the *schola* repeating the same in Latin, *Sanctus Deus.* The Cross shall then be borne before the altar by the two deacons, an acolyte following with a cushion upon which the holy Cross shall be laid. When that antiphon is finished which the *schola* has sung in Latin, the deacons shall sing *Quia eduxi vos per desertum,* the subdeacons responding *Agios* in Greek and the *schola Sanctus Deus* in Latin as before. Again the deacons, raising up the Cross, sing *Quid ultra* as before, the subdeacons responding *Agios* and the *schola Sanctus Deus* as before. Then, unveiling the Cross and turning towards the clergy, the deacons shall sing the antiphons *Ecce lignum crucis, Crucem tuam adoramus Domine, Dum Fabricator mundi* and the verses of Fortunatus, *Pange lingua.* As soon as it has been unveiled, the abbot shall come before the holy Cross and shall prostrate himself thrice with all the brethren of the right hand side of the choir, that is, seniors and juniors; and with deep and heartfelt sighs shall say the seven Penitential psalms and the prayers in honour of the holy Cross" (*Regularis Concordia,* 42–43).

87. *Rituale Cisterciense ex Libro Usuum Definitionibus Ordinis et Caeremoniali Episcoporum Collectum* (Westmalle, Belgium: Ex Typographia Ordinis, 1948), 135–42 [III.xxii].

88. *Regularis Concordia,* 43–44 (text reads: #47).

89. "Now since on that day we solemnize the burial of the Body of our Saviour, if anyone should care or think fit to follow in a becoming manner certain religious men in a practice worthy to be imitated for the strengthening of the faith of unlearned common persons and neophytes, we have decreed this only: on that part of the altar where there is space for it there shall be a representation as it were of a sepulchre, hung about with a curtain, in which the holy Cross, when it has been venerated, shall be placed in the following manner: the deacons who carried the Cross before shall come forward and, having wrapped the Cross in a napkin there where it was venerated, they shall bear it thence, singing the antiphons *In pace in idipsum, Habitabit* and *Caro mea requiescat in spe,* to the place of the sepulchre. When they have laid the cross therein, in imitation as it were of the burial of the

etc. {In} #47,[90] note {the} general communion {on} Good Friday, {and} shaving and bathing. {With regard to} *Easter*: {on} Holy Saturday, all is done at *none*;[91] {on} Easter {the} office {is} according to {the} Roman Rite;[92] #51 {describes the} Easter trope.[93]

On silence {see} #56.[94] *The circa* (circator) *totius claustri sub decano curam gerat*;[95] after compline {he is responsible for} picking up books and clothes in {the} cloister; during nocturns {he is} looking for sleepers with {a} lantern. {The} *daily mandatum of {the} poor* (#62[96]) {is performed} according to the *Rule*, chapter 53:[97] at least three poor {had their} feet washed and shared {the} food of {the} brethren; {on} Saturday {and} Sunday the *pueri* did it; {on}

Body of our Lord Jesus Christ, they shall sing the antiphon *Sepulto Domino, signatum est monumentum, ponentes milites qui custodirent eum*. In that same place the holy Cross shall be guarded with all reverence until the night of the Lord's Resurrection. And during the night let brethren be chosen by twos and threes, if the community be large enough, who shall keep faithful watch, chanting psalms" (*Regularis Concordia*, 44–45).

90. *Regularis Concordia*, 45–46.

91. I.e. the lighting of the new fire, the blessing of the paschal candle, the lessons and litanies, the singing of the Gloria and ringing of the bells, followed by Mass (##48–49 [*Regularis Concordia*, 47–48]).

92. #50 (*Regularis Concordia*, 49) (see above, n. 40).

93. I.e. the *Quem quaeritis* trope (see above, n. 41).

94. *Regularis Concordia*, 54–55; the text enjoins "strict silence in the cloister" and during the great silence from Vespers until chapter of the following day, notes that the *auditorium* is "excepted from the rule of silence" but is not therefore to be used for tales or gossip, and explains that "while the authority of the Rule bids us keep silence at all times, we nevertheless permit talking, as also does our patron the blessed Benedict, at the proper time and touching necessary affairs: not indeed in a loud voice but softly, on account of the importance of silence."

95. "[must be appointed] to look after the entire cloister, under the direction of the dean" (#57 [*Regularis Concordia*, 56]).

96. *Regularis Concordia*, 61.

97. McCann, *The Rule*, 120/121, which directs that the feet of all guests be washed, with "special attention" to be given in receiving "poor men and pilgrims."

other days, the monks, in turn—no one {was} exempt; {the} abbot washed {the} feet of {the} poor when he was free—also {the} feet of strangers and pilgrims. #63[98] {stresses that} all should be zealous to serve in {the} guesthouse; {the} abbot especially should have zeal to serve the poor (read;[99] read also {the} epilogue on not accumulating riches, but sharing with {the} poor[100]); when travelers leave, they are to be given supplies to take with them. #64[101] {treats of the} *mandatum* of {the} brethren and {the} *munditiae*;[102]

---

98. *Regularis Concordia*, 62.

99. "Moreover, when poor strangers arrive, the abbot and such of the brethren as he shall choose shall render to them the service of the Maundy in accordance with the ordinance of the Rule. Wherefore whenever he can, the father himself, no less than each of the brethren, shall be most zealous in providing every kind of service in the guesthouse; nor, seduced by boastful pride or deceived by idle thoughtlessness, shall he foolishly neglect anything commanded by the Rule in this regard. . . . All other duties, as we have said, the abbot shall fulfil most faithfully and with great gladness of heart; nor let him who is the vicar of the eternal Christ be slow and cold in the guesthouse of the monastery nor delay or neglect his ministrations to the poor while in the management of transitory affairs he shows himself swift and fervent in his desire to serve the rich."

100. "And, with his mind set on their well-being, [the king] urged and exhorted the Fathers and Mothers of monasteries that, with deep and lasting compunction, they should lay up as treasure in heaven, through the hands of the poor, whatever remains over and above necessary use; so that while they yet live on earth in the body their hearts may dwell now, and hereafter everlastingly abide, there where they have most rightly placed their treasure. And if, on the death of an abbot, there be found any superabundance of goods, his successor, instead of sharing it with relations or worldly tyrants shall, according to the command already given, use it as the grace of the Holy Ghost inspires him, for the needs of the brethren and poor, thus, with the counsel of the brethren, wisely disposing all things" (#69 [*Regularis Concordia*, 69]).

101. *Regularis Concordia*, 63.

102. I.e. the weekly "washing" of the towels and kitchen utensils, as mandated by the Rule, chap. 35 ("*munditias faciat*" [McCann, *The Rule*, 88/89]).

Cistercian History 19

all should be obedient and zealous to do chores (read[103]). #65[104] {considers the care of} *the sick and the dying*. #66[105] {is concerned with a monk's} death; burial, {the} tricenary {and} the *episticula* {are discussed in #67}.[106]

Dom T. Symons, {in} "Some Notes on English Monastic Origins" (*Downside Review*, January 1962),[107] {raises the question}: was {the} English Benedictine reform of {the} tenth century of totally continental origin?

1. Relations with {the} continent:[108] {in} 929, Bishop Cenwald heads a mission that visits German monasteries, especially St. Gall. {In} 944, monks of St. Bertin's who do not accept {the} reforms of Gerard of Brogne come to Bath. {There were} *contacts with Fleury*; Bishop Oda {may have gone there in} 936 (?); {later he} sends his nephew[109] there—Fleury {was} under *Odo* of Cluny. {The} third abbot of Einsiedeln {was} an Englishman,

---

103. "Let no one scorn to grease shoes or to wash garments or to minister water; but let these things be done by each, as the grace of the Lord enables him, at the proper time and in the accustomed way. Let each one according to his strength and with thanksgiving fulfil the duties of the kitchen and bakehouse as the Rule commands; lest by careless neglect of the smallest precept of the Rule he become guilty, as the apostle says, of all the commandments: which God forbid" (the references are to the Rule, chap. 35 [McCann, *The Rule*, 86, 88/87, 89] and to Jas 2:10).

104. *Regularis Concordia*, 64–65.

105. *Regularis Concordia*, 65.

106. *Regularis Concordia*, 65–66; the tricenary was the thirty-day commemoration of the recently deceased by the daily recitation of the office of the dead; the *episticula* was the brief notice (the form of which is provided) "sent to neighbouring monasteries informing them of the burial of [the dead] brother" (63).

107. Thomas Symons, OSB, "Some Notes on English Monastic Origins," *Downside Review* 80 (1962): 55–69; see also "The *Regularis Concordia* and the Council of Winchester," *Downside Review* 80 (1962): 140–56; "Notes on the Life and Work of St Dunstan," *Downside Review* 80 (1962): 250–61, 355–66.

108. "I. Ecclesiastical and Monastic Relations with the Continent" (56–60).

109. I.e. Oswald.

Gregory (964–996 {was the term of his} abbacy). {In} 956 {came the} exile of St. Dunstan in Flanders, after fifteen years as Abbot of Glastonbury; {he found refuge} in *St. Peter's, Ghent*, reformed by Gerard of Brogne. Monks {were} sent to Fleury {and} Corbie by Aethelwold, Abbot of Abingdon, who had also visited and studied abroad. {In} 962, Bishop Oswald of Worcester, {who had} trained at Fleury, founds {the} monastery of Westbury, and calls monks from Fleury to train {the community}. {In} 970 (about), monks from Fleury and Ghent assist in {the} Synod of Winchester and influence {the} *Regularis Concordia*. T. Symons' position {is that} (a) {the} early Glastonbury reform was *not* of continental inspiration, or Aethelwold etc. would not have {subsequently} gone to {the} continent to establish contact. In a word, foreign influence had *not* long been familiar at {the} time of {the} *Regularis Concordia*—it was beginning then. The *fame* of continental monasticism had long been known but details of observance were not. Before 956, no English reformer trained abroad. {The} English reform begins at Glastonbury and then, with this momentum, monks begin to look to {the} continent.

2. *Aethelwold and {the} Rule {of} Saint Benedict*.[110] It is stated that Aethelwold got {the} *Rule* {of} Saint Benedict from Fleury, implying {that} this was a first copy for England—contra: Aethelwold had been formed under {the} *Rule* {of} Saint Benedict at Glastonbury.

3. Monasticism of *Aelfheah* (Alfeth):[111] Aelfheah {was the} Bishop of Winchester who gave {the} monastic habit to Dunstan. Malmesbury tries to state {that} Aelfheah was an earlier abbot than Dunstan.[112] Was Aelfheah a monk of Glastonbury? Had monasticism died out at Glastonbury? It influenced Dunstan

---

110. "II. St Aethelwold and the Rule of St Benedict" (61–65).

111. "III. The Monasticism of Bishop Aelfheah: Glastonbury and Dunstan" (65–68).

112. William of Malmesbury, *Vita Dunstani*, in *Memorials of St Dunstan*, ed. William Stubbs, Rolls Series 63 (London: Longman, 1874), 260, quoted by Symons, "Notes," 66.

powerfully. Was {the} *Rule* {of} Saint Benedict unknown there in {the} time of Dunstan? T. Symons' contention is again that the first monastic inspiration for Dunstan was Benedictine life at Glastonbury. N.B. {on} pp. 68–69[113] {there is} question of a *topos*[114]— St. Odo in a panegyric of St. Benedict {writes}: "*O quanti sunt in etiam remotissimis trans maria regionibus*. . ."[115] who would rejoice to visit {the} relics of St. Benedict at Fleury—this is a *topos*, used (wrongly) as a source of scientific historical deductions by Mr. Eric John,[116] in *Revue Bénédictine* LXX, n. 1 (1960), p. 198—attacked by Symons.

Cluny

{At the} beginning of {the} tenth century, {the} Church {was} at its lowest ebb, {with the} break-up of {the} Carolingian Empire, {the} invasion of {the} Normans in {the} north {and the} Saracens in {the} south, laymen controlling abbeys, communities homeless. In some regions, monasteries almost completely disappear. Illiterate abbots and monks cannot even read {the} *Rule* (read PS, I.138[117]). {In} 910, Cluny {was} founded by William, Duke

---

113. "IV. St Odo and England" (68–69).

114. I.e. a traditional thematic or rhetorical literary device.

115. Symons, "Notes," 68 ("O how many are there, even in the remotest regions beyond the seas" [Symons, "Notes," 69]).

116. Eric John, "Sources of the English Monastic Reformation: A Comment," *Revue Bénédictine* 70, no. 1 (1960), 197–208.

117. "Là où un abbé laïque s'emparait d'un couvent et s'y installait avec sa femme et ses enfants, son palefrenier et sa meute de chiens, il ne pouvait plus être question de vie claustrale. Les moines imitaient leur abbé, se mariaient, vivaient avec leur famille et leur postérité sur les biens du couvent. Ainsi les monastères devinrent des maisons de famille ou des colonies de maisons familiales où régnaient le relâchement autant que les querelles et la jalousie. On allait bien encore à l'église, mais plus volontiers aux divertissements et aux exercices sportifs. Les jeunes gens s'exerçaient aux armes et à l'art de monter à cheval. Les dames soignaient leur extérieur et leur toilette. Les couvents qui passaient ainsi entre les mains des grandes étaient soumis au régime feodal. Comme tels ils devenaient héréditaires dans la famille de l'abbé laïque ou du propriétaire. Entre le propriétaire et l'abbé laïque, il y avait cette différence que le propriétaire avait, en général,

of Aquitaine, {with} *St. Berno* {as its} first abbot {and} following

---

un abbé sous ses ordres and le nommait. Mais, pour la communauté, souvent la différence n'était pas grande. Après que, dans l'Empire franc de l'Ouest, l'hérédité du fief de père en fils eut été reconnue suivant le capitulaire de Quiersy en 877, les abbés laïques cherchèrent à rendre héréditaires les monastères qui leur étaient confiés. Ainsi vit-on les ducs d'Aquitaine, les comtes d'Anjou, de Chartres, de Flandre conserver en héritage les abbayes qui leur avaient été autre fois données en fief par le roi, et les seigneurs transmettre les monastères à leurs femmes, à leurs enfants, à leurs brus ou à leurs gendres. La vie monastique disparaissait ainsi presque partout. Au début du Xe siècle, il était rare de trouver des moines réguliers. On se plaignait qu'il n'y eût pas dans toute la Francie un seul cloître regulier où pût entrer un moine sérieux" ("There where a lay abbot took possession of a religious house and was installed with his wife and children, his groom and his pack of dogs, there could no longer be a question of claustral life. The monks imitated their abbot, got married, lived with their family and their descendants on the goods of the house. Thus monasteries became family homes or colonies of familial homes where slackness reigned even to the point of quarrels and jealousy. Indeed, they still went to the church, but more willingly to entertainments and sporting events. The young men trained in arms and in the art of horseback-riding. The women took care of their outward appearance and their dress. Religious houses that thus passed into the hands of the great were subject to the feudal system. As such they became hereditary in the family of the lay abbot or the proprietor. Between the proprietor and the lay abbot there was this difference—that the proprietor generally had an abbot under his orders, and appointed him. But for the community, the difference often was not large. Once the inheritance of a fief passing from father to son had been recognized in the Frankish Empire of the West according to the capitulary of Quiersy in 877, the lay abbots tried to make the monasteries that had been entrusted to them hereditary. Thus one saw the Dukes of Aquitaine, the Counts of Anjou, of Chartres, of Flanders, keeping as inherited property monasteries that had been given to them at some point by the king as fiefs, and lords passing on monasteries to their wives, their children, their daughters-in-law or sons-in-law. Monastic life thus disappeared almost completely. At the beginning of the tenth century it was rare to find monks living according to the Rule. There were complaints that in all of Francia there was not a single regular cloister where a serious monk could enter") (Philibert Schmitz, OSB, *Histoire de l'Ordre de Saint Benoît*, 7 vols. [Maredsous: Éditions de Maredsous, 1948–1956]).

{the} customs and constitutions of *Aniane*; {it was named the} *Abbey of St. Peter and Paul*. Cluny {was} placed directly under {the} Holy See for temporal and spiritual things {and} hence {was} not at {the} mercy of lords or bishops ({it} can pick {its} bishop for {various} functions—{and is} not subject to episcopal censure). *This independence* led to prosperity (even practically {to} independence of {the} Holy See, {which was} weak and distant). St. *Odo* (d. 942) introduces reform in many monasteries at {the} request of bishops etc.—takes them over. These houses form *an "order" in practice*. St. *Mayeul* (d. 994) continues {this} work of reform everywhere. St. *Odilo* (d. 1049) consolidates {the} order, *initiates {the} commemoration of All Souls {on} November 2, {and} sold treasures of {the} Church to feed {the} poor, repeatedly*. St. *Hugh* (d. 1109), abbot for sixty years, entered at fifteen; {he was} active in *Church reform*. *Peter the Venerable* {was the last in this series of remarkable abbots}.

Life at Cluny {included} little or no manual work {and a} *very long liturgy* {marked by} liturgical splendor. {It was} a great center of fervor and a nursery of saints (see Cousin, pp. 250–251[118]). {Its} schedule {included} 138 psalms in each day's office—*sung*; {the} introduction of long lessons and *preces*;[119] two conventual Masses daily; {the} cult of Our Lady and {the} saints ({there were} *two processions daily to {the} Lady Chapel*). {There were} consequent alterations in {the} matter of food and clothing. {The} *great feudal power of {the} Abbot of Cluny* (!) {made him a} *bulwark of {the} Empire* as well as {of the} Church. Intellectual activity {was} very slight ({due to the} long offices), {but there was} considerable *artistic work*: manuscripts, sacred vessels, reliquaries, *Romanesque architecture*, *Romanesque sculpture*. {Cluny's was the} greatest church in Christendom until {the} Renaissance—St. Peter's. {As} *clerical monks*

---

118. Patrice Cousin, OSB, *Précis d'Histoire Monastique* (Paris: Bloud & Gay, 1956): Cousin provides a list of extra psalms added to the office, as well as extended readings during vigils, along with a detailed *horarium* for the typical day of a Cluniac monk (250–52).

119. "prayers"—collects.

increase in number, priests {celebrate} private Masses; {Cluny becomes a} nursery of bishops.
   Cluny: The Spirit of Cluny in the Golden Age (Leclercq, *TVM*, p. 447f.[120]). {The} Golden Age {extended} from *St. Odo* (d. 942) to *Peter {the} Venerable* (d. 1156). In this time Cluny was the greatest cultural, religious and civilizing force in Europe. {The} basic conviction {was}: *"le monachisme est la parfaite réalisation du mystère de l'Église"* (448).[121] Cluny {was} conscious of itself in {the} history of salvation. Penance {involved} washing out sin {and a} return to {a} paradisiacal state. {They were} building the *New Jerusalem*—{the} *Temple*—{the} *Tabernacle*—{this was the} ideal of cult. {The} monastery {was} a "church of the perfect"[122]—*poverty* {was central} at Cluny. Thus {it was} reorienting {the} whole of society to Christ, *Who is to return*. {There were} interests in {the} crusades, to deliver {the} Holy Sepulchre (see texts on {the} *Transfiguration* {of} Peter {the} Venerable—in *Pierre le Vénérable*, p. 326f.[123]). {The} Church {is considered} *an anticipation in time of the eternal Kingdom*

---

   120. Jean Leclercq, OSB, "Le Monachisme Clunisien," *Théologie de la Vie Monastique: Études sur la Tradition Patristique* (Paris: Aubier, 1961), chap. 22, 447–57.
   121. "Monasticism is the perfect realization of the mystery of the Church."
   122. "Église des parfaits" (Leclercq, *Théologie de la Vie Monastique*, 451, quoting Odo of Cluny, from Ovidio Capitani, *Motivi di Spiritualità Cluniacense e Realismo Eucaristico in Odone di Cluny* [Rome: Tipografia del Senato, 1959], 17).
   123. Jean Leclercq, OSB, *Pierre le Vénérable*, chap. 17, "Mort et Transfiguration" (Paris: Éditions Fontenelle, 1946), 325–40 (cited in Leclercq, *Théologie de la Vie Monastique*, 450, n. 13); Peter instituted the Feast of the Transfiguration at Cluny three centuries before the universal Church (1457) and wrote a good part of the office for the feast, associating the Transfigured Christ with the Old Testament figure of Wisdom and focusing on the Trinitarian dimension of the feast (326–28); his sermon on the Transfiguration is a long, lyrical commentary on the readings for the feast, focusing more on the literal than the allegorical sense of the text and describing the Transfiguration as an anticipation of the glorification of Christ's resurrected body, already united with the Divine Word (329–31).

of Heaven. Heaven will be a "vast monastery"[124] ({filled with} *praise*). {The} monastery {is the} *full realization* of {the} mystery of {the} Church—{the} *mystery of charity*. {The} *Blessed Virgin Mary* {is the} *model and protectress* of monasticism. {There was also} devotion to Sts. Peter and Paul: {the} Basilica of Cluny imitated St. Peter's {in} Rome, *with* {a} *close relationship to* {*the*} *Holy See* ({a} *direct dependence* on {the} Holy See)—{Cluny} tends to be {the} second capital of Christendom. *The monastery* {*is seen as a*} *school of charity* (Leclercq, *TVM*, p. 454); St. Benedict {is the} "*caritatis notarius*"[125] (Peter {the} Venerable) (454). Peter {the} Venerable {was} open to dialogue with Jews, Mohammedans etc. (454). {There was a} *special influence of Gregory the Great* informing {the} spirit of prayer at Cluny.[126] {The} splendor of worship {involved a} spirit of adoration and sacrifice, to remind us of {the} glory of {the} heavenly kingdom; "magnificence" {characterized} liturgical art; {worship was} centered on {an} eschatological conception of {the} Eucharist.

Monasticism in {the} High Middle Ages and at Cluny (J. Leclercq, *TVM*, {cc.} XXI,[127] XXII):

1. Sources for monastic ideas in this period {were found in} *lives of saints*: saints {were} considered as ideal models (perhaps even for liturgical use); {the} signification of hagiography {was located} in *doctrine* rather than history; two main themes in hagiography {were} exile {and} paradise (p. 438).

---

124. "Le ciel sera un vaste monastère, lorsque l'Église aura attaint son achèvement" ("Heaven will be a vast monastery, when the Church will have reached its fulfillment") (Leclercq, *Théologie de la Vie Monastique*, 453); see also Leclercq, *Théologie de la Vie Monastique*, 451: "L'Église est comme un vaste monastère; le monastère est un résumé de l'Église" ("The Church is like a vast monastery; the monastery is the epitome of the Church").

125. Peter the Venerable, *Epistola* 28 (to St. Bernard): "*Sed nec indignum est sancto charitatis vocari notarium*" ("But it is not unworthy for the saint to be called the recorder of charity") (PL 189:156C).

126. See Leclercq, *Théologie de la Vie Monastique*, 455–56.

127. "Le Monachism du Haut Moyen Age (viiie–xe siècles)," 437–45.

2. *Exile*:[128] Abraham {was} the model (Gen. 12:1); *peregrinatio*[129] {involved} going to an unknown land—{see} also the apostles. Often {monks were seen as} "unstable"[130]—{going} from {a} hermitage to {the} cenobium, etc.; some {were} *sent* as missionaries by {the} Church, others just went; but missionary monks are *the exception* (439). Priesthood {was} a rarity—{the} crown of the monk's ascetic life, fitting in one who is united to Christ crucified. {There was an} aspiration to martyrdom. *St. Boniface* {is} characteristic of the period, {and} fulfills all its aspirations.

3. *Paradise*[131] {is found as a} result of {a} struggle with {the} devil; the hermitage {is situated} in paradisiacal surroundings, {a} physical expression of the saint's interior beauty; {it includes a} life of friendship with the animals; *gentleness* has {a} great effect in {a} barbarian milieu—{it} delivers captives; {there is a} close union with the angels, {and a} love of sacred scriptures, themselves a "paradise."

Conclusion: {the} dominating idea "seems to be that of the freedom of the sons of God. The world groans in the pains of childbirth. The Christian participates in the cosmic suffering."[132] {See a} typical text: "*Statuit natales relinquere fines, quo liberius posset Domini servitiis operam dare*" (*Life of St. Wilfrid* by Eadmer).[133]

---

128. Leclercq, *Théologie de la Vie Monastique*, 438–41.

129. "pilgrimage."

130. "[L]a vie des saints moines d'alors est marquée par un instabilité qui est pleine de signification" ("The life of holy monks at that time was marked by an instability that is full of significance") (Leclercq, *Théologie de la Vie Monastique*, 439).

131. Leclercq, *Théologie de la Vie Monastique*, 441–44.

132. "L'idée que semble dominer toutes ces représentations est celle de la liberté des enfants de Dieu. Le monde gémit, il est dans les douleurs de l'enfantement. Le chrétien participe à cette suffrance cosmique" (Leclercq, *Théologie de la Vie Monastique*, 444).

133. "He decided to leave behind his native territory, so that he could more freely give his effort to the service of the Lord" (Leclercq, *Théologie de la Vie Monastique*, 445, n. 37, quoting *Acta Sanctorum Ordinis Sancti Benedicti*, ed. Jean Mabillon, OSB, 9 vols. [Paris: L. Billaine, 1668–1701], 3.1.198).

Norman Monasticism (Knowles[134])—{the Normans were} organizers {and} builders.

Normandy: {the} Normans {in the} tenth century {were still} largely pagan {when} monasteries begin: Jumièges {was founded in} 940 (from Aquitaine); St. Wandrille {was} refounded;[135] Mont Saint Michel (read H. Adams:[136] p. 1,[137] 46 top,[138] 48,[139] 50[140]) {and}

---

134. Knowles, *Monastic Order*, chap. 4: "The Norman Monasticism" (83–99).

135. This was done by Duke Richard I between 961 and 963.

136. Henry Adams, *Mont-Saint-Michel & Chartres* (1905; Garden City, NY: Doubleday Anchor, n.d.).

137. "The Archangel loved heights. Standing on the summit of the tower that crowned his church, wings upspread, sword uplifted, the devil crawling beneath, and the cock, symbol of eternal vigilance, perched on his mailed foot, Saint Michael held a place of his own in heaven and on earth which seems, in the eleventh century, to leave hardly room for the Virgin of the Crypt at Chartres, still less for the Beau Christ of the thirteenth century at Amiens. The Archangel stands for Church and State, and both militant. He is the conqueror of Satan, the mightiest of all created spirits, the nearest to God. His place was where the danger was greatest; therefore you find him here. For the same reason he was, while the pagan danger lasted, the patron saint of France. So the Normans, when they were converted to Christianity, put themselves under his powerful protection. So he stood for centuries on his Mount in Peril of the Sea, watching across the tremor of the immense ocean—*immensi tremor oceani*—as Louis XI, inspired for once to poetry, inscribed on the collar of the Order of Saint Michael which he created. So soldiers, nobles, and monarchs went on pilgrimage to his shrine; so the common people followed, and still follow, like ourselves. The church stands high on the summit of this granite rock, and on its west front is the platform, to which the tourist ought first to climb. From the edge of this platform, the eye plunges down, two hundred and thirty-five feet, to the wide sands or the wider ocean, as the tides recede or advance, under an infinite sky, over a restless sea, which even we tourists can understand and feel without books or guides; but when we turn from the western view, and look at the church door, thirty or forty yards from the parapet where we stand, one needs to be eight centuries old to know what this mass of encrusted architecture meant to its builders, and even then one must still learn to feel it. The man who wanders into the twelfth century is lost, unless he can grow prematurely young" (1–2).

St. Ouen {were begun, influenced by the} *Lotharingian* reform,

138. "The masculine, military energy of Saint Michael lives still in every stone. The genius that realized this warlike emotion has stamped his power everywhere, on every centimetre of his work; in every ray of light; on the mass of every shadow; wherever the eye falls; still more strongly on all that the eye divines, and in the shadows that are felt like the lights. The architect intended it all. Any one who doubts has only to step through the doorway in the corner into the refectory. There the architect has undertaken to express the thirteenth-century idea of the Archangel; he has left the twelfth century behind him."

139. "If any lingering doubt remains in regard to the professional cleverness of the architect and the thoroughness of his study, we had best return to the great hall, and pass through a low door in its extreme outer angle, up a few steps into a little room some thirteen feet square, beautifully vaulted, lighted, warmed by a large stone fireplace, and in the corner, a spiral staircase leading up to another square room above opening directly into the cloister. It is a little library or charter-house. The arrangement is almost too clever for gravity, as is the case with more than one arrangement in the Merveille. From the outside one can see that at this corner the architect had to provide a heavy buttress against a double strain, and he built up from the rock below a square corner tower as support, into which he worked a spiral staircase leading from the cellar up to the cloisters. Just above the level of the great hall he managed to construct this little room, a gem. The place was near and far; it was quiet and central; . . . monks might have illuminated missals there. A few steps upward brought them to the cloisters for meditation; a few more brought them to the church for prayer. A few steps downward brought them to the great hall, for business, a few steps more led them into the refectory, for dinner. To contemplate the goodness of God was a simple joy when one had such a room to work in; such a spot as the great hall to walk in, when the storms blew; or the cloisters in which to meditate, when the sun shone; such a dining-room as the refectory; and such a view from one's windows over the infinite ocean and the guiles of Satan's quicksands." Merveille ("Marvel"; "Wonder") is the name given to the multi-level proto-Gothic addition to the monastery along the northern side of the Mount, as planned by Abbot Jordan (1191–1212) and largely funded by King Philip Augustus, featuring on its main level the side-by-side great hall and a refectory that could seat 200 guests (see 42–50).

140. "The whole Mount still kept the grand style; it expressed the unity of Church and State, God and Man, Peace and War, Life and Death, Good and Bad; it solved the whole problem of the universe. The priest and the

from Ghent. ({The} Lotharingian reform, {centered} in Lorraine, {was} contemporary with Cluny; {its} two centers[141] {were at} Gorze, near Metz, {and at} Brogne, near Namur—which reformed {the} old monastery of Ghent.) {In} 1001, *Bl. William* of Volpiano,[142] abbot of St. Benignus of Dijon, comes to *Fécamp*—{he was} formed at Cluny, {but was} an *independent* abbot of St. Benignus. Fécamp reforms Mont St. Michel and St. Ouen and Jumièges; {there were} *many foundations* {and a strong} *intellectual revival*—contrast Cluny. *John of Fécamp* succeeded William as abbot; {he was the} *author of prayers in preparation for Mass ascribed to St. Ambrose*[143] {and the} greatest spiritual writer of this period[144]—see {the}

---

soldier were both at home here, in 1215 as in 1115 or in 1058; the politician was not outside of it; the sinner was welcome; the poet was made happy in his own spirit, with a sympathy, almost an affection, that suggests a habit of verse in the Abbot as well as in the architect. God reconciles all. The world is an evident, obvious, sacred harmony. Even the discord of war is a detail on which the Abbey refuses to insist. Not till two centuries afterwards did the Mount take on the modern expression of war as a discord in God's providence. Then, in the early years of the fifteenth century, Abbot Pierre le Roy plastered the gate of the châtelet, as you now see it, over the sunny thirteenth-century entrance called Belle Chaise, which had treated mere military construction with a sort of quiet contempt. You will know what a châtelet is when you meet another; it frowns in a spirit quite alien to the twelfth century; it jars on the religion of the place; it forebodes wars of religion; dissolution of society; loss of unity; the end of a world. Nothing is sadder than the catastrophe of Gothic art, religion, and hope. One looks back on it all as a picture; a symbol of unity; an assertion of God and Man in a bolder, stronger, closer union than ever was expressed by other art; and when the idea is absorbed, accepted, and perhaps partially understood, one may move on."

141. See Knowles, *Monastic Order*, 29.

142. D. 1031.

143. See André Wilmart, OSB, "L'Oratio Sancti Ambrosii du Missel Romain," *Auteurs Spirituels et Textes Dévots du Moyen-Âge Latin: Études d'Histoire Littéraire* (Paris: Bloud & Gay, 1932), 101–25.

144. "Dom Wilmart, indeed, does not hesitate to call John of Fécamp the greatest spiritual writer of the epoch before St Bernard" (Knowles, *Monastic Order*, 86).

book by Dom Leclercq.¹⁴⁵ {The} *Duke of Normandy* controlled {the} monasteries, appointed abbots, {and} could call on monks for military service.

{The Abbey of} *Bec* {became the} great center {of Norman monasticism and was} most influential in England after {the} conquest. Originally {it was} not Cluniac and social {but} more solitary, like Molesme (*read* Knowles, p. 89;¹⁴⁶ bottom 91¹⁴⁷). {On its}

145. Jean Leclercq, OSB, and Jean-Paul Bonnes, *Un Maître de La Vie Spirituelle au XIe Siècle: Jean de Fécamp*, Études de Théologie et d'Histoire de la Spiritualité 9 (Paris: Vrin, 1946).

146. "The circumstances of its origin sharply distinguish the early history of Bec from that of the other monasteries of Normandy. These were, as has been seen, largely the result of an earlier movement at Cluny which sprang into new life at centres such as Dijon and Fécamp, and considered as individuals they owed their existence to the initiative and fostering care of the Dukes of Normandy and their great vassals. Bec was a new and independent birth, almost a new order, and in its origin it is clearly seen to be one of that series of attempts to regain solitude and simplicity and austerity of life which are visible all over north-western Europe at the middle of the eleventh century, and which culminated at its close in the congregations of Tiron and Savigny and the order of Cîteaux. Had it not been for the arrival of the illustrious Lombard, it might well have remained an insignificant house, to disappear or to be merged in the life around it. Instead, after passing rapidly through phases of growth that normally fill many decades, it became the most typical black monk monastery of its day and exercised a widespread influence which has been felt, at least indirectly, throughout monastic history from that time to this."

147. "With Lanfranc's opening school the poor and primitive monastery of Herluin's first years embarked definitively upon a wholly different career, and it needed only the arrival of Anselm, some fifteen years later, attracted by Lanfranc but surpassing his master alike in sanctity of life and in purely intellectual gifts, to set the seal upon the new order of things. Thus Bec, in a little over a quarter of a century, from being a wholly obscure venture which was in a sense a reaction from the monasticism around it, came to rival and to surpass its neighbours in their most typical activities and to be the model and mistress of Norman monasticism."

foundation—read p. 90;[148] {the founder}, *Herluin*, {was} self-taught,

148. "Its founder, Herluin, whose name it bears, was not a child of the cloister. Of noble birth, excelling in arms and all physical pursuits, he lived for some twenty years—till past his thirty-seventh birthday—the life of a soldier in the retinue of Gilbert, count of Brionne. At the age of thirty-seven, about the year 1032, apparently as a result of some dangerous military adventure, he resolved to turn from the world and give himself to God. For some reason he did not immediately decide to become a monk. Remaining nominally a member of the circle of knights about the court of his lord he took every occasion for withdrawal and prayer, spending many hours in churches and fasting rigidly. He sought direction in vain from the priests and prelates of Normandy, who were at this time for the most part ignorant or worldly; failing to find what he sought, he resolved to give himself to the direct guidance of the Holy Spirit, obtained his release from his lord, and retired to an estate of his own where he spent his days in building a chapel and much of his nights in learning to read the psalter. After some two years, that is *c*. 1034, he decided to visit a number of monasteries in order to learn a monk's mode of life. At the time, only half a dozen houses existed in Norman territory, and it is possible that Herluin turned south to the older monasteries; in any case, his standards were doubtless exacting and he would at this period of his life have had little sympathy for an elaborate or wealthy institution; his experiences were therefore unfortunate enough, and he encountered worldly behaviour and rough treatment. Such a deep impression, we are told, did the sight of these disedifying lives make upon him in one abbey that he was on the point of despair, when an incident occurred which his biographer and disciple notes as an example of faith greater than miracles. In the depth of his discouragement Herluin remained after the night office praying in the church, as he thought, alone. There he saw one of the monks, who, like himself, imagined that the church was empty, remain instant in prayer from the depth of the night till full daylight. The example did its work. Leaving other houses unvisited, he returned to his own lands, was ordained priest, and with two others began his monastic life in complete poverty and seclusion. The little group worked all day clearing land, farming, gardening and building; as yet they had little in common with the tradition of Cluny or Dijon, and their beginning might well have been that of Tiron or Cîteaux, or of the early Carmelites in a later century. Recruits came, but the community remained simple, poor and laborious; the mother of the founder lived nearby and washed the garments of her son's followers. Herluin himself felt deeply his inability to guide the growing family. This

eager for learning (see {the} quote: DK, p. 96¹⁴⁹). *Lanfranc,* {a} lawyer from Lombardy, made Bec a center of learning; {he served} as {an} intimate counselor of Duke William. Lanfranc became Archbishop of Canterbury {in} 1070. Thus {Bec} attracted Anselm, who became prior of Bec three years after profession, then abbot. {In} 1066 {came the} Norman Conquest.¹⁵⁰ {In} 1070, Lanfranc {was} summoned from Caen to win over English monks to {the} new regime; {he was} appointing Norman monks from Bec and Caen as bishops and abbots. Norman abbots were great *builders* and *reformers;* {this period marks the} beginnings of the great cathedrals. Note {also} *Lanfranc vs. Berengarius*—{the} Eucharistic controversy.¹⁵¹ Lanfranc dies {in} May 1089. {In} 1093 *Anselm*

---

is a significant trait, for it shows not so much that he was a man of humility as that he had no definite programme of the monastic life to oppose to that current in France at the time, and that the simplicity of the early life was in a sense accidental. What would have become of his venture had his prayer for help received a different answer cannot be said. As it was, the whole history of the community was changed by one who sought admission about the year 1042, and who made of Bec for a short while the intellectual centre of Europe north of the Alps."

149. "An account of the spirit of Norman monasticism would, however, be scarcely complete which did not contain the passage in which Herluin's biographer narrates the zeal for letters of the self-taught founder of Bec. If [he writes] he came upon one of the brethren who was neglecting regular discipline and the study of letters . . . he would say: 'Of what use is a man who is ignorant of letters, and of the commandments of God?' . . . Many were incited to study rather by his encouragement than by a love for learning, for he inquired carefully who among the whole body of those being taught were possessed of keen minds and strong memories, who were making the most eager progress, and in what subjects of study. . . . If a man of letters came to him with a desire to become a monk, how gladly did he receive him, with what loving care and reverence did he entertain him!"

150. For these details Merton relies upon Knowles, *Monastic Order,* 106–13.

151. In his treatise *De Corpore et Sanguine Domini* (PL 150:407–42) Lanfranc affirmed the real presence of Christ in the Eucharist against the theories of Berengarius of Tours. See Jean de Montclos, *Lanfranc et Bérenger: La Controverse Eucharistique du XIᵉ Siècle* (Leuven: Spicilegium Sacrum Lovaniense, 1971).

{becomes} Archbishop of Canterbury—Anselm {is the author of the} *Monologion*[152] {and} *Proslogion*[153]—{with its} ontological argument.[154] *"Fides quaerens intellectum"*[155] {is his great motto}. {He is the} precursor of {the} scholastics.

{On} *Jean de Fécamp* {see the biographical study by} Dom Leclercq: {he was} born about 990 at Ravenna; {he was a} monk ({a} hermit) at Frutuaria; {he was then} sent to St. Benignus. {He was the} nephew of Bl. William of Volpiano, reformer of monks in Lorraine and Normandy {and} founder of St. Benignus. John {became a} monk of St. Benignus, {and was then} sent to Fécamp as prior by Bl. William. {He} became abbot {in} 1028 {and served as} abbot {for} fifty years ({in} 1052 {he was} abbot of St. Bénigne).

{The} *New Orders* {of the} tenth century etc.

{There were} "two tides"[156] starting from Italy and moving north—both primitive: (1) individual informal attempts at simplicity: St. *Nilus*; (2) organized solitude and primitivism: *St. Romuald*—{the} Camaldolese;[157] *St. John Gualbert*[158]—{the}

---

152. *S. Anselmi Cantuariensis Archiepiscopi Opera Omnia*, ed. F. S. Schmitt, OSB, 6 vols. (Edinburgh: Thomas Nelson, 1946–1951), 1.5–87.

153. Schmitt, *S. Anselmi Opera Omnia*, 1.93–122.

154. For Merton's reflections on this topic see "St. Anselm and His Argument," *American Benedictine Review* 17 (1966): 238–62; see also Thomas Merton, "Reflections on Some Recent Studies of St. Anselm," *Monastic Studies* 3 (1965): 221–34; Thomas Merton, *Cistercian Fathers and Forefathers: Essays and Conferences*, ed. Patrick F. O'Connell (Hyde Park, NY: New City Press, 2018), 102–33, 134–52.

155. "Faith Seeking Understanding," the original title given to St. Anselm's treatise now known as the *Proslogion* (see Schmitt, *Anselmi Opera Omnia*, 1.94).

156. In "The New Orders" (*Monastic Order*, 191–207), Knowles contrasts the "single tide" of the earlier renewal with "a two-fold current" at the beginning of the eleventh century: "there was the call to a solitary, penitential life, and the conscious recall to the spiritual legacy of the East" (191–92).

157. For Romuald (ca. 950–1027), see Knowles, *Monastic Order*, 193.

158. In his opening presentation for the November 1964 peacemakers' retreat Merton organized at the Abbey of Gethsemani, he "began by recounting the experience of St. John {Gualbert}. . . . This eleventh-century Florentine soldier on Good Friday met the murderer of his brother on a narrow bridge and moved to kill him in revenge. When the man fell to his knees and begged for mercy, {Gualbert} forgave him, threw his sword off the

Vallombrosans (*conversi* {were} introduced {here}).[159] St. *Nilus* (910–1005) {was a} Calabrian, in touch with Greek traditions; {he founded the} Basilian monastery of *Grottaferrata*, near Rome.[160] St. *Peter Damian*—cardinal, Doctor of {the} Church, hermit—{was the} dominant figure of eleventh-century monastic spirituality[161] ({for his} character, read Knowles, 195[162]). *St. Gregory* VII

---

bridge, and embraced him. It was an act, Merton felt, through which {Gualbert} essentially 'left the world,' and became '"cloistered" by his forgiveness,' as {Gualbert} would eventually establish a Benedictine monastic order" (Gordon Oyer, *Pursuing the Spiritual Roots of Protest: Merton, Berrigan, Yoder, and Muste at the Gethsemani Abbey Peacemaker Retreat* [Eugene, OR: Wipf and Stock, 2014], 111–12; Oyer has "Gaulbert" throughout).

159. For John Gualbert (ca. 993–1073), see Knowles, *Monastic Order*, 194; *conversi* are laybrothers, first introduced at Vallombrosa.

160. For Nilus, see Knowles, *Monastic Order*, 192–93.

161. See Thomas Merton, "St. Peter Damian and the Medieval Monk," *Jubilee* 8 (1960): 39–44, *Cistercian Fathers and Forefathers*, 26–40, for a brief overview of his life (ca. 1007–1072) and teaching.

162. "The greatest single influence . . . in what may be called the campaign of propaganda for a severely ascetical, quasi-eremitical monastic life was that of Peter Damian, who alike in writings, words and actions stands in something of the same prophetical relation to his age as does St Bernard to the age that followed a century later. Damian, at least until recent years, has probably been the object of less study and more misunderstanding than any other medieval figure of equal magnitude and significance. His fame has suffered both from the scantiness of records of the time, and from the reputation he acquired of an intransigence amounting to ferocity. When his activities and writings are regarded more closely, however, his mental and spiritual powers appear at better advantage; not only is his title of Doctor of the Church seen to be merited by his sane and central position in the controversy concerning simoniacal ordination, but his spiritual outlook while opening, so to say, in one direction upon the desert, can be recognized as including in its scope much of the devotional sentiment of the new age of which Anselm and Bernard were to be the masters. Peter Damian, like Romuald and Gualbert, came from a city family of Ravenna. Unlike them, he had as a youth entered fully into the new intellectual life of the schools of Lombardy before his conversion and entry into the Romualdine hermitage of Fonte Avellana, and this circumstance probably explains, as in similar

(1023–1085) ({was he a} Jew?[163]) becomes {a} Benedictine in Rome; {he takes a} job in {the} papal curia; {he is} anti-German {and} protects papal elections against imperial influence (under Leo IX). {In} 1073 Gregory {is} elected pope; {there follows the} struggle with Emperor Henry IV; Henry tried to demand {a} new election. {He is} (1) excommunicated {and does} penance at Canossa (three days outside {the} gate); (2) {a} second excommunication failed (it was *political*) and Gregory was driven out of Rome. ({The} Normans who came to rescue him sacked {the} city.) {His program was marked by a} *zeal* for {reform of the} clergy—celibacy; anti-simony; {the} clergy {were seen as} a levitical army; {he} exalted {the} *secular* power of {the} papacy, as well as {the}

---

cases throughout the ages, his frequent harshness of tone and exaggeration when criticizing the career he had abandoned. He early became a vehement advocate of a monasticism at once more austere and more eremitical than that of St Benedict and, trained as he had been in the schools that were so soon to develop into the universities of law, did not hesitate to defend his position with every kind of argument. More than once he met the critics who referred him to the words of the Rule which praise the common life by asserting roundly that the cenobitical life was a *pis aller* and had been recognized as such by the great legislator himself. Damian, like the Jerome to whom he bears some resemblance, wrote and acted with the fire of the moment rather than with the cold elaboration of logic, and in spite of his outspoken rejection of the traditional monastic life and his numerous controversies with abbots and monks, he retained a deep friendship and admiration for individuals and communities of the old model. . . . Damian, indeed, was not one of those spiritual teachers who build up a scheme for the soul's patient growth in perfection. His genius was to exhort and impel to the heroic, to praise striking achievements and to record edifying examples. Yet in him, as in Romuald, along with much that recalls past ages and other climates, the reader meets with many traces of the new intuitions and an intimacy of devotion to the mysteries of Christ's life on earth and of his Mother's."

163. According to an authoritative recent scholar, the rumored Jewish ancestry of Hildebrand, the future Gregory VII, is of doubtful historicity: see H. E. J. Cowdrey, *Pope Gregory VII, 1073–1085* (Oxford: Clarendon Press, 1998), 27–28.

spiritual. St. Peter Damian called him a Holy Satan.[164] {He was} canonized after {the} Counter-Reformation.

Molesme ({see} DK, 198 ff.[165])

{There were} *two centers of reform in France* {in the} eleventh century: (1) Maine—Tiron (Bernard[166]); Savigny (Vitalis[167])—{both} later than Cîteaux; (2) Burgundy—*Colan*: hermits here ask

---

164. "*Patri et filio papae et archidiacono, Petrus peccator monachus servitutem. Epistolam, de qua me insuggillastis, ad vos mitto, ut videatis, et quid in ea adversum vos egerim liquido comprobetis*. . . . *Si pro hac itaque epistola mori debeo, tendo cervicem, imprimite pugionem. De caetero sanctum Satanam meum humiliter obsecro, ut non adversum me tantopere saeviat, nec eius veneranda superbia tam longis me verberibus atterat; sed iamiam circa servum suum vel satiata mitescat*" ("Peter, monk-sinner, to the father and to the son, to the pope and to the archdeacon, humble service. I send to you the letter about which you have mistreated me, in order that you may see it, and may clearly decide what I have done against you in it. . . . If I ought to die because of this letter, I extend my neck—wield the sword. But for the rest I humbly beg my holy Satan not to rage so much against me; nor that his venerable pride wear me out with such extensive beatings; but that it may now be satisfied and abate toward its slave") (*Epistola* 16, to Pope Alexander II and the Cardinal Archdeacon Hildebrand [PL 144:235D–36A]); the letter in question had been written to the Archbishop of Cologne (PL 144:235C), urging him to summon a council to deal with a local schism, in Hildebrand's judgment unauthorized interference on Peter's part.

165. Knowles discusses the foundation of Molesme in "The New Orders" II (*Monastic Order*, 198–200) and those of Tiron and Savigny in Maine and Brittany in "The New Orders" III (200–202). For a detailed history of Molesme from its foundation through the departure for Cîteaux see also "Molesme, the Home of Cîteaux," the final chapter of Bede K. Lackner, *The Eleventh-Century Background of Cîteaux*, CS 8 (Washington, DC: Cistercian Publications, 1972), 217–76.

166. In 1109, Bernard (ca. 1060–1117), after serving as abbot of St. Cyprian in Poitiers, founded Tiron, which in turn generated a considerable number of daughter houses.

167. Vitalis began living as a hermit in the forest of Savigny ca. 1105, was joined by a group of disciples and founded the abbey there ca. 1112; he died in 1122. Savigny and its numerous foundations would merge with the Cistercians in 1147.

Robert, Abbot of St. Michel de Tonnerre, to be their superior; {in} 1075 Robert, with {a} brief from {Pope} Alexander II, becomes superior of {these} hermits and moves them *from Colan to Molesme*. {The} early reputation of Molesme draws St. Bruno (1080–1082) {and} draws Stephen Harding (read Dalgairns, p. 14 ff.–17[168]).

168. "Stephen was returning from his pilgrimage with his faithful companion, probably on his way back to Sherborne, when God conducted his steps to the place which was to be the scene of his labours. As he was travelling through a dark forest in the diocese of Langres in Burgundy, he came to a poor monastery situated on the side of a sloping hill, on the right bank of the little river Leignes. It could hardly be called a monastery, for it was a collection of huts, built by the monks themselves, of the boughs of trees, which they had cut down with their own hands, surrounding a small wooden oratory. Around this little knot of huts, more like an encampment than a settled dwelling, was an open space in the forest, which the monks had cleared, and which had been given them by a neighbouring baron. The brethren had no means of subsistence but the produce of this piece of ground, which they tilled with their own hands, and they were as much dependent upon it as the poorest serf who gained his own livelihood by the sweat of his brow; yet amongst this poor brotherhood were men of noble birth and of high intellectual attainments. The monastery had only been established a short time, and was struggling with all the difficulties which beset an infant community. Its history is a curious one, as showing how the reckless fury of the times was beaten down by an element of good even more energetic than the evil which it had to encounter. Two brothers of noble birth were one day riding through a solitary place in a forest not far from Molesme, called the forest of Colan; both were armed, for they were riding to take part in a tournament—a species of festivity, which with all its pageantry, its flutter of pennons and glittering of armour, was soon after condemned in strong terms by the Church. They were both worldly men, whose only object was honour, in pursuit of which they feared neither God nor man. As they were journeying on, the devil, aided by the solitude and darkness of the place, suggested horrid thoughts to each of them—of murdering the other in order to obtain his inheritance, and it cost them a struggle to put the temptation down. Shortly afterwards, on returning from the tournament, they passed through the same place. The wicked thoughts which had attacked them in that spot rose to the mind of each, and each trembled secretly at the dreadful power which Satan possessed over his mind. Without revealing to each

Cistercian History—Piety or Objectivity?

1. *The Foundation of Cîteaux* {came about as a} reaction against {the} accepted monasticism as practiced at *Molesme*. {It was} a new departure. What was Molesme? What was the new departure?

   a. {To understand} *Molesme* {we must consider} its founder, St. Robert, its foundation, and what changed? {It was a} fervent monastery—St. Stephen {and} St. Bruno {were} attracted to it; St. Warren

---

other their fears, they both hastened to the hut of a holy priest, who lived a hermit's life in the depth of the forest, and separately confessed their sin. They then revealed to each other the dreadful thoughts which had crossed their minds, and recognizing that they could not serve God and Mammon, but must either be like devils in wickedness or saints in holiness, they agreed to quit the world with all its honours, and to live in the forest under the direction of the holy hermit. The world soon heard of the conversion of these noble youths, who had quitted everything that it holds dear, to embrace a voluntary poverty, and to live a life of painful discipline; and a few others were induced to follow their example. At first they lived the life rather of hermits than of coenobites; afterwards, as their number increased to seven, they determined on adopting the rule of St. Benedict, and looked around them for someone to instruct them in it. They turned their eyes on Robert, then Abbot of St. Michel de Tonnerre, on the borders of Champagne and Burgundy. Robert, however was at that time unable to leave his post, and the hermits of Colan were disappointed in their hopes of obtaining him. Not long after, however, he was compelled to leave St. Michel by the incorrigibly bad lives of the monks, and to return to Celle near Troyes, his original monastery, from whence he was soon elected Prior of St. Aigulphus. At this place the hermits again sought him, and this time they applied to Rome for an order from the pope, commanding him to undertake the direction of them. Alexander II, the then reigning pontiff, pleased with their persevering zeal, granted their request, and Robert quitted St. Aigulphus to preside over this infant community. Under his guidance they gained frequent accessions to the brotherhood; and when at last their numbers amounted to thirteen, St. Robert saw fit to remove their habitation from the forest of Colan to Molesme. The new monastery was founded in honour of the Blessed Virgin, on Sunday the 20th of December, A.D. 1075. It was here that Stephen found the community, and he at once felt that he had reached the end of his wanderings" (John Bernard Dalgairns, *The Life of St. Stephen Harding, Abbot of Cîteaux and Founder of the Cistercian Order* [Westminster, MD: Newman, 1898]).

Cistercian History 39

goes out {from it} to {the} Alps.[169] But {it was} conventional—i.e. wealthy, comfortable, "enraciné."[170] {In} 1098 *the idea* of the foundation {of a new monastery arises}—from Robert? ({so} Orderic Vital[171]

169. Warren (Guarinus, Guerin) (d. 1150), monk of Molesme, in about 1090 was one of the founders of the hermitage of Aulps, in the Diocese of Geneva, which became a daughter abbey of Molesme in 1097 and eventually was accepted into the Cistercian Order in 1136; see Saint Bernard's letter to Warren at the time of the abbey's incorporation and his letter to the community two years later when Warren became bishop of Sion (Sitten) in Switzerland (*The Letters of St. Bernard of Clairvaux*, trans. Bruno Scott James [Chicago: Henry Regnery Company, 1953], 408–11 [#329], 219–21 [#151]; PL 182:459A–462C [#254], 297B–298C [#142]). For a brief biographical sketch (not completely accurate in all its details), see Thomas Merton, *In the Valley of Wormwood: Cistercian Blessed and Saints of the Golden Age*, ed. Patrick Hart, OCSO, CS 233 (Collegeville, MN: Cistercian Publications, 2013), 8–12.

170. "rooted"—i.e. well-established.

171. Ordericus Vitalis (1075–ca. 1143), *Historia Ecclesiastica*, III.8 (PL 188:637AC, 640AB): "*Ibi, tempore Philippi, regis Francorum, venerabilis Rodbertus abbas coenobium condidit, et inspirante gratia Spiritus sancti, discipulos magnae religionis aggregavit, studioque virtutum in sancta paupertate, juxta usum aliorum coenobiorum, comiter instruxit. Post aliquot annos, Sancti Benedicti regulam diligenter perscrutatus est, aliorumque sanctorum documentis Patrum perspectis, convocans fratres, sic affatus est: 'Nos, fratres charissimi, secundum Normam sancti Patris Benedicti professionem fecimus. Sed, ut mihi videtur, non eam ex integro tenemus. Multa, quae ibi non recipiuntur, observamus, et de mandatis eius plura negligentes intermittimus. Manibus nostris non laboramus, ut sanctos Patres fecisse legimus. Si mihi non creditis, o amici, legite gesta sanctorum Antonii, Macarii, Pacomii et ante omnes alios, doctoris gentium, Pauli apostoli. Abundantem victum et vestitum ex decimis et oblationibus ecclesiarum habemus, et ea quae competunt presbyteris, ingenio seu violentia subtrahimus. Sic nimirum sanguine hominum vescimur, et peccatis participamus. Laudo igitur ut omnino Regulam Sancti Benedicti teneamus, caventes ne ad dexteram vel ad sinistram ab ea deviemus. Victum et vestitum labore manuum nostrarum vindicemus. A femoralibus et staminiis, pelliciisque secundum Regulam abstineamus. Decimas et oblationes clericis, qui dioecesi famulantur, relinquamus. Et sic, per vestigia Patrum, post Christum currere ferventer insudemus.' His dictis, monachorum conventus non acquievit; immo praedecessorum quorum vita evidentibus miraculis insignita manifeste refulsit, exempla et instituta venerabilium vestigiis trita, virorum,*

moderatis novitatibus objecit. . . . *Abbas, in sua satis pertinax sententia, recessit ab eis, cum duodecim sibi assentientibus. Diuque locum quaesivit idoneum sibi suisque sodalibus, qui sancti decreverant Regulam Benedicti sicut Judaei legem Moysi ad litteram servare penitus. Tandem Odo, filius Henrici, Burgundiae dux, illis compassus est, et praedium in loco qui Cistercius dicitur, in episcopatu Cabilonensi, largitus est. Ibi Rodbertus abbas cum electis fratribus aliquandiu habitavit in eremo, nimiae districtionis et religionis coenobium construere coepit, Deoque donante, in brevi plerosque sanctitatis aemulatores habuit*" ("There, in the time of Philip, king of the French, the venerable Abbot Robert founded a monastic house, and inspired by the grace of the Holy Spirit, gathered followers in a noteworthy religious life; and he instructed them carefully in commitment to the virtues, in holy poverty, according to the usages of other monastic houses. After some years, he diligently examined the Rule of Saint Benedict, and after considering the texts of other holy Fathers, calling together his brothers, he spoke thus: 'We, most beloved brothers, made our profession according to the pattern established by our holy father Benedict. But as it seems to me, we do not hold to it in its fullness. We observe much that is not to be found there, and negligently we do not follow many of his commands. We do not work with our hands, as we read that the holy Fathers had done. If you do not believe me, O friends, read the deeds of the holy Anthony, Macarius and Pachomius, and before all others, of the teacher of the Gentiles, the apostle Paul. We have an abundance of food and clothing from tithes and offerings of the churches, and we draw on what belongs to priests, by sharp practice or by violence. Thus we are sated by the blood of men, and we participate in their sins. I therefore propose that we hold to the Rule of Saint Benedict completely, being careful that we might not deviate from it to the right or to the left. Let us procure our food and clothing by the work of our own hands. Let us abstain according to the Rule from undergarments and linens and furs. Let us give up tithes and offerings belonging to clergy who serve in the diocese. And thus, in the footsteps of the Fathers, let us endeavor to run fervently after Christ.' The community of monks did not go along with these words. Rather they opposed to such innovations the examples of their predecessors, whose distinguished life clearly shone forth in perceptible miracles, and the well-established practices on the moderate pathways of respected men. . . . The abbot, pertinacious enough in his own sentiment, withdrew from them, with twelve who assented to him. For a long time he searched for a suitable place for himself and his companions who had decided to keep the Rule of Saint Benedict to the letter as the Jews did the law of Moses. At last Odo, son of Henry the Duke of Burgundy, had compassion on them and bestowed on them an estate in a place called Cîteaux, in the diocese of Châlons. There Abbot Robert with his chosen

—read Lennsen,[172] p. 29[173]); or St. Alberic ({so} Gregor Müller,[174]

---

brothers lived for a while in solitude, and began to build a monastery of very great austerity and religious observance. Through the gift of God, in a short time he had numerous other sharers of this holy way of life.")

172. Séraphin Lenssen, "Saint Robert Fondateur de Cîteaux," *Collectanea Ordinis Cisterciensium Reformatorum* 4 (1937–1938): 2–16, 81–96, 161–77, 241–53; this article was reprinted as a 66-page pamphlet with consecutive pagination: *Saint Robert Fondateur de Cîteaux* (Westmalle: Imprimérie de l'Ordre Cistercien, 1937).

173. "*Quel* fut le premier auteur de l'idée créatrice de Cîteaux? Le coeur nous porterait à répondre: saint Robert. Orderic Vital, en effect, appuie ce sentiment; mais Guillaume de Malmesbury le combat. Nos documents de famille n'apportent aucune lumière. Cependant si Orderic Vital dit vrai, comment la piété filiale et la gratitude, la justice et la vérité ont-elles permis au compilateur du *Petit Exorde*, comme à nos autres historiens, de garder le silence sur ce point?—C'est là un objection sérieuse et que donne à réfléchir" ("Which one was the initial source of the creative idea of Cîteaux? The heart would urge us to answer: Saint Robert. Ordericus Vitalis, in effect, supports this view; but William of Malmesbury attacks it. Our documents from the Order do not provide any light. However, if Ordericus Vitalis is speaking the truth, how is it that filial piety and gratitude, justice and truth would have allowed the compiler of the *Exordium Parvum*, like our other historians, to keep silence on this point? There is a serious objection here, which prompts reflection") (Lennsen, "Saint Robert," 94–95 [Merton uses the pagination of the booklet rather than the article]). Lennsen's own position is that according to the *Exordium Parvum* the initial idea is owed not to any single person but to the conversations of various monks with their abbot, Robert ("l'idée fut le résultat des entretiens de plusieurs moines ensemble avec leur abbé" [96]). He presents Robert as the source not of the idea but rather of the ideal of Cîteaux (169), so that therefore Robert can be considered the "principal founder" ("le principal Fondateur") of the Cistercian Order, Alberic as the one who brought the project to full realization, as the *Exordium Parvum* states, Stephen Harding as the one providing the particulars of organization, and Bernard as the main propagator of the Cistercian vision: "Chacun des quatre a son mérite particulier. Mais au fond l'oeuvre des trois derniers est l'épanouissement de l'ésprit profondément monacal de Notre Père Saint Robert" ("Each of the four has his particular merit. But in the end the work of the last three is the expansion of the deeply monastic spirit of our Father Saint Robert") (169–70).

174. See Louis Lekai, *The White Monks: A History of the Cistercian Order* (Okauchee, WI: Our Lady of Spring Bank, 1953), 258–59: "In our century

Alberic found a strong champion in Gregor Müller, the founder and editor of the *Cistercienser-Chronik*. According to him: 'Alberic was appointed by Robert prior [of Molesmes (sic)]. . . . The more he delved into the study of the Rule, and compared its prescriptions with life in the abbey, the more he realized that it was not in satisfactory harmony with it and the more vigorously he labored to bring this about. . . . But because he also wished to suppress certain customs and usages . . . a storm broke loose. . . . Alberic wanted more than merely to remove abuses; his ideal was to secure full recognition to the prescriptions of the Rule . . . without any mitigation. . . . Some [of the monks] were ready to accept the plan the prior proposed to them. Particularly enthusiastic was the monk Stephen. . . . Since Alberic and Stephen realized that there could be no thought of realizing their plan at Molesme, they decided to implement it at another place. Now it was time to inform the abbot about their intention. . . . After mature reflection . . . . Robert declared himself . . . ready to participate in its execution' " (translation from Gregor Müller, *Vom Cistercienser Orden* [Bregenz: J. N. Teutsch, 1927], 9–10); Lackner adds: "In evaluating this conclusion one must now admit that it was drawn from documentary evidence which has since been proven debatable. It is not possible then to conclude that the Cistercian reform depends on the inspiration of St Alberic alone." It should be noted that in his adaptation of Müller's work Eugène Willems attributes this careful study of the Rule to Robert rather than to Alberic: "Plus Robert s'adonnait à l'étude du textus receptus de la Règle de saint Benoît, comparant les préscriptions avec la vie de l'abbaye, plus son zèle l'excitait à les remettre en plein valeur. Son but et ses aspirations le poussaient à ce que, dans la forme et les norms les plus pures, tout se fasse selon la Règle. Voilà comment il considérait la pureté monastique de la Règle—puritas Regula—Il ne voulait plus de compromis entre la tradition et la vie. Il désirait être un chevalier de la Règle. Cet idéal nouveau allant à l'encontre de la vie uniformément calme des monastères bénédictins de l'époque ne tarderait pas de provoquer l'étincelle d'un enthousiasme conquérant auprès de la jeunesse éprise d'héroïsme. Sa réaction contre la tendance qui dissociait de plus en plus la pratique matérielle des observances et coutumes monastiques de la vie spirituelle s'accentuait toujours. Sa charge de supérieur lui imposait le devoir délicat de remettre la Règle en valeur. Son prieur, Albéric, moine de talent and probablement ancien ermite de Colan, le suivra et le secondera dans la réalisation de ses vues" ("The more Robert devoted himself to the study of the standard text of the Rule of Saint Benedict, comparing its prescriptions with the life of the abbey, the more his zeal urged him to return to them in complete fidelity. His purpose and his aspirations pushed him to what, in

P. Othon[175]); or St. Stephen (William of Malmesbury[176]).

---

the form and the most pure norms, was to be done completely according to the Rule. See how he considered the monastic purity of the Rule—*puritas Regulae*—He no longer wanted any compromise between the tradition and life. He desired to be a knight of the Rule. This new ideal, encountering the uniformly calm life of the Benedictine monasteries of the period, was not slow to provoke the spark of an enthusiasm conquering the youth drawn to heroism. His reaction against the tendency that separated material practice of the observances and monastic customs more and more from the spiritual life became ever more evident. His responsibility as the superior imposed on him the delicate duty to return the Rule to its value. His prior, Alberic, a monk of talent and probably a former hermit of Colan, would follow him and support him in the realization of his views") (Eugène Willems, *Esquisse Historique de l'Ordre de Cîteaux*, d'après le Père Grégoire Müller, 2 vols. [Aubel: Notre-Dame du Val-Dieu, 1957–1958], 22); Willems subsequently affirms the priority of Robert in the foundation of the new abbey: "L'abbé Robert reste le vrai fondateur de Cîteaux" ("Abbot Robert remains the true founder of Cîteaux") (26); "On ne peut plus douter que l'abbé Robert fut le vrai INSPIRATEUR de la réforme. Un témoignage sûr, ancien, cistercien, officiel—l'Exordium Cistercii—montre avec insistance la communauté de vues entre Robert et sa communauté cistercianisante, déclarant que Cîteaux doit sa vie à saint Robert et à lui seul" ("One can no longer doubt that Abbot Robert was the true INSPIRER of the reform. A certain, early, Cistercian, official witness—the *Exordium Cistercii*—shows with insistence the community of views between Robert and his Cistercianizing community, declaring that Cîteaux owes its life to Saint Robert and to him alone") (29).

175. See Othon [Ducourneau], *Les Origines Cisterciennes* (Liguge: Imprimérie E. Aubin et Fils, 1933): "tous les documents primitifs donnent en effet le titre de premier abbé de Cîteaux à saint Aubri. . . . Pour bien préciser la part du saint abbé de Molesme dans l'oeuvre cistercienne, il faut dire qu'il fut simplement l'*installateur* du Nouvelle Monastère" ("all the early documents give the title of the first abbot of Cîteaux to Saint Alberic. . . . To specify exactly the role of the holy abbot of Molesme in the Cistercian work, one must say that he was simply the installer of the New Monastery") (71, 73).

176. See William of Malmesbury (ca. 1090–ca. 1143), *Gesta Regum Anglorum*, 4.334 (PL 179:1286C–1287A ["*De Cisterciensibus*"]): "*Ejus diebus religio Cistellensis coepit, quae nunc optima via summi in coelum processus et creditur et dicitur. De qua hic loqui suscepti operis non videtur esse contrarium, quod ad Angliae gloriam pertineat, quae talem virum produxerit qui hujusce religionis*

b. The struggle to make the foundation—Robert joins other hermits and is called back;[177] Alberic {is} imprisoned.

c. {Then comes} the departure, {the} foundation {and its} patrons, steps to get approval, {the} first days (read A. K. p. 5[178]),

---

fuerit et auctor et mediator. Noster ille, et nostra puer in palestra primi aevi tirocinium cucurrit. Quapropter, si non invidi sumus, eo illius bona complectimur gratiosius quo agnoscimus propinquius; simul et laudes ejus attollere mihi est animus, quia ingenua mens est si bonum in alio probes quod in te non esse suspires. Is fuit Hardingus nomine apud Anglos, non ita reconditis natalibus procreatus" ("In his days the Cistercian Order began, which now is both believed and said to be the best way to proceed to heaven. To speak about this does not seem to be incompatible with the work undertaken here, because it belongs to the glory of England, which produced such a man who was both author and promoter of this religious life. He belongs to us, and as a boy in our schools he ran the course of his first age. Therefore if we are not envious, we embrace his good qualities more graciously as we recognize them as closer to ourselves; at the same time my soul lifts up his praises, because the spirit is generous if you approve the good in another that you sigh not to find in yourself. He was named Harding among the English, and so not born of obscure parentage").

177. This was his withdrawal to Aux, at some period in the early 1090s (see Ducourneau, 36–40).

178. "St Robert, who led some 20 monks from Molesme to Cîteaux, had a varied monastic career; prior of Montier [sic] la Celle, abbot of St Michael of Tonnerre, prior of St Ayoul at Provins, and superior of a group of hermits in the forest of Colon [sic], whom he led eventually to Molesme, where a Benedictine house was established, of which he became abbot (1075–1098). On arrival at Cîteaux, the community renewed their obedience to Robert in the following formula: 'The profession and stability which I made in your presence at the monastery of Molesme, the same, I affirm before God and his Saints, I will keep in this place New Minster, in obedience to you and to your successors lawfully appointed.' St Robert himself, in accordance with the directions of the apostolic legate, Hugh, archbishop of Lyons, had been previously blessed as abbot by Walter, bishop of Chalon [sic]; while the generous material assistance given by the duke of Burgundy permitted the erection of a monastery. Manrique says of St Robert: *creatio prima convenit*, but the spearheads of the reform were rather St Alberic and St Stephen Harding: *resignons nous à refuser à saint Robert l'initiative de Cîteaux*" (Archdale A. King, *Cîteaux and Her Elder Daughters* [London: Burns & Oates, 1954]; the quotations are

{followed by the} return of Robert to Molesme (as {the} result of a provincial council).

d. {During} the administration of St. Alberic (1099–{1108}[179]) {the} *Privilegium Romanum*[180] {was obtained, assuring} protection of {the} monastery; {it provided a} statement of the *aims* of {the} foundation as approved by {the} Holy See, {including emphasis on} *solitude* {and} *austerity*. {The} *Instituta* {stressed} poverty {and included provisions for} laybrothers {and} future foundations.[181] {Regulations on the} *liturgy* {effected a} simplification of {the} office {and brought about a} reestablishment of balance {as a hallmark} of Cistercian life.

e. {The} administration of St. Stephen ({1108}–1133) {made clear the centrality of} solitude, {with the} exclusion of {the} Duke of Burgundy {from the cloister} ({the} Duke continues {to be} benevolent). Poverty—especially in liturgy—{was} pushed to {the} extreme; liturgical reform {focused on} chant {and} scripture translation. {The} CHARTER OF CHARITY (1118, 1119? approved 1152[182]), {the} original work of St. Stephen (see later[183]), creates {the} Cistercians *as {an} order*, {with a} General Chapter, {a system of} visitations, {a respect for the} autonomy of {individual} houses and of {the} Order {through} exemption {from secular control}. (N.B. {in}

---

from Angel Manrique, *Cisterciensium seu Verius Ecclesiasticorum Annalium a Condito Cistercio*, 4 vols. [Leyden: G. Boissat & Laurent Anisson, 1642–1659; rpt. Farnborough: Gregg International, 1970], chap. 3, *ad fin* ["the initial creation was due to him"] and Lennsen, "Saint Robert," 95 ["Let us resign ourselves to denying the initiative of Cîteaux to Saint Robert"]).

179. Copy text reads: "1109" here and below.
180. *Exordium Parvum*, chap. 14 (*Nomasticon Cisterciense, seu Antiquiores Ordinis Cisterciensis Constitutiones A.R.P.D. Juliano Paris . . .* Editio Nova, ed. Hugo Séjalon [Solesmes: E Typographeo Sancti Petri, 1892], 61–62).
181. I.e. the so-called *Instituta* of St. Alberic (*Exordium Parvum*, chap. 15: "*Instituta monachorum Cisterciensium de Molsimo venientium*" ["The Institutes of the Cistercian Monks Coming from Molesme"] [*Nomasticon*, 62–63]).
182. For the correct dating of the *Carta Caritatis Prior* (1119) and *Carta Caritatis Posterior* (1152), see below, page 66, n. 309.
183. See below, pages 66–67, 70–73.

1215 {the Fourth} Council {of the} Lateran, canon 12, {prescribed that} other orders should have {a} general chapter like Cîteaux.[184])

St. Robert:[185] *Anno milleno centeno bis minus uno / Sub Patre Roberto coepit Cistercius ordo.*[186] {There was} controversy about him (William of Malmesbury etc. contra[187]). {He was} born about 1028 ({see the} legend of {the} Blessed Virgin before {his} birth[188]). {He} entered *Moutier la Celle* at fifteen. {In} 1068, at about 40, {he}

---

184. See Lekai, *The White Monks*, 53: "The Fourth Lateran Council held in 1215, in a general reform of monastic constitution, pointed to the Cistercian Order as a model of perfect organization. The twelfth canon directs that the Benedictines in each province of a kingdom shall hold a chapter of abbots and priors every three years. Since they were unacquainted with the method of holding such meetings, it was suggested that two Cistercian abbots of the neighborhood be invited to give counsel and help in matters of procedure."

185. For Merton's early biographical sketch of Saint Robert see Merton, *Valley of Wormwood*, 143–52.

186. "In the year one thousand two hundred, minus one / Under Father Robert the Cistercian Order began" (Manrique, *Cisterciensium,* 1.11). The year indicated would thus be 1199, which is "of course absurd" as Herbert Thurston points out in his preface to Dalgairns (x).

187. William of Malmesbury, *Gesta Regum Anglorum*, 4.337: "*Haec abbas ille primo ingenti impetu et ipse faciebat et alios compellebat; sed temporis intercessu poenituit homo delicate nutritus, et aegre ferens iam diutinam ciborum parcimoniam. Cujus voluntatem monachi apud Molesmum residui cognocentes, verbis quibusdam incertum an et epistolis, per obedientiam papae astu quodam ad monasterium retrahunt, volentem cogentes. Quasi enim diffatigatus improbitate supplicum, angustos parietes reliquit pauperum, angustiorem repetens thronum. Secuti eum ex Cistellis omnes qui cum eo venerant, praeter octo*" ("This the abbot himself did under his initial strong impulse, and compelled the others to do, but with the lapse of time, he had a change of heart, being a man raised delicately and scarcely able to endure the long-lasting scarcity of food. When the monks remaining at Molesme became aware of his desire—whether by certain words or also by letters is uncertain—they drew him, through obedience to the pope, back to their monastery by a certain stratagem, compelling one who was willing. For as though worn down by the unrelentingness of their appeals, he left behind the narrow confines of the poor, seeking again a more elevated seat. All who had come with him followed him out of Cîteaux, except eight") (PL 179:1289BC).

188. "his mother Ermengarde . . . is supposed to have had a vision of the Blessed Virgin a little before her son's birth, in which Our Lady expressed

becomes abbot of *St. Michel de Tonnerre*; soon after *Colan* seeks him {but his} monks refuse {to let him go. He takes} refuge at *Saint Ayoul*. {In} 1074 Roman permission to get Robert {is granted; he} goes to Colan, then to Molesme (1175). (St. Bruno comes to Molesme about 1084). {In} 1088 (?) St. Stephen joins, returning from pilgrimage to Rome with Peter, his companion.

Development of Molesme—{there is} UNREST due to conflict between old and new; {there is} *not* {a} real lack of fervor, but dissatisfaction and division, {caused by} gifts of churches, tithes, children in {the} monastery, {oversight of} nuns in nearby houses. By 1098, Molesme had 35 dependent priories and granges, cells, nunneries; {the} COURT of nobles {was held} at {the} monastery. "Are we keeping the Rule?" *tepide ac negligenter*, {according to the} Letter of Hugh (*Exordium Parvum*[189]); *de transgressione Regulae . . . conquerebantur* (text of *Exordium Parvum*[190]). They claim (1) {the} necessity of penance and manual labor; of poverty; of fasting; of restoring the original balance of the {monastic} life (shortening {the} offices); (2) {there is a} reaction against *Cluniac observance*. {In} 1090, Guerin and Guy and Amadée {withdraw} to Aulps— cf. Subiaco.[191] {In} 1090 or 1093 (?) a first attempt {is made for a} hermitage of Aux or Auch—{a} foundation of nine priories and one abbey. {In} 1098 (January) {a} *delegation* {*goes*} *to* {*the*} *papal legate, Hugh*;[192] Alberic {is} imprisoned (?). {In} 1098, {in} March,

---

a desire to be espoused to the child that was soon to be born. This pious legend belongs to the thirteenth century" (Merton, *Valley of Wormwood*, 144).

189. "in a lukewarm and negligent fashion" (chap. 2 [*Nomasticon*, 54]).

190. "They were cast down by their violation of the *Rule*" (chap. 3 [*Nomasticon*, 55]).

191. The comparison is to St. Benedict's withdrawal to the cave at Subiaco in the Apennines, where he initially lives as a hermit and eventually attracts numerous disciples and establishes twelve monasteries there before moving to Monte Cassino (for a summary see Thomas Merton, *The Rule of Saint Benedict: Initiation into the Monastic Tradition* 4, ed. Patrick F. O'Connell, MW 19 [Collegeville, MN: Cistercian Publications, 2009], 21–29).

192. For the significance of the role of Hugh (d. 1106) as papal legate in the various reform efforts of the late eleventh century, see Lackner, *The Eleventh-Century Background*, 154–55.

{the} foundation of Cîteaux {is made}. {In} 1099 St. Robert {is} recalled to Molesme by {Pope} Urban—see *Exordium*, cap. 6;[193] reasons {are} given {in} cap. 7[194] (see the next page). {His} declining years {remain} active. {The} character of Robert {includes the following characteristics}: (1) quiet, gentle, self-effacing; (2) yet a good organizer ({this is} disputed); (3) Molesme {was} a great abbey and spiritual center. {In} 1111 {the} death of St. Robert {took place, on} April 17. {He was} succeeded {at Molesme}[195] by Guy de Chastel-Censoir (1111–1132)—{a} friend of St. Bernard; then {by} Giraut (1140–1148)[196]—again {there were} good relations with St. Bernard (n. b. {Bernard's sister} Humbeline[197] {went to} to Jully, {a convent associated with Molesme}). {By} 1198 Molesme {was} definitely decadent—{the} abbot of Clairvaux {was} appointed to make regular visitations, but {there was} an immediate revival under Gaucher.[198] Eudes II (1215–1227) works for {the} canonization of St. Robert, in harmony with {the} Cistercians ({he was} *canonized* {in} *1222*). {In} 1245 {the} title {of} first Abbot of Cîteaux and founder of {the} Cistercian Order {was} recognized by {the} General Chapter.[199]

193. This is Pope Urban's letter to Hugh of Lyons urging (but not requiring) that Robert return to Molesme (*Nomasticon*, 56).

194. The monks at Molesme were demanding Robert's return because since his departure the regular life at the abbey had degenerated, there was dissension among the monks, and the abbey was faced with ruin (presumably because of the hostility of the nobles and other neighbors mentioned in the pope's letter) (*Nomasticon*, 56–57).

195. For information on subsequent abbots of Molesme Merton relies on Lennsen, "Saint Robert," 82, n. 2.

196. The abbot between 1132 and 1140 was Evrard.

197. For a brief biographical sketch see Merton, *Valley of Wormwood*, 77–82.

198. Abbot of Molesme from 1197 to 1209.

199. Actually the first reference to Robert as founding abbot comes in the General Chapter of 1222 (#13): "*De beato Roberto primo abbate Cistercii fiat festum XV° kalendas maii cum XII lectionibus, sicut de beato Hieronmo, et una missa sicut de beato Benedicto*" ("Concerning blessed Robert, first abbot of

Cistercian History

Foundation of Cîteaux—{the sources include[200]}:
1) *Exordium Parvum*[201]—brief, official, definition of an ideal—but *early*;
2) *Exordium Magnum*[202]—relatively late—fanciful;
3) William of Malmesbury, *Gesta Regum Anglorum*[203]—{this is} biased—pro Stephen;
4) Ordericus Vitalis[204]—imaginative;
5) *Vita Roberti*[205] (thirteenth century) does not correspond with the others: e.g. {it} says Alberic and Stephen went to be hermits at *Vinicus*,[206] then went to Cîteaux and were found there by Robert + 22 {companions}.

Cîteaux, on April 17 let there be a feast of twelve lessons, like that of blessed Jerome, and of one Mass, like that of blessed Benedict") (J.-M. Canivez, ed., *Statuta Capitulorum Generalium Ordinis Cisterciensis ab Anno 1116 ad Annum 1786*, 8 vols. [Louvain: Bureaux de la Revue d'Histoire Ecclésiastique, 1933–1941], 2.15–16). The request from the Benedictines of Molesme to write to the pope in support of Robert's canonization is recorded in 1220 (#53) (Canivez, *Statuta*, 1.527); in 1254 (#1) Robert was called the "*Ordinis primi institutoris*" ("the first beginner of the Order") and included in the Cistercian litany following Saint Bernard (Canivez, *Statuta*, 2.398); in 1259 (#6) a feast of two Masses was instituted for Robert (Canivez, *Statuta*, 2.450).

200. Here Merton follows Jean de la Croix Bouton, *Histoire de l'Ordre de Cîteaux*, 3 vols. (Westmalle, Belgium: Notre Dame d'Aiguebelle, 1959, 1964, 1968), 53 (originally issued in pamphlet form as "Fiches Cisterciennes" in 120 installments).

201. *Nomasticon*, 53–65.

202. Conrad of Eberbach, *Exordium Magnum Cisterciense*, ed. Bruno Griesser (Rome: Editiones Cistercienses, 1961), 60–79 (1.10–21).

203. William of Malmesbury, *Gesta Regum Anglorum*, 4.334–37 (PL 179:1286C–1290C ["*De Cisterciensibus*"]).

204. Ordericus Vitalis, *Historia Ecclesiastica*, 8.26 (188:636D–642A).

205. PL 157:1278–88.

206. Ducourneau (51) discounts the historicity of this incident, particularly as it has Alberic and Stephen going directly from Vinicus (or Vivicus) to Cîteaux when it is clear from contemporary sources that they were at Molesme at the time of the withdrawal.

Evolution of {the} Early Constitution—{an} outline based on {the} *Exordium Parvum* (*Lekai*[207]):

1) 1098 (January?)—Robert, with Alberic {and} Stephen, {as well as} Odo, Letald, John and Peter—goes to {the} papal legate, asking permission to make a new foundation under his protection; he approves: {see the} *letter of Hugh* (Lekai, p. 252—read[208]); {he} encourages and blesses {the} project to go elsewhere and keep {the} *Rule* of St. Benedict more perfectly. 21 March 1098 {is the} date of {the} consecration of {the} monastery.

2) {In} 1100, {on} April 18, Paschal {II}[209] grants the *Privilegium Romanum*;[210] {its} purpose {is} to insure *peace for the Cistercian*

---

207. The *Exordium Parvum*, trans. Robert E. Larkin (Lekai, *The White Monks*, 251–66).

208. "Hugh, Archbishop of Lyons and Legate of the Apostolic See, to Robert, Abbot of Molesme, and to the brethren who together with him desire to serve God according to the Rule of Saint Benedict. Be it known to all those who rejoice in the advancement of our Holy Mother the Church that you and some of your sons, brethren of the community of Molesme, appeared before us at Lyons and pledged yourselves to follow from now on more strictly and more perfectly the Rule of the Most Holy Benedict, which so far in that monastery you have observed poorly and neglectfully. Since it has been proven that because of many hindering circumstances you could not accomplish your aim in the aforementioned place, we—keeping in view the spiritual welfare of both parties, namely of the departing and of the remaining—consider that it would be expedient for you to retire to another place which the Divine Munificence will point out to you, and there serve the Lord undisturbedly in a more wholesome manner. Therefore, to you who presented yourselves: Abbot Robert, and the brethren Alberic, Odo, John, Stephen, Letald and Peter as well as all others who properly and by unanimous consent have decided to join you, we advise and commend to persevere in this holy endeavor which we, through the impression of our seal corroborate forever by the Apostolic authority" (252–53 [*Nomasticon*, 54]).

209. Text reads: "III" (probably taken from Lekai, *The White Monks*, 19, where the same error is found).

210. This decree of Pope Paschal declares the New Monastery forever free from all interference by secular or clerical authority, under pain of excommunication, and confirms the ruling of Pope Urban II requiring mutual

reform. {These} steps {are taken}: (a) John and Ilbodus {are} sent to Rome (*Exordium Parvum*[211]—Lekai, p. 258); (b) with {a} *letter of two cardinals*, John and Benedict (p. 258), {in which they} ask that {the} previous protection granted by Urban (254, 255?) be confirmed;[212] {as well as a} *letter of {the} legate, Hugh*,[213] describing {their} observance and persecution by {the} Benedictines, asking {for their} protection;[214] {and also a} *letter of Walter of Châlons*[215] {saying that} everything is in order, {that} all has been carried out according to {the} orders of Urban II;[216] protection {is} requested, *under {the} bishop* (260–61).

{The} Foundation of Cîteaux—{the} story based on charters etc. (Fiches[217]):

1. That the place was wild and desolate—{this is} something of a midrash. There were two families of serfs *in the neighborhood*. They and {the} land they were on {were} given to Cîteaux between 1134 {and} 1143 (Fiches[218]); possibly {there was} a *chapel* {already there}.

1a. That they got there on March 21: {this is} oversimplified; March 21 {is} the official date ({the} "community {was} erected" {then}?);

2. The monks began to use the chapel for {the} office—it is (re)dedicated in 1098, {during the} summer or fall—{was it an} old chapel or new?

---

forbearance by Molesme and the New Monastery (*Exordium Parvum*, chap. 14 [*Nomasticon*, 61–62; Lekai, *The White Monks*, 261–62]).

211. Chap. 10 (*Nomasticon*, 58–59).

212. Chap. 11 (*Nomasticon*, 59).

213. Actually, under Paschal, the new pope, Hugh had been replaced as legate in 1099 by Cardinals John and Benedict: see *Narrative and Legislative Texts from Early Cîteaux*, ed. and trans. Chrysogonus Waddell, Studia et Documenta, vol. 9 (Cîteaux: Commentarii Cistercienses, 1999), 430.

214. Chap. 12 (*Nomasticon*, 60–61; Lekai, *The White Monks*, 259–60).

215. The bishop of the diocese in which Cîteaux was located.

216. Chap. 13 (*Nomasticon*, 60–61; Lekai, *The White Monks*, 260).

217. Bouton, *Histoire*, 54–55.

218. Bouton, *Histoire*, 54.

3. {The} support of {the} legate, Hugh, a zealous reformer and {a} friend of Robert, {was important, along with the} support of Odo (Eudes), Duke of Burgundy, who bought more land and added to {the} property {and} helped {the} monks finish {the} wooden buildings; {he} liberates them from feudal obligation and grants {them the} use of (his) woods.

4. Robert {was} installed at Châlons; {the} monks make stability at Cîteaux.

5. {At} Christmas, 1098, Odo presents Robert with a vineyard, in {the} presence of a great multitude of lords (comment—Fiches, p. 55[219]—{a} silly remark! They were *there*!)

Return of Robert to Molesme:

1. {The} new abbot, Geoffrey, {was} blessed while {the} others go to Cîteaux.

2. After {the} new foundation, benefactors stop giving gifts to Molesme; one of them burns down a grange.

3. Geoffrey, fearing {the} ruin of {the} monastery, appeals directly to {the} pope, who tells {the} legate to look into it and *permits* {the} return of Robert.

4. {A} synod at Port Anselle decides that Robert *must* return to govern Molesme.

5. Robert turns over interim administration of Cîteaux to {the} Bishop of Châlons. {The} Bishop of Langres restores to Robert the abbacy of Molesme—Geoffrey has {the} right of

---

219. "Enfin la dernière charte où paraît S. Robert à Cîteaux date de la solennité de Noel (1098). En ce jour, en présence d'une grande multitude de seigneurs, le duc Eudes fit don au Nouveau Monastère d'une vigne qu'il possédait à Meursault. On a prétendu que le duc avait tenu sa cour à Cîteaux. Rien ne l'indique. Il n'est pas vraisemblable qu'en plein hiver cette multitude se soit rencontrée dans le 'désert' de Cîteaux" ("The last charter in which Robert appears at Cîteaux dates from the feast of Christmas in 1098. On that day, in the presence of a large crowd of nobility, Duke Eudes made a gift to the New Monastery of a vineyard which he owned at Meursault. It has been assumed that the duke had held his court at Cîteaux. Nothing indicates this to be the case. It is unlikely that in mid-winter this multitude would have gathered in the 'desert' of Cîteaux").

succession. {The} monks of Cîteaux {are} released from {their} promise of obedience to Robert; those who wish may return with Robert to {Molesme}.[220] Neither monastery will receive monks of {the} other without authorization of {the} abbot.

6. Judgements: (a) {in the} ancient sources {there is simply the} plain statement of fact; (b) William of Malmesbury accuses Robert of defection, because of {the} strict life at Cîteaux; he plotted secretly with {the} monks of Molesme to bring about his return;[221] (c) Conrad of Eberbach, {in the} *Exordium Magnum*, wrote, "if Robert had really wanted to stay, he could have";[222] he fled poverty; this was suppressed by {the} General Chapter[223] {and} rediscovered[224] and adopted by Fr. Othon Ducourneau[225]

220. Text reads: "Cîteaux."
221. See above, n. 187.
222. "*cum secundum tenorem litterarum ab apostolico missarum se excusare potuisset, si heremiticam paupertatem dilexisset*" ("although he could have excused himself according to the tone of the letter sent by the apostolic legate if he had loved solitary poverty") (Griesser, ed., *Exordium*, 68).
223. The modern editor of the *Exordium Magnum*, Bruno Griesser, believes it more likely that this material was not deliberately suppressed but lost due to the absence of one or more folios from the major manuscript tradition (see Paul Savage, "Introduction," *The Great Beginning of Cîteaux— A Narrative of the Beginning of the Cistercian Order: The Exordium Magnum of Conrad of Eberbach*, trans. Benedicta Ward and Paul Savage, ed. E. Rozanne Elder, CF 42 [Collegeville, MN: Cistercian Publications, 2012], 32, referring to the revised edition: *Exordium Magnum Cisterciense sive Narratio de Initio Cisterciensis Ordinis*, ed. Bruno Griesser, CCCM 138 [Turnhout, Belgium: Brepols, 1994], 10–11).
224. See Tibertius Hümpfner, "Der Bisher in den Gedruckten Ausgaben Vermisste Teil des Exordium Magnum S. O. Cist.," *Cistercienser-Chronik* 20 (1908): 97–106 for the discovery of the manuscript with the missing material (MS Innsbruck, Universitätsbibliothek 25) and the text of these seven chapters.
225. "Il y aurait donc eu de la part de l'abbé, non seulement découragement de l'oeuvre enterprise et regret des sacrifices accomplis, mais encore intrigues secrètes pour parvenir à se retirer honorablement sous le couvert de l'autorité pontificale. Des agissements aussi peu dignes son trop incompatibles avec la sainteté indiscutable de Robert pour qu'il n'y ait pas là une

{but} disputed by Laurent,[226] Mahn,[227] Lenssen;[228] (d) pro Robert opinions today {include comments on his} "heroic obedience" (Lenssen[229]) {and the} "reparation of scandal" (Turk[230]).

---

exaggération calomnieuse, mais, pour exagérées et malveillantes qu'elles soient, ces assertions n'en renferment pas moins un grand fond de verité, au moins quant au désir de Robert d'abandonner Cîteaux" ("Thus there would have been on the part of the abbot not only discouragement about the work undertaken and regret at the sacrifices made, but also secret intrigues to reach the point of withdrawing honorably under the cover of pontifical authority. Such manipulations so unworthy are too incompatible with the indisputable sanctity of Robert for it not to be a calumnious exaggeration, but however exaggerated and ill-natured they may be, these assertions none the less rest on a great basis of truth, at least as to the desire of Robert to abandon Cîteaux") (*Origines Cisterciennes*, 70).

226. See Jacques Laurent, "Le Problème des Commencements de Cîteaux," *Annales de Bourgogne* 6 (1934): 213–29; this article is a sustained critique of Dom Othon's position concerning Robert's motives for returning to Molesme.

227. See Jean-Berthold Mahn, *L'Ordre Cistercien et son Gouvernement des Origines au Milieu du XIIIe Siècle (1095–1265)* (Paris: E. de Boccard, 1945), 44, where Mahn points out (as have other scholars) that Dom Othon mistakenly translates the clause "*Haec omnia Abbas ille laudavit & fecit*" from Archbishop Hugh's letter to the Bishop of Langres on Robert's return to Molesme (*Exordium Parvum*, chap. 7 [*Nomasticon*, 57]) as "Robert 'loua et approva,'" alors que le mot *laudare* n'a qu'un sens de confirmation, d'acceptation formelle, comme on le voit dans des milliers de chartes de l'époque" ("Robert 'praised and approved,' while at that time the word *laudare* simply had the meaning of confirmation, of formal acceptance, as is seen in thousands of charters of the period").

228. Much of Lennsen's article "Saint Robert" is a critique of Père Othon's assumption that the negative attitude toward Robert found in William of Malmesbury and in the *Exordium Magnum* represented the consensus judgment of the twelfth century.

229. "une obéisance *heroique*" (Lenssen, "Saint Robert," 241).

230. "*At contra Conradum dicendum est non agi de macula inobedientiae, sed de macula scandali, quod Molismenses in egressu Cisterciensium passi sunt quodque etiam eo maius erat, quia monasterium Molismense etiam abbas dereliquit. Hoc scandalum autem tum* Exordium Cisterciensii coenobii *tum* Exordium Magnum *caute silentio praetereunt, quia difficile negari poterat. Quod autem Molis-*

{The} *Exordium Magnum*:

1. {In} I.10[231] he says he is defending {the} Order against {the} accusations of Black Benedictines in Germany that the founders left Molesme in an *act of disobedience*—"*contra voluntatem abbatis sui de Molismensi coenobio egressos fuisse.*"[232] His text will prove this {to be} an *impudens mendacium*[233] (p. 61). Two arguments {are presented, supported} by papal documents etc., to show: (a) *quam rationabiliter quamque auctorabiliter* humano iudicio *probatus est*;[234]

---

menses attinet, cum reditum Roberti postulassent, nonne eodem iure utebatur, quo v.g. Bernardus reditum Arnoldi abbatis Morimundi, et monachorum eius postulabit" ("But contrary to Conrad, it should be said to be a matter not of the stain of disobedience but of the stain of scandal that the monks of Molesme were allowed to leave for Cîteaux, and that this was even more serious, because the abbot also deserted the monastery of Molesme. This scandal both the *Exordium Cisterciensis Coenobii* [i.e. the *Exordium Parvum*] and the *Exordium Magnum* cautiously passed over in silence, because it could be denied only with difficulty. Because what concerned the monks of Molesme when they demanded the return of Robert, was it not using the same law by which, for example, Bernard demanded the return of Arnold, Abbot of Morimond, and his monks?") (Josip Turk, "Cistercii Statuta Antiquissima," *Analecta Sacri Ordinis Cisterciensis* 4 [1948]: 103–4). This position is not then "pro Robert" but a claim that since Robert had deserted his post without the permission of the Bishop of Langres just as Arnold, the founding abbot of the Cistercian Abbey of Morimond, would later desert his in his wild plan to go to the Holy Land in 1124 (see PL 182:89B–91C [#4]; James, *Letters*, 19–22 [#4]), his return was the reparation of a scandalous act. This is however a tendentious argument since Robert and his companions had in fact received permission for the foundation of the New Monastery from the papal legate Hugh of Lyons, the ecclesiastical superior of (the unsympathetic) local bishop Robert of Langres (see Waddell, *Narrative and Legislative Texts*, 420), so that there was no question of scandal and no parallel with the situation of Arnold.

231. Griesser, ed., *Exordium*, 60–63.

232. "they had gone forth from the cenobium of Molesme against the will of their abbot" (Griesser, ed., *Exordium*, 61).

233. "shameless lie."

234. "how reasonably and how authoritatively it was approved by human judgment" (Griesser, ed., *Exordium*, 61, which reads: "*probatus et approbatus sit*").

(b) *qualiter divino iudicio approbatus sit*[235] (by miracles, graces and virtues, and {the} wonderful expansion of {the} Order—especially graces of prayer).

2. The brethren at Molesme, inspired by {the} Holy Spirit: (1) realize that the *Rule* read in chapter is not being kept; hence they are not living up to their vows; (2) they discuss the matter, it gets around, they are opposed by the weaker brethren; (3) *they go to {the} abbot* (he is represented as having nothing to do with {this}); (4) he is *ad horam compunctus*[236] and not only approves but even says he will go with them; hence they are glad; they "know it is {the} work of God";[237] (5) {the} brethren and Robert go to Hugh, {the} Legate, who says they are right and *exhorts* them to follow their inspiration ({the} text of {the} letter[238] {is given} as in {the} *Exordium Parvum*[239]); (6) they return to Molesme and select socios remissioris vitae blanditias respuentes et ad *puritatem simplicitatemque* sanctae Regulae pure simpliciterque tenendam prompto animo flagrantes elegerunt . . . *qui perfectioris vitae et regulae Sancti Patris Benedicti* ad litteram *tenendae desiderio arctam et angustam viam ingressi sunt.*[240] See other language (p. 65): *laetantibus angelis . . . Christianam philosophiam . . .* etc.;[241] the Good Shepherd and wandering sheep (n.b. tendentious!) {along with} other symbols: the desert flowers; the first tree grows etc.

235. "how it was approved by divine judgment" (Griesser, ed., *Exordium*, 61).

236. "pierced at that hour" (Griesser, ed., *Exordium*, 63).

237. "*sed dexteram Dei vivi virtutem operantis in eis*" ("but the power of the right hand of the living God working in them") (Griesser, ed., *Exordium*, 63).

238. 1.12 (Griesser, ed., *Exordium*, 64).

239. See above, n. 208.

240. "they selected companions rejecting the allurements of a laxer life and burning with resolute mind to hold fast to the purity and simplicity of the holy *Rule* purely and simply . . . who entered upon the strait and narrow way with a desire of keeping the more perfect life and *Rule* of their holy Father Benedict to the letter" (Griesser, ed., *Exordium*, 64).

241. "rejoicing angels . . . Christian philosophy" (Griesser, ed., *Exordium*, 1.13).

The Return of Robert:
1. Note in {the} documents, Urban says: *si fieri possit*;[242] Hugh says: *restituere* DECREVIMUS[243] for Robert; *dedimus licentiam redeundi*[244] for others who wish, but *qui eum secuti fuerint*[245] implies they want to be WITH ROBERT. But *ut si deinceps eandem ecclesiam* SOLITA LEVITATE *deseruerit* . . . (p. 68).[246]

2. Comments of {the} *Exordium Magnum* (banned by {the} General Chapter): (1) Robert {is} *horrorem et vastitatem heremi pertaesus*;[247] (2) {and is} *pristini honoris et commoditatis male memor*;[248] (3) *secundum tenorem litterarum . . . se excusare potuisset* [true] *si hereiticam paupertatem dilexisset*;[249] (4) others who went also "did not love solitude"![250] (5) *the point* {is that} he declares it was not those who left Molesme to come to Cîteaux who were disobedient, but those who left Cîteaux to return to Molesme: *quoniam maius bonum eligendo minus bonum sibi illicitum fecerunt, apostasiae nota non careant.*[251] They try to cover their tepidity by

242. "if it can be done" (1.14 [Griesser, ed., *Exordium*, 67]; *Exordium Parvum*, chap. 6 [*Nomasticon*, 56]).
243. "we have decreed he is to return" (1.15 [Griesser, ed., *Exordium*, 67]; *Exordium Parvum*, chap. 7 [*Nomasticon*, 57]).
244. 1.15 (Griesser, ed., *Exordium*, 67, which reads: "*dedimus etiam licentiam cum eo redeundi*" ["we also give permission to return with him"]; text identical to *Exordium Parvum*, chap. 7 [*Nomasticon*, 57]).
245. "who had followed him" (1.15 [Griesser, ed., *Exordium*, 67]; *Exordium Parvum*, chap. 7 [*Nomasticon*, 57]).
246. "that if he should abandon that same community again with his customary instability . . ." (1.15; *Exordium Parvum*, chap. 7 [*Nomasticon*, 57]).
247. "wearied of the awesomeness and desolation of the wilderness" (1.15 [Griesser, ed., *Exordium*, 68]).
248. "recalling with regret his earlier honor and comfort" (1.15 [Griesser, ed., *Exordium*, 68]).
249. "in accord with the substance of the letter he could have excused himself if he had loved solitary poverty" (1.15 [Griesser, ed., *Exordium*, 68]).
250. "*qui heremum non diligebant*" (1.15 [Griesser, ed., *Exordium*, 68]).
251. "Because by choosing a greater good they made the lesser good illicit for themselves, they may not escape the mark of apostasy" (1.15 [Griesser, ed., *Exordium*, 68]).

{an} appeal to papal documents, which only *permit their* return (but see above: *decrevimus*). Then {there is} a tirade on the comforts of Molesme by which Robert was deceived and seduced; {he} lost the honor of being called {the} founder of Cîteaux and of {the} Cistercian Order. Hence they were all weak {and} did not want to share in {the} Passion of Christ. *Conclusion*: the reason why Divine Providence allowed Robert to be moved at least to come to Cîteaux was to show {that} the first founders were not doing their own will.

St. Alberic[252]—{his} proper name {was} *Aubrey*. {He} was one of the seven hermits who lived at Colan in 1071 and asked for Robert as {their} superior.[253] {He was} active in {the} foundation of Molesme. {In} 1075 {he was} prior of Molesme.[254] When Robert retired to Aulps (Auch, Aux, Aures, Aulph ??) ({see} *DHGE*[255]), Alberic remained in charge {but} was beaten and imprisoned (*DHGE*[256]). {He} then left Molesme with St. Stephen and one or two others to be hermits at Vinicus ({in the} Diocese of Langres) ({there is a} false story that {the} Bishop of Langres excommunicated him).[257] Robert and Alberic {were} recalled to Molesme, but {the} situation remains impossible. {In} 1098 Alberic {is} one

252. For a biographical sketch see Merton, *Valley of Wormwood*, 37–51.

253. Lennsen points out ("Saint Robert," 96, n. 1) that in fact there is no documentary evidence to support this traditional assumption.

254. In the same note Lennsen shows that Alberic could not have been the first prior of Molesme since charters from the years 1075–1080 indicate that someone named Hugh was prior during this period.

255. J.-M. Canivez, "Aulps," *Dictionnaire d'Histoire et de Géographie Ecclésiastiques*, ed. Alfred Baudrillart et al. (Paris: Letouzey et Ané, 1912–), 5.671–74; here Merton is combining two different places: Aures (Auch, Aux) is the hermitage to which Robert retired briefly in the early 1090s; Aulps (Aulph) is the hermitage in the Alps founded by Saint Guerin and others that eventually joined the Cistercian Order, where Robert never lived.

256. P. Fournier, "Alberic," *Dictionnaire d'Histoire et de Géographie Ecclésiastiques*, 1.1407–8.

257. This historically doubtful material comes from the *Vita Roberti* (see above, nn. 205, 206).

of those who go to {the} legate, Hugh, in January (*EP* I[258]). {In} 1099 {he is} elected Abbot of Cîteaux (*EP* IX[259]). See {the description of his} *character*—study {this}; study {the} THREE LETTERS to Rome in favor of Cîteaux (chs. 11-12-13[260]). {He} sends John and Ilbodus to Rome. {In} 1100 {is issued the} *Privilegium Romanum* (*EP* XIV[261])—*study this*: does it constitute {an} *exemption* or *protection* only?? ({this is} disputed).[262]

Exordium Parvum IX: (1) *virum* litteratum, *in* divinis *et* humanis *satis* (?) *gnarum*;[263] (2) *amatorem regulae et fratrum*;[264] (3) {he} was prior of Molesme, {noteworthy for} his labors and sufferings for {the} Cîteaux project (cf. Manrique[265]—{the} three Fathers, etc.); (4) *multum renitens*[266] ({he} receives {the} abbacy); (5) *vir mirabilis prudentiae*[267]—{he} thinks of {the} *Privilegium Romanum*; (6) note: *antequam ipse PP. Paschalis . . . peccaret*??[268]

---

258. *Nomasticon*, 53–54; the participants are named in chap. 2 (Hugh's letter), 54.

259. *Nomasticon*, 58.

260. *Nomasticon*, 59–61.

261. *Nomasticon*, 61–62.

262. See Lekai, *The White Monks*, 19: "in his letter dated April 18, 1100, addressed to Alberic, [the pope] took the 'New Monastery' under immediate Papal protection. Although the letter cannot be regarded as exempting the monastery from diocesan jurisdiction, the formal Papal approval finally secured the peaceful and quiet development of the community." See also Mahn, *L'Ordre Cistercien*, 131–33, who distinguishes between the apostolic protection extended by the *Privilegium* and exemption from episcopal jurisdiction (in opposition to the position taken by Ducourneau).

263. "a literate man, sufficiently learned in divine and human matters."

264. "a lover of the *Rule* and of the brothers."

265. Manrique, *Cisterciensium*, 5 (I.3).

266. "resisting strongly" (chap. 10 [*Nomasticon*, 58]).

267. "a man of remarkable prudence."

268. "before Pope Paschal himself had sinned" (see *Nomasticon*, 59, n. 1, which points out that the pope is said to have sinned by conceding to Emperor Henry V under duress the right of investiture of benefices).

The three letters: XI:[269] {the letter of} John and Benedict {secures the} confirmation of {the} privilege granted by Urban II: *de quiete et suae religionis stabilitate;*[270] XII:[271] {the} Epistle of Hugh {gives the} *reasons for {the} new foundation: propter arctiorem et* sanctiorem [*sacratiorem*; *secretiorem*] *vitam*[272] *secundum Regulam beati Benedicti*[273]; *depositis quorumdam . . . consuetudinibus, imbecillitatem suam iudicantium* [or *iudicantes*] . . . *etc.;*[274] *utpote pauperes Christi.*[275]

{The} *Privilegium:*[276] *Desiderium quod ad religiosum propositum et animarum salutem pertinere monstratur, auctore Deo sine aliqua est dilatione complendum;*[277] *pro quiete monastica* [*eorum*] *elegistis;*[278] {to secure the} protection of {the} new *cenobium; meminisse debetis*—

269. *Nomasticon*, 59.
270. "concerning the tranquility and stability of their religious life."
271. *Nomasticon*, 59–60.
272. "for the sake of a more austere and holier life" (*Nomasticon*, 60, which reads, "*secretiorem*" ["more hidden"]); the reading "*sanctiorem*" is found in the Laibach (or Ljubljana) manuscript that Merton will discuss below: see the transcription in Canisius Noschitzka, "Codex Manuscriptus 31 Bibliothecae Universitatis Labacensis," *Analecta Sacri Ordinis Cisterciensis* 6 (1950): 12, which also includes "*sacratiorum*" ["more sacred"] as a possible alternative reading in its apparatus.
273. In context, the reference to the Rule in Hugh's letter is not to any particular passage but rather, as the subsequent phrases make clear, to the accretion of additional duties and practices, particularly liturgical, not found in the Rule, which made the original Benedictine balance of prayer, *lectio divina* and manual labor impossible.
274. "the customs of certain [monasteries] having been set aside, judging their own frailty [unequal to bearing so great a weight]" (*Nomasticon*, 60, which reads: "*judicantes*"; the reading "*iudicantium*" is found in the Laibach ms. [Noschitzka, "Codex Manuscriptus 31," 12]).
275. "as being the poor of Christ" (*Nomasticon*, 60).
276. *Exordium Parvum*, chap. 14 (*Nomasticon*, 61–62).
277. "A desire that is shown to pertain to a religious commitment and to the salvation of souls, with God as its origin, should be fulfilled without any delay" (*Nomasticon*, 61).
278. "[the place] you have chosen for monastic quiet" (*Nomasticon*, 61).

alligaistis—saeculares latitudines, monasterii laxioris minus austeras angustias;[279] hence {the} love of God—*quanto . . . liberiores tanto amplius placere Deo . . . anheletis.*[280]
{Was there an} apparition of Our Lady in 1101, ordering {a} change of habit? {This is} legendary. Did Alberic change {the} color of {the} habit?[281]

279. "you should remember—[some of you have left behind a] worldly environment, [others] the less austerely narrow paths of a less strict monastery" (*Nomasticon*, 61).
280. "so that the more free you are . . . the more you may yearn to please God" (*Nomasticon*, 60).
281. See King, *Cîteaux*, 10: "there is no evidence for the tradition which would connect St Alberic with the change in the color of the habit, beyond providing for the wool to be of a natural colour, and for many centuries there was no suggestion of anything supernatural about the discarding of black." See also Merton, *Valley of Wormwood*, 49–50: "One of the Cistercian innovations that caused the most criticism of the new monastery was something quite accidental to the reform itself: the change in the color of the habit from black to white. The black Benedictines threw up their hands in horror when they saw these monks wearing, as they said, the color of joy in the region of penance. Their horror at this presumption was only equaled by their horror at the eccentricity with which these fanatics were fasting and abstaining from flesh meat and devoting so much of their days to hard penitential labor in the fields. The Cistercians rightly retorted that theirs was indeed a life of joy, for since they had left everything else behind them for the love of God, they were already receiving the hundredfold promised by Christ; but it is hard to see the reason for the change unless we admit the old tradition that the Blessed Virgin herself appeared to Saint Alberic and asked him that the monks of the new monastery dedicated to her should wear white in her honor. The only other explanation is perhaps that unbleached wool would be grey, and their poverty suggested that they use no dyes, but the usual explanation offered by the Cistercians is that Our Lady intervened in the affair. Unfortunately the origin of this tradition is extremely obscure. . . . the first documentary evidence of it is not to be found before the fifteenth century, when the forty-third Abbot of Cîteaux, Jean de Cirey, appealed to it in an exhortation to his brethren, referring to it as something with which they were very well acquainted and which went back to the early days of the Order."

{The} *Instituta* (study) (*EP* XV[282]) {establishes the} introduction of *laybrothers*.

{In} 1108, {on} January {26}[283] {the} death of Alberic {takes place}. {He was} buried in {the} *church* ({there are} restrictions on this at first); then {in the} cloisters (with thirteen other abbots under {the} *altar*?—{or a} statue?—of {the} Blessed Virgin[284]). (1109—the date given by Manrique[285]—{is} not correct.) {Was there a formal} canonization? "*communi acclamatione et consensus ecclesiae*" says Manrique[286]—picked up by {the} *DHGE*;[287] actually—[288]

---

282. *Nomasticon*, 62–63.

283. Text reads: "2"; for the correct date see King, *Cîteaux*, 11.

284. See King, *Cîteaux*, 11, who writes, "The tomb of Alberic, shared by Stephen Harding and 13 other abbots, was in the cloister by the door into the church, where an altar had been erected in honour of the Blessed Virgin"; the "statue of our Lady of Mercy, of a type frequently reproduced from the 14th century onwards" (90), was apparently a later addition.

285. Manrique, *Cisterciensium*, 49 (1109, 1.2–3).

286. "by the common acclamation and consensus of the Church" (Manrique, *Cisterciensium*, 50 [1109, chap. 9], which is much more verbose than this concise summation).

287. Fournier, "Alberic," 1.1408, which repeats both the erroneous date and the canonization by acclamation.

288. Merton leaves this sentence unfinished, but in *Valley of Wormwood* he had written, "The liturgical veneration of this great Father of the Order, like that of his companions, Robert and Stephen, was more or less in abeyance for a time. The only Cistercian whose canonization was enthusiastically backed by the whole Order in those days was Bernard of Clairvaux. Saint Alberic had to bide his time until the eighteenth century, when he was finally beatified *per modum favoris* with the title of saint" (51–52). Here he is evidently following A Father of the Abbey of Gethsemani, Kentucky [Alberic Wulf, OCSO], *Compendium of the History of the Cistercian Order* (Trappist, KY: Abbey of Gethsemani, 1944), who notes that a number of those venerated as saints in the Order "were not canonized or even beatified in any real sense of these terms, unless we extend their meaning to the simplest of all methods, a sort of gracious extension of the old time 'local canonization,' that, is *per modum favoris*" (335), and notes specifically that "one of the most ancient fathers of

St. Stephen Harding[289] (*DS*[290]) (cf. William of Malmesbury, *PL* 179, 1287A[291]): {He was} born in England before 1066. {He} entered Sherborne, {then} left to study in Scotia (Scotland or Ireland?[292]). On {his} return from {a} pilgrimage to Rome, {he} enters Molesme. {He became} a leader in the movement to go to Cîteaux.

{In} 1107 (about),[293] {he} succeeds Alberic {and} works to *consolidate* the reform: (1) {he keeps} seculars out of {the} monastery ({see} *Laibach*—p. 15[294]); (2) {he stresses} poverty and simplicity: *ne quid in Domo Dei* {. . .} *quod superbiam aut superfluitatem redoleret* {. . .} *aut paupertatem custodem virtutum . . . corrumperet*;[295] (3) {he makes} foundations {in the} spirit of the new monastery (Laibach 16[296]); (4) {he founds a community for} nuns {at} Tart {in} 1125. {In} 1133, nearly blind, he resigns. {In} 1134, {on} March 28, {Stephen} dies. {There was} no liturgical feast until {the} seventeenth century; {the} General Chapter {of} 1623 (45) = April 17;[297]

---

the Order, St. Alberic, co-founder and the second Abbot of Citeaux, came unto his own after having patiently bided his time during six centuries" (336), when in the early eighteenth century Pope Clement XI officially approved his cult within the Order. The phrase *per modum favoris* [lit. "through the mode of favor"] may be interpreted "according to the criterion of broad acceptance."

289. For a biographical sketch see Merton, *Valley of Wormwood*, 262–77.

290. Maur Standaert, "S. Étienne Harding," *Dictionnaire de Spiritualité Ascétique et Mystique* [*DS*], ed. F. Cavallera et al., 17 vols. (Paris: Beauchesne, 1932–1995), 4.1489–93.

291. See above, n. 176.

292. See below, page 121, for evidence favoring Scotland.

293. More precisely, 1108.

294. *Exordium Parvum*, chap. 17 (Noschitzka, "Codex Manuscriptus 31," 15; *Nomasticon*, 64).

295. "lest anything in the House of God [remain . . .] that smelled of pride or excess, to corrupt poverty, the guardian of virtue" (Noschitzka, "Codex Manuscriptus 31," 15; *Nomasticon*, 64).

296. Noschitzka, "Codex Manuscriptus 31," 16; *Nomasticon*, 64.

297. Canivez, *Statuta*, 7.353.

{the} General Chapter {of} 1683 (87) = July 16;[298] {the} General Chapter {of} {1960} = January 26[299] (with Robert and Alberic).

Doctrine: William of Malmesbury reports "speeches" of Stephen Harding on the reform—{these are} not genuine (*PL* 179, 1287 etc.); {there is also a} spurious sermon on St. Alberic (*PL* 166, 1375–1376[300]). *Genuine* {works[301] include a} *monitum* on {the} Bible text for {the} Cistercian office (1109) (cf. *Citeaux* 10 [1959] p. 40[302]) (his care for good editions of books); {and a} *Preface to* {the} *Hymnal* (*Collectanea* 10 [1948] p. 100[303]). ({What is the} status of studies on St. Stephen's chant reform??[304])

298. Canivez, *Statuta*, 7.550.

299. See *Cinquente-sixième Chapitre Général (Plénier) de l'Ordre des Cisterciens de la Stricte Observance (Sept. 12–17, 1960)—Compte Rendu de Séances* (Westmalle: Imprimerie de l'Ordre des Cisterciens de la Stricte Observance, 1960), 23; text reads: "1962."

300. "*Sermo Beatissimi Stephani in Obitu Praedecessoris Sui*," taken from Manrique, *Cisterciensium*, 1.50 (1109, 1.19).

301. See also the one authentic surviving personal letter of Stephen, written to the abbot and community of Sherborne, his own original monastery as a youth, at the time of the first Cistercian foundations in England: C. H. Talbot, "An Unpublished Letter of St Stephen," *Collectanea Ordinis Cisterciensium Reformatorum* 2 (1936): 66–69; Chrysogonus Waddell, "Notes toward the Exegesis of a Letter by Saint Stephen Harding," in *Noble Piety and Reformed Monasticism*, ed. E. Rozanne Elder, Studies in Medieval Cistercian History 7, CS 65 (Kalamazoo, MI: Cistercian Publications, 1981), 10–39.

302. Charles Oursel, "La Bible de Saint Étienne Harding et le Scriptorium de Cîteaux (1109–vers 1134)," *Cîteaux* 10 (1959): 34–43.

303. B. Kaul, "Le Psautier Cistercienne," *Collectanea Ordinis Cisterciensium Reformatorum* 10 (1948): 83–106.

304. The official commission of the Order appointed to research this matter had issued a brief overview more than a decade earlier: see Commission de Chant, "Conspectus Historicus de Cantu in Ordine Cisterciensi," *Collectanea Ordinis Cisterciensium Reformatorum* 12 (1950): 212–16. At the very time Merton was writing this, his former student Chrysogonus Waddell was in Europe (1962–1965), engaged in studies on the early Cistercian liturgical tradition that would make him the most significant modern scholar on this material. See in particular Chrysogonus Waddell, "The Origin and Early Evolution of the Cistercian Antiphonary: Reflections on Two Cistercian Chant Reforms," in *The Cistercian Spirit: A Symposium in Memory of Thomas Merton*,

Writings of St. Stephen—Exordium and *Carta Caritatis*:
{The} *Exordium Parvum* {was} attributed to St. Stephen {in} about {the} seventeenth century. J. Lefèvre[305] attacks {its} authenticity today—{he} says it was written about 1152, {and that its} narratives {are} tendentious, {though its} documents {are} genuine; others admit {the} whole *Exordium Parvum* as substantially by Stephen;[306] {we should} distinguish {this document from the} *Exordium Cistercii*, {which} dates from 1119 {and} is authentic, says Lefèvre (see Lefèvre, *Collectanea* 16 [1954], 97-98).

To situate {the} *Exordium Cistercii*, it is part of the official document of 1119:[307] A = the 1119 document, containing {the} *Summa Carta Caritatis*; B = *Carta Caritatis Prior* ({see} Turk,

---

ed. M. Basil Pennington, CS 3 (Spencer, MA: Cistercian Publications, 1970), 190–223; Chrysogonus Waddell, "The Early Cistercian Experience of the Liturgy," in *Rule and Life: An Interdisciplinary Symposium*, ed. M. Basil Pennington, CS 12 (Spencer, MA: Cistercian Publications, 1971), 77–116; *The Twelfth-Century Cistercian Hymnal*, ed. M. Chrysogonus Waddell, 2 vols. (Trappist, KY: Abbey of Gethsemani, 1984); also *The Summer Season Molesme Breviary*, ed. M. Chrysogonus Waddell (Trappist, KY: Abbey of Gethsemani, 1984).

305. J.-A. Lefèvre, "La Véritable Constitution Cistercienne de 1119," *Collectanea Ordinis Cisterciensium Reformatorum* 16 no. 2 (1954): 77–104.

306. The latest and most thorough investigation of the authorship of the *Exordium Parvum* attributes the original version (the Prologue and chapters 1–2, 4–14) to Saint Stephen, who composed it as a directory for those entering Cîteaux around 1113 (e.g., Bernard and his companions in particular) and chapters 3, 15–18, along with the chapter titles, to Bl. Raynald de Bar, Abbot of Cîteaux from ca. 1134 to 1150, who used the *Exordium Parvum* as a historical introduction to the Cistercian customary, or usages, of ca. 1147: see Waddell, *Narrative and Legislative Texts*, 414, 416–40, 197–231.

307. This claim by Lefèvre has been rejected by subsequent scholars, particularly on the basis that it is virtually inconceivable that a summary of the foundational document (the *Summa Carta Caritatis*) would have been submitted to the pope, Callistus II, to gain his approval, rather than the complete text (i.e., the *Carta Caritatis Prior*): see Waddell, *Narrative and Legislative Texts*, 137–75, 398–413, who dates this material to the mid-1130s, when it was composed by Abbot Raynald to serve as the introduction to the second recension of the Cistercian customary or usages.

*ASOC*³⁰⁸): {it is} not official, *but traditional and early*, and *not* {the} text approved by Callistus; C = *Carta Caritatis Posterior*—approved by Eugene III in 1152³⁰⁹—{which is an} evolution of {the} above—official and definitive.

The Carta Caritatis, according to Lefèvre (as opposed to {the} traditional view of {the} *Carta Caritatis Prior* {as} written in 1119 by St. Stephen³¹⁰ and approved by Callistus II):

A. Against Turk, this—{i.e. the *Carta Caritatis Prior*}—was NOT the original text approved by Callistus II; the text approved

---

308. Ioseph Turk, "Charta Caritatis Prior," *Analecta Sacri Ordinis Cisterciensis* 1 (1945): 11–61.

309. Lefèvre's position is that it was the *Carta Caritatis Prior* that was submitted to Eugenius III in 1152 rather than the *Carta Caritatis Posterior*, which he dates to the late twelfth century; this position is refuted by Waddell, *Narrative and Legislative Texts*, who demonstrates that the *Carta Caritatis Prior* is the official document submitted for papal approval in 1119 and a slightly earlier version of the *Carta Caritatis Posterior* that was submitted in 1152 (the text that has been passed down dates from a subsequent papal approval in 1165). For Merton's previous discussion of the *Carta Caritatis*, including Lefèvre's article "La Véritable Carta Caritatis Primitive et Son Évolution," *Collectanea Ordinis Cisterciensium Reformatorum* 16 (1954): 5–29, see Thomas Merton, *Charter, Customs, and Constitutions of the Cistercians: Initiation into the Monastic Tradition 7*, ed. Patrick F. O'Connell, MW 41 (Collegeville, MN: Cistercian Publications, 2015), xvi–xxi, 1–14.

310. Technically this was not the "traditional" position in that the existence of the *Carta Caritatis Prior* was not known before the discovery of the Laibach manuscript, though it is more consistent with the traditionally accepted assumption that a complete text of the *Carta* was approved by Pope Callistus in 1119. According to Waddell (*Narrative and Legislative Texts*, 261–73, 414, 441–50) the core of the *Carta Caritatis Prior* (chaps. 1–3) probably dates to ca. 1113, with the text as transmitted dating to 1119, when it was confirmed by Pope Callistus II; the preface and chapter headings were probably added by Abbot Raynald de Bar around 1147, shortly before it was replaced by the *Carta Caritatis Posterior*, approved by Pope Eugenius III in 1152. This is basically in accord with the position of Msgr. Turk rejected by Lefèvre.

by Callistus was the *Summa Carta Caritatis* and *Exordium Cistercii* and {the} *Capitula* (of {the} General Chapter {of} 1119).

B. This is Turk's *Carta Caritatis Prior* in Laibach; {it consists in}:

    a. a primitive kernel—chapters 1-3—written {in} 1114 at {the} time of {the} foundation of Pontigny; *this {is} certainly by Stephen himself*—{its rhetoric is} monarchic and traditional: Stephen is the *boss*;

    b. {this is the} first "contract" block (cc. 4-7), written about 1115-1116—chapters 4-7—{it} includes an annual meeting of abbots of direct filiations—in the chapter of Cîteaux; where there is a chapter of faults for the abbots, but {the} monks of Cîteaux cannot proclaim them;

    c. {this is the} second contractual block (1118-1119)—chapters 8-11—{the} annual meeting extends to all abbots of filiations; further precisions {are added} on relationships of abbots and on corrections.

The three-fold text above indicates different hands or interventions—{according to} Lefèvre—but it is *not {an} official text*.

C. {The} *Carta Caritatis Posterior*: this is in {the} usages[311] and {the} *Nomasticon*.[312] However it does go back further—{it} is the *traditional* text; and it EVOLVES, is changed, glossed etc. until {it is} *officially approved* by Eugene in 1152, replacing A.[313]

---

311. The *Carta Caritatis* is not found in the contemporary volume of the Cistercian Usages—*Regulations of the Order of Cistercians of the Strict Observance Published by the General Chapter of 1926* (Dublin: M. H. Gill & Sons, 1927); the reference is evidently to the more generic use of the term to refer to the Cistercian customary, for which *Liber Usuum* was used as an alternate title to *Consuetudines* (see King, *Cîteaux*, 10; Wulf, *Compendium*, 57, 168); this traditional version of the *Carta Caritatis* was included as introductory material—see for example Canivez, *Statuta*, 1.xxvi–xxxi.

312. *Nomasticon*, 68–81.

313. N.B. that this is not the position of Lefèvre but that of Turk, and likewise the conclusion of Waddell (*Narrative and Legislative Texts*, 371–89, 415, 498–505).

N.B. in {the} *Summa Carta Caritatis* (take in detail later) (*Collectanea* [1954], p. 99[314]) {the} details on {the} General Chapter.

The Spirituality of the *Exordium Cistercii* (*Collectanea* 1954[315]):

I. *De Egressu*:[316]

a. Molesme is *fama celeberrimum, religione conspicuum*[317] (p. 97). God made it *nec minus amplum possessionibus quam clarum virtutibus* {. . .}. *Ceterum* quia possessionibus virtutibusque diuturna non solet esse societas. . . .[318]

b. The founders of Cîteaux {were} *viri sapientes altius intelligentes* (*ex illa sancta congregatione*);[319] (1) *elegerunt potius studiis celestibus occupari quam terrenis implicari negociis*;[320] (2) Unde et mox virtutum amatores de PAUPERTATE FECUNDA VIRORUM *cogitare ceperunt*;[321] (3) they note that though they live holily at Molesme, *minus tamen pro sui desiderio atque proposito ipsam quam professi*

---

314. Lefèvre includes the the *Summa Carta Caritatis* along with the *Exordium Cistercii* and the *Capitula* (found as an undivided text of twenty-six chapters, of which the first two constitute the *Exordium Cistercii* and the following four the *Summa Carta Caritatis*), from the Ste. Geneviève MS, as an appendix (entitled "Le Dossier Présenté à Calixte II en 1119") to his article "La Véritable Constitution Cistercienne de 1119" (96–104). For a more recent edition and translation, see Waddell, *Narrative and Legislative Texts*, 176–91, 399–413.

315. Lefèvre, "Véritable Constitution," 97–98.

316. Chap. 1: "*De egressu cisterciensium monachorum de molismo*" ("The Departure of the Cistercian Monks from Molesme") (Lefèvre, "Véritable Constitution," 97).

317. "most famous in reputation, outstanding in religious observance."

318. "not less ample in possessions than distinguished in virtues. However, because the daily association of possessions and virtues is not customary."

319. "wise and more deeply intelligent men (of that holy congregation)" (text reads: "*ex illa sancta congregatione viri nimirum* [certainly] *sapientes altius intelligentes*").

320. "they chose rather to be occupied with heavenly concerns than to be involved in earthly matters."

321. "Thus the lovers of the virtues soon began to to reflect on poverty, fruitful source of men."

fuerant regulam observari;[322] (4) They discuss together *qualiter illum versum adimpleant. Reddam tibi vita mea q. d. l. m.;*[323] (5) they leave with *beati memorie Roberto {. . .} communi consilio, communi perficere nituntur assensu, quod uno spiritu conceperunt*[324] (n.b. {the} common life); (6) they suffer many labors *quas omnes in Christo pie vivere volentes pati necesse est;*[325] (7) they come to Cîteaux, *locus horroris et vaste solitudinis.*[326] *Sed milites Christi loci asperitatem ab arto proposito quod jam animo conceperant non dissidere judicantes ut sibi divinitus preparatum* tam gratum habuere locum quam carum propositum.[327]

II. *De Exordio Cisterciensis cenobii:*[328]

a. Backed by Hugh, writer of {the} epistle, and Duke Odo: *inventam heremum in abbatia construere ceperunt;*[329]

b. return of Robert to Molesme *Papae Urbani secundi iussu;*[330]

---

322. "nevertheless the very rule they had professed was being kept less than according to their desire and commitment."

323. "how they may fulfill that verse, I will pay you my vows which my lips have uttered" (Ps 65 [66]:13-14; the initials are an abbreviation for "*quae distinxerunt labia mea*").

324. "Robert of blessed memory, they press on with united resolution and united assent to accomplish what they had conceived in one spirit."

325. "which it is necessary for all who wish to live piously in Christ to suffer."

326. See Deut 32:10: "*Invenit eum in terra deserta, in loco horroris et vastae solitudinis*" ("He found him in a desert land, in a place of horror, and of vast wilderness").

327. "a place of horror and vast solitude. But the soldiers of Christ, judging the harshness of the place not to be at odds with the strict resolve they had already conceived in their mind, held the place as divinely prepared for them, just as welcome as their resolve was precious" (text reads: "*locum tunc scilicet horroris*").

328. Lefèvre, "Véritable Constitution," 97–98.

329. "they began to build the wasteland they had found into an abbey" (text reads: "*abbatia construe*" with the alternative "*construere*" in the notes).

330. "by the order of Pope Urban II."

c. arrangements {are made} for peace between Molesme and Cîteaux;

d. under Alberic—*non mediocriter Deo cooperante* in sancta conversatione profecit opinione claruit rebus necessariis crevit (98);[331]

e. Stephen succeeds Alberic: *natione anglicus; religionis, paupertatis, disciplinaeque regularis ardentissimus amator fidelissimus aemulator*[332] (p. 98) (would this be by Stephen himself?[333]);

f. the trial of Stephen: *Nam cum pusillus grex hoc solum plangeret quod pusillus esset . . . etc;*[334] Bernard {makes an} intervention to bring thirty novices;

g. Twelve monasteries {are} now founded;

h. {The} *Carta Caritatis* has been written by Stephen: *Sagacitate pervigil mire providerat discretionis scriptum tamquam putationis ferrum ad praecidendos scismatum suculos unde et . . . cartam caritatis voluit nominari;*[335] {this} is approved by the abbots—{the} *Summa Cartae Caritatis* follows.

Differences between {the}

Carta Caritatis Prior (Laibach)[336] and   {the} *Carta Caritatis Posterior (Nomasticon)*[337]

---

331. "with God at work with them, they progressed in no average fashion, shone in reputation, increased in things that were needed."

332. "English in nationality, a most ardent lover and most faithful model of religious life, of poverty, of the discipline of the rule."

333. See n. 307 above.

334. "For when the paltry flock lamented only this: that it was paltry" (text reads: "*solum quod plangeret quod*").

335. "with a marvelously foresighted wisdom he had provided a text marked by discernment, like a tool for pruning to cut off shoots of schisms and so wished it to be called the *Carta Caritatis*" (text reads: "*putationis ferramentum ad precendos* ["*prescindendos*" [sic] as a variant] *videlicet scismatum suculos. . . . Unde et*").

336. Noschitzka, "Codex Manuscriptus 31," 109–14; Turk, "Carta," 53–61.

337. *Nomasticon*, 68–73; the division into five chapters is first found in the original 1664 edition of the *Nomasticon* and is retained in the 1892 updated

1. Prologue[338] and chapters 1-3[339]	Prologue,[340] chapters 1-3 are chapter 1:[341] all {the} same text, but ADDS at {the} end: *nec aliqua ecclesia . . . adversus communia ordinis instituta privilegium a quolibet postulare audeat* etc.[342]
2. chapters 4-7[343]	forms chapters 2, 3 of {the} *Carta Caritatis Posterior*
chapter 4 remains substantially {the} same	chapter 2[344]
chapter 5	on visitations—{they} can be made *by {some} other delegated abbot* Cîteaux {is} to be visited by {the} Four First Fathers.[345]
chapter 6 remains the same, with additions	end of chapter 2: *Carta Caritatis Posterior* on protocol between abbots who are equal (this is *Carta Caritatis Prior*, cap. 10)— the seniority {is determined} according to {the} abbey; daughters

---

edition; it has no basis in the manuscript tradition, in which in fact there are originally no chapter divisions at all (see Waddell, *Narrative and Legislative Texts*, 498–99).

338. Noschitzka, "Codex Manuscriptus 31," 109; Turk, "Carta," 53.
339. Noschitzka, "Codex Manuscriptus 31," 109; Turk, "Carta," 53.
340. *Nomasticon*, 68.
341. *Nomasticon*, 68–69.
342. "Let no community . . . contrary to the institutes common to our Order, dare to seek a privilege from anyone" (*Nomasticon*, 69, which reads: "*ecclesia vel persona Ordinis nostri* [or person of our Order] . . . *communia ipsius Ordinis*").
343. Noschitzka, "Codex Manuscriptus 31," 110–11; Turk, "Carta," 54.
344. *Nomasticon*, 69–70.
345. I.e., the abbots of the first four daughter houses of Cîteaux: La Ferté, Pontigny, Clairvaux and Morimond.

chapter 7[346]—on {the} General Chapter—{there are} *many changes* n.b. in *Carta Caritatis Prior* {the} term *generale capitulum* {is} not used[348]—they just *tractent de salute animarum*,[349] but cf. cap. 8 of *Carta Caritatis Prior*—{it} has much that {the} *Carta Caritatis Posterior* has left out: they are excused by sickness or {the} *profession of a novice* (cf. *Summa Cartae Caritatis*); {they} can send {the} prior instead—who will explain and bring back news of Cîteaux can make foundations and visit them *but {they are} not {to} hold general chapters of filiations.*

chapter 3; omnes *abbates* {. . .} *singulis annis* {. . .} *omni postposita occasione*;[347] only {the} sick {are} excepted {and they} must send {a} message; those *in remotioribus partibus*[350] {may come} less frequently; {there are} penances for absence; Important—*Si aliqua controversia . . .*[351] (1) {the} chapter decides; (2) if {the} chapter can't decide then {the} Abbot {of} Cîteaux and those of *sanioris consilii*[352] {do so}.

---

346. Noschitzka, "Codex Manuscriptus 31," 110–11.

347. "all the abbots . . . every year . . . with every excuse having been put aside."

348. N.B. it is found in the chapter titles (7, 8), which were added to the original text by Abbot Raynald de Bar, but not in the text itself (see above, n. 299).

349. "They consider the salvation of souls" (text reads: "*animarum suarum* [their own souls]").

350. "in distant locations" (*Nomasticon*, 70).

351. "If there is any dispute" (*Nomasticon*, 71, which reads: "*Si forte* [by chance] *aliqua*").

352. "wiser judgment" (*Nomasticon*, 71).

of statutes passed; {the text} speaks of a *magister capituli*[353] who gives penances for absence
chapter 9[354] {provides} MUCH MORE DETAIL on {the} election of abbots (see deposition of abbots; episcopal intervention {is} possible.

chapter 4[355] (see *Carta Caritatis Prior*, c. 11).

chapter 5:[356] beginning—resignation of abbots; deposition—{the} language {is} less strong; {there are} details on Cîteaux and how to depose {the} Abbot of Cîteaux.

Analecta SOC (1950) 1-4:[357] the Laibach codex 31 dates from before 1191, after 1150, *probably before 1175*—{it is the} source for {the} *Carta Caritatis Prior* (edited by Turk: *ASOC*, 1945[358]). *Priora Instituta*; {an} early version of {the} *Exordium Parvum* (cf. Turk: *ASOC*, 1948[359]); {there is a} special emphasis on *early legislation that was dropped*; {the} codex contains: (1) *Exordium Parvum*;[360] (2) *Carta Caritatis* PRIOR;[361] (3) *Instituta Generalis Capituli apud*

353. "master of the chapter."
354. Noschitzka, "Codex Manuscriptus 31," 111–13; Turk, "Carta," 55–56.
355. *Nomasticon*, 71–72.
356. *Nomasticon*, 72–73.
357. Noschitzka, "Codex Manuscriptus 31," 1–124.
358. See above, n. 308.
359. Josip Turk, "Cistercii Statuta Antiquissima," *Analecta Sacri Ordinis Cisterciensis* 4 (1948): 1–159; the article includes discussion of the *Instituta Generalis Capituli apud Cistercium* (i.e. the *Priora Instituta*) (1–31), the *Exordium Parvum* (32–108), and the *Carta Caritatis* (109–59).
360. Noschitzka, "Codex Manuscriptus 31," 6–16.
361. Noschitzka, "Codex Manuscriptus 31," 16–22.

Cistercium;[362] (5) *Ecclesiastica Officia (Consuetudines)*[363] (NOT {the} *Usus Conversorum*[364]).

{The} *Carta Caritatis*[365]—{its} aim {is} peace by clarity and definition of aims.

Prologue:[366] (a) to avoid conflicts with bishops—clarify their aims and have them approved before a foundation is attempted; (b) for mutual peace and charity, {there must be} a basis of *like understanding* in {the} interpretation of {the} *Rule*; {they are} to live *corporibus divisi animis indissolubiliter conglutinati;*[367] (c) hence {the} *Carta* {is} devised as a guarantee for *charity and {the} good of souls in divine and human spheres.* Comment: {note the} importance {of this} for {the} spirit of {the} Order; practicality and logic {are} united with charity, {in} overall simplicity.

Cap. 1:[368] (a) daughter houses do not have to contribute anything to {the} mother house; the relation of mother and daughter houses {is} purely for {the} good of souls; (b) how? {through} uniform observance of {the} *Rule* as interpreted by {the} first founders of Cîteaux; comment—how {can they} determine {the} validity of changes since that time? (c) monks can be received in other monasteries of {the} Order (n.b. stability)—hence *una caritate, una regula, similibus vivamus moribus;*[369] (d) independent action of a house getting {a} special privilege direct from {the} Holy See is against this charity.

Cap. 2[370]—*Visitations:* (a) precedence; (b) {there should be} prudence and reserve in making corrections—{the} Abbot {of}

362. Noschitzka, "Codex Manuscriptus 31," 22–38.
363. Noschitzka, "Codex Manuscriptus 31," 38–124.
364. I.e. the *Laybrothers' Usages.*
365. For Merton's earlier summary of the provisions of the *Carta Caritatis,* see *Charter, Customs, Constitutions,* 1–14.
366. *Nomasticon,* 68.
367. "divided in body, inseparably joined together in spirit" (text reads: "*conglutinarentur*").
368. *Nomasticon,* 68–69.
369. "let us live with one love, under one rule, with like customs" (*Nomasticon,* 69).
370. *Nomasticon,* 69–70.

Cîteaux visits *all* monasteries if he likes {and} *corrects in union with* {*the*} *local abbot*; (c) {there are} regular annual visitations; (d) questions of precedence {are dealt with}.

Cap. 3[371]—{the} *General Chapter*: (a) all must attend except those in remote places ({who} come to {the} plenary); (b) {its} main business {is} *de salute animarum*;[372] changes of observance; *bonum pacis et caritatis inter se reforment*[373] (comment: cf. visitations etc.—hashing things out—{this is the} best way to peace); (c) correction of faults, proclamation of abbots, penances; (d) settling controversies—n.b. {the} Abbot of Cîteaux has preeminence here; (e) getting together to help impoverished abbeys.

{The} *Spirituality of* {*the*} *Exordium Magnum*:[374]

(a) {It is} *late*—it records {the} death of Peter Monoculus,[375] which occurred in 1186—{it was} written in Germany—by one or more writers?? {It is} ascribed to Conrad, {a} monk of Clairvaux, {later} Abbot of Eberbach—{this is} *disputed*;[376] (b) {it is} not "history" but rather "temoignage"[377] (cf *Fioretti*[378])—{an} *apology for strictness* (against OSB detractors).

Distinctio I[379] starts with {a} résumé of monastic history, going back to {the} Gospels, Acts and Egypt;[380] {it expresses} high

---

371. *Nomasticon*, 70–71.

372. "concerning the salvation of souls" (*Nomasticon*, 71, which reads: "*animarum suarum* [their souls]").

373. "they reform among themselves the good of peace and charity" (*Nomasticon*, 71).

374. Merton relies here on "The *Exordium Magnum Cisterciense*," chapter 5 of Watkin Williams, *Monastic Studies* (Manchester: Manchester University Press, 1938), 52–60.

375. 2.33 (Griesser, ed., *Exordium*, 146).

376. This authorship is now generally accepted.

377. "witness"; "testimony."

378. The famous collection of legendary stories on Saint Francis and his early companions (see *The Little Flowers of St. Francis*, ed. and trans. Raphael Brown [Garden City, NY: Image Books, 1958]).

379. Griesser, ed., *Exordium*, 48–97.

380. 1.1–3 (Griesser, ed., *Exordium*, 48–51).

esteem for Cluny,[381] which saved the monastic *ordo*—but it lapsed into *voluptas* and *vanitas*, the daughters of *negligentia*;[382] hence {the} need for {the} foundation of Cîteaux ({which was} NOT an illicit departure); but Cîteaux itself has by now begun to decline from its pristine perfection—*hence {the} need of a reminder*; there are *filii degeneres*,[383] though the Order is still whole and healthy; *Distinctio* I covers {the} "first five Abbots of Cîteaux, ending with Raynald" (W. Williams[384]); actually {it} goes down to the tenth abbot,[385] omitting two (Bl. Lambert and Bl. Gilbert "the Great"): St. Robert,[386] St. Alberic,[387] St. Stephen,[388] Guy (one month: 1134),[389] Bl. Raynald de Bar,[390] Bl. Goswin ({who} commanded Bernard to work no more miracles after death—except such as would not disturb regularity),[391] Bl. Fastrad ({the} seventh),[392] [Bl. Lambert (memorial: July 12)], [Bl. Gilbert], Bl. Alexander (1166-1175) ({whose} extraordinary conversion and vocation {occurred} when Bernard preached {the} crusade in Germany).[393]

Distinctio II[394] {discusses the} first eight Abbots of Clairvaux:

---

381. 1.6–9 (Griesser, ed., *Exordium*, 54–60).

382. "*duas filias ipsa matre [negligentia]* . . . *voluptatem scilicet et vanitatem*" ("two daughters of the same mother (negligence)—namely pleasure and vanity") (1.9 [Griesser, ed., *Exordium*, 59]).

383. "degenerate sons" (1.10 [Griesser, ed., *Exordium*, 61]).

384. "we are given records of the first five Abbots of Cîteaux, ending with that of Raynald" (Williams, *Monastic Studies*, 56).

385. See King, *Cîteaux*, 5–28, for information on all these early abbots.

386. 1.11–15 (Griesser, ed., *Exordium*, 63–69).

387. 1.16–20 (Griesser, ed., *Exordium*, 69–77).

388. 1.21–31 (Griesser, ed., *Exordium*, 77–89).

389. 1.31 (Griesser, ed., *Exordium*, 88–89).

390. 1.34 (Griesser, ed., *Exordium*, 94–95); Raynald (or Rainard) is mentioned only briefly in the context of the story of Christian of l'Aumone.

391. 2.20 (Griesser, ed., *Exordium*, 116–18); Goswin is actually not mentioned by name, and the story is found in the second rather than in the first *Distinctio*; see also King, *Cîteaux*, 26.

392. 1.32 (Griesser, ed., *Exordium*, 89–93).

393. 1.33 (Griesser, ed., *Exordium*, 93–94).

394. Griesser, ed., *Exordium*, 98–147.

St. Bernard (+1153),[395] Bl. Robert of Bruges (+1157),[396] Bl. Fastrad (to Cîteaux {in} 1161),[397] Geoffrey (to 1165),[398] Pontius (to 1170),[399] Bl. Gerard (+1175),[400] Henry de Marcy (cardinal) (to 1179)[401] (read—character[402]); Peter Monoculus (from Igny: 1179—+1186).[403]

395. 2.1–20 (Griesser, ed., *Exordium*, 98–118).
396. 2.21–23 (Griesser, ed., *Exordium*, 118–23).
397. Fastrad is briefly mentioned at the beginning of 2.24 (Griesser, ed., *Exordium*, 123), but discussed only in 1.32 (see n. 392 above).
398. Geoffrey of Auxerre, Bernard's former secretary and the author of the three final books of the *Vita Prima* of Saint Bernard, is mentioned only in passing at the beginning of 2.24.
399. 2.24–26 (Griesser, ed., *Exordium*, 123–29).
400. 2.27–29 (Griesser, ed., *Exordium*, 129–36).
401. 2.30–31 (Griesser, ed., *Exordium*, 136–41).
402. "*Hic venerandus pater nobilis quidem genere, sed longe nobilior virtutum generositate a primis adolescentiae suae annis in sanctuario Domini locatus manum misit ad fortia magis eligens ferre iugum Domini suave et onus eius leve quam dici et esse filius Belial, id est absque iugo, plus appetens pro Christo Domino humiliari cum mitibus quam dividere spolia cum superbis ac per hoc in sortem illius cadere, qui est rex super omnes filios superbiae. Porro dies adolescentiae suae tanta puritate et innocentia pertransiit, sicque canos sapientiae in annis tenerioribus induerat, ut, dum vix adhuc limen virilis aetatis atigisset, merito magis religionis et prudentiae quam aetatis sequester inter Deum et homines constitueretur et vicarius filii Dei factus nomen pariter et officium patris et pastoris adipisci mereretur. Quam tamen praerogativam honoris vel potius pondus sollicitudinis semel susceptum tanta fidei et devotionis alacritate amministravit, ut internus ille iudex, discretor cogitationum et intentionum cordis, qui in manu omnium hominum signat, ut noverint singuli opera sua, fidelem in minori dispensatione probans maiori eum charismatum gratia sublimare decerneret. Nempe maturiori iam aetate virtutibusque in habitum versis abbas Claraevallis factus rigorem disciplinae, per quem alios ad tramitem iustitiae cogebat, in seipso minime neglexit, sed quantum dignitas officii sui patiebatur, ad communis vitae socialitatem se constringens ipsi etiam labori manuum aliquoties pro tempore cum ceteris fratribus insudabat. Ceterum quam sanum consilium dederit sapiens omnibus in sublimitate constitutis dicens: Quanto magnus es, humilia te in omnibus, quamque acceptum sit Deo, si praelatus propter timorem ipsius duris etiam et vilibus laboribus carnem suam castigare non dedignetur, pius Dominus huic famulo suo demonstrare dignatus est*" ("This venerable Father, certainly noble in ancestry but far more noble in the generosity of his virtues, placed from the earliest years of his adolescence in the sanctuary of God, sent forth his

Distinctio III[404] {considers some} special distinguished monks of Clairvaux: Bl. Gerard,[405] Bl. Humbert of Igny,[406] Bl. Guerric,[407] Eskil,[408] Gunnar,[409] Achard,[410] William,[411] Boso.[412]

---

hand to vigorous acts, choosing to bear the easy yoke and light burden of the Lord rather than to be called, and to be, a son of Belial, that is, one without a yoke; seeking to be humbled for the sake of Christ the Lord with mildness rather than to divide the spoils with the proud and through this to fall under the sway of the one who is king of all the sons of pride. Moreover he passed the days of his youth in such purity and innocence and so had put on the gray hairs of wisdom in his more tender years, so that, while he had scarcely reached the threshold of adulthood, he was appointed a mediator between God and men, due more to the merit of his religious way of life and his prudence than of his age, and having been made vicar of the Son of God, he equally deserved to acquire the name and the office of father and shepherd. He administered this position of honor, or rather weight of responsibility, undertaken with such promptness of faith and devotion, that the inner Judge, discerner of the thoughts and intentions of the heart, Who puts a sign on the hand of all men so that they might each know His works, finding him faithful in small matter, decided to raise him up by a greater grace of spiritual gifts. Having become abbot of Clairvaux at a more mature age, when his virtues had become habitual, he certainly did not in the least neglect in himself the rigor of discipline through which he compelled others along the pathway of righteousness, but to the extent the dignity of his office allowed, binding himself to the sharing of the common life, on occasion he even used to sweat for a while in manual labor with the other brothers. The blessed Lord deigned to show in this his servant how sage the advice the wise man had given to all those established in a high position, saying: To the degree that you are great, humble yourself in all things, and how acceptable it is to God if a prelate does not distain to curb his flesh even with hard and lowly labors because of love for Him") (2.30 [Griesser, ed., *Exordium*, 136–37]).

    403. 2.32–33 (Griesser, ed., *Exordium*, 141–47).
    404. Griesser, ed., *Exordium*, 148–223.
    405. 3.1–3 (Griesser, ed., *Exordium*, 148–54).
    406. 3.4–6 (Griesser, ed., *Exordium*, 154–62).
    407. 3.8–9 (Griesser, ed., *Exordium*, 163–66).
    408. 3.27–28 (Griesser, ed., *Exordium*, 210–17).
    409. 3.29 (Griesser, ed., *Exordium*, 217–18).
    410. 3.22 (Griesser, ed., *Exordium*, 201–3).
    411. 3.16 (Griesser, ed., *Exordium*, 183–87).
    412. 3.34 (Griesser, ed., *Exordium*, 223).

Distinctio IV[413] {looks at} more obscure monks, including laybrothers, often not named: Bro. Lawrence;[414] the brother who saw Jesus guiding the oxen.[415]

Distinctio V[416] {consists in} *salutaria monita*:[417] on {the} evil of proprietorship;[418] on dying in the cowl;[419] on openness;[420] on wakefulness at divine office;[421] on not desiring sacred orders;[422] on obedience;[423] on {the} danger of conspiracy,[424] etc.

Dist. VI[425] {has more of} the same: W. Williams says, "These two distinctions constitute something of a treatise on moral theology in some of its monastic aspects."[426]

---

413. Griesser, ed., *Exordium*, 224–72.

414. Sent from Clairvaux on business to the king of Sicily, Lawrence discovered on the way that the king had died; with no knowledge of the new king, he was plunged in desolation, but prayed to St. Bernard and the next morning encountered merchants on their way to the Sicilian court, where he was graciously treated by the king and successfully fulfilled his mission; on passing through Rome on his return he was given further gifts, loaded on ten buffaloes and brought safely back to Clairvaux through land controlled by brigands, by Bernard's intercession (4.34 [Griesser, ed., *Exordium*, 268–70]).

415. This anonymous laybrother at one of the granges of Clairvaux had a vision of Jesus helping him to herd his cows, and died happily soon afterward, having told his dream to St. Bernard, who declared that the brother had indeed walked with God (4.18 [Griesser, ed., *Exordium*, 243–44]).

416. Griesser, ed., *Exordium*, 273–338.

417. The title of this distinction as found in the Patrologia text, but omitted (with other section titles) in the critical edition, is *"Distinctio Quinta. Continens salutaria Monita exemplis probata, de quorumdam vitiorum periculo, et punitione"* ("Fifth Distinction: Containing Beneficial Warnings, Supported by Examples, of the Danger of Certain Vices and their Punishment") (PL 185:1124C).

418. 5.2 (Griesser, ed., *Exordium*, 274–76).

419. 5.3 (Griesser, ed., *Exordium*, 276–77).

420. 5.5 (Griesser, ed., *Exordium*, 278–81).

421. 5.6 (Griesser, ed., *Exordium*, 281–84).

422. 5.7 (Griesser, ed., *Exordium*, 284–86).

423. 5.8–9 (Griesser, ed., *Exordium*, 286–92).

424. 5.10 (Griesser, ed., *Exordium*, 292–98).

425. Griesser, ed., *Exordium*, 339–70.

426. Williams, 56, which reads: "In fine these last two *Distinctiones* constitute something of a treatise on moral theology in various of its monastic aspects."

Spirituality of {the} Exordium {Magnum[427]}:

Trust in Providence {is a central characteristic} of St. Stephen and {the} early Fathers (also {of} Robert at Molesme)—{for example} sending {a} brother to town to buy horses, wagons, supplies—without money;[428] *"in paupertate sua de misericordia Dei magnifice praesumens"*[429] (*magnificentia*)—{he} gave him three pennies—the brother is taken to a dying rich man who gives all his money to the monks. St. Stephen {is called} *animo semper in Domino laetus* (William of Malmesbury).[430] St. Stephen {is} described as *"eremi amator et ferventissimus sanctae paupertatis aemulator"* (*Exordium Magnum*;[431] cf. *Exordium Parvum*[432]). {He is marked by} his fidelity to his practices ({for example praying} the psalter on the voyage to Rome with Peter[433]) cf. in regard to St. Bernard, his trial in regard to vocations—their sadness, near despair—the vision of the dead brother;[434] {a} bird flies in with a big fish when St. Stephen had been bled;[435] the Feast of Pentecost when they have no food[436] (cf. {the} early Franciscans). *The Cistercian community* is Jesus himself ({cf. the} vision of Fastrad when he flies to {the} Carthusians—{the} Blessed Virgin puts {the} Infant Jesus

---

427. Text reads: *"Parvum."*

428. 1.28 (Griesser, ed., *Exordium*, 84–86).

429. "in his poverty relying marvelously on the mercy of God" (Griesser, ed., *Exordium*, 85).

430. "always joyful of soul in the Lord" (*Gesta Regum Anglorum*, 4.337 [PL 179:1289D]).

431. "a lover of the wilderness and most fervent devotee of holy poverty" (1.21 [Griesser, ed., *Exordium*, 77, which reads: *"heremi amatorem et ferventissimum sanctae paupertatis aemulatorem"*).

432. *"quique amator Regulae & loci erat"* ("who was a lover of the Rule and of the place") (chap. 17 [*Nomasticon*, 64]).

433. 1.21 (Griesser, ed., *Exordium*, 77).

434. In response to the abbot's request at his deathbed, a dead monk appears in a vision to Stephen to assure him of God's approval of the Cistercian project and of the imminent entry of a multitude of new recruits (1.22 [Griesser, ed., *Exordium*, 80–82]).

435. 1.24 (Griesser, ed., *Exordium*, 83).

436. An unexpected gift of food shows up as the monks are celebrating Mass (1.25 [Griesser, ed., *Exordium*, 83]).

Cistercian History 81

in his arms[437]); {it} prays with angels ({cf. the} vision of Christian of l'Aumone[438]); to go to another order {is} regarded as apostasy.

{There is a} *special love of {the} community of Clairvaux*, {marked by}: *poverty*—to have a better cowl is equivalent to excommunication (Fastrad);[439] {a} sacramental concept of {the} common life; {note the} portrait of Peter Monoculus;[440] love of {the} poor— Bl. Alquirinus, a doctor, very austere with himself, {is} sought by all {but} preferred the poor, seeing Christ in {the} poor; {he was} encouraged in this by {his} superiors and {by} visions; {he had} visions of Christ crucified, {and was} told all {his} sins {were} forgiven (Dist IV.1[441]); *labor*—Henry de Marcy, {due to} exaggerated zeal, neglects {his} dying brother;[442] Humbert of Igny {was renowned for a} love of manual labor;[443] *Our Lady*: {note the} vision of Raynald;[444] {and the} one who wanted to see Our Lady but was only worthy to see St. Mary Magdalene;[445] *other*

---

437. He had fled when he heard the report that he had been elected abbot of Clairvaux (1.32 [Griesser, ed., *Exordium*, 90]).

438. Summoned to Cîteaux by Abbot Raynald, Christian has a vision on the way of the community at prayer with an angelic congregation praying above, the abbot in their midst (1.34 [Griesser, ed., *Exordium*, 94–95]).

439. 1.32 (Griesser, ed., *Exordium*, 91).

440. The description stresses Peter's gentleness, his pastoral sensitivity, his temperance and humility, and his strict observance of the Cistercian way of life (2.32 [Griesser, ed., *Exordium*, 141–43]); for a brief biographical sketch, see Merton, *Valley of Wormwood*, 371–79.

441. Griesser, ed., *Exordium*, 224–25.

442. In a vision, a brother who had died shortly before this monk appears to Abbot Henry and tells him God requires him to pray the seven penitential psalms daily for the rest of his life for this neglect (2.30 [Griesser, ed., *Exordium*, 137–38]).

443. Even as a retired abbot, Humbert sought out the manual labor that younger men could scarcely endure (3.4 [Griesser, ed., *Exordium*, 156]).

444. Raynald, a monk of Clairvaux, had a vision of the Blessed Virgin, along with Saints Elizabeth and Mary Magdalene, visiting the monks as they worked in the fields, as well as a vision of the Virgin preparing clothing for him to wear in heaven (3.13 [Griesser, ed., *Exordium*, 176–79]).

445. The monk is told in his vision that he is not yet worthy to see the Blessed Mother and should work diligently to become worthy (4.11 [Griesser,

visions—one brother {had} visions of demons, and of St. Augustine showing him hell and heaven and saying "choose which one you want—read my books if you want to go to heaven";[446] *lectio*: Fastrad {was noted for this}.[447]

Consuetudines[448]

To follow *Carta Caritatis*[449]—the *Instituta*:[450] Part II of {the} *Consuetudines*—{a} summary of decisions of {the} General Chapter during St. Stephen's time.

---

ed., *Exordium*, 236]).

446. "*Elige, quod bonum est in oculis tuis! Si viam iustitiae, quae in libris meis copiose digesta est, tenere decreveris, portionem accipies in terra viventium cum omnibus istis. Si vero post concupiscentias tuas ire volueris, in gladio numerandus es cum iis, quos vidisti terribili quidem, sed tamen iusto Dei iudicio proiectos in anathema oblivionis*" ("Choose which is good in your eyes. If you decide to hold to the way of righteousness, which is abundantly summarized in my books, you will receive a share in the land of the living with all these. If you wish to go after your desires, you must be numbered with those whom you have seen in wretched death, hurled by the just judgment of God into the curse of oblivion") (4.4 [Griesser, ed., *Exordium*, 230]).

447. Fastrad is described as "*Qui liberalibus studiis non mediocriter initiatus, sacris tamen litteris ardentiori desiderio semper inhaesit, ita ut, cum postmodum sapientia et aetate proficeret, eas prae oculis et manibus incessanter haberet et ne ad mensam quidem sine lectione divina discumbere vellet*" ("One who had been introduced to liberal studies in no half-hearted way and was always dedicated to sacred letters with a more ardent desire, so that, when he had eventually progressed in wisdom and age, he had them constantly before his eyes and in his hands, and was unwilling even to sit down at table without spiritual reading") (1.32 [Griesser, ed., *Exordium*, 89]).

448. *Nomasticon*, 84–241; see Merton, *Charter, Customs, Constitutions*, 15: "As given in the *Nomasticon*, the text of the *Consuetudines* is divided into three parts: (i) *Ecclesiastica Officia*; (ii) *Instituta Generalis Capituli*; (iii) *Usus Conversorum*." In that volume Merton discusses the last three of the five "*distinctiones*" of the *Ecclesiastica Officia*, or "religious duties" (15–56), passing over the liturgical materials of the first two distinctions.

449. This material may have been used earlier as a sequel to the material on the *Carta Caritatis* in the *Charter, Customs, Constitutions* volume; see the Introduction above (xvii–xviii).

450. *Instituta Generalis Capituli* (*Nomasticon*, 212–33).

I. Monasteries {are} to be {located} in remote places, not in towns or villages.[451]

II. *Ut inter abbatias unitas indissolubilis perpetuo perseveret*:[452] {there should be} unity in {the} interpretation of {the} *Rule*, unity in books, {in} food, {in} all customs (cf. LVI[453]).

Books {must be} the same: III.[454]

Manual labor: V allows us to own land, {with} restrictions on {the} type of animal owned[455] (cf. XXII[456]).

VI. Monks {are} not to live on granges permanently[457] (cf. XXI,[458] LXXI;[459] LI: *De Nundinis*[460]).

VII. {There are to be} no female servants or workers.[461]

---

451. "*Quo in Loco Sint Construenda Coenobia*" ("In What Place Monasteries Should Be Built") (*Nomasticon*, 212).

452. "That among the abbeys an unbreakable unity might last forever" ("*De Unitate Conversationis in Divinis & Humanis*" ["On the Unity of the Way of Living in Divine and Human Matters"] [*Nomasticon*, 212]).

453. "*De Mensura Pulmentorum*" ("On the Amount of Food") (*Nomasticon*, 225).

454. "*Quos Libros non Licet Habere Diversos*" ("Which Books Are Not Permitted to Have Different Texts") (*Nomasticon*, 212).

455. "*Unde Monachis Debeat Provenire Victus*" ("Whence Subsistence for the Monks May Be Obtained") (*Nomasticon*, 213): deer, cranes and other "useless" animals are excluded.

456. "*Quod Animalia Vitium Levitatis Ministrantia non Nutriantur*" ("That Animals Contributing to the Vice of Levity May not Be Raised") (*Nomasticon*, 217): this statute adds bears to deer and cranes as being in this category.

457. "*Quod non Debeat Monachus extra Claustrum Habitare*" ("That a Monk Must Not Dwell outside the Cloister") (*Nomasticon*, 213).

458. "*Ut extra Portam Domus non Habeatur*" ("That No Dwelling Be Located outside the Gate") (*Nomasticon*, 217).

459. "*De Domibus Quae in Villis Sunt*" ("Concerning Dwellings That Are in Towns") (*Nomasticon*, 229): the statute forbids living in towns or villages.

460. "Concerning Fairs" (*Nomasticon*, 223–24): while warning of the dangers of attending fairs, this statute notes the necessity of doing so, within the distance of a three- or four-day journey, to sell monastery goods and purchase necessities.

461. "*Quod in Ordine Nostro Feminarum Cohabitatio Interdicta Sit, & Ingressus Etiam Portae Monasterii Eis Negatus*" ("That in Our Order Women Are

VIII. Laybrothers {are to be regarded as} *"coadjutores . . . participes."*[462]

IX-X. Poverty[463] (cf. {the} *Instituta* of St. Alberic[464]).

XI. Relations between monasteries—not stealing postulants; not taking those who have been turned away without letters of {reference}[465] ({see also} XVI: fugitives;[466] LXX,[467] XXX: quarrels in {the} General Chapter;[468] XXXII: granges;[469] XXXV: abbots who don't obey {the} General Chapter;[470] XXXIX: {a} traveler {should}

Forbidden to Live within the Monastery, and even Entering within the Gate of the Monastery Is Denied to Them") (*Nomasticon*, 213).

462. "helpers . . . fellow workers" ("*De Conversis*" [*Nomasticon*, 213]).

463. "*Quod Reditus non Habeamus*" ("That We May not Have Revenues"); "*Quod Liceat vel non Liceat Nobis Habere de Auro, Argento, Gemmis & Serico*" ("What Is Permitted or not Permitted for Us to Have of Gold, Silver, Gems and Silk") (*Nomasticon*, 214).

464. *Exordium Parvum*, chap. 15 (*Nomasticon*, 62–63), which specified poverty, simplicity and the renunciation of sources of outside income.

465. "*Ut Nemo Recipiat Aliquem ad Aliam Ecclesiam Ire Volentem*" ("That No One May Accept Anyone Wishing to Go to Another Monastery") (*Nomasticon*, 214).

466. "*De Monacho vel Converso Fugitivo*" ("On a Fugitive Monk or Laybrother") (*Nomasticon*, 216): monks or brothers who refuse to return to their own monastery are to be deprived of their religious habit (except in the case of a monk who had been a member of another order before becoming a Cistercian).

467. "*Qualiter Terminari Debeat si Qua Forte Controversia inter Abbates Orta Fuerit*" ("How a Controversy Should Be Settled if by Chance One Should Arise between Abbots") (*Nomasticon*, 228): neighboring abbots are to be summoned for arbitration; if this fails, the matter is to be raised at the next General Chapter, whose decision is binding.

468. "*Quomodo Causae in Generali Capitulo Exortae Definiantur*" ("How Disputes Arising at a General Chapter Are to Be Settled") (*Nomasticon*, 219): the matter is to be settled if possible by the common consent of all the abbots assembled; if this does not happen, the abbot of Cîteaux appoints four abbots to settle the matter and all are to abide by their decision.

469. "*De Vicinitate Grangiarum*" ("On the Distance between Granges") (*Nomasticon*, 219): there are to be at least two leagues between granges.

470. "*Quae Poena Injungatur Negligentibus Instituta*" ("What Punishment Is to Be Imposed on Those Disregarding the Institutes") (*Nomasticon*, 221):

not impose on other monasteries;[471] XLII: abbots {should} not bring monks to {the} General Chapter[472] [cf. LXXVI[473]]).

XII. Foundations: how {they are} made—{what are the} minimum requirements?[474] dedication {of all monasteries} to Mary (XVIII[475]).

Poverty—no white bread for common use (XIV[476]); no expensive clasps on books (XIII[477]); no pittances for abbots at {the} General Chapter (XIX[478]); no sculptures etc. only {a} painted

---

an abbot is to be proclaimed at the annual chapter of faults at the General Chapter, and his performance of the assigned penance to be checked the following year.

471. *"Quod Monachi vel Conversi in Alia Abbatia Nihil Quaerant"* ("That Monks or Laybrothers Are to Seek Nothing at Other Abbeys") (*Nomasticon*, 221).

472. *"Quot Sociis Abbas Veniens ad Capitulum Contentus Esse Debeat"* ("How Many Companions an Abbot Coming to the General Chapter Should be Content With") (*Nomasticon*, 222): an abbot should be accompanied by a single laybrother.

473. *"Quod Monachi vel Conversi ad Generale Capitulum Venientes Verberentur"* ("That Monks or Laybrothers Coming to the General Chapter Should Be Beaten") (*Nomasticon*, 229): the reason is that such unauthorized presence would put an intolerable burden on the resources of Cîteaux during the General Chapter.

474. *"Quomodo Novella Ecclesia Abbate & Monachis & Ceteris Necessariis Ordinetur"* ("How a New Monastery Is to Be Arranged as to the Abbot, the Monks and Other Necessities") (*Nomasticon*, 213): a minimum of twelve monks plus the abbot are needed to begin a new foundation, which should be provided with all material and liturgical necessities to observe the Rule from the beginning of life there.

475. *"Quod Omnia Monasteria in Honorem Beatae Mariae Dedicentur"* ("That All Monasteries Are to Be Dedicated to the Blessed Mary") (*Nomasticon*, 216).

476. *"De Pane Quotidiano"* ("On Daily Bread") (*Nomasticon*, 215).

477. *"De Firmaculis Librorum"* ("On Clasps of Books") (*Nomasticon*, 215).

478. *"Ut Pitantiae non Administrentur in Refectorio apud Cistercium Tempore Generalis Capituli"* ("That Pittances Are not to Be Given in the Refectory at Cîteaux at the Time of the General Chapter") (*Nomasticon*, 216).

cross (XX[479])—cf. liturgy: simple; special buildings and privileges (XXXI[480]); fairs (LI[481]).

De Forma Visitationis: XXXIII.[482]

Liturgical simplicity (no special community devotions: XLIX;[483] windows and ms.: LXXX).[484]

Various: not writing new books: LVIII;[485] *De Falsis Vocibus*: LXXIII;[486] young students: LXXVIII;[487] scriptoria: LXXXV;[488] silence even with {a} visiting abbot: LXXXIX;[489] commemoration {of the} Blessed Virgin: XCI.[490]

479. "*De Sculpturis & Picturis, & Cruce Lignea*" ("On Sculptures and Pictures, and the Wooden Cross") (*Nomasticon*, 217).

480. "*De Privilegiis*" ("On Privileges") (*Nomasticon*, 219): any violation of this renunciation of special privileges is to result in the demolition of the monastery buildings and the end of the foundation.

481. "*De Nundinis*" (*Nomasticon*, 223–24).

482. "Concerning the Form of Visitation" (*Nomasticon*, 219-20): this statute provides instruction both for the visitor, who is to be both diligent and discerning in discovering faults to be corrected, and the superior and the community of the house being visited, who are to be receptive, docile and obedient.

483. "*Quod Psalmi vel Alii Quaelibet Orationes praeter Assuetas in Conventu pro Quavis Necessitate non Dicantur*" ("That Psalms and Any Other Prayers beyond the Accustomed Ones Are not to Be Said in the Common Assembly for Any Reason Whatsoever") (*Nomasticon*, 223).

484. "*De Litteris & Vitreis*" ("On Letters and Windows") (*Nomasticon*, 230).

485. "*Si Liceat Alicui Novos Libros Dictare*" ("Whether It Is Permitted to Anyone to Dictate New Books") (*Nomasticon*, 225): new books are to be produced only with the permission of the General Chapter.

486. "Concerning Falsetto Voices" (*Nomasticon*, 229): this artificial singing style is strictly forbidden.

487. "*De Pueris Litteras Discentibus*" ("On Boys Learning Their Letters") (*Nomasticon*, 230): only novices or newly professed monks are to be students in Cistercian monasteries.

488. "*De Scriptoriis*" ("On the Scriptoria") (*Nomasticon*, 231): silence is to be observed in scriptoria, where monks are employed copying manuscripts.

489. "*Cum Quot Monachis Liceat Abbati Hospiti Simul Loqui*" ("With How Many Monks a Visiting Abbot Is Allowed to Speak at One Time") (*Nomasticon*, 232): only two at a time are permitted.

490. "*Quibus Diebus Commemoratio Beatae Mariae Intermittenda Sit, & Quibus Dicenda*" ("On Which Days the Commemoration of Blessed Mary Is

Consuetudines Part III: *Usus Conversorum*[491]

Prologue: {the} problem of {the} laybrothers—some {were} neglected, overworked and underfed; others {were} pampered physically, yielded to on points of food etc. in order to be worked harder; summary: too many abbots just *use* the laybrothers for their own purposes and do not consider their interests.[492]

I. Their *office* {consists of} *Paters* and *Aves* and *Glorias*.[493]

II. They rise for vigils at {the} last psalm of {the} first nocturn of {the} choir (or at {the} beginning of {the} second nocturn on feasts); {in the} summer, after {the} end of choir vigils—they go to work; {in the} winter {they} sleep until lauds; {they} do not attend day hours in church, but come to compline; {on} feast days and Sundays when {there is} no work, {they} rise with {the} monks; those who come from granges can go to bed after {the} fourth responsory; in {the} granges {there is a} special time table.[494]

IV. {They} come to {the} conventual Mass on feasts of two Masses, {for} funerals, {on} special fast days like Ash Wednesday and ember days.[495]

V. {They receive} communion seven times a year—for more, {they} need *special* permission of {the} abbot and this {is} to be rare![496]

---

to Be Omitted, and on Which It Is to Be Said") (*Nomasticon*, 233): periods around major feasts, including Christmas, Easter, the Ascension, Pentecost, All Saints and the Assumption omit the commemoration.

491. "Customs of the Laybrothers" (*Nomasticon*, 234–41).

492. *Nomasticon*, 234.

493. "*Qualiter Se Habeant Fratres in Grangias*" ("How the Brothers Are to Conduct Themselves at the Granges") (*Nomasticon*, 234–35; no mention is made of "*Aves*" ["Hail Marys"] in the text).

494. "*Quo Tempore Surgant ad Vigilias*" ("At What Time They Are to Arise for Vigils") (*Nomasticon*, 235–36).

495. "*Quo Tempore Missas Teneant*" ("At What Time They Are to Attend Mass") (*Nomasticon*, 236).

496. "*De Communione*" ("On Holy Communion") (*Nomasticon*, 236–37).

VI. Silence: {there are} regulations to insure silence at work, *especially* {for the} tailors—brothers {are} not to talk with those to whom they talk at *work* when not working (cf. feasts etc.); {in} answering a traveler, {they} can tell him the way, but beyond that they can't talk.[497]

IX. *Nullus habeat librum vel discat aliquid nisi Pater, Ave, Gloria, Miserere* etc.[498]

XI. Chapter: (a) {they} go to morning chapter for {a} feast of sermon *only*; (b) {they} have {a} special sermon in their own chapter by {the} abbot on Sundays and days after Christmas, Easter and Pentecost, after matutinal Mass; {a} novice {is} received here {and the} chapter of faults {takes place here};[499] (c) profession {is made} in {the} monastic chapter; *after that* {a brother is} never received as {a} monk; if he goes to another order he can be received back unless he is ordained *"quod absit."*[500]

XV. {They} eat like {the} monks but can take mixt; {there is} less fasting in {the} granges;[501] {they} can wear sheepskins etc. but not fur of wild animals (rabbits etc.)[502] {and} no boots;[503] {there are} no bells in {the} granges.[504]

---

497. *"Ubi Teneant Silentium"* ("When They Are to Keep Silence") (*Nomasticon*, 237).

498. *"Quid Debent Discere"* ("What They Are to Learn") (*Nomasticon*, 238, which reads: *"Nullus habeat librum nec discat aliquid, nisi tantum Pater noster & Credo in Deum, Miserere mei Deus, & cetera quae debere dici ab eis statutum est; & hoc non littera sed corde tenus"* ["No one may have a book or learn anything, except only the Our Father and the 'I believe in God,' the 'Have mercy on me O God' [Ps 50 [51]], etc., which it is decreed must be recited by them, and this by heart, not by the written word"]).

499. *"De Capitulo"* ("On the Chapter") (*Nomasticon*, 239).

500. "during the time he is away" (*"De Professione"* [chap. XIII] ["On Profession"] [*Nomasticon*, 239–40]).

501. *"De Victu"* ("On Food") (*Nomasticon*, 240).

502. *"De Vestitu"* (chap. XVI) ("On Clothing") (*Nomasticon*, 240–41).

503. *"De Botis"* (chap. XIX) ("On Boots") (*Nomasticon*, 241).

504. *"De Campanis"* (chap. XX) ("On Bells") (*Nomasticon*, 241).

Appendix to Cistercian History
Appendix—*Historians in the Twelfth Century*
(Chenu[505]) (perspectives)

The universal history of man as a unity—a "sacred history," {the} history of salvation—{was} already a central idea in Augustine, {and} returns to prominence in the twelfth century. (A Cistercian, Otto of Freising, is very important here.)

1. Hugh of St. Victor stresses the *lectio* of the historical sense of Scripture and of course also the spiritual sense, based on it. *Series narrationis*[506] {is the} object of intelligibility of history, the articulated connections of events intended by God, revealing His salvific plan. *Haec enim quattuor praecipue et in historia requirenda sunt: persona, negotium, tempus et locus. . . . Noli contemnere minima haec. Paulatim deficient, qui minima contemnunt* (Hugh {of} St. Victor, *Didascalion*, VI. 3 [PL 176.799]).[507] {An} example {is the} movement from east to west: history moves like the sun—when the historical activity of man is centered in the west, it is near *sunset*.[508] {Hence the} common conviction, based on {the} Bible, that we are in the "last age," and that the *motives of men*, in historical *causality*, are significant and reveal something of God's plan.

2. Anselm of Havelberg, a canon, seems to have had a sense of evolution and progress within the Church, {a} divine pedagogy

---

505. Marie-Dominique Chenu, OP, *La Théologie au Douzième Siècle* (Paris: J. Vrin, 1957), chap. 3, "Conscience de l'Histoire et Théologie" (62–89); Marie-Dominique Chenu, *Nature, Man, and Society in the Twelfth Century: Essays on New Theological Perspectives in the Latin West*, ed. and trans. Jerome Taylor and Lester K. Little (Chicago: University of Chicago Press, 1968), chap. 5: "Theology and the New Awareness of History" (162–201); this translation includes nine of the nineteen chapters of the original French edition.

506. Chenu, *La Théologie*, 65 ("narrative sequence" [Taylor and Little, trans., 167]).

507. Chenu, *La Théologie*, 67, n. 3 ("For these are the four things which are especially to be sought for in history—the person, the business due, the time, and the place. . . . Do not look down upon these least things. The man who looks down on such smallest things slips little by little" [Taylor and Little, trans., 169, n. 16]).

508. See Chenu, *La Théologie*, 79 (Taylor and Little, trans., 186–87).

in {the} gradual adaptation of {the different} states of life.[509] {He was an} adversary of Rupert of Deutz (+ 1130) {on} the question of states of life in {the} twelfth century.[510] For Rupert and the monks, the *monastic life* is the *vita vere apostolica* (see PL {170}: 611-664[511]). {A} contrast {was made between} VITA and OFFICIUM:[512] *vita* = the common fraternal life of {the} first Christian communities, reproduced in monasteries—*regula monastica* = *regula apostolica*[513] (cf. Acts 4:32); *vita apostolica* = *vita communis*[514] ({the} Gregorian reform canonizes this term—in reaction against {the} decadence of clerics). But {the} monk lives "from the altar";[515] priestly life {is} more "normal"—{it is} "apostolic perfection"; manual labor {is} downgraded. {The} *problem* of the monastic life {is that it is} "instilled" in power in {the} fabric of feudal society and {is in tension with} the pressure of evangelical grace calling {the monk} to poverty: "inquiétude que la ferveur ne faisait qu'exasperer" (Chenu[516]). {This is} solved (as above) by {the} splendor of worship.

---

509. See Chenu, *La Théologie*, 69–70 (Taylor and Little, trans., 173–75).

510. See Chenu, *La Théologie*, chap. 10: "Moines, Clercs, Laïcs: Au carrefour de la vie évangélique" (225–51) (Taylor and Little, trans., chap. 4: "Monks, Canons, and Laymen in Search of the Apostolic Life" [202–38]).

511. Chenu, *La Théologie*, 227 ("the truly apostolic life" [Taylor and Little, trans., 205, which has the correct volume number; Chenu, followed by the copy text, reads "165"]). Chenu notes that there are serious doubts about the authenticity of the *De Vita Vere Apostolica* as a work of Rupert; John Van Engen's authoritative work *Rupert of Deutz* (Berkeley: University of California Press, 1983) declares the work definitely not by Rupert (300, n. 5).

512. Chenu, *La Théologie*, 228 ("function . . . mode of life" [Taylor and Little, trans., 206]).

513. Chenu, *La Théologie*, 228 ("The monastic *regula* was in fact the *regula apostolica*" [Taylor and Little, trans., 206]).

514. "the apostolic life = the common life" (Chenu, *La Théologie*, 228 [Taylor and Little, trans., 206]).

515. I.e. from revenues generated by liturgical service (see 1 Cor 9:13-14; Chenu, *La Théologie*, 230 [Taylor and Little, trans., 208–9]).

516. Chenu, *La Théologie*, 230 ("an uneasiness of soul which his fervor tended only to exacerbate" [Taylor and Little, trans., 208]).

3. "Shocks": {the} crusades and missionary expansion of {the} thirteenth century awaken a new historical conscience of worlds beyond the closed world of Patristic historical speculation[517] (cf. {the} article of Bede Griffiths[518]).

4. The traditional view of history in {the} twelfth century {includes}:

   a) The *aetates* = six "days" of the new creation (read Daniel 7[519]).

---

517. See Chenu, *La Théologie*, 80 (Taylor and Little, trans., 188–89).

518. Probably a reference to Bede Griffiths, "The Ecumenical Approach to Non-Christian Religions," *Catholic World* 193/1157 (August 1961): 304–10.

519. "In the first year of Baltasar king of Babylon, Daniel saw a dream: and the vision of his head was upon his bed: and writing the dream, he comprehended it in few words: and relating the sum of it in short, he said: I saw in my vision by night, and behold the four winds of the heaven strove upon the great sea. And four great beasts, different one from another, came up out of the sea. The first was like a lioness, and had the wings of an eagle: I beheld till her wings were plucked off, and she was lifted up from the earth, and stood upon her feet as a man, and the heart of a man was given to her. And behold another beast like a bear stood up on one side: and there were three rows in the mouth thereof, and in the teeth thereof, and thus they said to it: Arise, devour much flesh. After this I beheld, and lo, another like a leopard, and it had upon it four wings as of a fowl, and the beast had four heads, and power was given to it. After this I beheld in the vision of the night, and lo, a fourth beast, terrible and wonderful, and exceeding strong, it had great iron teeth, eating and breaking in pieces, and treading down the rest with its feet: and it was unlike to the other beasts which I had seen before it, and had ten horns. I considered the horns, and behold another little horn sprung out of the midst of them: and three of the first horns were plucked up at the presence thereof: and behold eyes like the eyes of a man were in this horn, and a mouth speaking great things. I beheld till thrones were placed, and the Ancient of days sat: his garment was white as snow, and the hair of his head like clean wool: his throne like flames of fire: the wheels of it like a burning fire. A swift stream of fire issued forth from before him: thousands of thousands ministered to him, and ten thousand times a hundred thousand stood before him: the judgment sat, and the books were opened. I beheld because of the voice of the great words which that horn

spoke: and I saw that the beast was slain, and the body thereof was destroyed, and given to the fire to be burnt: And that the power of the other beasts was taken away: and that times of life were appointed them for a time, and a time. I beheld therefore in the vision of the night, and lo, one like the son of man came with the clouds of heaven, and he came even to the Ancient of days: and they presented him before him. And he gave him power, and glory, and a kingdom: and all peoples, tribes and tongues shall serve him: his power is an everlasting power that shall not be taken away: and his kingdom that shall not be destroyed. My spirit trembled, I Daniel was affrighted at these things, and the visions of my head troubled me. I went near to one of them that stood by, and asked the truth of him concerning all these things, and he told me the interpretation of the words, and instructed me: These four great beasts are four kingdoms, which shall arise out of the earth. But the saints of the most high God shall take the kingdom: and they shall possess the kingdom for ever and ever. After this I would diligently learn concerning the fourth beast, which was very different from all, and exceeding terrible: his teeth and claws were of iron: he devoured and broke in pieces, and the rest he stamped upon with his feet: And concerning the ten horns that he had on his head: and concerning the other that came up, before which three horns fell: and of that horn that had eyes, and a mouth speaking great things, and was greater than the rest. I beheld, and lo, that horn made war against the saints, and prevailed over them, till the Ancient of days came and gave judgment to the saints of the most High, and the time came, and the saints obtained the kingdom. And thus he said: The fourth beast shall be the fourth kingdom upon earth, which shall be greater than all the kingdoms, and shall devour the whole earth, and shall tread it down, and break it in pieces. And the ten horns of the same kingdom, shall be ten kings: and another shall rise up after them, and he shall be mightier than the former, and he shall bring down three kings. And he shall speak words against the High One, and shall crush the saints of the most High: and he shall think himself able to change times and laws, and they shall be delivered into his hand until a time, and times, and half a time. And judgment shall sit, that his power may be taken away, and be broken in pieces, and perish even to the end. And that the kingdom, and power, and the greatness of the kingdom, under the whole heaven, may be given to the people of the saints of the most High: whose kingdom is an everlasting kingdom, and all kings shall serve him, and shall obey him. Hitherto is the end of the word. I Daniel was much troubled with my thoughts, and my countenance was changed in me: but I kept the word in my heart."

Cistercian History

b) The *aetates* = six ages of man (*infantia, pueritia, adolescentia, juventus, senectus,* decrepitude)[520] (cf. De Lubac, *Catholicisme,* p. 104–106[521])—hence {there is a} *pedagogy of "states"* appropriate to each age. (See *Garnier de Rochefort, Sermo* 19 [PL 205[522]]: Garnier of Rochfort[523] {was the} ninth abbot of Clairvaux {and was} elected Bishop of Langres {in} 1187; Sermon 19 {is} an Easter sermon on Numbers 7, where the chiefs of Israel bring gifts for six days at the dedication of the Tabernacle; history {is} seen in the seven days of creation, and {the} seven days of the week, applied to the seven Sundays from Septuagesima to Laetare Sunday; among other things this {is applied to the} three main languages—see {the} sign on {the} cross:[524] Greek {is} said with {the} lips; Hebrew {is} said in {the} throat; Latin {is} in between—*therefore* Latin {is} the language of {the} Kingdom of God, which is to *unite* Greek and Jew!!) See also {the} transposition of the *aetates* into Church history {and} applied to monastic orders: Cluny = {the} last one, which will collapse and give place to new (canonical—later mendicant) life in {the} perfect (see Chenu, p. 234[525]).

520. See Chenu, *La Théologie*, 75, n. 3 (Taylor and Little, trans., 181, n. 29).

521. Henri De Lubac, SJ, *Catholicisme: Les Aspects Sociaux du Dogme* (Paris: Éditions du Cerf, 1938), cited in Chenu, *La Théologie*, 74, n. 1; English translation: *Catholicism: A Study of Dogma in Relation to the Corporate Destiny of Mankind*, trans. Lancelot C. Sheppard from 4th ed. (1947; New York: Longmans, Green, 1950), 73–76, cited in Taylor and Little, trans., 180, n. 37. De Lubac summarizes the various symbolic stages of the Christian conception of history—the four "times" and six (or seven, or eight) "ages"—and contrasts them with pagan perspectives.

522. PL 205:694D–700A (see Chenu, *La Théologie*, 75, n. 1 [Taylor and Little, trans., 180, n. 37]).

523. See King, *Cîteaux*, 258–60, for an overview of his abbacy (1186–1193); for Merton's opinion of Garnier, compared with Guerric of Igny, see *Cistercian Fathers and Forefathers*, 197–99.

524. PL 205:697A.

525. Chenu quotes from the commentary of Rupert of Deutz on the Rule of Saint Benedict (PL 170:535–36), rejecting the analogy between the succession of pagan kingdoms and Christian history (*La Théologie*, 234–35 [Taylor and Little, trans., 215]).

c) Other views {distinguish between} *ante legem, sub lege* {and} *sub gratia*.[526] But {there is a} danger of regarding true "*sub gratia*" as complete, as a marking of time to await the end: (α) St. Thomas speaks[527] of an *incrementum temporis*[528] in which men will learn the full meaning of {the} Gospel; (β) Otto of Freising, however, takes a pessimistic view of the "*senectus" mundi: Mundum* jam deficientem et tamquam ultimi senii extremum spiritum trahentam cernimus (*Chron.* V: Prologue[529]); (γ) Anselm of Havelberg {writes}: *Sancta Ecclesia pertransiens per diversos status sibi invicem paulatim succedentes,* usque in hodiernum diem, sicut juventus aquilae {renovatur et semper} renovabitur (*PL* 188.1149);[530] (δ) Adam Scot {describes} four ages of the Church (*PL* 198.144):[531] (1) receiving {the} Word of salvation; (2) {the} struggle with adversaries, and conquest; (3) peace "planting the vines on the mountains"[532]—i.e. *explaining* {the} word of God; (4) *Dies Domini—dum in caritate laetatur beatae et beatificantis visionis*.[533]

---

526. See Chenu, *La Théologie*, 76 ("the time before the Law (of Moses), the time of the Law, and the time of Grace" [Taylor and Little, trans., 182]).

527. *In Epistolam ad Hebreos* 1.1 (*Sancti Thomae Aquinatis Doctoris Angelici Ordinis Praedicatorum Opera Omnia, secundum Impressionem Petri Fiaccadori Parmae 1852–1873 Photolithographice Reimpressa*, 25 vols. [New York: Misurgia, 1948], 13.668), cited in Chenu, *La Théologie*, 76, n. 2 (Taylor and Little, trans., 182, n. 43).

528. "increment of time" (Taylor and Little, trans., 182).

529. Chenu, *La Théologie*, 77, n. 1 ("we see the world . . . already on the decline and exhaling the final breath, so to speak, of advanced old age" [Taylor and Little, trans., 183]).

530. *Dialogi* 1.6, quoted in Chenu, *La Théologie*, 77 ("The holy church, passing through various stages which in turn gradually succeed themselves up to this present day, is renewed just as the eagle's youth [is renewed; and it always] will be renewed" [Taylor and Little, trans., 184]).

531. *De Triplici Sanctae Ecclesiae Statu*, Sermo 8, quoted in Chenu, *La Théologie*, 77, n. 3.

532. "*vineam plantat in montibus*" (not quoted in Taylor and Little, trans.).

533. "the Day of the Lord—while there is rejoicing in love of the blessed and beatific vision" (not quoted in Taylor and Little, trans.).

5. The *"Roman" World* (especially Otto of Freising[534]): all admit {the} providential role of {the} Roman Empire, {which} unifies {the} human race. {The} predestined vocation of Rome {was}

---

534. For a biographical overview of Otto (d. 1158), son of the Duke of Austria, uncle of Frederick Barbarossa, monk of the Abbey of Morimond, which he entered in 1132 and where he briefly served as abbot in 1138 before becoming Bishop of Freising that same year, see King, *Cîteaux*, 338–41. See also Merton's journal entry of December 11, 1962: "Otto of Freising was so convinced that Constantine had finally inaugurated the Kingdom of God, that he spoke at last only of *one city* in his history of the 'Two Cities.' When the Emperor became Catholic, then Christendom = the Kingdom of God, i.e. the Christian politico-religious world is the kingdom of God. Hence there is no more to be done, but to preserve the status quo of the kingdom, if necessary by violent repression, coercion rather than apostolate. The apostolate of united coercion!! And as the genuine Christian spirit must *necessarily* resist the identification of the Kingdom of God with a limited human society, then the focus of 'Christendom' did in fact tend to repress those movements which tended to genuine development, thrusting them outside the 'city' where their evolution became distorted and unhealthy. Hence another Cistercian, Joachim of Fiore, rises up against Otto of Freising's Constantinian theory with an apocalypse of the 'Spirit.' He was in fact expressing the stirrings that were to bring about the birth of a new age and break down medieval society. Two temptations, then: to evade the responsibilities of a Christian in history by saying that the kingdom has arrived and medieval Christendom is/was the kingdom, or to do the same by saying the kingdom will arrive only at the end of, or outside of time. The true responsibility—to receive the Holy Spirit and cooperate with His transforming work in time now. (I have a doubtless rather good little publication on/for Catholic intellectual and social movements. It is called what? *Pax Romana!* And the uneasiness with which I cannot help viewing Don Giovanni Rossi's Pro Civitate Xtiana and all other such movements, comes to the same thing!) Already Catholics with this mentality but tired of western capitalism, are beginning secretly to dream of a Constantine in Moscow and a new Muscovite Christian Kingdom of God! As if this were a *new* dream!" (Thomas Merton, *Turning Toward the World: The Pivotal Years. Journals, vol. 4: 1960–1963*, ed. Victor A. Kramer [San Francisco: HarperCollins, 1996], 273–74; Merton is reflecting here on Chenu, *La Théologie*, 81–82).

to set {the} stage of {the} universality of {the} Gospel: Catholic = Roman. {According to} Otto:

a) {there was a} *translatio imperii*[535] to the predestined *German* race to maintain the unity of the collapsed empire (cf. Holy Russia—Moscow {as the} Third Rome[536]). Note: for Rupert,[537] now that the Church occupies the whole world, the new state of {the} Church calls for a multiplication of priests—NOT {for} penance, but {for the} glorification of God in cult, {a} manifestation of Christian victory. But he stops short at preaching and administering sacraments. The monastery is the "City of God" in which the city of the world has been totally absorbed and consecrated. {The} monastery is then the "true Church." The only genuine Christian is the monk, for Rupert.[538] There is therefore no confrontation between {the} monk and {the} world, in preaching,

---

535. Chenu, *La Théologie*, 79 ("transference of the empire" [Taylor and Little, trans., 186]).

536. In the aftermath of the fall of Constantinople (the "second Rome") to the Ottoman Turks in 1453, the claim that Moscow was its legitimate successor became widely held in Russia, based both on the fact that Grand Duke Ivan III had married the niece of the last Byzantine Emperor and on the reputation of Russia as the great remaining bastion of Orthodox Christianity. This position was bolstered by the assumption of the title of *tsar* (i.e. Caesar) by the Russian ruler in the mid-sixteenth century. See Merton's comments on the continuing pertinence of such theories in his December 9, 1962, journal entry: "How much we have done to lead ourselves astray with theories about ages of the world, and extrapolations from prophecies of Daniel about the Roman Empire to Charlemagne—to Barbarism [probably a misreading for "Barbarossa"] and what not. This was the contribution of a Cistercian, Otto of Freising. We have never given up thinking in such terms. No one, however, has yet formulated anything about the 'Western' realm of America being the heir of the Holy Roman Empire—or perhaps some Spaniard did. Yet that is how we think, still, and it is built in to our Christianity as a permanent delusion. So also the delusion of Holy Russia. There are too damn many holy empires with archimandrites to shower them in holy water" (*Turning Toward the World*, 272–73).

537. See Chenu, *La Théologie*, 230–31 (Taylor and Little, trans., 210).

538. See Chenu, *La Théologie*, 232 (Taylor and Little, trans., 212).

according to Rupert (says Chenu[539]); and yet in practice there was great ferment in the lower classes, especially in towns, which *were already beginning to lose contact with the Church* (233[540]). Monks refuse to confront them and speak. N.B. in this stable society there are *"ordines"* of laypeople—{with} fixed and sacred responsibility—the order of knighthood {has a} sacred function—{the} knight is "ordained." {There is an} order of judges and lawyers {and an} order of farmers; but the *mercatores* do not constitute an *ordo*[541]—see {the} quote from Gratian (p. 240, n. 4[542]).

b) There is now in practice *one city*. The temporal city is *within* the Church, for the Emperor is Catholic; {cf. the} exaltation of Charlemagne (canonized {in} 1168[543]). Peace {is} to be imposed by Christian armies, for {the sake of the} spread of {the} Gospel; the King = Christ; {the} destiny of man = {the} destiny of {the} Empire. To rebel against the social setup is to rebel against Christ ({cf. the} trial by ordeal). {This view promotes a} *static* attachment to feudal society (with insensibility to new needs and trends).

6. {The} Trinity and History: {the} idea of {the} Age of {the} Father, {and of the} Son and {of the} Holy Ghost is traditional (cf.

---

539. "À la limite, dans cet univers sacralisé, dans une terrestre cité de Dieu totale, le prosélytisme de la parole de Dieu, le *ministerium verbi inter gentes*, deviendrait sans objet et sans raison. . . . La *vita apostolica*, enfin réalisée, laisse hors sa réflexion institutionelle l'affrontement au monde, que requiert l'Évangile" (Chenu, *La Théologie*, 232–33) ("The end result of this sacralized universe, of this perfected terrestrial city of God, would be to make proselytizing, the *ministerium verbi inter gentes*, pointless and unnecessary. . . . In its final realization, this *vita apostolica* left out of its consideration that confrontation of the world which the gospel demanded" [Taylor and Little, trans., 212–13]).

540. Taylor and Little, trans., 213.

541. Chenu, *La Théologie*, 241–42 (Taylor and Little, trans., 225–26).

542. "*Mercator vix aut nunquam potest placere Deo*" (*Decretum*, 1.88.11) ("A merchant is rarely or never able to please God" [Taylor and Little, trans., 224, n. 45]).

543. I.e. by an antipope, through the influence of the emperor, Frederick Barbarossa (see Chenu, *La Théologie*, 84 [Taylor and Little, trans., 194]).

Rupert of Deutz[544]). *Joachim of Flora*[545] has a revolutionary application {of this}—{the} idea of {the} new age of the Spirit, to begin in 1200, {which} breaks up {the} accepted unity of the current Christian view of history; this will be a totally new development—{a} *false* progressivism; but, in contrast to {the} above, *now the monk will preach and fulfill his prophetic mission.*[546]

7. Progressive views {are represented by} Orderic Vital {and} John of Salisbury,[547] {who exhibits} political maturity, {along with

---

544. *De Trinitate et Operibus Ejus* (PL 167:199–200; cited in Chenu, *La Théologie*, 82, n. 1 [Taylor and Little, trans., 191, n. 60]).

545. For a largely positive evaluation of the controversial Calabrian abbot (originally a Cistercian) Joachim (1132–1202) as "*one of the most important figures in the Middle Ages*" because of his eschatological teaching of the coming "third age" of Christianity, ruled by the Holy Spirit, see Thomas Merton, *An Introduction to Christian Mysticism: Initiation into the Monastic Tradition* 3, ed. Patrick F. O'Connell, MW 13 (Kalamazoo, MI: Cistercian Publications, 2008), 172–73; see also the comments in Thomas Merton, *Conjectures of a Guilty Bystander* (Garden City, NY: Doubleday, 1966), 40–41, 188, as well as his journal entry for May 7, 1961, when he mentions becoming "more and more fascinated by the mysticism of the late Middle Ages . . . going back to the Cistercians, Joachim, St. Francis, the Béguines, the Cathari, the Spirituals, *assimilated* fully by the Church in the great Rhenish mystics. . . . We have not even begun to understand all this or appreciate its purport" (*Turning Toward the World*, 117).

546. See Chenu, *La Théologie*, 82 (Taylor and Little, trans., 191).

547. Merton calls John (ca. 1115–1180), a native of England, student in Paris, friend and supporter of Thomas Becket, moral and political philosopher, and finally bishop of Chartres, "one of the key names in the humanism of Christendom" (*Conjectures*, 163). Merton's interest in John was part of his broader fascination with the School of Chartres during the early 1960s; see also his reflections on a passage from Vergil's *Georgics* learned as a schoolboy and rediscovered in a volume of John, who, he writes, "rightly sees that to have gained something of this Classic temper leaves one ready for faith and for the highest truth because, he says, 'It is not possible for one who with his whole heart seeks and embraces truth, to love and cultivate what is merely empty'" (*Conjectures*, 236–37; see also the original version of this passage in Merton's journal entry for September 29, 1962 [*Turning Toward the World*, 251–52], which quotes the original Latin).

a} sense of *politics*: {he} separates politics and theology {and has a} sense of secondary causes; {for him the} Empire {is} not divine.[548]

8. {The} twelfth century {is a} time when {the} term *vita apostolica* is revolutionized to mean the *itinerant preaching life*. Luke 10:1-12 becomes the great text; {the} common life (poverty) {is} still the basis, but now {there is} a new dynamism of action;[549] canonical life appeals to Augustine and Jerome as its founders;[550] activity *of laymen* {becomes significant, at times with} wrong tendencies (Waldo[551]), {at others} correctly channeled (St. Francis); but {there is evident a} beginning of {a} sense of {the} *lay-state* and {the} *lay-vocation* (in seed).[552]

* * * * * * *

Decline of {the} Cistercian Order
(cf. Dom Leclercq—*Revue Bénédictine*, 1954[553])

Monastic Decline in General: in {the} thirteenth century, {there was an} *intellectual* decline of the monks, {who had} no vitality to set as {a} counterpoint to {the} theological activity of {the} schools. {Likewise there was a} *spiritual* decline—rich established groups {were} out of touch with new movements, as opposed to {the} poverty and fervor of the friars.

548. See Chenu, *La Théologie*, 85–86 (Taylor and Little, trans., 196–97).
549. See Chenu, *La Théologie*, 234 (Taylor and Little, trans., 214–15).
550. See Chenu, *La Théologie*, 235 (Taylor and Little, trans., 216).
551. Peter Waldo (or Valdez) (ca. 1140–ca. 1205) was the leader of a radical mendicant movement known as the Poor Men of Lyons, or the Waldensians, strongly critical of the institutional Church and rejecting some doctrines including transubstantiation and purgatory; eventually he and his followers were excommunicated and settled for security in the mountainous region of the Piedmont in northern Italy, where the movement continued to exist until the time of the Protestant Reformation, of which it was considered a forerunner. A small Waldensian Church still survives in Italy today.
552. See Chenu, *La Théologie*, 237–38 (Taylor and Little, trans., 219–22).
553. Jean Leclercq, "Épitres d'Alexandre III sur les Cisterciens," *Revue Bénédictine* 64 (1954): 68–82; for a discussion of this article, see below, pages 168–70.

Special features of {the} Cistercian decline {include}: (1) {the} struggle of first four fathers with {the} Abbot of Cîteaux—activities (n.b. exemption?); (2) business and *tithes*; (3) the laybrothers' crisis; (4) the missionary failures—against {the} Albigensians—{for the} *crusade*, cf. *DHGE*[554] 926f.;[555] Canivez 1218;[556] {for the} crusades in {the} Holy Land {see} *DHGE* 931;[557] {for} abbots out

554. J.-M. Canivez, "Cîteaux (Ordre)," *Dictionnaire d'Histoire et de Géographie Ecclésiastiques*, 12.874–997.

555. After briefly touching on the Fourth Crusade of 1202, for which the Cistercians were asked to provide prayers and funds, and for which the Abbot of Sambucina was appointed by Pope Innocent III as principal preacher, there follows an overview of the Cistercian involvement in the Albigensian Crusade, in which Cistercians preached against the Cathars (joined in 1203 by Bishop Diego of Osma and Dominic Guzman, soon to found the Order of Preachers). Shortly after the decision was made to launch a military crusade against the heretics, the Cistercian Peter of Castelnau was assassinated on January 15, 1208. The crusade, initially successful, eventually foundered after Simon de Montfort, its leader, was killed on June 25, 1218, at the siege of Toulouse (cols. 926-29).

556. The General Chapter enjoined the Abbots of Bithaine, Noirlac and Chalivois to investigate the conduct of abbots and monks who were preaching the crusade, and to make those who were unsatisfactory or had not been officially authorized to do so return to their monasteries (Canivez, *Statuta*, 1.491 [#35]).

557. For the new crusade in 1218 the Abbot of Villers was authorized by the General Chapter to accompany the Duke of Brabant to the Holy Land; the king of Hungary asked to be attended by two monks and a laybrother; various financial contributions were made by monasteries of the Order. More interest was shown in the crusades of King Louis IX (Saint Louis), beginning with a penitential procession in 1247 and special prayers of intercession; the Cistercians were exempted by the king from financial impositions for this expedition of 1248. In 1267, the Order gave a gift of 20,000 livres to the king for a proposed crusade and was exempted from taxes as a consequence. This second crusade of Saint Louis ended with his death from illness on August 25, 1270, in North Africa (Canivez, "Cîteaux," 12:931–33).

Cistercian History

on Church business {see} *DHGE* 933;[558] Canivez 1211;[559] (5) the College of St. Bernard.[560]

Causes of Decline *According to the Compendium*[561]

1. *Visitations?* {On} p. 164-5 {it is stated}: "from the year 1130 to the death of St. Bernard (1153) the annual Regular Visitation of monasteries was not made"; {this} "was morally impossible"[562]

---

558. Innocent III sent Cistercians to evangelize northern Europe and often appointed them judges in ecclesiastical courts (Canivez, "Cîteaux," 12:933–35).

559. The General Chapter instructs the Abbot of Cîteaux to beg the pope to spare them these appointments, or at least not to assign priors, subpriors or cellarers to these duties—to no avail (Canivez, *Statuta*, 1.385 [#34]).

560. For a discussion of this house of studies in Paris, see below, pages 212–25.

561. Merton makes frequent reference to the author of the *Compendium*, Fr. Alberic Wulf, in his journal in the period leading up to and following the latter's death on March 23, 1947: see Thomas Merton, *Entering the Silence: Becoming a Monk and Writer. Journals, vol. 2: 1941–1952*, ed. Jonathan Montaldo (San Francisco: HarperCollins, 1996), 32–33, 48, 50–51, 52, 126, 281, 368 [12/24/1946, 3/18/1947, 3/23/1947, 3/25/1947, 10/16/1947, 2/13/1949, 9/14/1949]. He calls Wulf "a kind, and simple and solitary little person" (32), "a very saintly little man" (50), with whom he had developed "a sort of pact about saying prayers for one another" (51), and who was "writing the history of the Order on scraps of paper in the infirmary!" (368). He notes in a May 2, 1947, entry that he had been given, among other tasks, "that of continuing Fr. Alberic's work by revising the *Compendium of the History of the Order*" (69), which was never done, though *The Waters of Siloe* (New York: Harcourt, Brace, 1949) might be considered Merton's own version of this history. (In the revised text of this passage Merton writes only that "Father Abbot gave me the notes that Father Alberic was working on, for the revised edition of his history of the Order," and goes on to mention having "finished three chapters of *The Waters of Siloe*"—not referred to in the original journal passage—suggesting that the assignment had been altered to an original work that might draw on some of Fr. Alberic's research [Thomas Merton, *The Sign of Jonas* (New York: Harcourt, Brace, 1953), 45–46]).

562. Wulf, *Compendium*, 165, which reads, "rendered that observance of a very important ordinance of the Charter of Charity morally, at least, impossible."

but "did not result in any declination of monastic fervor" (171)—a fantastic statement. *Knowles* says[563] that Bernard never visited his filiations in England *personally*—yes—but {conducted visitations} by proxy; {there is} evidence that Ailred {of Rievaulx} made his visitations conscientiously (Knowles, *MOE*, p. 262[564]); evidence shows that the system during {the} first century of expansion worked efficiently (read *MOE*, p. 637[565]). In *Religious Orders in England* 1, p. 110,[566] Knowles says: "Visitations can kill germs of decay before they do irreparable harm; {. . .} it can graft new life upon the old stock. *Never in the history of the Church has this been seen more clearly than in the first century of the Cistercian order* . . ."[567] and {he} describes {the} power of visiting abbots—to depose, to bring in monks from other houses, to {impose} penance etc. "The Cistercian visitation ceased to be powerful only when political and ecclesiastical changes had weakened the cohesion of the Order, and when the constitutions were no longer kept

---

563. Knowles, *Monastic Order*, 262, n. 2, which actually says: "Bernard, it would seem, never in person visited Rievaulx or any of the Clairvaux foundations in the British Isles, nor have I met with any reference to substitutes sent by him to Rievaulx."

564. "Ailred, in the course of each year, had the obligation of visiting Cîteaux, Clairvaux, Woburn, Revesby, Rufford, Melrose and Dundrennan, and though no doubt dispensations or sheer impossibility relieved him from time to time of some of these visits, there is evidence from a number of sources that none of his charges were neglected, and that he was continually on the road."

565. "Perhaps the most distinctive and valuable contribution of the *Carta Caritatis* to ecclesiastical discipline was its institution in clear and simple decrees of a system of regular visitation. The evidence of Cistercian sources, of casual references and of hostile criticism all combines to show that this system, during the first century of the plantation in England and Wales, worked regularly and efficiently, and continued to be an effective instrument for maintaining or restoring discipline."

566. David Knowles, *The Religious Orders in England*, 3 vols. (Cambridge: Cambridge University Press, 1948–1959).

567. Text reads: "It can kill . . . harm; it can rid the body of a cancer; it can graft a new life . . . century of the life of" (emphasis added).

according to the letter" (p. 111). (When was this?) {There is} evidence of a *special visitation*—special visitors in England in 1188 changed several abbots. {There are} records of abbots deposed, or resigning, as {a} result of visitations, {as well as} abbots punished by {the} General Chapter for not making regular visitations. {In} 1215 {the} *Fourth Lateran Council* extends Cistercian-type visitation to other monastic orders (obviously because it worked).[568]

2. {The} *General Chapter*: {according to the} *Compendium*: "Some abbots were unable to assist at General Chapter . . . while others remained away through indolence or lack of interest in the general affairs of the Order."[569] This is preposterous. However, {the} beginning of trouble {can be} seen[570] in statutes of 1190,[571] 1193,[572] 1194,[573] 1196.[574] *Knowles* says[575] attendance was strictly enforced; more than one abbot died at Cîteaux or on the road. {In} 1157[576] three abbots of Scotland have permission to come every four years. {The} same permission {was} REFUSED to abbots of England (1201)[577] (contrast *Compendium* p. 183[578]); {it was} granted to Irish abbots in 1190.[579] Reprimands and penances {were issued}

---

568. *Disciplinary Decrees of the General Councils*, ed. and trans. H. J. Schroeder, OP (St. Louis: B. Herder, 1937), 253–54 (canon 12). See above, n. 184.

569. Wulf, *Compendium*, 171, which reads: "Then some abbots were unable to assist at the annual General Chapters at Cîteaux; while . . ."

570. See Canivez, "Cîteaux," 12:907.

571. Canivez, *Statuta*, 1.126–27 (##42, 64): penances for abbots not attending General Chapters or not making visitations to daughter abbeys.

572. Canivez, *Statuta*, 1.160, 165, 166–67 (##16, 44, 48): an abbot fails to come to the General Chapter because of a bishop's wish.

573. Canivez, *Statuta*, 1.179–80 (#54).

574. Canivez, *Statuta*, 1.205 (#41).

575. See Knowles, *Monastic Order*, 638–39.

576. Canivez, *Statuta*, 1.67 (#62); see Knowles, *Monastic Order*, 639.

577. Canivez, *Statuta*, 1.272 (#45); see Knowles, *Monastic Order*, 639.

578. "When in the middle of the twelfth century, some 340 abbots were wont to attend the General Chapter every year, dispensation from annual attendance was readily granted to those residing in distant countries."

579. Canivez, *Statuta*, 1.122 (#17); see Knowles, *Monastic Order*, 639.

for defaulting abbots. Those from Syria {were} allowed to come every seventh year.[580]

3. {The} *decline of poverty* {is} vaguely stated {on} p. 171: "abbots became implicated in secular affairs, to the detriment of their subjects,"[581] suggesting only that abbots were away on business; see what really happened below.

4. {The} *principal cause* {is presented as}: "The spirit of dissension which animated *certain major abbots*" (!).[582] Again {there is a} characteristic vagueness: "particularly many {of} the successors of St. Bernard."[583]

Thirteenth Century Abbots: (1) they are great feudal lords—the post is enviable—{it} implies great power and prestige; (2) his job is to maintain the power of his monastery; he is often elected or appointed due to influence outside {the} monastery.

{N.B. the} Donation {in} 1157 by Geoffrey de la Roche, as Bishop of Langres—{he} gives {a} church and {its} revenue to Quincy.[584] *Poverty* {is compromised}: {cf. the} donation of {the} church of Scarborough by Richard Coeur de Lion {in} 1190 to pay expenses of {the} General Chapter;[585] {in} 1196, Clairvaux has {a} church of Boulogne; {by} 1231, Clairvaux has three villages and {their} inhabitants (as serfs?).[586] {With regard to} *tithes*, {in} 1170,

---

580. So Lekai, *The White Monks*, 66; according to the General Chapter of 1216, n. 49, abbots from Syria and Palestine were to come every five years (Canivez, *Statuta*, 1.459) (n.b. in Mahn, *L'Ordre Cistercien* [179], the reference to Syria is found in n. 7; might Lekai—followed by Merton—have found it there and inadvertently substituted the note number for the proper number of years?).

581. Text reads: "abbots became more and more implicated."

582. Wulf, *Compendium*, 172, which reads: "dissension that animated" (emphasis added).

583. Wulf, *Compendium*, 172, which reads: "particularly the successors."

584. See Canivez, "Cîteaux," col. 919.

585. See C. H. Talbot, "Cîteaux and Scarborough," *Studia Monastica* 2 (1960): 95–158.

586. See Canivez, "Cîteaux," cols. 919–20.

Bois-Grolland has tithes on salt-pits;[587] {in} 1230 {the} General Chapter sanctions them.[588]

The Cistercian Decline

I. {For} the Cistercians in the early thirteenth century, see Knowles, *Religious Orders in England*: (1) nothing remarkable {is evident}: the houses are not set apart by special fervor or notable decline; they retain a reputation for austerity {and} still attract some {recruits} from {the} Benedictines etc. The contemplative fervor has died down, "sunk into the countryside" {amid} prosperity (read *ROE*, p. 316—bottom[589]).

The Agrarian Economy of the Cistercians (p. 64ff.[590]—{a} typical case of English Cistercians): special characteristics {of the Cistercians

---

587. See Canivez, "Cîteaux," col. 921; Mahn, *L'Ordre Cistercien*, 116–17.

588. The reference immediately following in Mahn, *L'Ordre Cistercien*, 117, is not specifically to Bois-Grolland but to the formal acceptance by the General Chapter (1230.3 [Canivez, *Statuta*, 2.84]) of the common practice of a Cistercian monastery levying tithes on property owned by others (as Bois-Grolland did with regard to the mines owned by the Benedictine house of Orbestier).

589. "Of the Cistercian abbeys, only a very few in the thirteenth century show distinguishing characteristics. Thus Beaulieu in Hampshire, by reason of its recent plantation from abroad under royal patronage, and Hayles, chiefly on account of the relic which made it one of the most frequented shrines of England, had a certain celebrity, and the Cistercians in general retained something of their reputation for austerity until the middle of the century, as is shown by the occasional recruits they still drew off from the black monks and canons, but in general their abbeys had sunk into the countryside and lost for ever that compelling charm which had once made them seem like outposts of Jerusalem, the vision of peace. Even the great Yorkshire abbeys, Fountains and Rievaulx, were now distinguished by little save their larger flocks and the superior magnificence of their fabric. Nevertheless, a few notices remain to show that many of them, especially in the north, still stood high in general esteem."

590. "Nothing, in fact, is more certain than the success of the early Cistercians in reclaiming waste and woodland to cultivation, and the new abbeys, after some twenty or thirty years, were all surrounded with arable and pasture admirably cultivated and fertile. In the few cases where the poverty of the soil baffled every effort, the monastery was transferred

include} land worked by monks and brothers—not rented out; monasteries isolated in {the} midst of farm land; granges (land reclaimed from waste); centralized control of {the} cellarer, instead of many officials; greater order and efficiency than {among the} Benedictines; {the} most powerful group of large-scale wool producers for export (read *ROE* p. 66[591]); *ROE* p. 67 {speaks of an eventual}

---

wholesale to a more promising site, and the complete control of the lay-out of the fields was so profitable in itself and so essential on all land that was to be cultivated by the monks in person, that it was the habit of the Cistercians, wherever possible, to acquire all rights over a manor or village and then 'reduce it to a grange' by exiling the previous inhabitants and pulling down their cottages. This free, ring-fence or enclosure type of husbandry was throughout the middle ages typical of the Cistercians and other orders modeled upon them. In ways perhaps not foreseen by its originators it decreased overhead costs, simplified administration, economized labour and made possible all the transferences of stock and implements, and all the specialization of production necessary for successful large-scale commercial farming. The Cistercian system of granges articulated upon the home-farm and each developing to the full local advantages, for particular types of produce was, indeed, almost as influential and as efficient an instrument in the rejuvenating of European agrarian life as was the constitutional scheme of the *Carta Caritatis* in renewing religious discipline. In the fertile and ordered, yet spacious and not wholly developed, corn-growing districts north of the Humber the grange as a unit of agriculture stood outside the normal open-field strip-cultivation. Elsewhere, in the midlands, East Anglia and the south, Cistercian husbandry was perhaps less distinctive, particularly when gifts or purchases of land from among normal manors could not be adapted to any grange. Finally, the Welsh abbeys, standing outside any ordered system of cultivation, were usually free to choose sites for plough-land and granges in the open valleys of Carmarthen and Cardigan, or in the straths of Merioneth and Carnarvon. Here, especially in south and west Wales, conditions were favourable to large-scale sheep-farming, in which, indeed, the larger abbeys engaged from the start when they had peace in their borders" (1.64–65).

591. "The pasturing of sheep had always been an integral part of English husbandry. The sheep, indeed, had more uses than any other animal. Besides the wool, which was carded, spun and woven in every village, the ewes gave milk for direct consumption and for cheese-making. . . . The precise moment at which English wool was first grown for export is difficult to mark. . . . There is, however, little evidence of an organized trade or

"breach in the simple economy of Cistercians"[592] {brought about by} *surplus wool*, {the} *need of cash*, {a} *desire to build*; {the presence of} wool merchants at the gate; involvement in business of a greater and greater scope; {establishment of} agencies in towns and abroad; {the} multiplication of distant granges; buying up wool from peasants to add to {a} bulk contract ({the} brothers get it together); "traffic *far too lucrative to be dropped*" (p. 68); contracting for years ahead (really a loan—with interest charged by {the} lowering of price) {n.b. the} mortgaging {of} the abbey of Fountains {in} 1276.[593]

{The} *General Chapter* strives to stop the process:[594] {in} 1157[595] {it} forbids {the} purchase of wool for resale; {in} 1214[596] {it} investigates purchasing of wool for resale by {the} brothers; {in}

---

large-scale sheep-farming for the wool market before the arrival of the Cistercians. Settling as they did away from cultivation and free of the shackling organization of manor and village, with limitless pasture for their sheep on mountain, moor, wold and marsh, with abundant service and an efficient central control, they began very early to have a large surplus from the year's clip which exporters and foreign merchants were willing to buy *en masse* for the looms of the new towns of the continent. They had, at least throughout the twelfth century, heavy advantages over the black monks who in the majority of cases kept their sheep scattered over their manors and exploited by half a dozen different obedientiaries, even if they had not been leased out with the land. The estimation and collection of the crop were therefore alike more difficult, and in fact the black monks did not as a rule deliver their wool graded, as did the Cistercians, but mixed and in bulk. Among the new orders, on the other hand, conditions were ideal for large-scale buying: the woolmonger could ride up to the abbey, learn at once the number and quality of fleeces to be shorn and the probable yield in sacks of wool; he could, if he wished, ride round the sheep-walks and inspect the flocks himself; he could fix the date of delivery, settle the price and cross the moors to the next abbey. The attention of the exporting merchants was thus quickly attracted to the white monks and canons" (1:66–67).

592. Text reads: "of the early Cistercians."
593. See Knowles, *Religious Orders*, 1.68.
594. See Knowles, *Religious Orders*, 1.69.
595. Canivez, *Statuta*, 1.61 (#19).
596. Canivez, *Statuta*, 1.426 (#45).

1181[597] {it} forbids agreements for more than a year ahead—payment {is} to be accepted on delivery; {in} 1277[598] {this provision is} reenacted; {in} 1279[599] {monasteries are} allowed to collect in advance when money {is} needed for debts. *The failure of the great Italian merchant houses at {the} end of {the} thirteenth century put an end to the peak business of the Cistercian monasteries.* (N.B. on the mania for cutting down trees, see ROE, I.74 bottom.[600])

Conclusion: {with} *rising costs {and the} decline of laybrothers' vocations, Cistercians rent their land and live on the revenues.*

Debts:[601] {in} 1186 {the} usurer Aaron of Lincoln dies; nine Cistercian abbeys, including Rievaulx, owe him 6400 marks; n.b. sometimes monasteries accepted gifts of mortgaged land along with {the} mortgage. John Lackland[602] mulcts the Order in England of 24,027 marks; one abbey, Meaux, is fined 1000 marks. Meaux and Waverly had to disband and take refuge in other houses until {a} good year {arrives}.

Decline of the Cistercian Order[603]

1. *Rivalry between abbots of the first four foundations and {the} abbot of Cîteaux* {develops}: (a) before 1152 {the} right of {the} four proto-abbots to visit Cîteaux is *inserted* in {the} *Carta Caritatis*. This

---

597. Canivez, *Statuta*, 1.89 (#10).
598. Canivez, *Statuta*, 3.169 (#30).
599. Canivez, *Statuta*, 3.184 (#2).
600. "The grange of Croo—so named, it would seem, from the most vocal of its tenants—lay in the open, wind-swept country by Beeforth near the sea. Despite its exposed position, it was completely sheltered and hidden by a thick grove of oak and ash and other trees which harboured a large colony of rooks. A certain villein who was administering the grange found the crying and calling of the birds so exasperating that he approached the abbot and obtained permission to deal with the nuisance. His method, effective if drastic, was to fell every stick of timber in the place, so that the farm buildings, now visible from afar, lay open to the four winds. Nothing could more clearly show the complete control exercised by one in charge of a grange of this kind."
601. See Knowles, *Monastic Order*, 353–54.
602. I.e. King John.
603. For this information Merton follows Lekai, *The White Monks*, 55–58.

Cistercian History 109

is "the first sign of an unfortunate rivalry for power" (Lekai[604]); (b) {at the} turn of the twelfth century, {in} 1215, Innocent III suppresses the conflict; (c) {the} 1262 election of James II of Cîteaux {is} contested by Philip of Clairvaux, {with the} intervention of Urban IV and St. Louis not availing; {in} 1264 Philip calls a separate chapter of *his* abbots at Clairvaux; (d) {in} 1265 *Parvus Fons* of Clement IV[605] {is issued} to settle this dispute by CENTRALIZATION; {the} aim {is} to reestablish {the} central authority of {the} General Chapter {by} means {of} restricting {the} rights of visitors, especially in regard to depositions of abbots {and} creating a *definitorium* of 25 abbots—{the} abbot {of} Cîteaux and {the} four proto-abbots, with four {additional members} from each one's foundation; {Clement} *wanted* them {at} first to be elected representatives like {the} Order {of} Preachers—{there was strong} OP influence. {The} result {is that the} *definitorium* actually runs and swings the General Chapter; {it} undermined its prestige and discouraged abbots from attending; (e) {in} 1303—{a sign of} centralization—{the} first reference to a Procurator General in Rome {is made}.

* * * * * * *

Privileges of {the} Cistercian Order[606]

{These were granted} especially as {a} recognition of {the} work of St. Bernard and {the} presence of Cistercian cardinals and {the} general favor shown by {the} hierarchy to the Order:

1. Exemption from episcopal control {was the} work of Eugene III?—{Cistercian} rule and administration could not be touched by outsiders, except {the} Holy See. Exemption {meant

---

604. Lekai, *The White Monks*, 56.

605. *Nomasticon*, 366–76; Canivez, *Statuta*, 3.22–30; for a discussion of this document, see below, pages 189–91.

606. See *Institutiones Capituli Generalis Collectae Annis 1240 et 1256, Distinctio IV*: "*De Privilegiis et Immunitatibus et Indulgentiis Ordinis*" (*Nomasticon*, 300–309); *Liber Antiquarum Definitionum, Distinctio II*: "*De Libertatibus, Privilegiis, Immunitatibus et Indulgentiis*" (*Nomasticon*, 376–94).

that} bishops could not make visitations[607] or preside over {the} election[608] or deposition[609] of abbots, {and} could not excommunicate Cistercians or their familiars (1184)[610] ({this} begins with {the decree of} 1100—{the} *Privilegium Romanum*,[611] made definite in 1132 {and again in} 1184).

2. Exemption from tithes,[612] {granted by} Innocent II {in} 1132,[613] {which} caused {a} struggle; {the} reason {for the exemption was that the} monks shared with {the} poor their surplus. {On} *tithes* first see {the} *Exordium Parvum*;[614] {the} exemption from tithes granted by Innocent II {in} 1132 {was made out of} gratitude to St. Bernard[615] {and a} recognition of {the} labors of {the} Cistercians; {there were} complaints from Cluny {but the} popes support Cîteaux and forbid exaction of tithes under pain of excommunication;[616] Richard Archbishop of Canterbury writes

---

607. See Mahn, *L'Ordre Cistercien*, 97–98.

608. See Mahn, *L'Ordre Cistercien*, 74–75: in 1160 Pope Alexander III makes clear that bishops are not to interfere with abbatial elections, a directive repeated a number of times through the following decades.

609. See Mahn, *L'Ordre Cistercien*, 85; this was also decreed by Alexander III in 1160.

610. See Mahn, *L'Ordre Cistercien*, 80, which dates the prohibition of excommunication of monks to 1184 and of their "serviteurs" to the following year.

611. *Exordium Parvum*, chapter 14 (*Nomasticon*, 61–62).

612. For a detailed discussion of this topic see Mahn, *L'Ordre Cistercien*, part 2, chapter 3: "Les Cisterciens et la Dîme" (102–18).

613. I.e. in the bull *Habitantes in Domo Dei* of February 10, 1132 (PL 179:122–26) (see Mahn, *L'Ordre Cistercien*, 99, 104).

614. "*decimas aliorum hominum . . . abdicaverunt*" ("they renounced the tithes of other men") (*Exordium Parvum*, chapter 15 [*Nomasticon*, 62]).

615. See Canivez, "Cîteaux," col. 902, and Mahn, *L'Ordre Cistercien*, 94; see also King, *Cîteaux*, 26: "The privilege had been granted by Innocent II in the constitution *Habitantes in Domo Dei* in 1132, as a reward for the services of St Bernard in obtaining the overthrow of the anti-pope Anacletus. Opposition to the favour, especially on the part of Cluny, had, however, continued for 20 years."

616. See Mahn, *L'Ordre Cistercien*, 111, citing bulls of Alexander III.

Cistercian History

to {the} General Chapter about 1179 {and with} bitter reproaches says {that the} Order {of} Cîteaux can no longer in conscience refuse to pay tithes;[617] {the} reaction of {the} General Chapter {of} 1180[618] {was to agree to} pay tithes on new lands; {see also} 1190—*de non acquirendo*;[619] {the} Fourth Lateran Council settles it.[620] (N.B. {the} complaints of Alexander III {and the} action of {the} General Chapter {in} 1175-1182.[621])

3. {The Order receives the} privilege of celebrating {the} office in spite of {a} local interdict {in} 1152.[622]

4. {The} privilege for abbots to exercise their function without episcopal benediction if {a} bishop refuses unduly {is granted in} 1165 (provided they are priests).[623]

5. Exemption from excommunication by bishops {is given in} 1184.[624]

---

617. PL 207:252–55; see Mahn, *L'Ordre Cistercien*, 110, which says the letter is addressed to the abbot of Cîteaux rather than the General Chapter.

618. See Mahn, *L'Ordre Cistercien*, 111; Canivez, *Statuta*, 1.86–87 (#1).

619. "on not acquiring [property]" (Canivez, *Statuta*, 1.117–18 [#1]); the Order decided that no new purchases of land would be allowed; only pure and simple donations of land would be accepted (see Canivez, "Cîteaux," col. 920; Mahn, *L'Ordre Cistercien*, 111).

620. In canon 55, this council of 1215 restricted the exemption of the Order from tithes to lands acquired before the council and to lands newly brought under cultivation, whether in the past or the future (see Mahn, *L'Ordre Cistercien*, 112–13, 115).

621. See Mahn, *L'Ordre Cistercien*, 111: Alexander warns the Cistercians of the danger to their reputation of taking undue advantage of their privileges and exemptions, which leads to the voluntary limitations of the rights of the Order on the part of the General Chapter.

622. See Canivez, "Cîteaux," col. 903; Mahn, *L'Ordre Cistercien*, 94, 137; King, *Cîteaux*, 26, n. 5 (which refers to a "general interdict"), and *Nomasticon*, 300.

623. See Canivez, "Cîteaux," col. 903, and Mahn, *L'Ordre Cistercien*, 76–79, for the development of this provision; see also King, *Cîteaux*, 28.

624. See Canivez, "Cîteaux," col. 904; Mahn, *L'Ordre Cistercien*, 138, 148–49; King, *Cîteaux*, 30 (the pope was Lucius III).

6. {The} privilege of *Nominal Mention* {of} 1169 {meant that} no law from Rome affects Cistercians unless {they are} expressly named.[625]

(N.B. Innocent III personally composed the *orationes* used still today in {the} Mass of St. Bernard[626]).

7. Exemption from special expensive receptions of papal legates etc., {in favor of} ordinary hospitality, {is granted by} Honorius III.[627]

({In} 1245 bishops at {the} Council of Lyons try to get Cistercian privileges revoked {but} Innocent IV upholds them.[628])

8. Monks presented for ordination are exempt from episcopal examination {in a decree of} 1245.[629]

(Encouragement and support of the College of St. Bernard {is given} by Innocent IV.[630])

625. See Canivez, "Cîteaux," col. 904; Mahn, *L'Ordre Cistercien*, 156.
626. See Canivez, "Cîteaux," col. 934; King, *Cîteaux*, 246.
627. See Canivez, "Cîteaux," col. 935; Mahn, *L'Ordre Cistercien*, 157.
628. See Canivez, "Cîteaux," col. 938: "Au cours d'une des sessions conciliares, certains évêques, et notamment Robert Grossetête, avaient demandé de réduire les privilèges et les immunités de l'ordre de Cîteaux. Le pape maintint les moines dans leur ancienne position juridique" ("In the course of one of the sessions of the council, certain bishops, Robert Grosseteste in particular, had requested the reduction of the privileges and exemptions of the Order of Cîteaux. The pope kept the monks in their old legal position"). See also Schroeder, 321–22 (First Council of Lyons: second series, canon 6), which specifies that "Those exempt may in the matter of transgressions in non-exempt localities be summoned before the local ordinaries; in exempt localities, not. Over monasteries enjoying immunity against interdict, suspension, and excommunication, ordinaries in these matters have no jurisdiction, unless monks of such monasteries are sent to priories subject to the ordinaries."
629. See Canivez, "Cîteaux," col. 938; see also Mahn, *L'Ordre Cistercien*, 93, which indicates that Pope Innocent IV restricted episcopal inquiry concerning monastic ordinands to two points—whether they had committed an egregious offence (*"notorium crimen"*) and whether they were subject to a major vice of the flesh (*"enorme corporis vitium"*).
630. See Canivez, "Cîteaux," cols. 938–39; see also King, *Cîteaux*, 271: "Pope Innocent IV in the bull *Virtutum intenta* (January 5, 1245) approved

9. {An} abbot can confer minor orders on his subjects {according to a decree of} 1260[631] (major orders? not Cîteaux[632]); {In} 1265 *Parvus Fons* {mandates a} governmental reform of {the} Order;[633] {in} 1312 Cîteaux fights successfully for privileges of *all* regulars.[634]

10. Mendicants entering {the} Order {of} Cîteaux were to be deprived of {a} vote and {were} ineligible {to act} as superiors ({this ban} lasted until 1917).[635]

11. {From} 1474, Cistercian confessors have {the} privilege of absolving from censures reserved to bishops (not *ab homine*[636]).

* * * * * * *

Dialogus:[637] {The} Account of {the} Foundation of Cîteaux in {the} *Dialogus* (1593):

---

the venture. . . . A further bull, *Diligentiae studio contemplantes* (September 4, 1245), sought to put pressure on the general chapter, which had been incensed at not being consulted about the establishment of the college."

631. See Canivez, "Cîteaux," col. 939; King, *Cîteaux*, 41–42, 274 (the pope was Alexander IV, on the recommendation of the Cardinal John of Toledo, a Cistercian).

632. According to King (*Cîteaux*, 64–65, 131), the bull *Exposcit* of Pope Innocent VIII (1489) gave to the abbot of Cîteaux the right to ordain any member of the Order to the subdiaconate and diaconate, and to the four "first fathers" (the abbots of La Ferté, Pontigny, Clairvaux and Morimond) the same right with respect to religious of their own filiations.

633. See Canivez, "Cîteaux," col. 950; Mahn, *L'Ordre Cistercien*, 234–38.

634. See Canivez, "Cîteaux," col. 961; the occasion was the Council of Vienne.

635. See Canivez, "Cîteaux," col. 961; the change came with the promulgation of the 1917 Code of Canon Law.

636. "by a person": i.e. a censure made by an ecclesiastical superior against a particular person (as distinguished from a censure *"a jure"*: according to a general law).

637. *Dialogus inter Cluniacensem Monachum et Cisterciensem de Diversis Utriusque Ordinis Observantiis* (*Dialogue between a Cluniac Monk and a Cistercian about the Differing Observances of Each Order*), in *Thesaurus Novum Anecdotorum*, ed. Edmond Martène and Ursinus Durand, 5 vols. (Paris: Lutetiae

1. {A} fervent minority at Molesme *Dei gratia adspiratione de transgressione regulae . . . loquebantur, conquerebantur, contristabantur, videntes se . . . hanc regulam solemni professione servaturos promississe* eamque minime custodisse et ob hoc periurii crimen scienter incurisse (1593).[638]

2. {They} got {the} permission of {the} Holy See to come *"'ad hanc solitudinem,' ut professionem suam observantia sanctae regulae adimplerent, veniebant."*[639]

3. They arrange their life according to {the} *Rule*, rejecting *"quidquid Regulae refragabatur."*[640] Here follows {a} long word-for-word quote from {the} *Exordium Parvum*.[641]

* * * * * * *

Cîteaux and Cluny in {the} Twelfth Century:

1. The conflict was *real* but must not be exaggerated (cf. Protestants and Catholics—{a} disgraceful schism in {the} family of St. Benedict): (a) in certain quarters {there was} a very hot divergence over *observance*; (b) in other quarters {it was a

---

Parisiorum, 1717), 5.1569–1654. Merton would have been familiar with the *Dialogus* from the article by Watkin Williams in his *Monastic Studies*, "A Dialogue between a Cluniac and a Cistercian" (61–74). For a contemporary translation, which includes a substantial introduction identifying the author and providing the context of the work, see Idung of Prüfening, *Cistercians and Cluniacs: The Case for Cîteaux*, trans. Jeremiah F. O'Sullivan, CF 33 (Kalamazoo, MI: Cistercian Publications, 1977).

638. "Inspired by the grace of God concerning the violation of the Rule, they spoke, they complained, they lamented, seeing themselves as having promised by their solemn profession to keep this Rule, as having observed it to a minimal extent and as having knowingly committed the crime of perjury because of this" (text reads: "*adspirati*").

639. "they came to this solitude, in order to fulfill their profession by observance of the holy rule."

640. "whatever was contrary to the Rule" (text reads: "*quicquid*") (*Exordium Parvum*, chapter 15 [*Nomasticon*, 62]).

641. *Exordium Parvum*, chapter 15 (*Nomasticon*, 62–63), the so-called "*Instituta* of St. Alberic."

matter of} *political* and *economic* conflict: {e.g.} Gigny {and} le Miroir,[642] {the} Bishop of Langres election;[643] (c) in others, {it was a question of} mere *local jealousies*: cf. {the} problem of Robert, Bernard's cousin;[644] all these must not be lumped together and made a "great issue" in which one must take sides, "stand up and be counted": (d) {the} personal divergence between Peter the Venerable and St. Bernard brings out "profound aspects of their personalities" (Dom Leclercq[645]): Peter {the} Venerable {is} more urbane, {marked by} human understanding, peace, charity; St. Bernard {is} more aggressive, powerful, carried away by burning zeal, passionate, {with a} single-minded attachment to his ideal. *Note* {however the} *fraternal affection* of these saints and {of} many others of both orders.

{The} VALUE of {the} controversy {is that it} focused on important issues {and} helped {the} Order {of} Saint Benedict to revaluate some points {and} helped {the} Order {of} Cîteaux to be more humble.

642. Because the Cluniac Abbey of Gigny had lost revenue from tithes from the Cistercian abbey of Miroir, now exempted by the pope from paying them, some of the Gigny monks invaded Miroir and did extensive damage, for which they were ordered to pay compensation (see Saint Bernard's letter to Pope Eugenius [*Letters*, 429–30 (#353); PL 182:489B–490A (#283)]).

643. See James, *Letters*, 249–59 [##179–86] (PL 182:322A–331C [##164–70; the letter to Umbald, #184, does not appear in Migne]) with a detailed headnote concerning this disputed election, in which Geoffrey de la Roche, Saint Bernard's prior at Clairvaux, was eventually consecrated in October 1138.

644. James, *Letters*, 1–10; PL 182:67D–79C; for a discussion of this letter, in which Bernard begs his cousin Robert to return to Clairvaux from Cluny, see Thomas Merton, *The Cistercian Fathers and Their Monastic Theology: Initiation into the Monastic Tradition* 8, ed. Patrick F. O'Connell, MW 42 (Collegeville, MN: Cistercian Publications, 2016), 126–33.

645. Leclercq provides an extensive discussion of the relationship between Saint Bernard and Peter the Venerable in "La Rencontre des Saints," chapter 5 of *Pierre le Vénérable* (67–87), but the precise French equivalent of this phrase is not found there or elsewhere in the volume.

2. *Critics of Cîteaux*: *Peter the Venerable* (a) REPLIES to Cistercian attacks; (b) lays down {a} basic distinction, adopted by St. Bernard and now {the} common teaching of theologians, between ESSENTIALS of observance which cannot change, and ACCIDENTALS which can; *Abelard* {raises} mostly liturgical questions {and} points out anomalies: v.g. {the use of} Ambrosian hymns every day;[646] *Rupert of Deutz*[647] {notes} further liturgical anomalies, {the} dubious color of {the} habit,[648] lack of daily Mass in {the time of} harvest, etc.;[649] *Hugh of Amiens* defends OSB "humanism."[650]
Cîteaux and Cluny

Letter 221 (among {the} letters of St. Bernard) of Peter {the} Venerable[651] laments that those who have in common their Christian faith and their monastic profession should be *divided by dissension*—this is diabolical. {He notes} the absurdity of bickering over diversities of observance. There must be diversities of customs in the Church; for instance he finds no reason for discord between East and West in {the} fact that leavened and unleavened

---

646. See Abelard, *Epistola* 10 (to Bernard, ca. 1131), PL 178:335B–340D.

647. See Rupert of Deutz, *Super Quaedam Capitula Regulae Divi Benedicti Abbatis*, PL 170:477–538; for an extensive discussion of Rupert and the Cistercians, see Van Engen, 314–23: "Defender of the Black Monks 3. Ministry at the Altar: Rupert against the New Monks."

648. Rupert, *Super Quaedam Capitula*, 3.13 (PL 170:520D–522A).

649. Rupert, *Super Quaedam Capitula*, 3.10 (PL 170:517D–518C).

650. For Hugh's treatise, see André Wilmart, "Une Riposte de l'Ancien Monachisme au Manifeste de Saint Bernard," *Revue Bénédictine* 46 (1934): 296–344; the attribution to Hugh is challenged by Jean de la Croix Bouton, "Bernard et l'Ordre de Cluny," *Bernard de Clairvaux*, Commission d'Histoire de l'Ordre de Cîteaux (Paris: Éditions Alsatia, 1953), 193–217; it is supported by C. H. Talbot in "The Date and Author of the 'Riposte,'" in *Petrus Venerabilis, 1156–1956: Studies and Texts Commemorating the Eighth Centenary of His Death*, ed. Giles Constable and James Kritzeck (Rome: Herder, 1956), 72–80.

651. PL 182:398B–416D; the same letter is included among Peter's own correspondence in PL 189:321A–344A (*Epistola* 2.17); for a discussion of this and Peter's earlier letter to Saint Bernard on Cluniac and Cistercian observances, see Merton, *Cistercian Fathers and Their Monastic Theology*, 134–39.

bread are used. Different interpretations of the *Rule* are perfectly legitimate—"many roads leading to the same end."[652] Why get angry if another order follows a different path? {The} *principle* {should be}: let each abbot arrange all things so that souls may be saved, and let the brethren not murmur (*Rule*, c. 41[653]). What matters is the *simplex oculus*[654] of faith and pure intention and *sincere charity*. Then the disputed questions are brought up (col. 406)—all are more or less indifferent to Peter {the} Venerable: (1) a year's novitiate? Cîteaux: yes; Cluny: no; (2) clothing (furs—with reason, why not?) {the} black monks {are} laughing at {the} white as if {at} a monster or {a} centaur; (3) Cîteaux receives back fugitives *only* three times, Cluny more; (4) fasting: Peter {the} Venerable reproves Cistercians for fasting during {the} Christmas holidays; (5) manual labor; (6) reception of all guests according to {the} *Rule*[655] (Cîteaux: yes, Cluny: no); (7) {the} abbot's table (Cluny has given it up).

{A} *distinction* {is made} between commands of {the} *Rule* that are necessary for charity and cannot be changed and those which for charity's sake *can* be changed. The true monk is he who in all things seeks charity. (Bernard agrees on this principle {in} *De Praecepto* {et} *Dispensatione*.[656]) Those who wound charity for {the} sake of black or white habits are absurd and blameworthy and {act} against {the} *Rule*, which says the monks are not to

---

652. "*Quid plane refert, quid obest, si vario tramite ad eamdem regionem, si multiplici via ad eamdem vitam, si multiplici itinere ad eamdem, quae sursum est*" ("What does it really matter, what is the harm, if one goes by a different path to the same region, if by a diverse way to the same life, if by a varied route to the same goal that is above?") (PL 182:404CD; PL 189:327B).

653. McCann, *The Rule*, 98.

654. "*Si oculus tuus fuerit simplex, totum corpus tuum lucidum erit*" ("If thy eye be single, thy whole body will be lightsome" [Luke 11:34]) (PL 182:405C; PL 189:328A); Peter repeatedly uses this image to distinguish between essentials of the Rule and customs that are matters of prudence and charity (PL 182:405C–408C; PL 189:328A–331A).

655. Rule, chapter 53 (McCann, *The Rule*, 119–23).

656. PL 182:859D–894C; for a discussion see Merton, *Cistercian Fathers and Their Monastic Theology*, 214–24.

worry about {the} color of {their} habit.[657] However he adds that *he* prefers {the} black habit as penitential and humble, {the} white as signifying glory. The *true cause* of dissension {is the} jealousy of {the} black monks at {the} success of Cîteaux, {as well as the} vanity of Cistercians at their popularity. Let us imitate {the} humility of Christ.

* * * * * * *

Cistercian Nuns[658]

{For} antiquity {there is a} lack of material (cf. double monasteries—Fontevrault;[659] St. Gilbert {of} Sempringham[660]).

1. *Molesme* and *Jully*: St. Robert had nuns under his direction; mostly *wives* of husbands who had entered {the} monastery. {They} lived in separate cottages, not in a cloister. His successor was thinking of disbanding them when several wives of men entering Cîteaux with Bernard presented themselves. {In} 1113 Miles of Bar hands over {the} castle of Jully for {the} nuns ({was} St. Bernard influential in this?). {The} nuns lived on dowries, labor and alms; {they had an} austere observance. Pierce, or Pron, {was} one of four monks of Molesme in charge of these nuns; a claustral prior {was} designated by {the} abbot of Molesme {and} assisted the prioress. {The} first prioress {was} Elizabeth, wife of Bernard's brother Guy. {The} community {was} limited to seventy

---

657. Rule, chap. 55 (McCann, *The Rule*, 125).

658. Merton relies principally in this section on Bouton, *Histoire*.

659. See Lekai, *The White Monks*, 13: "Robert of Arbrissel founded c. 1100 a community on the model of the Apostolic Church at Fontevrault in Anjou. A phenomenal success, it became a fully organized order with three groups of members—the contemplative nuns, the lay sisters, and priests who served as chaplains. The abbess of Fontevrault had jurisdiction over the whole organization"; see also Knowles, *Monastic Order*, 204.

660. See Lekai, *The White Monks*, 14: "Direct Cistercian influence was working in England in the reform of Gilbert of Sempringham, involving communities for both men and women. In 1147, the founder himself proposed the fusion of his growing congregation with the Cistercians. Cîteaux, however, opposed to the establishment of any legal connection with convents, declined the offer"; see also Knowles, *Monastic Order*, 205–7.

nuns and four laysisters. *Humbeline* enters here {and} becomes {the} second prioress about 1128.[661]

2. Tart[662] {was} founded about 1120 (Tartum), {a} special project of St. Stephen Harding; {it was} founded by nuns from Jully (n.b. not Humbeline or other sisters of Cistercians?). {It followed} Cistercian observances.

3. *Foundations*[663] {of} various kinds {were subsequently made}: (a) {those} founded by a Cistercian abbot—v.g. Belfays—from Morimond; (b) {those} founded directly by Tart—v.g. Belmont (1127); (c) {those} taken under {the} protection of an abbot of {the} Order, *in spiritualibus*[664] (*temporarily* in {the} Order).

3a. {*General*} *Chapters* {tried to deal with the} situation, {which was} confused and irregular, {with} varying degrees of observance. {In} 1187, *Las Huelgas* (Burgos) {was} founded by Alfonso VIII of Castile. {In} 1189 {the} first General Chapter of abbesses of Castile and Leon {was held}.[665] {In} 1188 *St. Sacerdos*, formerly abbot of Huerta and Bishop of Siguenza,[666] obtains {the} permission of {the} General Chapter[667] {for this} and was present at {the} first meeting.[668] {In} 1191 {the} General Chapter refuses to *oblige* {the} abbesses of Castile and Leon to attend but *urges* them to.[669] *This led to assemblies of French abbesses at Tart*—annually, {on the} Feast of St. Michael, under {the} presidency of {the} abbot of Cîteaux.[670] {In} 1199 Las Huelgas {was} placed under {the} direct control of Cîteaux and {its} immediate daughter house of Tart; then {a} chapter of Las Huelgas {was held} on {the} eleventh {of}

661. See Bouton, *Histoire*, 118.
662. See Bouton, *Histoire*, 121.
663. See Bouton, *Histoire*, 121.
664. "in spiritual matters," i.e. not juridically connected to the Order.
665. See Bouton, *Histoire*, 122.
666. Popular name of St. Martin Mãnoz y Finojosa (1139–1210); for a brief biographical sketch, see Merton, *Valley of Wormwood*, 164–66.
667. Manrique, *Cisterciensium*, 3.218; see King, *Cîteaux*, 33, n. 3 (not found in Canivez, *Statuta*).
668. See Bouton, *Histoire*, 122.
669. Canivez, *Statuta*, 1.139 (#7).
670. See Bouton, *Histoire*, 122–23.

November with all {the} Spanish abbots present.[671] {In} 1192,[672] abbots of Spain {were given a} penance for traveling with abbesses.

4. *Benedictines and Cistercians?*[673] {There were} cases of convents which *did not know their status*; Malquet (Paderborn) wanted to find out if they were {under} Cluny or Cîteaux; *Meissen* {has} six charters {that} say {they are subject to the} Order {of} Cîteaux, twelve charters {that} say {the} Order {of} Saint Benedict, but {they} refused a Cistercian visitor {and} thenceforth {were} recognized as OSB. {A major} *reason* {for this confusion was that} many convents adopted {the} usages and habit of Cîteaux without being admitted juridically to the Order. *Helfta* {is} a case in point. The saints of Helfta (St. Gertrude {the} Great[674] and St. Gertrude of Hackborn, St. Mechtilde of Hackborn[675] {and} St. Mechtilde of Magdeburg) {exemplify the} difference in {the} mysticism of thirteenth-century nuns and twelfth-century men: visions, affectivity ({devotion to the} Sacred Heart) {and} Eucharistic {piety characterize the women}. Other Cistercian nun saints {include, in} *Flanders*: St. Lutgarde,[676] Bl. Aleth,[677] {the} three Idas;[678] {in}

---

671. See Bouton, *Histoire*, 123.

672. 1192:6 (Canivez, *Statuta*, 1.147); see Merton, *Charter, Customs, Constitutions*, 44 for details.

673. See Bouton, *Histoire*, 44.

674. For a brief biographical sketch of Saint Gertrude (1256–ca. 1302), see Merton, *Valley of Wormwood*, 401–11.

675. For a brief biographical sketch of Saint Mechtilde of Hackborn (b.1241), see Merton, *Valley of Wormwood*, 412–17.

676. In addition to his brief biographical sketch of Saint Lugarde (d. 1246) in Merton, *Valley of Wormwood*, 213–29, see the full-length biography: Thomas Merton, *What Are These Wounds? The Life of a Cistercian Mystic, Saint Lutgarde of Aywières* (Milwaukee: Bruce, 1950).

677. The reference here is not to the mother of Saint Bernard but to Bl. Aleyde of Scharbeek (d. 1250), who suffered from leprosy for most of her adult life; for a brief biographical sketch, see Merton, *Valley of Wormwood*, 204–9.

678. For brief biographical sketches of Bl. Ida of Louvain (d. ca. 1300), Bl. Ida of Leeuwen (d. 1260), and Bl. Ida of Nivelles (d. 1231), see Merton, *Valley of Wormwood*, 131–37, 380–87, 424–30.

Portugal: Sts. Theresa, Sancha, Mafalda;[679] cf. {also} St. Hedwig[680] ({at} Trebnitz).

* * * * * * *

St. Stephen Harding (Archdale King[681]—his source: William of Malmesbury [see *PL* 179, col. 1287[682]]; {for the} writings of St. Stephen Harding, see Migne, *PL* 166[683]). {He was} born in England {and was a} Benedictine "oblate" {{according to} Archdale King[684]) at Sherborne. {He} went to Scotia—Ireland or Scotland? William of Malmesbury says Hibernia for Ireland {and} does not say *transfretavit*[685] (Archdale King[686]). {In} 1088 (?) {he makes a} pilgrimage to Rome; on {his} return {he} enters Molesme {and} joined {the} "reforming party."[687] {In} 1108 {he} becomes Abbot {of Cîteaux}, after Alberic. {The community endures} great poverty; {it is} starving at Pentecost {but is} "miraculously" fed ({see the}

---

679. The three daughters of King Sancho I of Portugal, all of whom became Cistercian nuns; for brief biographical sketches of Sancha (d. 1229), Mafalda (d. 1252) and Teresa (d. 1250), see Merton, *Valley of Wormwood*, 101–5, 159–61, 230–36.

680. Never officially a member of the Order because she retained title to her property as Duchess of Silesia in order to use it for the poor, Saint Hedwig (ca. 1174–1243) founded the monastery of Trebnitz and lived there the same life as the nuns; for a brief biographical sketch, see Merton, *Valley of Wormwood*, 357–62.

681. King, *Cîteaux*, 11–22.

682. William is the source for King's information on Stephen's youth in England in particular (see 12, n. 3).

683. For a discussion of Stephen's authentic and spurious writings, see above, pages 64–65.

684. King, *Cîteaux*, 12.

685. "he crossed the sea."

686. King, *Cîteaux*, 12, n. 3.

687. King, *Cîteaux*, 12.

Exordium Magnum, I.18[688]); {N.B. the} *apparition of the monk* {and his} prophecy of vocations (*Exordium Magnum*, I.16[689]).
{In} 1112, {at} Easter, {comes the} arrival of St. Bernard and {his} thirty companions. {In} 1113 {comes the first foundation}, *La Ferté*. {In} 1119 {Stephen} presents {the} *Exordium* and *Carta Caritatis* to Callistus II at Saulieu (Callistus had been {a} friend of Cîteaux as Bishop of Vienne, and wanted his heart buried there [1124][690]). Callistus II approves {the} *Carta Caritatis* {on} December 23, 1119—twelve abbeys had now been founded ({for the} *Carta*—see *Collectanea* 1954 #1;[691] {the} earliest manuscript, {dating from} 1194, {is} from Cîteaux, {now} at Dijon;[692] {the text} was divided into chapters in 1201[693]—{it} was to be read each year in chapter; {see also} Bouton, "*Negotia Ordinis*," in *Bernard de Clairvaux*, p. 180[694]). {The} *Consuetudines* {are} also by St. Stephen;

---

688. PL 185:1014D–1015A (Griesser, ed., *Exordium*, 83 [1.25]); the use of the chapter numbers from the Migne edition indicates that this was written before the critical edition of Griesser had been published [1961]); see above, n. 436.

689. PL 185:1012C–1014D (Griesser, ed., *Exordium*, 80–82 [1.22]); see above, n. 434.

690. See King, *Cîteaux*, 20.

691. Lefèvre, "La Véritable Carta Caritatis," cited by King, *Cîteaux*, 14, n. 2.

692. So Philippe Guignard, ed., *Les Monuments Primitifs de la Règle Cistercienne* (Dijon: Imprimerie Darantière, 1878), lxx, cited by King, *Cîteaux*, 13, n. 5.

693. See King, *Cîteaux*, 13, who proposes this date to coincide with the direction of the General Chapter that the *Carta* be read in sequence over the course of a week at the daily chapter (Canivez, 1.265 [1201:9]).

694. Jean de la Croix Bouton, "Negotia Ordinis," Commission d'Histoire de l'Ordre de Cîteaux, *Bernard de Clairvaux* (Paris: Éditions Alsatia, 1953), 172–82; the reference in King, 15, n. 1, is to Bouton's enumeration of the successive bulls of Eugenius III (1152), Anastasius IV (1153), Adrian IV (1157) and Alexander III (1165) that were issued to confirm the various slightly modified versions of the *Carta Caritatis* as it evolved into the final form that became the definitive text.

{on the} *revision of {the} Vulgate* see Archdale King, p. 16 (*PL* 166.1373-76[695]). {Cistercian} bibliographical asceticism {was} not due to Stephen but to *Bernard*—{it} dates from 1125 {with the writing of the} *Apologia*;[696] Stephen's breviary, {from} 1130, still has pictures.[697] {In} 1133, Stephen, nearly blind, resigns. {On} March 28, 1134, Stephen dies; {his} feast, {of} twelve lessons, {was} first observed in 1623; {in} 1628, {a feast with} *sermo* {was established and in} 1683 {a feast} with octave.[698]

{The initial} *foundations of Cîteaux* {include}: 1113—*La Ferté*; 1114—*Pontigny*, a hermitage twelve miles from Auxerre {that was} taken over by Stephen Harding {on} May 31, {with} Hugh of Mâcon {as} superior (one of Bernard's companions);[699] 1115—*Clairvaux* (June 25) {with} St. Bernard, his brothers, Gerard, Guy, Bartholomew {and} Andrew, and {also his} uncle Gaudry {and his} cousin Geoffrey de la Roche; later Tescelin and Nivard {also came} ({for a} description {see} Archdale King, 213;[700] read {the}

---

695. "*Censura de Locis Bibliorum.*"

696. PL 182:895D–918A (see King, *Cîteaux*, 17); for an extensive discussion of this text see Merton, *Cistercian Fathers and Their Monastic Theology*, 141–56.

697. See King, *Cîteaux*, 18.

698. King, *Cîteaux*, 21–22. On these distinctions see Lekai, *The White Monks*, 174: "During the course of the twelfth century feasts were ranked according to the manner in which they were observed. Thus, some of the feasts (originally about 20) were celebrated with two official Masses, which were later called 'Feasts of Two Masses' (*Festum Duarum Missarum*). On the greatest festivities the abbot delivered a sermon in the chapter hall, consequently these became distinguished as 'Feasts of Sermon' (*Festum Sermonis*), while the remaining simple feasts were known as 'Feasts of Twelve Lections' (*Festum Duodecim Lectionum*)."

699. See King, *Cîteaux*, 149.

700. "The *monasterium vetus* was of the simplest character. The building had two floors: on the ground floor were the refectory and the kitchen; on the upper floor, the dormitory, which was reached by a ladder. To the southwest lay the chapel [which] had two doors, both on the east side, the one leading from the ladder to the dormitory, the other from the outside. The simple furnishings included three altars: the high altar dedicated to our Lady, an altar on the left, between the two doors, to St Benedict, and one in

letter of Peter de Roya[701]); 1115—*Morimond*, on {the} site of another hermitage (July 11), {in a} narrow valley in {a} marshy forest (*Moiremont*); {there was} a line through {the} refectory {that} divided France and Lorraine; {the monks} prayed in France and ate in Germany; Abbot *Arnold* entered Cîteaux with St. Bernard {in} 1112; {he was} German {and made} foundations in Germany and Poland; {he} leaves {in} 1125 (*see {the} letter of St. Bernard*[702]). {From} Cîteaux[703] {there were} 28 foundations; {from} La Ferté, five foundations (Italy); {from} Pontigny, 16 foundations; {from}

---

the south-east corner to St Laurence. . . . The floor of the refectory was the bare earth; while the beds of the community consisted of rough wooden enclosures on the floor, made of four planks, about six feet by three in area and strewn with straw or dry leaves. At the top of the ladder were two small cells which served as the abbatial apartment and the guest room. The single seat in the abbot's cell was a ledge in the wall under the slant of the roof, too low to admit the raising of the head when seated, while the bed consisted of a framework of planks, with a block of wood for a pillow."

701. "Although Clairvaux is in appearance situated in a valley, its foundations are upon the holy hills, whose gates the Lord loves more than all the dwellings of Jacob. . . . They (the religious) eat and drink reverently the other gifts of God which are set before them: no exquisite delicacies, but that which they have cultivated with their own hands; vegetables and pulse. Their drink is a kind of beer; if this is wanting, they use plain water instead. Wine they seldom use; and then mixed with much water" (King, *Cîteaux*, 214–15; the full letter is found in PL 182:710–12); at the time of writing Peter de Roya was a novice at Clairvaux.

702. PL 182:89B–91C (#4) (James, *Letters*, 19–22 [#4]).

703. In the typescript the five first houses are arranged in a cross, with Cîteaux in the center, La Ferté below, Pontigny to the left, Clairvaux above, and Morimond to the right, representing the geographical arrangement of the houses; see King, *Cîteaux*, 329: "In relation to the Cistercian centre of unity (Cîteaux), the four premier houses were situated at the four cardinal points within a radius of 100 kilometres—La Ferté to the south, Pontigny to the west, Clairvaux to the north, and Morimond to the east. The disposition is interesting, although it can hardly have been the outcome of any deliberate policy." In the upper right quadrant of this arrangement there is also a cryptic note: "59" or "to 9" followed by an indecipherable abbreviation, with an arrow beneath it.

Clairvaux, 80 foundations (Belgium, England, Sweden, Denmark, Italy, Spain); {from} Morimond, 30 foundations.[704]

****

{For} St. Ailred,[705] {see the} story of {his} life at Hexham[706] {and at the} court of David,[707] his "conversion" to Rievaulx (read

---

704. For these numbers see King, *Cîteaux*, 121. The total for Morimond is apparently somewhat uncertain: King says "29 or 30" here, and "about 30 daughters" later (*Cîteaux*, 339), but lists 27 specific foundations (333); Wulf, *Compendium*, 71–72, drawing on Leopold Janauschek, *Der Cistercienser-Orden: Historische Skizze* (Brünn: Benedictiner-Buchdruckerei, 1884), 11, provides numbers of direct filiations of all five of the earliest abbeys, identical with these except for those of Morimond, which number 28 in this accounting.

705. For Merton on Aelred (1110–1167), see Thomas Merton, "St Aelred of Rievaulx and the Cistercians," ed. Patrick Hart, *Cistercian Studies* 20, no. 3 (1985): 212–23; 21, no. 1 (1986): 30–42; 22, no. 1 (1987): 55–75; 23, no. 1 (1988): 45–62; 24, no. 1 (1989): 50–68; *Cistercian Fathers and Forefathers*, 253–400, which also includes transcriptions of two conferences and a book introduction.

706. "Ailred of Rievaulx came of one of the few Saxon Christian families that still gave priests to the Church in Yorkshire in the darkest ages. In that outlying wilderness, Church discipline was not very strictly observed because it was mostly unknown, and Ailred's father Eilaf was a hereditary priest, the scion of a long line of priests who sound rather more like the Old Testament than the New. His benefice was the ruined abbey of Hexham. He lived in the gutted buildings, half of which were unroofed so that the rain was washing the old frescoes off the walls and grass had overgrown the shrines of the Saxon saints. Ailred was probably born at Hexham in 1110, and is supposed, in his childhood, to have manifested some of the precocious signs of future sanctity which abound in the medieval *Vitae Sanctorum*" (*Cistercian Fathers and Forefathers*, 279–80).

707. "Ailred . . . went off to the Court of Prince David at Edinburgh when he was about fourteen. It was a good place for a young man of his talents to seek training and a career. . . . David himself came to the throne of Scotland about the time Ailred entered his household, and the young boy grew up with the King's son and his stepson, Waldef. With the latter in particular he formed ties of the most intimate friendship. . . . Waldef was more retiring than Ailred and was the first to leave for the cloister, when he travelled south and entered the monastery of Austin Canons at Nostell, Yorkshire, in 1130. Ailred was

from {the} life⁷⁰⁸). His character {was marked by} tenderness,

---

twenty years old at the time, and he seems to have been concentrating with single-minded purpose on a court career so that when Waldef went off to the monastery it disturbed and upset his own soul and made him begin to wonder if he, too, belonged in the cloister. At the moment, however, everything pointed to a prominent position at the court. He was already Seneschal, which meant that he had a busy and important post as *major domo* in the King's palace. It was not necessarily a job that gave full scope to his intellectual talents, but nevertheless there was a strong active and practical side to his nature which found some satisfaction in managing the royal household. It meant that he had his fingers on the pulse of court life and perhaps also that he had something to do with the actual tempo of that life. Since he was an intensely sociable person, vivacious and friendly and steeped in the enthusiasm for that 'courtly' living which marked the spirit of the time, he probably found no little satisfaction in his position as Seneschal. There was, in fact, no reason why he should not have been intensely happy—except that he was one of those fortunate people who are incapable of deluding themselves that they find happiness in the prosperity and pleasures of the world" (*Cistercian Fathers and Forefathers*, 280–81).

708. "Shortly afterwards he was in the neighbourhood of the city of York where he was come on business to the archbishop of the diocese. By a happy chance he heard tell, from a close friend of his, how, two years or more before, certain monks had come to England from across the sea, wonderful men, famous adepts in the religious life, white monks by name and white also in vesture. . . . They set up their huts near Helmsley, the central manor of their protector, Walter Espec, a very notable man and one of the leading barons of King Henry I. The spot was by a powerful stream called the Rie in a broad valley stretching on either side. The name of their little settlement and of the place where it lies was derived from the name of the stream and the valley, Rievaulx. . . . Such was the story—and a true story—which Ailred was told by his friend. At this point he exclaimed, 'And where, oh where, is the way to those angelic men, to these heavenly places?' 'Don't be disturbed,' said his friend, 'they are close to you, and you know it not. You have only to ask and they can easily be found.' He replied, 'O, how greatly do I desire, how ardently I thirst for the sight of them, and to see for myself what you have told me about that happy place.' 'Go thither,' returned the other, 'but seek first the leave of the archbishop and receive his blessing, and, if you wish, God will satisfy your desire before the sun sets.' Carried away by eager desire for the things to come he hurries to the prelate, obtains

his leave and blessing, rushes back to his lodging, mounts his horse, does not stop to go in, and, with the hastiest of farewells to his hosts, speeds his mount he knows not where. But his informant makes him follow behind and, spurring their horses to a gallop, they reach before nightfall the castle of Helmsley, two miles from Rievaulx. There the lord, Walter Espec, the founder of the abbey, gave them a triumphant welcome. They spent the night with him very happily, and as he told him still more about the life of the monks Ailred's spirit burned more and more with inexpressible joy. Next morning the lord Walter, accompanied by a few people of the vicinity, goes with him to the monks. Ailred meets the prior, the guestmaster and the keeper of the gate. They take the young man to prayers, his face washed with tears, his heart consumed in humble confession to his Lord. After prayers they preach the word of God. The power of their talk of spiritual things is almost too great for him to bear. He gives full vent to the outpourings of his breast; the fountain of his tears gushes forth like a deluge flooding the earth. His heart of flesh was so full of pious affections and moist with the dew of continual mercies, that it was easier to refuse a smile at urbane jests and honest pleasantries than to restrain his tears at words of admonishment and the talk that edifies. Yet it was not on that day that the call of the place made him choose it as his home. He returned with the lord Walter Espec to the castle and spent another night there, like the last. After some talk among the company about a number of things they went to bed until the morning star appeared. Then, aroused from sleep, he called to his servants to bridle, saddle and harness the horses and, when all was ready, he said farewell to the most noble Walter and set out on the journey to his lord the King in Scotland. Now he had to pass along the edge of the hill overlooking the valley, where a road led down to the gate of the monastery, and when he reached the spot, still aflame with the heat of the Holy Spirit, that is to say, with the love of the Lord Jesus, he asked one of his servants, whom he called his friend, if he would like to go down to the abbey and learn something more than he had seen the day before. Oh, the mercy of our God, ever to be proclaimed by those who wish to make their home in Christ! Oh, how faithful is our God in clemency and kindness! For, as our father would tell us, if the friend he had asked if he wished to go down to the monastery or not had said 'I have no mind to go,' he himself in that hour would not have gone down with him as he actually did. Take note here of the outshining humility of this gentlest of men, whose own will depended on the will of his servant. God indeed opened the mouth of that servant. He said, 'I am for going down,' and what the servant preferred to do the lord decided should be done. So they went down to the monastery of Rievaulx. Today as

simplicity {and} ardent charity. His works {available} in English[709] {include}: *De Jesu Duodenni*;[710] {the} letter to {his} sister;[711] *Spiritual Friendship*;[712] in Latin:[713] Sermons;[714] *Speculum Charitatis*.[715]

---

yesterday the prior, with the guestmaster, and the keeper of the gate and a great company of the brethren hasten to meet him and to do him honour. They have a shrewd suspicion that the will of the visitor, who has come to them again, has been prompted by longing for his well-being; and, since he listens to their words with an eager and unreserved attention, making them his own with tears as things to be embraced, they are led on to probe his mind with more searching admonitions. I need say no more. He agrees at last to become a monk" (Walter Daniel, *The Life of Ailred of Rievaulx*, ed. and trans. F. M. Powicke [New York: Thomas Nelson, 1950], 10, 12–15).

709. For a complete list of current English translations in the Cistercian Fathers series, see the bibliography in Merton, *Cistercian Fathers and Their Monastic Theology*, 456.

710. Aelred of Rievaulx, *On Jesus at Twelve Years Old*, trans. Geoffrey Webb and Adrian Walker (London: Mowbray, 1956).

711. Aelred of Rievaulx, *A Letter to His Sister*, trans. Geoffrey Webb and Adrian Walker (London: Mowbray, 1956); this is a translation of Aelred's *De Institutione Inclusarum*, or *Rule for Recluses*.

712. *Of Spiritual Friendship: A Translation of the De Spirituali Amicitia of Saint Aelred (1109–1166)*, trans. Sr. M. Francis Jerome (Patterson, NJ: St. Anthony's Guild Press, 1948).

713. At that time, the standard edition of Aelred's works was found in PL 195. (For the modern critical edition, see *Aelredi Rievallensis Opera Omnia*, vols. 1–7, CCCM I–III [Turnhout: Brepols, 1971–2017].)

714. Probably a reference to *Sermones Inediti B. Aelredi Abbatis Rievallensis*, ed. C. H. Talbot (Rome: Apud Curiam Generalem Sacri Ordinis Cisterciensis, 1952); Aelred's previously known sermons were included in PL 195:209–500.

715. As there was no new Latin edition of the *Speculum* at this time, this reference is probably a slip on Merton's part for the recently published edition of Aelred's treatise on the soul: Ailred of Rievaulx, *De Anima*, ed. C. H. Talbot (London: Warburg Institute, 1952). (The first critical edition of the *Speculum* text is found in *Aelredi Rievallensis Opera Omnia I: Opera Ascetica*, CCCM 1, ed. C. H. Talbot [Turnhout: Brepols, 1971], 3–61.) An English translation of the *Speculum* was published in 1962: Aelred of Rievaulx, *The Mirror of Charity*, trans. Geoffrey Webb and Adrian Walker (London: Mowbray, 1962), which suggests that this brief note was written before that date.

****

Cistercian Easter Sermons—{The} Spiritual Sense of Scripture
St. Ailred (*PL* 195) *Sermo 11 in Dei Paschae 1*:[716] "*Quasi modo geniti infantes*. . ."[717]
Lac = dulcedinem Jesu Christi[718] (271)—{there are} two kinds:
1. In {the} contemplation of His Passion: they have experienced His sweetness in {the} Passion: "*haec omnia multo melius vidistis, et clarius oculis cordis, quam multi tunc viderunt oculis corporis, quando facta sunt*" (272)[719]—specifically, His arms open to embrace them, His breast bared to nourish them.
2. In the Eucharist: (a) *dulcissima esca in qua Judaei miscuerunt fel*[720] (Judas); (b) *Calix vini meri, pleni misto*[721] ({the} law {as understood} with the *spiritual sense*); "*Istud vinum est spiritualis intelligentia, quae fuit in illis institutionibus, quae erant in veteri lege*" (273).[722] David, drunk with this wine, danced before {the} ark;[723] Isaias, drunk with this wine, went naked.[724] {This symbolizes the} institution of {the} Eucharist—*inclinavit ex hoc in hoc*[725]—{the wine was} poured out from {the} old chalice ({the} paschal lamb) into {the} new chalice (His Body and Blood), {with the} old

---

716. PL 195:271D–278A.

717. "As newborn babes, [desire the rational milk without guile, that thereby you may grow unto salvation]" (1 Pet 2:2) (PL 195:271D).

718. "milk . . . the sweetness of Jesus Christ."

719. "You have seen all this much better and more clearly with the eyes of the heart, than many saw with their bodily eyes at the time when the events took place."

720. "the sweetest food in which the Jews mixed gall" (PL 195:272B).

721. "The chalice of pure wine, full of mixture" (PL 195:272D, which reads: "*Calix in manu Domini vini meri, plenus misto*" [Ps 74 [75]:9: "For in the hand of the Lord there is a cup of strong wine full of mixture"]).

722. "That wine is spiritual understanding, which was in those institutions that were in the old law."

723. PL 195:273A (see 2 Sam 6:14-16).

724. PL 195:273B (see Isa 20:2-3).

725. "And he hath poured it out from this to that" (Ps 74 [75]:9) (PL 195:273C).

chalice remaining empty, except for the lees; *commemoratio passionis Domini in agno, quasi vinum in calice* (274);[726] (the lees {are} the remains of literalism in {the} old chalice: {the} Jews drank {the} lees; we drink the wine); *lactucae agrestes*[727] (274) {is} to be eaten with {the} paschal lamb, signifying humility born of suffering; Jesus {in} washing {the} feet of {His} disciples feeds them with this "lettuce" {and so} prepares {the} disciples for the bitterness of life. (N.B. {the} quote from Isaias 52 (275) {with its} unusual form[728] {perhaps} indicates {a} translation from English??) All these {are} examples of the powerful effect of the *memoria passionis Domini*[729] ({the} Passion in this sermon outweighs {the} Resurrection): {it} dwells again on the opprobrium, the humiliation of the Crucified Christ—a sweetness mixed with bitterness—seeing His humility and mercy but also His bitter sufferings (*quam dulcedinem potuit haurire cor vestrum, quando interiori oculo vidistis ipsum Dominum portare crucem suam?* [275])[730]). Then {it} passes to His glorious

---

726. "The remembrance of the passion of Christ in the lamb, like wine in the cup" (text reads: "*Commemoratio ergo passionis*").

727. "wild lettuce."

728. "*Sicut, inquit, obstupuerunt super te multi sic inglorius erit inter viros aspectus eius et forma eius inter filios hominum*" ("As many have been astonished at Thee, so shall His visage be inglorious among men, and His form among the sons of men") (Isa 52:14). Rather that the Vulgate "*obstipuerunt*," Aelred's text reads "*obstupuerunt*," also used repeatedly in the sentence immediately following: "*Multi quidem obstupuerunt, quando pavit quinque millia hominum de quinque panibus et duobus piscibus (Ioan. VI); multi obstupuerunt, quando caecum natum illuminavit (Ioan. IX); multi obstupuerunt, quando Lazarum suscitavit (Ioan. XI). Obstupuerunt, laudaverunt, gloricaverunt*" ("Many were astonished when he fed five thousand men with five loaves and two fish [John 6]; many were astonished when he gave sight to the man born blind [John 9]; many were astonished when he restored Lazarus to life [John 11]. They were astonished, they praised, they gave glory").

729. "memory of the Lord's passion" (PL 195:273C, which reads, "*memoriam ejusdem* [the same] *passionis Domini*").

730. "How much sweetness your heart can drink when you have seen with your inner eye the Lord himself carrying His cross."

exaltation: "*Ideo qui hoc vinum mordens gustastis,* id est memoriam passionis Domini, modo lac concupiscite, id est suavitatem resurrectionis illius" (276)[731] (n.b. {the} ambiguity—wine {is} better than milk). *Milk* {is the} sweet contemplation of Jesus eating with {His} disciples AFTER {the} resurrection. N.B. *Abraham* "saw this day"[732] of His resurrection and rejoiced when he received the three angels[733] ({a} type of {the} Eucharist?) (276).

{Then the focus shifts to} *the women at the tomb—eamus cum istis sanctis mulieribus . . . ad monumentum Scripturarum;*[734] again, the spiritual meaning of Scripture {is paramount}—with ointments of devotion; who will roll away the stone of the literal sense? *Here he suddenly and inexplicably switches to a* TREE on which hangs the bunch of grapes = Christ on the cross (276). (Here, {is this} ANOTHER sermon? no: Abraham {is mentioned again}.) Then {the} hearth cake {is presented} as {a} type of {the} Eucharist and {also a} type of {the} burial of Christ (buried under ashes); {the} three measures {represent the} three days in {the} tomb (277) (compare finding {a} typology of {the} Passion and Resurrection in Abraham's meal for his guests).

Conclusion: {the} disciples {are} nourished with {the} milk of {the} Resurrection because they could not face the Passion (!!) and {the} invisible things of His divinity (277). *Necesse ergo erat ut, quasi parvuli etiam oculis carnis viderent resurrectionem ejus, sicque quasi quodam lacte nutrirentur, ut idonei essent invisibilia credere, invisibilia contemplari* (277).[735] The women announce it, for

---

731. "Therefore, you who have tasted this bitter wine—that is, the memory of the Lord's passion—aspire now to milk—that is, the sweetness of His resurrection."

732. *"Hunc diem vidit"* (PL 195:276B) (see John 8:56).

733. Gen 18:1-8.

734. "Let us go with those holy women . . . to the memorial of the Scriptures" (PL 195:276C).

735. "It was necessary that they still saw His resurrection with the eyes of the flesh, like children, and so were nourished as with a kind of milk, that they were suited to believe the unseen, to contemplate the unseen."

it is woman's role to give milk to children. *In isto lacte crescite, et crescite in salutem* (277).[736] (Easter grace {means a} growth in faith.) *Colligite de lacte hoc, id est de memoria resurrectionis Domini, pinguedinem amoris Christi.*[737] {Note the mention of} *butter* ({an} Easter food in monasteries) {in the} context of {the} Easter apparitions: *"debemus quasi impinguari in dilectione ejus."*[738]

St. Ailred, *In Die Paschae* (*Sermones Inediti*, p. 94[739]).

The Easter feast on earth {is the} shadow of the *perfect Paschal Supper in heaven. Ibi edunt pauperes et saturantur. Nobiscum vero bene agitur si esurimus et sitimus justitiam, ubi esurientes et sitientes in terra tandem satiemur in patria.*[740] His desire for heaven {is} as yet denied (94). But let some crumb fall from the heavenly table to the whelps (cf. P. de Celles[741])—*ad canem istum mortuum et pulicem*

---

736. "Grow in that milk, and grow in salvation."

737. "Gather from this milk, that is, from this memory of the resurrection of the Lord, the richness of Christ's love" (PL 195:277D, which reads, "*de hac memoria*").

738. "We should be enriched in His love" (PL 195:278A, which reads, "*debemus quasi impinguari*").

739. Talbot, ed., *Sermones Inediti*, 94–100.

740. "There the poor eat and are satisfied. Truly it goes well with us if we hunger and thirst for righteousness; when hungering and thirsting on earth, we will finally be satisfied in the fatherland" (Ailred, *In Die Paschae*, 94).

741. Peter of Celles, *Sermo 81, De Apostolis* (PL 202:885C–886A): "*Dat itaque escam in tempore opportune, non uno simul . . . Sub mensa vero publicani et peccatores, qui sicut canes famem patiuntur et convertuntur ad vesperam, dicentes cum illo evangelico Pharisaeo: Domine, non sum dignus levare oculos meos ad coelum (Luc. XVIII, 13); et: Non sum dignus vocari apostolus (I Cor. XV, 1); et: Non sum dignus ut intres sub tectum meum (Matth. VIII, 8). Isti nec a mensa recedunt desperatione sicut ille qui dixit: Maior est iniquitas mea, quam ut veniam merear; ecce eiicis me hodie a facie terrae et a facie tua abscondar (Gen. IV, 14). Nec irruunt ad mensam fronte meretricis et rabie immoderata, sed tempus opportunum exspectant, ut cum filii saturati fuerint; excutiat pater bonus sinum suum, et micas quae non negligentia, sed copiosa abundantia in gremium distillaverat, canibus quasi non ex industria proiiciat. Sic itaque catelli et canes edunt de micis quae cadunt de mensa dominorum suorum*" ("Therefore he gives food at the appropriate time, not all at one time. . . . Beneath the table the publicans and sinners, who like the

unum.[742] May the crumb from heaven sweeten the "bitter herbs"[743] prescribed for the feast. *De hac vita mortali sine lactucis agrestibus, videlicet, sine amaritudine pascha celebrare non possumus.*[744]

Pascha transitus interpretatur[745]—{in a} three-fold {sense}: (1) {the} Jews from Egypt—from fleshpots to manna—immolation of Lamb; (2) Christians from desire to Christ and to the Eucharist—immolation of Christ; (3) from mortality to immortality—*Pascha sanctorum ac perfectorum* (95):[746] *de miseria ad felicitatem, de labore ad requiem, de timore ad securitatem*[747]—{This is} the perfect *glorification of Christ, non immolatur sed potius manifestatur Christus;*[748] *in primo illo pascha passio Christi praefiguratur,* in altero exhibetur, in tertio fructus ipsius passionis per virtutem resurrectionis ostenditur.[749] *Ita,*

---

dogs endure hunger and are converted at evening, saying with that Pharisee evangelist, 'Lord, I am not worthy to lift my eyes to heaven' [Luke 18:13], and 'I am not worthy to be called an apostle' [1 Cor 15:1], and 'I am not worthy for you to enter under my roof' [Matt 8:8]. Those do not withdraw from the table in despair like the one who said, 'My iniquity is greater than I can bear. Behold, you banish me today from the face of the earth, and I hide from your face' [Gen 4:14]. They do not rush to the table with the boldness of a harlot and an unbridled fury, but await the proper time, so that when the sons have been satisfied, the good Father may open his breast and, as though not on purpose, throw to the dogs the crumbs that he had held in his bosom, not with negligence but with copious abundance. Thus the puppies and the dogs eat of the crumbs that fall from the table of their masters").

742. "to that dead dog and one flea" (Ailred, *In Die Paschae*, 94).

743. "*lactuce . . . amare*" (Ailred, *In Die Paschae*, 94).

744. "From this mortal life we are not able to celebrate the pasch without wild lettuce, that is, without bitterness" (Ailred, *In Die Paschae*, 94).

745. "Pasch is interpreted passage" (Ailred, *In Die Paschae*, 94).

746. "Passover of the saints and the perfected."

747. "from misery to happiness, from labor to rest, from fear to safety" (Ailred, *In Die Paschae*, 95).

748. "Christ is not immolated but rather revealed" (Ailred, *In Die Paschae*, 95, which reads: "*manifestabitur* [will be revealed]").

749. "In that first pasch the passion of Christ is foreshadowed, in the next it is shown forth, in the third the fruit of the passion itself is revealed through the power of the resurrection" (Ailred, *In Die Paschae*, 95).

sapientia vincit malitiam (95 ff.):[750] {There is a} three-fold cord—*sapientia, fortitudo, suavitas*[751]—these three {are} necessary against the diabolical three—*voluptas, vanitas, cupiditas*,[752] *the temptations of Christ* (97), binding Christ, like Samson, in the passion; {thus this is} a commentary on the three temptations suggested by Satan and other temptations suggested by {the} Pharisees—always {with} Christ as Samson and {the} Philistines trying to "bind" him; Christ—Samson (*Philistiim super te Samson!*[753])—{He} breaks these bonds, but they are *my* bonds not His. {As for} the woman taken in adultery, "I" am this woman, says Ailred.[754] In the Passion Samson's "hair" is shaved (the disciples leave Him) and He is taken; dying on {the} Cross He breaks the "two columns"[755]—the devil and original sin. The Philistines (devils) are destroyed in His death (100).

Isaac of Stella—Sermo XL in Die Paschae[756]

The *bonds* that unite men {are} compared to the bond uniting man and God, restored by the Resurrection:

1. {The bond} between man and wife—man who has left God and "fornicated"[757] with idols is restored to divine union (Jerem. 3). Now God embraces man {and} introduces him to the wine cellar (1824).[758]

2. {The} bond between mother and child—cf. Isaias 49: a mother *cannot not love* her son. We have forgotten Him; He has not forgotten us. He created us without any merit on our part, and redeemed us likewise.[759]

---

750. "Thus, wisdom overcomes malice" (Wis 7:30).
751. "wisdom, fortitude, sweetness."
752. "pleasure, vanity, cupidity."
753. "The Philistines are upon you, Samson" (Judg 16:12, 14, 20) (97; text reads: "Sampson").
754. Cf. John 8:1-11.
755. "*duas columpnas*" (99).
756. PL 194:1824B–1827D.
757. "*fornicata est*" (PL 194:1824C).
758. See Song 2:4.
759. PL 194:1824D–1825A.

3. {The} bond of love between man and himself: a man cannot not love himself. God broke this bond in Himself, delivering Himself to death for us, and broke it first in {the} Incarnation. *Quid magis, rogo, exinanire se potuit Deus, quam ut homo fieret; homo, quam ut moreretur, Deus Dominus, quam ut servus efficeretur; servus, quam ut turpiter moreretur?* (1825).[760] {Here is} *admiration of the divine mercy in the Passion of Christ*—compassion for His enemies (ourselves) (1825).

Our death and resurrection {is} double:

1. As we died by disobedience, so we live by faith, *considered as obedience to God.* Mors itaque prima est animae, quando propter inobedientiae malum a vita sua Deo deseritur: *quam absorbet per resurrectionem vita, qua justus ex fide vivit. Manente enim corpore mortuo propter peccatum,* vivit tamen spiritus propter justificationem, cum se per obeditionem subdit Deo (1825)[761] ({this is} very dense and important: *Resurrection* {is} *obedience to God as Life*); *cum accedit ad Deum, accedit ad vitam, et invenit resurrectionem primam.*[762]

2. *Resurrectio secunda, regenerans totum simul hominem ad vitam,*[763] by reason of the obedience of the *dilecta anima Christi*[764] (1826): *Dilecta autem illa, et benedicta Salvatoris anima, quae venit solvere, quae non rapuit . . . sicut in peccati mortem nequivit cadere, ita nec de peccato in justitiae vitam resurgere. Semel verbo vitae unita, sicut*

---

760. "What more, I ask, could God do to empty himself than to become human: could a human being do, than to die; could the Lord God do, than to become a slave; could a slave do, than to die shamefully?"

761. "Therefore the first death is that of the soul, when because of the evil of disobedience it is abandoned by God its life; this death life swallows up through the resurrection, the life which the just person lives by faith. For although the body remains dead because of sin, the spirit lives because of justification when through obedience it submits itself to God" (PL 194:1825D–1826A).

762. "When he draws near to God he draws near to life and he finds the first resurrection" (PL 194:1826A).

763. "The second resurrection, at once restoring the whole person to life" (PL 194:1826A).

764. "the beloved soul of Christ" (not in text).

personali unione, ita et justitiae dilectione insolubiliter adhaesit, prae omnibus exsultans, et dicens: Mihi adhaerere Deo bonum est (1826).[765]

Christ's soul, united to the Person of the Word and to the divine will, {is} *separated from its body by a surrender of His will* in order to reunite us to God. *Ego, qui aedificavi vestrum [templum], reaedificabo meum. Vos, qui solutionem meruistis vestri, solvite meum. Solvite non merito iniquitatis meae, nec imperio potestatis vestrae, sed positione voluntatis meae* (1826).[766] This {was} possible because *et divinitati humanitas inseparabilis personali copula adhaesit, et a delectatione et amore Verbi nullo peregrino amore anima ad punctum abscessit. Vixit itaque mortuus, qui obiit vivus* (1827).[767] His obedience was such a perfect union with life that He lived even when soul and body were separated.

Our risen life in Christ—*in veris vera [quaerere], in spiritualibus spiritualia, in coelestibus coelestia, et in divinis divina, sapientes quae Dei sunt, et in novitate vitae ambulantes, complantati similitudini mortis Christi, dum peccato et carni et mundo mortui sunt,* configurati resurrectioni Christi . . . *in carne quodammodo supra carnem degunt,* consedentes cum eo in coelestibus, dum eorum requies et conversatio in coelis est, et conregnantes illi, dum omnia sua

---

765. "That beloved and blessed soul of the Savior, which comes to pay back what it did not snatch away . . . as it could not fall into the death of sin, so it could not arise from sin into the life of righteousness. For united once for all with the Word of life, it thus was attached unbreakably as by a personal union, so too by a delight in righteousness, exulting beyond all others and saying: For me, to be united to God is My good" (Ps 72 [73]:28) (PL 194:1826B, which reads: "*Semel enim verbo.*").

766. "I, who have built your [bodily temple], will rebuild mine. You, who have deserved the destruction of yours, destroy mine. Destroy it not as the consequence of my iniquity, not by the power of your authority, but by the disposition of my will."

767. "By a personal union humanity inseparably bonded with divinity, and the soul did not withdraw for a single instant from the delight and love of the Word for any wandering love. Thus he was alive when dead, who was dead while living."

ad spiritualem profectum deservire compellunt (1827).⁷⁶⁸ *Quod in nobis adimplere dignetur is, cujus resurrectionem colimus et imitamur, quoad possumus: sine quo nihil, et in quo omnia possumus, Christus Dominus* (1827).⁷⁶⁹

Isaac of Stella—*Sermo II de Resurrectione* (PL 194:1827ff.)⁷⁷⁰

*Ego hodie genui te*⁷⁷¹ {is} used by St. Paul for {the} resurrection. Why?

1. Resurrection = a birth to a new life (1828). We have three births: (1) carnal; (2) spiritual (baptism); (3) to immortality (resurrection of the body). *Quales enim renascimur de fonte, talis natus est Christus ex Virgine: qualis regeneratus est Christus de tumulo, tales renascemur in futuro.* Et hic est status, ad quem factus est homo: *nec antea erit homo consummatus, donec perficiatur in eo, ad quod fuit inchoatus. Tunc enim generatus proprie dicetur, cum fuerit pergeneratus; tunc factus, quando completus.*⁷⁷²

---

768. "[To seek] the truth in true things, the spiritual in spiritual things, the heavenly in heavenly things, the divine in divine things, tasting what is of God, walking in newness of life, rooted in likeness of the death of Christ, while they have died to sin and the flesh and the world, conformed to the resurrection of Christ . . . in the flesh they live somehow above the flesh, also seated with Him in the heavens, while their rest and citizenship is in heaven and reigning together with Him, as they strive to devote everything belonging to them to spiritual progress" (text reads: "*consedentes quoque cum*").

769. "May He whose resurrection we worship and imitate as much as we are able, deign to bring it to fulfillment in us—Christ Jesus, without whom we can do nothing and in whom we can do all."

770. "*Sermo XLI in Eodem Festo II.*"

771. "This day have I begotten thee" (Ps 2:7) (PL 194:1828A).

772. "As we are reborn at the font, so Christ was born of the Virgin; as Christ was reborn from the tomb, so we will be reborn in the future. And this is the condition for which the human person has been made; man will not be perfected until the purpose that had been begun in him is accomplished. For then will generation be properly named, when it will be regeneration; then properly considered complete, when it is fulfilled" (PL 194:1828BC).

2. Nourishment—in carnal life, {is} material food; in spiritual life, {the} sacraments; in {the} resurrection, God Himself, without sacraments. Christ takes material food and makes of it a sacrament, the *Eucharist. Nova creatura, nova esca* (1828).[773] *Post primam regenerationem opus habet alimonia, qua vivat in ea, et crescat, ac corroboretur, qua regenerata est vita, non ut post baptismi gratiam, aliam sumat vitam, sed ne per indigentiam perdat acceptam* (1829).[774] In {the} risen life, God is our food. *Tunc enim immediate ac sufficienter vivet de anima sola caro tota; immediate ac perfecte de Deo solo anima {tota}, ubi nec caro indiga erit alimentis, nec anima sacramentis* (1829)[775] (cf. infra 1829: IPSE DE FACIE MEA VIVAT SINE SACRAMENTO[776]). *Hodie genui te. Hodie talem te genui in statu tertio, propter quem te creavi in primo, et vivificavi in secundo* (1829).[777] We must suffer with Christ to live this risen life with Him.

---

773. "New creature, new food."

774. "After the first regeneration [the soul] has need of food, through which it lives and grows and becomes strong in that life by which it has been reborn, not in order to receive, after the grace of baptism, another life, but in order not to lose through deprivation the life it has received."

775. "For then the entire flesh will live immediately and sufficiently from the soul alone, the entire soul immediately and sufficiently from God alone, when neither will the flesh be in need of food nor the soul of the sacraments" (copy text reads: "*anima sola*").

776. "He himself shall live before my face without a sacrament."

777. "Today I have begotten you. Today I have begotten you in a third state, because of which I created you in the first and brought you back to life in the second."

THE CISTERCIAN ORDER FROM THE DEATH OF SAINT BERNARD TO THE REFORM OF BENEDICT XII (1153–1335)

Introduction: this is a difficult and rather complex study, and a very important one, for it embraces the whole *maturity of the Order*. It has not been satisfactorily studied as a whole in English, though there are many detailed studies of some aspects of it, especially some of the theses being published by Fordham— v.g. Donnelly on the laybrothers.[1] At best we have brief and correct surveys, or even very incorrect surveys of the whole area. Much of this material is completely omitted from manuals at our disposal. The history of the Order, we remember, can be conveniently divided as follows (all such divisions have something arbitrary about them): (1) The Formation of the Order: 1098 to 1119; (2) The Growth of the Order: 1119 to 1153; (3) The Maturity of the Order: (a) apogee: 1153 to 1265 (*Parvus Fons*[2] of Clement IV); (b) centralization and decline: 1265–1335 (this period is what we are now studying); (4) Decadence: 1335; (5) Reform: sixteenth–twentieth centuries. A few remarks will enable us to place this study of the maturity of the Order in its perspective:

---

1. James S. Donnelly, *The Decline of the Medieval Cistercian Laybrotherhood* (New York: Fordham University Press, 1949).

2. *Nomasticon Cisterciense, seu Antiquiores Ordinis Cisterciensis Constitutiones A.R.P.D. Juliano Paris . . .* Editio Nova, ed. Hugo Séjalon (Solesmes: E Typographeo Sancti Petri, 1892), 367–76.

1. This period is seldom really studied, at least in our monasteries, especially in our novitiates. We tend to concentrate on the formative period, and to discuss very sketchily the basic legislation, the *Exordium Parvum*,[3] the *Carta Caritatis*.[4] We do not even take cognizance of the fact that the versions of these basic texts we study belong in reality to the period after 1153,[5] so that even what we have studied of the earliest period is seen through the glass of this later period. We tend to study the formative period also with our own Trappist prejudices about it, in the light of the Trappist reform.

2. The maturity of the Cistercian Order is not the *ideal* Cîteaux but it is the *actual* Cîteaux of its greatest period. This actual Cîteaux, being rather different from the ideal, must nevertheless be taken into account. Here we are dealing with the two centuries of greatest spiritual and material prosperity, when the Order was fully and strongly established and flourished everywhere. It is however not the period of first fervor any more. Nor is it the period of St. Bernard and of the Cistercian writers (Guerric, Ailred, William, etc.[6])—only minor writers. Yet it is the period of Cistercian mysticism in the Low Countries and Germany, a

---

3. *Nomasticon*, 53–65.

4. *Nomasticon*, 68–81.

5. This idea stems from the theories of J.-A. Lefèvre, who considered both the *Exordium Parvum* and the final version of the *Carta Caritatis* to be late-twelfth-century documents, a position no longer generally accepted. For a thorough discussion of the evidence and new editions of the relevant texts, with translations, see *Narrative and Legislative Texts from Early Cîteaux*, ed. and trans. Chrysogonus Waddell, OCSO, Studia et Documenta, vol. 9 (Cîteaux: Commentarii Cistercienses, 1999).

6. I.e. Guerric of Igny, Aelred (Ailred) of Rievaulx, William of Saint-Thierry, often described (with Saint Bernard) as the four Cistercian evangelists; for an overview of Merton's interest in and writings on these early classic Cistercian authors, see the Introduction to Thomas Merton, *The Cistercian Fathers and Their Monastic Theology: Initiation into the Monastic Tradition 8*, ed. Patrick F. O'Connell, Monastic Wisdom [MW] vol. 42 (Collegeville, MN: Cistercian Publications, 2016), xliv–xlix; see also Thoms Merton, *Cistercian Fathers and Forefathers: Essays and Conferences*, ed. Patrick F. O'Connell (Hyde Park, NY: New City Press, 2018).

period which is more fully Cistercian perhaps than we realize. Some of the inner spirit of this great period has been preserved more authentically by our brothers of the Common Observance than by ourselves.

3. Finally we have to face the fact that we are dealing with the *actual decline* of the Order in all its complexity. This has to be treated prudently and humbly, but quite frankly and objectively.

Since there is not {a} fully satisfactory treatment of this whole subject easily available in English at the present moment, it is necessary to attempt a systematic study of the question, at least in outline. There will be inevitable gaps, errors and limitations, but perhaps this will serve as a general introduction to the question, and will prepare the way for a better understanding of the problems. Obviously these rough notes will call for many corrections.

A few preliminary remarks on the *decline of the Cistercians*:

1. The decline of the Cistercian Order was part of the general decline of the whole monastic order in the late Middle Ages. More than that, it must be seen in the context of a general upheaval of Christian society that took place throughout the thirteenth to fifteenth centuries and culminated in the Protestant Reformation, the Enlightenment, the French Revolution, etc.

2. Once this has been said, we must beware of easy generalizations that attempt to explain these phenomena. It would be foolish to expect that any institution of men should maintain a uniformly high standard of perfection over many centuries. There must be change and decline and then renewal. Here we seek only to state historical facts, not to judge. Note the inevitable subjectivity of this kind of study. Try as we will, we cannot avoid projecting into it our own ideals and our own misgivings. But we must beware of using the history of the Order as a cloak for criticism and discontentment about our own present-day situation. Still less should we allow it to be a self-justification and a complacent glorification of our present state of prosperity, or of our hopes for the future and our pet policies. Such "history" belongs to the Communist variety—making the events mean what you want them to mean.

3. Yet nevertheless there is a fact to be taken into account. The orders that did not become inordinately large were better able to preserve their original standards. The Carthusians are a case in point. But the Carthusians were exceptional, and the mere fact that they were not a large order is no sufficient explanation. Other small orders fell apart and disappeared. Other eremitical orders declined and had to be reformed (the Camaldolese). It is true then that the Cistercian Order was "too big." Nevertheless, although this explains many of the difficulties of the Order, it does not explain everything, nor does it entitle us to say that if St. Bernard had never existed, and if the tremendous expansion of the Cistercians had not taken place, the Order would not have declined. It might not even have survived. It was the coming of St. Bernard with his thirty companions that saved Cîteaux.

4. One thing is certain. In the early period, from 1098 to about 1130, the Cistercians were *ahead of their times, full of extraordinary vitality and originality in every sphere.* Until the death of St. Stephen, the original impetus of the Holy Spirit remained most powerful, and the Order was an unusual, charismatic phenomenon in the Church. Men were so impressed with this that they credited the Order with this inspired quality long after the inspiration was gone. In the period from 1130 to 1200, the Order is full of spiritual vitality, and is fully *with* the times. It dominates the life of the age, and is fully part of it. Yet there are signs of rigidity and decline beginning to be evident. In this period the Order becomes *identified with established power and the status quo*—it is rich and strong—at the same time fervent, but no longer progressive. *In the thirteenth century, the Order represents the immediate past.* It is *regressive,* and its power is something of a *brake* on the Church.

5. It would be a mistake to say that everything that happened during the period of decline somehow contributed to that decline in a very positive way. For instance, the fact that the College of St. Bernard was founded and Cistercians were sent to study in different universities is not necessarily a "cause" of the decline of the Order. This probably had many different effects—good and bad. If we discuss the colleges in these notes, it is not to blame

the decline on them. They *may* perhaps have been symptomatic of the decline.

6. These notes will then concern themselves with how the decline actually took place, and with the various aspects of the history of the Order during the twelfth to fifteenth centuries. There will inevitably be repetitions and perhaps inconsistencies. We make no claims to perfection. Rather these notes should be taken as an encouragement to further personal studies on the part of each one in our group.

The Cistercian Order from the Death of St. Bernard
to the Reform of Benedict XII
(1153–1335)

Background and Outline.

1. 1147—*Before the Death of St. Bernard*:[7]

A. {There was a} crucially important meeting of the General Chapter.[8] Pope Eugene III was present. {The Chapter decided on}:

a. {the} admission of Savigny with its twenty-seven dependencies into the Order of Cîteaux. {The} object {was} to save the family of Savigny from dissolution. The English abbots were breaking away from Savigny. Some of the English abbots resisted the move. The pope deposed the Abbot of Furness. *Serlo*, Abbot of Savigny, entered Clairvaux. St. Bernard was the guiding spirit of this incorporation of Savigny into the Order and the filiation of Clairvaux. (La Trappe was one of the Savignian houses.)

b. {the} admission of Obazine, with two filiations, headed by *St. Stephen Obazine*.[9]

---

7. For this material Merton closely follows Eugène Willems, *Esquisse Historique de l'Ordre de Cîteaux*, d'après le Père Grégoire Müller, 2 vols. (Aubel: Notre-Dame du Val-Dieu, 1957–1958), 1.90–99.

8. See J.-M. Canivez, ed., *Statuta Capitulorum Generalium Ordinis Cisterciensis ab Anno 1116 ad Annum 1786*, 8 vols. (Louvain: Bureaux de la Revue d'Histoire Ecclésiastique, 1933–1941), 1.37–38.

9. For a brief biographical sketch, see Thomas Merton, *In the Valley of Wormwood: Cistercian Blessed and Saints of the Golden Age*, ed. Patrick Hart,

c. the request of St. Gilbert of Sempringham to have his congregation affiliated to the Order was refused, because he had double monasteries (i.e., monasteries of women united with monasteries of men).

{In} 1152,[10] {the} General Chapter seeks to arrest {the} expansion of {the} Order. No new foundations {were} to be made; 349 foundations had been made in forty years. {A} *new text of {the} Carta Caritatis*[11] {was} approved by Eugene III in {the} bull *Sacrosancta*:[12]

1) {The} Abbot of Cîteaux is still the *one* head of the Order. Cîteaux is still not visited by anyone.

a. Several other abbots are to be present at {the} election of {the} Abbot of Cîteaux, as advisors and witnesses.

b. In case an Abbot of Cîteaux is incorrigible, he is to be *warned* by {the} Abbots of La Ferté, Pontigny and Clairvaux, then denounced to {the} Bishop of Châlons, who deposes him.

c. {The} Abbot of La Ferté is {the} administrator of Cîteaux when there is no abbot.

2) Abbots of other monasteries (than Cîteaux) {were} formerly corrected only by {their} Father Immediate and {their} bishop. Now {the} Abbot of Cîteaux can intervene. {The} bishop will depose {the} delinquent if necessary. The intervention of bishops, not yet restricted, creates problems.

3) There is as yet no statute saying Fathers Immediate must visit daughter houses every year (according to Willems[13]).

OCSO, Cistercian Studies [CS] vol. 233 (Collegeville, MN: Cistercian Publications, 2013), 93–101.

10. Canivez, *Statuta*, 1.45 (#1).

11. N.B. the *"new text"* being described here is actually the *Carta Caritatis Prior*, dated by Lefèvre to 1152 but by most scholars today to 1119; see below, n. 22.

12. *Nomasticon*, 74–78 (1152); reissued with slight revisions by Anastasius IV in 1153 (*Nomasticon*, 79), by Adrian IV in 1156 (*Nomasticon*, 80) and by Alexander III in 1165 (*Nomasticon*, 80–81).

13. Willems, *Esquisse Historique*, 1.98.

The Cistercian Order (1153–1335)

4) {The} first text of *Usus Conversorum*[14] is approved.

2. 1153 {brought the} death of St. Bernard and of Eugene III, {who were} still both under a cloud, due to the failure of the (Second) Crusade. The failure of the crusade dashed Eugene's hopes of a reunion with the Byzantine and other Eastern Christians.[15]

3. In 1158, the Order of Calatrava began.[16] Cistercian monks of Fitero volunteered to take over this undefended town, abandoned by the Templars. They joined with lay soldiers. A rule was formed for this military group. Later, after the death of St. Raymond[17] (1163) there was a disagreement between the monks and laymen and the monks withdrew. The lay order continued under the Rule of Calatrava, affiliated to the Order of Cîteaux. In 1193, Calatrava fell to the Moors and remained in their power until 1212, when Arnold, Abbot of Cîteaux, then Bishop of Narbonne, came with troops he had been using against the Albigensians.[18]

Note: after 1150 there is a great spread of Cistercian convents of nuns in Spain: Las Huelgas (Burgos), founded in 1187, became a rich and splendid "royal monastery." The Kings of Castile wanted the abbesses of Spain to meet annually in a General Chapter at Las Huelgas. In 1191, the General Chapter *permitted* this but did not make it obligatory.[19]

4. 1160 to 1177 {saw the} schism of Victor IV against Alexander III.[20] Cistercian abbots {were} occupied in travel to advance {the} cause of Alexander. The Order {was} divided—some houses were at first for the anti-pope (especially under imperial

---

14. *The Customary of the Laybrothers* (*Nomasticon*, 234–41).

15. See Willems, *Esquisse Historique*, 1.99.

16. See Willems, *Esquisse Historique*, 1.110–11; copy text reads "1150"; see also below, page 209.

17. The Abbot of Fitero who initiated the Order of Calatrava; for a brief biographical sketch, see Merton, *Valley of Wormwood*, 69–72.

18. See Willems, *Esquisse Historique*, 1.136.

19. See Willems, *Esquisse Historique*, 1.138.

20. See Willems, *Esquisse Historique*, 1.112–13.

pressure). St. Peter of Tarentaise was one of the most zealous defenders of the interests of Alexander.

5. {In} 1163 and 1165, Alexander III renews *Sacrosancta*,[21] with significant changes: (a) There are now *four* First Fathers: Morimond is added to La Ferté, Pontigny and Clairvaux; (b) The four First Fathers *make regular visitation of Cîteaux*; (c) {the} power of {the} Abbot of Cîteaux in correcting {the} abbots of {the} Order is diminished; (d) {the} power of {the} General Chapter to inflict punishment is increased; (e) {the} election of {the} Abbot of Cîteaux becomes an affair concerning the whole Order; (f) {the} Abbot of Cîteaux {is} not deposed by {the} bishop but by {the} General Chapter; (g) exemption from episcopal control is established. *Summary*: {there is} growth of the power of the General Chapter. Is this {the} *Carta Caritatis Posterior*? Is {the} date correct, or should it be 1190?[22]

6. {In} 1166, St. Thomas à Becket takes refuge at Pontigny.[23] {The} King of England[24] puts pressure on the Order through threats against English abbeys, and St. Thomas is forced to leave Pontigny at {the} request of the General Chapter. This year

---

21. See Willems, *Esquisse Historique*, 1.105–6.

22. Willems dates the *Carta Caritatis Posterior* to ca. 1190 (*Esquisse Historique*, 1.125), based on the theories of Lefèvre, who considered the brief *Summa Cartae Caritatis* to be the text presented to Pope Callistus II for approval in 1119 and the *Carta Caritatis Prior* that presented to Pope Eugene III in 1152, with the *Carta Caritatis Posterior* (the standard text) actually a late, tendentious and polemical revision (see above, pages 65–68, 70–75). This theory has been generally rejected by more recent scholars, who date the *Carta Caritatis Prior* to 1119 and the *Carta Caritatis Posterior* to 1152, with minor revisions in 1153, 1156 and 1165; see Waddell, *Narrative and Legislative Texts*, 162–66, 183–86, 261–82, 371–88, 441–50, 498–505.

23. See Willems, *Esquisse Historique*, 1.114–15; for a thorough discussion of the complicated relations between Becket and the Cistercians, see Bernard McGinn, *The Golden Chain: A Study in the Theological Anthropology of Isaac of Stella*, CS 15 (Washington, DC: Cistercian Publications, 1972), 34–50.

24. Henry II (1133–1189), whose reign began in 1154.

St. Ailred died. By 1166 the great writers of the Order are all dead (Guerric {in} 1157; William {in} 1148; Isaac[25] probably about 1160).

7. {In} 1174, Alexander III, in gratitude for the support of the Cistercians in the schism, canonizes St. Bernard.[26] From this time on it is clear that the original character of the Order has been considerably modified. The rule is the same, the life in the monastery is the same, but in effect the Order of Cîteaux has become a *great active force* rather than a purely contemplative body of monks.

8. {In} 1184, Lucius III definitively confirms {the} Cistercian exemption from episcopal control.[27]

9. {In} 1198, Berthold, Abbot of Loccum (Saxony), is killed by pagans in Livonia.[28] This is the period of *Cistercian missionary activities* in Prussia, Poland and the Baltic region. Some great abbeys were founded—v.g. Dargun, Eldena, Oliva, Colbaz.[29] {There were} many Cistercian bishops and martyrs. The monks preached, in spite of {the} unwillingness of {the} General Chapter. In 1212 the pope intervened so that the Cistercians might continue preaching.[30] This pope was Innocent III, elected in 1198.

Cistercians at the Beginning of the Thirteenth Century:

1. *Expansion*: the Order is at the apogee of its power and greatness. It consists of over five hundred monasteries of men. (*Note*: in the seventeenth century, there were sixteen hundred[31] monasteries, seven hundred of men and nine hundred of women.) *Clairvaux* has 355 dependent monasteries (in 1147 Savigny and

---

25. For Merton's interest in and writings on Isaac of Stella, the other great Cistercian author of the "Golden Age," see the Introduction to *Cistercian Fathers and Their Monastic Theology*, xlix–l; *Cistercian Fathers and Forefathers*, 402–18.

26. See Willems, *Esquisse Historique*, 1.116.

27. See Willems, *Esquisse Historique*, 1.127–28; see also Jean-Berthold Mahn, *L'Ordre Cistercien et son Gouvernement des Origines au Milieu du XIIIe Siècle (1095–1265)* (Paris: E. de Boccard, 1945), 138, 148–49; text reads: "Lucian."

28. See Willems, *Esquisse Historique*, 1.134–35; typescript reads "Berthord."

29. Typescript reads "Darun, Elbena . . . Colonz."

30. See Willems, *Esquisse Historique*, 1.135.

31. Typescript reads "1500."

twenty-nine dependencies joined the filiation of Clairvaux). *Morimond* has 193 dependent abbeys, *Cîteaux* 109, *Pontigny* 43, *La Ferté* 17. The early and rapid expansion of the Order outside France in the twelfth century can be judged by the following statistics:[32] {in} Italy, {the} first monastery {was} founded by La Ferté {in} 1120—eventually {it} had 88 Cistercian monasteries; {in} Germany, {the} first monastery {was} founded by Morimond {in} 1123; {in} England, {the} first monastery {was} founded by Aumône {in} 1128—eventually {it} had 122 (with Ireland); {in} Austria, {the} first monastery {was} founded {in} 1130; {in} Spain, {the} first monastery {was} founded {in} 1132—eventually {it} had 56; {in} Belgium, {the} first monastery {was} founded {in} 1132—eventually {it} had 20; {in} Switzerland, {the} first monastery {was} founded {in} 1133; {in} Scotland, {the} first monastery {was} founded {in} 1136; {in} Portugal, {the} first monastery {was} founded {in} 1138—eventually {it} had 13; {in} Hungary, {the} first monastery {was} founded {in} 1142; {in} Poland, {the} first monastery {was} founded {in} 1143; {in} Denmark, {the} first monastery {was} founded {in} 1144; {in} Norway, {the} first monastery {was} founded {in} 1146. Many of these monasteries are (in 1200) still in the slow process of being built: for instance, Longpont, founded in 1131, dedicated its church in 1227; St. Louis[33] was present. They are lavishly endowed with lands and other donations. We shall see that for (already) fifty years, these donations have sometimes {been} violations of the original *Instituta* of the *Exordium Parvum*.[34] Clairvaux received 1771 donations of land, etc. in its first hundred years, and made many purchases besides. Its property was centered around twelve granges and two cellars (*cellaria*—i.e. vineyards and buildings attached).

---

32. See Louis Lekai, *The White Monks: A History of the Cistercian Order* (Okauchee, WI: Our Lady of Spring Bank, 1953), 37–38.

33. King Louis IX (1214–1270), canonized 1297.

34. *Exordium Parvum*, chap. 15 (*Nomasticon*, 62–63).

Attempts to slow down expansion:

a. The General Chapter had long ago seen {the} danger in this rapid and far-flung expansion. {In} *1152*[35] a statute forbade further foundations; the statute of 1152 was enacted under a new Abbot of Cîteaux, Goswin. He had just succeeded Raynald, friend of St. Bernard and {a} promoter of expansion. St. Bernard was ill at the time. This statute reflects conflict in the Order over the policy of expansion {and} probably expresses the desires of a group that disagreed with St. Bernard and Raynald[36] on this point. But the Bernardine outlook still was very strong and predominated: *1158* {saw} five foundations, {and} *1162* fourteen foundations.

b. Furthermore, the General Chapter had seen {the} danger in the acquisition of more and more land. {In} 1180 it passed a statute *de non acquirendo*.[37] This was ineffective and by 1248 it was set aside.[38]

c. The General Chapter had seen {the} danger in the ever-increasing building programs and the too-ambitious building projects. Legislation to prevent this is found in 1188, n. 10;[39] 1191, n. 90;[40] 1192, n. 4[41] etc.

Special Dangers: the danger was all the greater because some of the monasteries were going into debt while acquiring more land and putting up larger buildings. In 1182[42] it was forbidden to a monastery in debt to start any more building. {With regard to} visitations, naturally it was difficult for Fathers Immediate to visit all these foundations, but as we shall see, it was not the visitors that failed. Visitations were regularly and conscientiously made. Undoubtedly in the large number of postulants that were received, there may perhaps have been many who were not fully

---

35. Canivez, *Statuta*, 1.45 (#1).
36. Typescript reads "Raymond."
37. "on not acquiring [property]" (Canivez, *Statuta*, 1.86–87 [#1]).
38. Canivez, *Statuta*, 2.327 (#1).
39. Canivez, *Statuta*, 1.109–10.
40. Canivez, *Statuta*, 1.146.
41. Canivez, *Statuta*, 1.147.
42. Canivez, *Statuta*, 1.90–91 (#9).

suited to the monastic life, and who, once they were under vows, were kept for life even though mentally ill, or of scandalously evil life. But in the twelfth century, Cîteaux took the elite. In the thirteenth century the best vocations went rather to the friars. However, one fact cannot be doubted: among the large numbers received into the Order *comparatively few were destined to be contemplatives*. On the contrary it would seem that the majority were of a type who, able to lead a good strict and regular life in the cloister, definitely needed to be kept busy. Hence the Order more or less consciously renounced the desire to remain purely contemplative and entered, with its eyes open, into *active participation in the contemporary struggles of the Church*, as the "Order of St. Bernard" (read Lekai, p. 42-43[43]). The post of *abbot* in the Cistercian Order is one of great power and prestige. It is enviable, and sometimes influence outside {the} monastery is already brought to bear in obtaining it. The abbot is a feudal lord. He is very much engaged in public life, as we shall see. He is very much interested in maintaining[44] the power and wealth of his monastery. The Cistercian *cellarers* were in actual fact important and busy men. They travelled much, with their aides, and were influential in what we would now call the business world. The Cistercian monasteries were drawn upon for *bishops*: {there were} 160 Cistercian bishops in the thirteenth century. We shall see that on the continent they were also drawn upon by the popes,

---

43. "To meet the challenge of a changing civilization, theoretically, there were only two possible procedures: the first would be to reduce systematically and proportionately to the decreasing contemplative vocations the number of houses and their membership, in order to attempt to secure as far as possible the primitive spirit and discipline; the second would be to maintain the preeminent position of the Order in the Church and society in its full extent, providing the whole organization with the necessary vocations by a compromise, namely, the adaptation of the Rule to the contemporary religious needs and desires. Since the first course was practically impossible and in fact, never happened in monastic history, there was no real choice but to take the second alternative."

44. Typescript reads "maintain."

especially Innocent III, for special missions, and particularly to preach and fight against the Albigensian heresy. Generally, even in decline the situation was peaceful and outwardly regular, and we can see what is probably the condition of the Order in its average monasteries: there is nothing outwardly remarkable, neither special fervor or notable decline; the monasteries still maintain a reputation for austerity and regularity, and still attract some from other monastic families—v.g. the Benedictines; also later the Carmelite friars, when the Carmelites have their problems about action–contemplation in {the} mid-thirteenth century, will turn to Cîteaux as a haven of contemplation. (*Note*: even in the fifteenth century, *The Imitation of Christ*[45] can still point to the Cistercians as edifying by their austere monastic life of prayer.) However the contemplative fervor has largely died down, says Knowles of the English monasteries. Note however the *Cistercian convents of nuns in the Lowlands* were centers of mystical life, related to the spirituality of the Béguines in preparing the way for {the} Rhenish mystics of the fourteenth century. In general it can be said that the average Cistercian monastery is a quiet, prosperous, well-ordered religious house "sunk in the countryside" (READ Knowles, *Religious Orders*, I, p. 316[46]).

45. "Consider how other religious persons act who are strictly governed under the rules of their religious order. They seldom go forth; they live severely; they eat poorly, and are clothed roughly. They labor much, speak little, watch long, arise early, make long prayers, read frequently, and keep themselves always in some holy doctrine. Consider the Carthusians and the Cistercians, and many other monks and nuns of different orders—how they rise every night to serve our Lord" (Thomas à Kempis, *The Imitation of Christ*, trans. Richard Whitford, ed. Harold C. Gardiner, SJ [Garden City, NY: Doubleday Image, 1955], 71 [bk. 1, chap. 25]).

46. "Of the Cistercian abbeys, only a very few in the thirteenth century show distinguishing characteristics. Thus Beaulieu in Hampshire, by reason of its recent plantation from abroad under royal patronage, and Hayles, chiefly on account of the relic which made it one of the most frequented shrines in England, had a certain celebrity, and the Cistercians in general retained something of their reputation for austerity until the middle of the

Expansion in Eastern Europe: this presented a very special problem. It was here that the *Instituta* regarding property and sources of income were *violated on a large scale*. This was considered justified because the monasteries had a missionary function among pagan peoples. Note: in Portugal also, where the monasteries were spearheads against Mohammedanism, vast properties were also acquired. {For} example, Leubus, in Poland, in its charter of foundation has churches, rents, sharecroppers and villages. By 1239 this monastery had acquired 950,000 acres of land.

Growth of the Order in the Thirteenth Century: about 170 abbeys of men were added in the thirteenth[47] century. Abbeys of other orders wanted frequently to be incorporated in the Order of Cistercians, but the Order is now very cautious in receiving them. {The} General Chapter {of} 1231 ({n.} 52[48]) does not want {to} be accused of "grabbing." {In} 1253 three abbeys which apply are officially visited[49] {but} only one is accepted.[50] {In} 1236 a Cistercian cardinal "presented" two abbeys to the Order, but in the end they were refused (1236:16[51]). It is an error to think that the Priory of Val de Choux[52] was affiliated with the Order in 1214: a

---

century, as is shown by the occasional recruits they still drew off from the black monks and canons, but in general their abbeys had sunk into the countryside and lost for ever that compelling charm which had once made them seem like outposts of Jerusalem, the vision of peace. Even the great Yorkshire abbeys, Fountains and Rievaulx, were now distinguished by little save their larger flocks and the superior magnificence of their fabric. Nevertheless, a few notices remain to show that many of them, especially in the north, still stood high in general esteem" (David Knowles, *The Religious Orders in England*, 3 vols. [Cambridge: Cambridge University Press, 1948–1959]).

47. Typescript reads "14th."
48. Canivez, *Statuta*, 2.100.
49. Canivez, *Statuta*, 2.392 (#16).
50. 1254:10 (Canivez, *Statuta*, 2.401).
51. Canivez, *Statuta*, 2.155–56.
52. A Burgundian hermitage site that became a monastery and the motherhouse of a small monastic order, which eventually was incorporated into the Cistercian Order in the eighteenth century.

statute of the General Chapter (1214:34[53]) refers only to association *with the prayers* of the Order; Val de Choux was founded by a Carthusian in 1193, and it had some Cistercian features also.

Foundations in Syria and Greece: {in} *Syria and {the} Holy Land*, {it is} difficult to say exactly when and where monasteries were founded; {the} initiative {was} usually taken by lords on crusades. There were six monasteries in Syria—they had a short life. {With respect to} *Greece*, Cistercian monasteries in Greece were founded during the iniquitous Latin Empire of Constantinople.[54] There are records of five or six monasteries, which were soon destroyed.

The Nuns and Recluses {were} never fully accepted by the Order without reservations. {The} General Chapter {of} 1228:16[55] authorizes any convent to live by Cistercian rules, but disclaims all responsibility. This {statute} refuses to admit new convents into the Order; this favored the *Béguines*. Some abbeys, however, maintained a close relationship with communities of recluses and Béguines—v.g. Marienstatt had care of a group of recluses. {The} Abbot of Sichem had the recluse Blessed Hazeka under his care. {The} Abbot of Villers supported {the} Béguines of Nivelles, Tirlemont, etc. {The} Abbot of Locus Sancti Bernardi took care of Béguines in Brussels and Malines.

Expansion declines about the middle of the thirteenth century. From 1263 to 1267 only five foundations {are made} (one a year); {from} 1267 to 1335, {there are a total of} thirty-two foundations (less than one every two years).

{With regard to the} *size of monasteries*, at the peak of the expansion the monasteries were not as large as we think. Clairvaux was an exception, {with its} monks under St. Bernard. Rievaulx under Ailred had 140 monks and 600 brothers; {as for} other English houses, Fountains {had} 80 monks {and} 200 brothers, Waverly 70 monks {and} 120 brothers; *most* monasteries {had

---

53. Canivez, *Statuta*, 1.424.
54. I.e. in the aftermath of the Fourth Crusade (1204).
55. Canivez, *Statuta*, 2.68.

about} 30 monks {and} 40 to 60 laybrothers, says Knowles[56] (this seems low).

2. THE ECONOMIC SITUATION OF THE ORDER {at the} end of {the} twelfth century {and the} beginning of {the} thirteenth century:

1) Review here the basic legislation of the *Exordium Parvum, capitum* XV—{the} *Instituta*:[57] they renounced *ecclesias* (parish churches), *altaria seu oblationes* (Mass stipends and especially foundations?), *sepulturas* (burial privileges for benefactors), *decimas* (tithes on the produce of others' work and land), *furnos* (manorial bakeries), *molendina* (mills where peasants were charged for the corn ground), *villas* (villages), *rusticos* (later *coloni*?).[58]

2) *Thesis*: during the later twelfth and early thirteenth centuries, the Cistercians reached a peak of phenomenal economic prosperity, due first of all to their very efficient economic system, and to the work done by monks and especially by brothers in developing the great monastic properties. At the same time the respect in which they were held by all brought them many donations, not only of land, which they were entitled to accept, but also of some of the sources of revenue that they had renounced. By the end of the twelfth century the Cistercians were (a) very rich; (b) the object of widespread criticism for their wealth; (c) the General Chapter was striving to maintain the policy of the founders but without full success; (d) many of the points of the *Instituta* in the *Exordium Parvum* XV were habitually violated; (e) the storm center was the question of *tithes*, which will have to be considered in detail; (f) another source of problems was the *laybrotherhood*, obviously central in the economic functioning of the Order.

3) The Efficiency of the Cistercian System: the Cistercian monks acquired large properties, usually in forest areas, which they opened up for cultivation, draining marshes etc. They did not originally rent their land out but farmed it themselves. The original fervor of the monks and the numerous laybrothers' voca-

---

56. See Knowles, *Religious Orders*, 2.258–59, which also mentions Furness (70 and 120) and Louth Park (66 and 150).

57. *Nomasticon*, 62–63.

58. "countryfolk," i.e. sharecroppers (see below, page 168); "farmers."

tions ensured that the work done was zealous and productive. The system of *granges*, which ideally had to be within a day's journey of {the} monastery, enabled the monks to reach out over a wide territory (granges could be twenty miles away). Seven or ten granges were normal for an abbey of moderate size; larger houses had many more. The whole productive enterprise of the monastery was centralized under the control of the cellarer and not divided among many officials as in the Benedictine monasteries of the time. Under the cellarers were bursars and other business men, grange masters, and monks sent on journeys for business.

> During the first fifty years of Cistercian life in England the economic and social significance of the monasteries underwent a very considerable development. In the sphere of material things, the great innovation of the white monks had been the introduction of agricultural work as an essential of the monastic life. In origin the move was largely due to a desire to escape from the possession of the complex sources of income of the black monks and to return to a simple life in which the community should live by the labour of its own hands, This, however, was soon recognized as being impossible once a family had passed the pioneer stage, for the hours of heavy labour needed for farm, field and forest work, especially if at any distance from the monastery, would have left insufficient time for the prayer and reading of the Rule. To escape from this difficulty the early fathers of Cîteaux had recourse to the employment, truly epoch-making in its consequences, of lay brothers. When the order was still in its cradle no eye could have foreseen what important economic consequences were to result from this system, and how these were to react in time upon the order itself. A small religious house, buried in the forest or in an upland valley, of which some members, not in orders, devoted the greater part of their time to rearing beasts and cultivating the scanty fields of the monastery, had as innocent an appearance as the first crude pieces of steam-driven machinery in the mills of the north six hundred years later. But when the houses of the order were multiplied a hundredfold, and when the monks and *conversi* in many of the larger ones could

themselves be counted by the hundred, and when these powerful forces of labour could cease from reducing a wilderness to order and devote themselves to exploiting to the extreme limit all the resources of a territory already under cultivation, and when this territory, originally perhaps a waste, but now fertile and increased by gift after gift, was treated as a single economic unit and became something very considerable upon the map of the district, the full implications of the system were, if not fully realized, at least experienced far and wide. The wheel had come full circle, and the expedient {originally devised to isolate the monastery from the life of the world} was now something which affected at least indirectly the lives of all around. From being a small Christian household, exhibiting the dignity of toil and of direct production in the midst of a feudal society, the great Cistercian abbeys had become ranches, *latifundia*, the enemies of their small neighbours. In the districts of intense cultivation of vine and olive in the south of Europe, and even in the purely agricultural lands, harmful consequences were long in making themselves felt, but in north England and (though less notably) in Wales, circumstances combined to make of the white monks mass-producers of the raw material which formed the basis of much of the country's industry, trade and credit during the later centuries of the Middle Ages. All this came about in large part before the order had been established for a hundred years in England; later, the process was to go a stage farther when the class of *conversi* who had been its mainspring disappeared, leaving the Cistercian monks as capitalists in the full sense of the word. This rapid economic development is of such importance that its beginnings deserve to be traced in the scanty records of contemporary documents (Knowles, *Monastic Order in England*, p. 348f.;[59] READ Knowles, *Religious Orders*, I, p. 66[60]).

---

59. David Knowles, *The Monastic Order in England: A History of its Development from the Times of St Dunstan to the Fourth Lateran Council 940–1216* (Cambridge: Cambridge University Press, 1940) (line omitted in the text restored).

60. "The pasturing of sheep had always been an integral part of English husbandry. The sheep, indeed, had more uses than any other animal. Besides

4) Irregularities: in 1147, when Savigny and its twenty-nine dependencies join the Order, they are allowed to continue practices which were against the original *Instituta* of Cîteaux—for instance, tithes {and} parish churches. This was also true of dependencies of Cadouin, like Fontguilhem,[61] which received a church in 1141 (and probably others) and was affiliated to Cîteaux in 1147. Another monastery, Grosbois, received a church in 1150 and was affiliated to the Order in 1166. But this had its effect on the other houses of the Order. However, not everything is to be blamed on the Savigny houses. In 1145, Bellevaux, an original Cistercian foundation, received the gift of a parish church, *before* the affiliation of the Savigny congregation (see Knowles, *Monastic*

---

the wool, which was carded, spun and woven in every village, the ewes gave milk for direct consumption and for cheese-making. . . . The precise moment at which English wool was first grown for export is difficult to mark. . . . There is, however, little evidence of an organized trade or large-scale sheep-farming for the wool market before the arrival of the Cistercians. Settling as they did away from cultivation and free of the shackling organization of manor and village, with limitless pasture for their sheep on mountain, moor, wold and marsh, with abundant service and an efficient central control, they began very early to have a large surplus from the year's clip which exporters and foreign merchants were willing to buy *en masse* for the looms of the new towns of the continent. They had, at least throughout the twelfth century, heavy advantages over the black monks who in the majority of cases kept their sheep scattered over their manors and exploited by half a dozen different obedientiaries, even if they had not been leased out with the land. The estimation and collection of the crop were therefore alike more difficult, and in fact the black monks did not as a rule deliver their wool graded, as did the Cistercians, but mixed and in bulk. Among the new orders, on the other hand, conditions were ideal for large-scale buying: the woolmonger could ride up to the abbey, learn at once the number and quality of fleeces to be shorn and the probable yield in sacks of wool; he could, if he wished, ride round the sheep-walks and inspect the flocks himself; he could fix the date of delivery, settle the price and cross the moors to the next abbey. The attention of the exporting merchants was thus quickly attracted to the white monks and canons" (1:66-67; previously quoted above, p. 106, n. 591).

61. Typescript reads "Fontguilhen."

Order, p. 350 and ff.[62]). {With regard to} *villages*, what could an abbey do with the gift of a village? (a) one course which kept the letter and spirit of the *Instituta* {was that} it could refuse; (b) another course {was that} it could accept and then satisfy the letter of the *Instituta* by sending the inhabitants elsewhere, tearing down the buildings, and using the land for a grange—this was bitterly criticized and happened often[63] (*n.b.* {the} case of a parish church thus destroyed, and the action upheld by {a} Cistercian bishop [Murdac] and pope [Eugene III] [Knowles, *Monastic Order*, 350]); (c) simply accept the village and use it as a source of income, {a} violation of both letter and spirit, but in some sense more honest than (b). {As for} *serfs*, it was licit to hire laborers, but not to own serfs. Already in 1157[64] there is legislation to correct abuses on this point. The practice of owning serfs grew because *they were acquired with land*. Between 1154 and 1157 Rievaulx acquired *all the serfs* with a property given by Roger de Mowbray.[65] Similar transactions, including *purchase* of serfs, {are} noted at Kirkstall in {the} second half of {the} twelfth century. In 1210, Meaux had sixteen serfs on one part of its lands (see {the} article by Coburn Graves[66] [ASOC, 1957, fasc. 1-2[67]]). *Advowson* {refers to} accepting a church, appointing the pastor, and collecting revenues. {See the} example of Byland, which in 1143 *refused* a gift of several churches because {this would have been} contrary to the *Instituta*.[68] Note: there may well have been many more such

---

62. Knowles discussed the Cistercian ownership of churches here (350–51, 354–55) but not the specific instance of Bellevaux, for which see Mahn, *L'Ordre*, 48–49, n. 3, which mentions the other cited instances as well.

63. See Knowles, *Monastic Order*, 350–51, *Religious Orders*, 1.64.

64. Canivez, *Statuta*, 1.68 (#70).

65. Roger de Mowbray (ca. 1120–1188) was a major supporter of the Cistercians in Yorkshire. He was also the one who offered the three churches to Byland Abbey, mentioned below.

66. Coburn V. Graves, "The Economic Activities of the Cistercians in Medieval England (1128–1307)," *Analecta Sacri Ordinis Cisterciensis* 13 (1957): 7.

67. Graves, "Economic Activities," 3–62.

68. See Graves, "Economic Activities," 9; Knowles, *Monastic Order*, 355.

refusals than we realize. *Acceptances were recorded*, refusals generally not so. How many sacrifices for the sake of monastic purity are unknown to us? It is possible that the English Cistercians were the first to lose the original spirit, due to economic expansion. Yet the original spirit lived in the communities.

> Thus by the end of the twelfth century an atmosphere of commerce and litigation was beginning to surround the white monks in England. As will be seen elsewhere, there is some reason to think that in this respect the Cistercians of this country were among the first to lose the original purity of their order. How far discipline and observance were affected for the worse is not so clear; this point, also, will receive further treatment on another page; here it may suffice to remark that the summary judgments that have sometimes been made do not sufficiently distinguish between century and century, house and house, and that in general the life of the order would seem to have been still vigorous at the death of John. The Yorkshire families, in particular, with all their ramifications, were still a powerful spiritual force in 1200. Rievaulx, Fountains and Byland were the luminaries of the north; Byland had only recently lost her founding abbot, Roger, and Rievaulx, which had called a succession of superiors from her daughter-houses to rule as abbots, was flourishing and observant. As for Fountains, the centenarian Serlo who could remember the first beginnings was able to assert *c.* 1206 that the spirit of the original fathers of the house still lived on there. This abbey, indeed, deserves more than a passing reference, for the origin of Fountains gives to it such a unique position among the Cistercian houses of England that it is of interest to follow its history to the end of the period with which we are concerned, so far as the scanty records permit. (Knowles, *Monastic Order in England*, p. 356)[69]

---

69. Fountains was founded in 1132 by a group of black monks from St. Mary's Abbey, York, led by Richard, the prior, in a secession that is often compared to that of the first Cistercians from Molesme (see Knowles, *Monastic Order*, 231–39).

Churches—churches were a most profitable source of income, also of political patronage. By {the} end of {the} twelfth century it was common for Cistercians to own parish churches—v.g. in England: Byland, Meaux, Pipewell, Stanley, Wardon, Woburn.[70] Cleeve *rented* a nearby church owned by {the} Abbey of Bec.[71] The possession of churches involved many problems. In 1157, Geoffrey de la Roche, St. Bernard's friend, secretary and biographer,[72] when he became Bishop of Langres, gave the Abbey of Quincy (Cistercian) a church and its revenues.[73] In 1196, Clairvaux has the church of Boulogne[74] and its revenues. In 1189, Salley was broke {and} visitors recommended the house close down or move. Lady Percy, {the} daughter of {the} founder, gave three churches to support and save {the} monastery.[75] In 1189 {came} the famous case of the *church of Scarborough*,[76] donated to the Order by Richard I of England to defray expenses of {the} annual General Chapter. Cîteaux had to offer hospitality to over 500 abbots by {the} beginning of {the} thirteenth century. The church of Scarborough, {in} Yorkshire, was presented to the Order, {but the} king reserved

---

70. See Graves, "Economic Activities," 9.

71. See Graves, "Economic Activities," 9.

72. Merton is combining two early disciples of Saint Bernard here: his cousin Geoffrey (or Godfrey) de la Roche, one of the original companions who entered Cîteaux with Bernard, who later became prior of Clairvaux, and then in 1138 Bishop of Langres (Bruno Scott James calls him "Bernard's alter ego" [*The Letters of St. Bernard of Clairvaux*, trans. Bruno Scott James (Chicago: Henry Regnery Company, 1953), 249]), and Geoffrey of Auxerre, former student of Abelard who became Bernard's secretary and was one of the three authors of the first biography of Bernard (*Vita Prima*, bks. 3–5); he was also abbot of Clairvaux in 1161–1165, after serving as Abbot of Igny, and would subsequently hold the same office at Fossanova and Hautecombe (see Archdale A. King, *Cîteaux and Her Elder Daughters* [London: Burns & Oates, 1954], 249–51).

73. See J.-M. Canivez, "Cîteaux (Ordre)," *Dictionnaire d'Histoire et de Géographie Ecclésiastiques*, 12.919.

74. Typescript reads "Bonlogne."

75. See Graves, "Economic Activities," 11.

76. See C. H. Talbot, "Cîteaux and Scarborough," *Studia Monastica* 2 (1960), 95–158.

{the} right to appoint {its} vicar. He was under {the} surveillance of {the} Abbot of Rievaulx. As pastor he was responsible to {the} Archbishop of York for his ministry, {to} Cîteaux for the revenues. Revenues *included all the tithes* in Scarborough, including those of the fishing industry. Later, the Abbot of Cîteaux also appoints the vicar. He supervised the affairs of this church by a monk who was "proctor" and lived at Scarborough with some companions. (For some of the affairs conducted by the proctor, see C. H. Talbot, "Cîteaux and Scarborough," in *Studia Monastica*, vol. 2, #1, p. 100ff.) *Note*: he successfully kept the Friars Minor from establishing themselves in Scarborough in 1239 (see {the} same article, p. 101-102). However the mendicants moved in successfully in 1252 (Dominicans) and 1267 (Minors). The people now went to them and the revenues of the parish church diminished seriously. This created a long and bitter struggle between Cistercians and mendicants in Scarborough. The Cistercians gave up their resistance at the end of the thirteenth century. Gradually, during the Hundred Years War, the Scarborough parish becomes detached from Cîteaux and affiliated to an English house; the proctors are now representatives of the *king*. Cîteaux battled for a long time, ineffectually, trying to recover its rights. They were still fighting for this parish when the Reformation swept everything away.

{With regard to} *tombs*, a statute of the General Chapter {of} 1194 (#7)[77] indicates that already it is quite common for *founders of monasteries* and bishops to be interred in the cloisters—also laymen. With these tombs went certain gifts, including in many cases *pittances* on the anniversary of the departed.[78] {As for} *mills*

---

77. Canivez, *Statuta*, 1.172.

78. See Thomas Merton, *Monastic Observances: Initiation into the Monastic Tradition* 5, ed. Patrick F. O'Connell, MW 25 (Collegeville, MN: Cistercian Publications, 2010), 186: "All monasteries in fact have benefactors, and in the ancient monasteries sometimes benefactors left sums of money to be used for 'pittances' ('relief') to be served in the refectory on certain days, and the monks prayed for them in a special way in consequence. Pittances could be specified by the benefactor—that the monks should have a dish of eggs, or even of fish, or some wine of good quality, etc."

{and their} violations, see 1157, n. 36.⁷⁹ Abbeys had manorial mills which they rented to others or gave to a third party for his lifetime, provided they would return it at death. Meaux was running mills at a loss {during the period} 1249-1269.⁸⁰

The Problem of Tithes: although all the above were significant, the greatest and most complex problem was that of tithes. This problem is involved in many of the others we have seen above, for instance churches and villages. Because of tithing, the Cistercians entered very early into conflicts with Benedictines and the secular clergy, as well as with secular lords:

a) The ordinary practice {was that} all property was normally tithed. The revenues were divided between the bishop, the local clergy, the poor, and the upkeep of the church.

b) The Cistercians renounced tithes as a source of income. They did not receive tithes. They did not originally renounce the payment of tithes.

c) But from the beginning, since they did not receive tithes, it was conceded to them by generous donors that they would be exempt from *paying* tithes on certain properties. But this means that the properties were donated and at the same time the obligation to pay tithes was removed. They received the land free of tithes. However, on other land they continued to pay tithes.

d) {In} 1132, {in} *Habitantes*,⁸¹ Innocent II exempts the Cistercians from paying any tithes, and the phrase *sane laborum*⁸² is introduced.⁸³ It acquires a certain importance.

---

79. Canivez, *Statuta*, 1.64.
80. See Graves, "Economic Activities," 8.
81. The bull *Habitantes in Domo Dei* of February 10, 1132 (J.-P. Migne, ed., Patrologiae Cursus Completus, Series Latina [PL], 221 vols. [Paris: Garnier, 1844–1865], 179:122C–123D); see Mahn, *L'Ordre*, 99, 104.
82. "Certainly of [your] works, [no one may presume to demand tithes from you]" (i.e. on lands cultivated by their own labor).
83. "Dans tous les cas visés, l'exemption de dîmes est introduite par l'emploi d'une formule qui débute par ces mots: *Sane laborum*" ("In all the instances considered, exemption from tithes is introduced by using a formula which begins with these words: *Sane laborum* ") (Mahn, *L'Ordre*, 105).

e) {In} 1156, Adrian IV,[84] because of {the} problem of the large amount of land thus exempted from tithing, makes a distinction. New lands acquired by the Order which are *already under cultivation* are to be tithed if they are so already. But new land brought under cultivation by the Cistercians is not to be tithed. The expression *sane novalium*[85] appears here, as distinct from *sane laborum*. Exemption *sane novalium* is exemption of new land opened up for cultivation.[86]

f) This leads to a hot debate: are the Cistercians really to be confined strictly to exemption *sane novalium* or have they a right to insist on exemption *sane laborum*? Obviously it makes a big difference, because in the second case all the land they work themselves is exempt; in the other case only land opened up for cultivation by them is exempt.

g) In 1168,[87] Alexander III supports the Cistercians in their claim for exemption *sane laborum*.[88] Hence the favorable decision increases {the} hostility of enemies of Cîteaux. There is a renewal of physical struggle, which had been known in the lifetime of St. Bernard in the celebrated case of the Benedictine monks of

---

84. See Mahn, *L'Ordre*, 106–7.
85. "Certainly of [lands] newly [brought under cultivation]."
86. "la formule restrictive d'exemption (*Sane novalium*) n'apparaissant dans les privileges concédés aux Cisterciens au lieu de la formule générale (*Sane laborum*), qu'à partir d'Adrien IV" (Mahn, *L'Ordre*, 107) ("the restrictive formula of exemption (*Sane novalium*) appearing in the privileges granted to the Cistercians in place of the general formula (*Sane laborum*), only from the time of Adrian IV").
87. Typescript reads "1160."
88. "[P]ar la bulle *Audivimus et audientes,* donc les terms seront souvent reproduits au cours de son pontificat, puis par ses successeurs, le pape Alexandre III, notifiait dès 1168 au plus tard, que, s'il n'avait entendu exempter les Cisterciens que des dîmes novales, il n'aurait pas parlés de leurs *labores*, mais seulement de leur *novalia*" (Mahn, *L'Ordre*, 108) ("In the bull *Audivimus et audientes,* whose terms would often be repeated in the course of his pontificate, then by his successors, Pope Alexander III let it be known from 1168 onward that if he had only intended to exempt the Cistercians from new tithes he would not have spoken of their *labores* but only of their *novalia*").

Gigny, who attacked the Cistercians of Le Miroir because the latter refused to pay them tithes.[89] Monks of Noirlac were attacked during harvest by Benedictines of Bourg Dieu for {the} same reason.[90] {These were} typical incidents.

h) Archbishop Richard of Canterbury writes to the Abbot of Cîteaux reproving him for accepting this exemption. It was justified in the early days, when the Order was poor, but {he asserts} that now the only legitimate exemption is *sane novalium*.[91]

i) {In} 1179, the Third Lateran Council does nothing about the question of the tithes of the Cistercians, although it is a burning issue. However, Alexander III himself writes a letter (June 6, 1179) urging the Cistercians to moderate their activities in this regard. He urges the following moves: (a) Cistercians should not extend the exemption from tithes to newly acquired lands already under cultivation (a modification of the *sane novalium*—a solution which respects the privilege granted to lands they already possess but affects what they are to acquire from then on); (b) English Cistercian abbots are to cease taking over parish churches; (c) in general the Cistercians must moderate their acquisitions of land and must come to friendly agreements with those who have legitimate complaints against them.[92]

j) {In} 1180, the General Chapter follows up this instruction by deciding that cultivated land acquired by the Order is not exempt from tithing, except by special agreement.[93] The statute is very strong and detailed. It reads in part:

---

89. Because the Cluniac Abbey of Gigny had lost revenue from tithes from the Cistercian Abbey of Miroir, now exempted by the pope from paying them, some of the Gigny monks invaded Miroir and did extensive damage, for which they were ordered to pay compensation (see Mahn, *L'Ordre*, 105, and Saint Bernard's letter to Pope Eugenius [*Letters*, 429–30 (#353); PL 182:489B–490A (#283)]).

90. See Mahn, *L'Ordre*, 110.

91. PL 207:252; see Mahn, *L'Ordre*, 110–11, and Graves, "Economic Activities," 50–51.

92. See Mahn, *L'Ordre*, 111.

93. See Mahn, *L'Ordre*, 111.

Since the words of God and men alike admonish us to put a rein to our cupidities and a limit to our acquisitions, we have hitherto hesitated to impose a strict norm on our brethren because of the various conditions of the monasteries and in order that their good might be the fruit of voluntary action. We have also felt it was necessary to deliberate upon this question at length. Meanwhile because of the serious scandal which grows from day to day concerning our keeping back of tithes, we provide and firmly command that whosoever among you from this day forth shall have acquired fields and vineyards from which . . . tithes were collected, etc.[94]

We see from this that it is a partial and emergency measure, pending a fuller study and more complete legislation on the whole problem of acquisitions.

k) {In} 1189 (see Canivez, 1190, n. 1[95]), the more definitive and final solution is promulgated, and renewed in brief form in 1191, n. 42.[96] It is a statute *de non acquirendo*, and applies a perpetual ban on all purchases of new real estate (*possessiones immobiles*) with the exception of pasture lands, which are still left undecided. Exceptions {are} also {made that} those who have "problems with tithes"[97] *can* acquire new land ({this is} not clear), and those with distant and less good lands can get rid of these and replace them with better and more convenient lands.

---

94. "*Cum divina pariter et humana verba nos admoneant, ut studeamus cupiditatibus nostris imponere frenum, et modum acquisitionibus nostris propter varios status monasteriorum, adhuc veremur necessitatem fratribus nostris imponere, optantes bonum eorum voluntarium esse, et diuturna deliberatione super hoc credimus opus fore. Interim autem propter scandalum gravius, quod super retentione decimarum undique crescit in dies, providemus et firmiter praecipimus, ut quicumque ex vobis ab hoc die, et deinceps acquisierit agros vel vineas, ex quibus . . . percipere hactenus decimas consueverant . . .* " (Canivez, *Statuta*, 1.86–87 [#1]).

95. Canivez, *Statuta*, 1.117–18; see Mahn, *L'Ordre*, 112.

96. Canivez, *Statuta*, 1.142.

97. "*de decimis inquietantur*" (Canivez, *Statuta*, 1.118).

l) {In} 1203,⁹⁸ the General Chapter penances abbots who pay tithes from which they are exempt. Therefore the Order intends to cling to its privilege.

m) {In} 1213 {comes the} notorious affair of a monastery in Hungary which was carrying on a large-scale wine operation, and was buying many vineyards {but} not paying tithes on them. The affair was brought to Pope Innocent III and he decided to refer it to the coming Lateran Council.⁹⁹

n) {In} 1215 the FOURTH LATERAN COUNCIL legislates finally concerning the Cistercians' tithes.¹⁰⁰ Canon 55¹⁰¹ exempts the Cistercians from tithes on lands acquired before that time and cultivated by the monks or their hired help (*sane laborum* {is} confirmed). *But not exempt are all lands acquired after 1215, even if cultivated by monks.*¹⁰²

o) However this settlement was not absolutely definitive. Many cases arose which required that it be restated over and over again. Meanwhile, privileges were granted once again, and exceptions crept in. For instance {in} *1224* Honorius III exempts from tithes, unconditionally, Cistercian gardens, orchards and fisheries.¹⁰³ {In} *1244* Innocent IV exempts salt flats, mills, forage, wool, milk, lambs.¹⁰⁴ {In} *1261*, lands rented to others and acquired before {the} Lateran Council of 1215 are exempt from tithes.¹⁰⁵

We can stop this survey here. It shows how the Order clung tenaciously to this very important and profitable privilege, and maintained it against all comers. But this was a constant source

---

98. Canivez, *Statuta*, 1.287 (#15); see Mahn, *L'Ordre*, 112.
99. See Mahn, *L'Ordre*, 112; Lekai, *The White Monks*, 216.
100. See Mahn, *L'Ordre*, 112–13.
101. *Disciplinary Decrees of the General Councils*, ed. and trans. H. J. Schroeder (St. Louis: B. Herder, 1937), 283.
102. I. e. all lands already under cultivation.
103. See Mahn, *L'Ordre*, 113–14.
104. See Mahn, *L'Ordre*, 114.
105. See Mahn, *L'Ordre*, 114–15.

of conflict. The fact that the Order was severely criticized does not mean that all the wrong was on one side. The privilege had been granted for good reasons, and those who saw it from a certain point of view could insist that it was perfectly legitimate. It was in any case a right which the Order felt itself obliged to defend stoutly.

Cistercians as Collectors of Tithes:[106] the Cistercians could certainly justify their conduct in defending their privilege of *exemption from paying tithes*. But as collectors of tithes they were less fully justified. Tithes were clearly forbidden as a source of income in the *Exordium Parvum*.[107] The data that follows is perhaps not complete. It is a simple indication of the trend in the Order. The way tithes came into the Order was usually through the acquisition of parish churches that collected tithes on other land not belonging to the Order. The houses of the Savigny family brought into the Order with them many parish churches. There are rare indications of houses actually in the Order receiving churches before 1153—for instance, *Bellevaux* received a church in 1145. {In} 1186, Colbaz ({in} Eastern Europe) receives tithes from villages; {in} 1202, four brothers enter Gimont, bringing with them their share in some tithes; {in} 1211, Ourscamp receives {a} gift of tithes on certain lands, not the lands themselves; {in} 1220, {there is a} similar donation to Ter Doest. {At the} 1230 General Chapter, statute 3[108] speaks explicitly of abbeys of our Order acquiring {the} right to collect tithes on land, and approves of it, in special cases. {In} 1248, a lord entering Cîteaux brings in with him a share of some tithes. The MOST FAMOUS CASE of tithes and other church incomes was {in} 1189—the gift of the (parish) church of Scarborough, Yorkshire, by Richard I to Cîteaux to cover the expenses of the annual General Chapter. All the revenues of this church went to Cîteaux, and a monk of Cîteaux with some brothers lived at Scarborough to manage {the} property (not {as a} parish priest).

---

106. See Mahn, *L'Ordre*, 116–18.
107. *Nomasticon*, 62 (chap. 15).
108. Canivez, *Statuta*, 2.84.

Much trouble and litigation {developed} over this property in later years, {including} fights with {the} mendicants (see above[109]).

Letters of Alexander III criticizing the Cistercians: Dom Leclercq[110] has produced two letters of Alexander III[111] in which important sections had been left in the dark and not reproduced in Cistercian collections because they were unfavorable to the Order. Other sections, more favorable, had been preserved. *Revue Bénédictine*, 1954, p. 68 gives a section added to some copies of the letter (*Aeterna et Incommutabilis*[112]) specially in reference to certain English Cistercians who were favoring the schism of Victor IV. More important for our purpose {is the} letter *Inter Innumeras* to the General Chapter (1169),[113] only once published in its entirety,[114] and this one text is little known and has hitherto been ignored or remained unknown to Cistercian historians ({a} partial text is in Canivez, *Statuta*, for 1170[115]). This text reproaches some of the Cistercian monasteries for having *villas et rusticos*. This applied especially to two Savignian houses in England— Swineshead and Furness. Were *villages* and *sharecroppers* among legitimate sources of income for these houses, like tithes and churches? evidently not. Also, the monasteries not only own parish churches but distribute benefices like secular lords. They are told to discontinue this practice. {Likewise pertinent are} newly discovered statutes of {the} General Chapter: in a manuscript of Vauclair,[116] Dom Leclercq has also discovered statutes of General Chapters, some of which are in Canivez, others not. Some refer

---

109. See page 160, n. 76.
110. Jean Leclercq, OSB, "Épitres d'Alexandre III sur les Cisterciens," *Revue Bénédictine* 64 (1954): 68–82.
111. Pope from 1159 to 1181.
112. A papal bull issued in October 1159 (Leclercq, "Épitres d'Alexandre III," 69).
113. See Leclercq, "Épitres d'Alexandre III," 70–74.
114. By A. Duchesne (see Leclercq, "Épitres d'Alexandre III," 71).
115. Canivez, *Statuta*, 1.76–79.
116. See Leclercq, "Épitres d'Alexandre III," 74–82.

The Cistercian Order (1153–1335) 169

to liturgical simplicity and simplicity in buildings. {There are} important ones regarding {the} economic situation of the Order, and {which are} a response to the letter of Alexander III, thinks Leclercq:

1. 1175[117] {decrees that} those who have mills must get rid of them in a year. 1180 {rules that} *villas* must not be received and must be got rid of.[118] {On the} question of mills, {the Chapter determines} under what special conditions a mill may be kept, {making a} distinction between "abbeys founded in the Order,"[119] which must get rid of mills, and others (Savigny etc.) which may keep them under certain conditions—*ergo* abbeys not of {the} Savigny congregations also had mills by 1180. {From} 1182[120] {comes an} important statute from {the} Vauclair manuscript, not in Canivez: "It is evident to all that from the great expansion of our possessions there arise to us both within the order and outside it a multitude of scandals and that this *expansion is the greatest if not the sole source and origin of all our troubles* [ET EA NOBIS VEL SOLA VEL MAXIMA OMNIUM EST ORIGO ET CAUSA MALORUM]. . . . Hence by the grace of God and with His mercy we are striving to put a check to cupidity, an end to acquisitions, and limit to possessions [CUPIDITATIBUS FRENUM, ACQUISITIONIBUS FINEM, POSSESSIONIBUS MODUM]."[121] The following measures are then taken:

(1) They will be content with what they now have, and not acquire (i.e. buy) any new land, whether cultivated or not. However this is not absolute, if they wish to exchange a certain tract of land for better land, or if they have already planned to buy a larger tract, and they can recover land that has been rented out or somehow alienated. Also the restriction does not bind the

---

117. Canivez, *Statuta*, 1.83 (#15); Leclercq, "Épitres d'Alexandre III," 78.

118. Canivez, *Statuta*, 1.87 (#1); Leclercq, "Épitres d'Alexandre III," 78.

119. "*Abbatie . . . create in ordine*" (Leclercq, "Épitres d'Alexandre III," 79).

120. Typescript reads "1181."

121. Leclercq, "Épitres d'Alexandre III," 79–81.

small, poor monasteries which have not yet reached a normal size (which is not specified).

(2) Those who have mills and other possessions forbidden to the Order must not rent them out to others and then later recover them.

(3) N. 51 of the *Instituta*[122] in the *Exordium Parvum* is repeated, about *mercatores*, the monks going to fairs: *"Multa est de mercatoribus nostris querela, multa confusio."*[123] It is not complete—{it} demands only honest transactions and forbids shipping overseas.

How this important text came to be excluded from collections of the statutes is not explained. We have seen above, however, that the General Chapter, 1190, n. 1,[124] promulgated a long statute *de non acquirendo*, renewed in brief form in 1191, #42.[125] The latter reads: AD TEMPERANDAM CUPIDITATEM IN ORDINE NOSTRO ET NOTAM SEMPER ACQUIRENDI QUA IMPETIMUR REPELLENDAM, PROPOSUIMUS FIRMITER TENENDUM AB OMNIBUS UT DEINCEPS OMNINO ABSTINEAMUS AB OMNI EMPTIONE TERRARUM ET POSSESSIONUM ET MOBILIUM.[126] Note that this is much stricter, more precise and more absolute than the prolix and heavily qualified text given by Leclercq for 1182. There, many reservations are allowed and many exceptions made. Here there are none: *firmiter tenendum ab omnibus; omnino abstineamus ab omni emptione*—of what? *terrarum—possessionum—mobilium.* The General Chapter of 1190 (#14)[127] had already taken account of the *danger of large debts* by forbidding monasteries to borrow

---

122. The reference should be to the *Statuta* of 1134, rather than to the *Exordium Parvum* (*Nomasticon*, 223-24; Canivez, *Statuta*, 1.24).

123. "There is a great deal of complaint, a great deal of confusion about our merchants" (Canivez, *Statuta*, 1.24, which reads *"multa de . . . querela est"*; Leclercq, "Épitres d'Alexandre III," 80, which reads *"mercationibus"*).

124. See page 165, n. 95.

125. See page 165, n. 96.

126. "In order to moderate the avarice in our Order and to remove the stigma of always acquiring for which we are criticized, we have decided that all must be bound firmly to renounce completely all exemption of lands and possessions and moveable property."

127. Canivez, *Statuta*, 1.120-21.

money from Jews, who charged a high rate of interest. In 1186 the Jewish usurer Aaron of Lincoln died. Nine Cistercian abbeys, including Rievaulx, owed him 6400 marks, a very large sum. It was already usual to accept gifts of mortgaged land, along with the mortgage. *Note*: Jews were chattels of the king, and when a Jew died the king took over his credits {and} could make a favorable settlement with debtors.[128]

5) *Criticisms of the Order*—and of the twelfth century: note— the statute refers to the frequent criticism of the Order for "always buying," or broader, always acquiring (lands, buildings, perhaps even villages etc.). What were these criticisms? Were they from irresponsible people? Did others besides Pope Alexander III reprove the Cistercians? Many of the criticisms came from *friends* of the Order. It was these which moved the General Chapter more than anything else. Alexander III was a good friend of the Order. He had great respect for the Cistercians and canonized St. Bernard. The statute of 1191 was occasioned by several criticisms of the Cistercians.

a) A better known text of Alexander III, which is in *PL* 200:1004-1005[129] (quoted in Donnelly, *Decline of the Medieval Cistercian Laybrotherhood*[130]), reproves Cistercians for appointing priests to churches—hence of having churches. He forbids them to acquire any more churches, and gives his love for the Order as the reason. This letter dates from between 1161 and 1175; however this is not referred to in {the} General Chapter {of} 1191.

b) {A} letter of Richard, Archbishop of Canterbury (written before 1184) refers to the question of tithes (which will be taken up in more detail[131]) (see *PL* 207:252, quoted in Donnelly, *ibid.*[132]).

---

128. See Knowles, *Monastic Order*, 353–54; Graves, "Economic Activities," 42–44.
129. *Epistola* 1152.
130. Donnelly, *Decline*, 46, n. 38; see also Knowles, *Monastic Order*, 355, who dates the letter to ca. 1170.
131. Already discussed above, page 164.
132. Donnelly, *Decline*, 47, n. 39 (cols. 252–55).

c) {There is a} further letter of Alexander III taking up the same question of tithes (quoted in Donnelly, ibid.[133]). It includes these words: CESSATE ITAQUE IN ILLIS PRAESERTIM DUOBUS REGNIS [i.e. England and France] ACQUIRERE DE CETERO MONASTERIA UEL FUNDARE AUT DILATARE POSSESSIONES SEU CONGREGARE ANIMALIA IN IMMENSUM, SED MEDIOCRITATEM SEQUAMINI.[134] Hence {the} reference is to further foundations, to affiliation of monasteries of other orders, to acquisition of new lands, to enormous flocks (we shall see the English monks had huge flocks of sheep). This letter is dated June 6, 1179 (or '78).

d) {In} 1190, Abbot Stephen of St. Geneviève complained of {the} Abbot of Longpont to {the} Archbishop of Rheims and said scathingly: CREDO PATER QUIA CISTERCIENSES DE NUMERO SUNT EORUM QUI VIOLENTI DIRIPIUNT COELUM SED UTRUM VIOLENTER EIS TERRAM RAPERE LICEAT, NONDUM LEGI.[135]

e) Later King Richard I of England would criticize his friends the Cistercians for avarice (about 1197).[136] This criticism of Richard I was hardly fair. In 1193 the Cistercians of England had contributed the *wool crop of an entire year* to the sum for the ransom of their king, held prisoner by the Emperor. When he was set free he immediately tried to raise more money on the security of the 1194 crop and the monks, to avoid ruin, raised money themselves to pay this debt and save their main source of income.[137]

---

133. Donnelly, *Decline*, 47–48, n. 40.

134. "Therefore cease, especially in those two realms, to found monasteries or to acquire them from another, or to expand possessions or to collect animals without number, but follow the way of moderation."

135. "I believe, Father, that the Cistercians are among the number of those who seize heaven by violence, but whether it be permitted to them to seize the earth by violence, I have not yet read" (PL 211:351, quoted in Donnelly, *Decline*, 38, n. 3).

136. See Donnelly, *Decline*, 38, n. 4; Graves, "Economic Activities," 51.

137. See Graves, "Economic Activities," 20, 37–38.

f)[138] *Clerical writers* criticize the monks—{these were} forerunners of the Reformation, {writing} satirical literature, based on classical models, {as} an outlet for literary talent and social resentment. A new class {was} arising—the rootless and talented cleric. He takes the monks as his target and is not always careful to be true or just. His criticism is often exaggerated and unfair. A "satirical legend," {a} caricature or midrash, is created (see Graves, *ASOC* 13, p. 47). {For example, there is} *Gerald of Wales*[139] (see {the} description of him in Knowles, {*Monastic Order*}, p. 663), {a man of} charm, talent, activity, resentment, frustration and waste. His disappointments are reflected in his writing. His contrast between black and white monks {is found} in the *Itinerarium Kambriae*:[140]

> For the black monks he [Gerald of Wales] has little praise. They are rich, yet their riches serve no good purpose, for in part they are wasted in luxurious living, and in part they slip between the fingers of the many who have a share in their administration. The white monks, on the other hand, are excellent men of business and all is centred in the hands of one procurator; they do not live on rents and charges, but on their own work; they are most sparing in their diet and therefore able to practise the most abundant works of charity to the poor and travellers. Their fault is a grasping anxiety to acquire more and more land. The methods of the two bodies, Gerald continues, are utterly opposed one to the other. If you were to make a present to a community of black monks of a fully equipped abbey in the enjoyment of ample revenues, it would be dilapidated and poverty-stricken in a very short time. Give the Cistercians a wilderness or a forest, and in a few years you will find a dignified abbey in the midst of smiling plenty. Consequently, whereas the black monks will let a crowd of paupers starve at their

---

138. Typescript reads "e."
139. D. 1223.
140. *Journey through Wales*.

gates rather than give up one of their thirteen courses, the white will abandon one of their two scanty dishes rather than see a single poor man in want. Best of all, and combining the good qualities of black and white monks, are the canons. (Knowles, *Monastic Order in England*, p. 664–65)

In this book he is favorable to the Cistercians, compared to Cluniacs. His attacks on the Order are due mostly to personal conflicts with members of the Order, especially struggles for advantage and preferment (v.g. the case of the vacant See of St. David, in which Cistercians competed with him for the episcopacy). His criticisms usually apply to certain monasteries with which he is in conflict. It is always difficult to assess the real value of his statements (see Knowles, {*Monastic Order*}, p. 668). *Summary of Gerald's criticism of the monks*:

(a) {For the} black monks {he} criticized isolated cells where one or two monks lived without regularity and without fulfilling any special function. {He} also attacked their diet, much as St. Bernard had.[141] He reports cases of incontinence. He suggested they ought to have visitations "like the Cistercians," and this coming from a critic of the Order shows that the system was generally recognized to work well. *Cuncta supervacua et honestatis ordini contraria per visitatores et capitula resecare curant.*[142]

(b) {Regarding the} white monks, his stories about Cistercians do not indicate any laxity in the matter of austerity in the monastic life. {His} chief accusation {was} avarice. They are land-grabbers, he says. If you have a property near a Cistercian monastery, you are likely to suffer the fate of Naboth.[143] {He} resents their sound business methods, {and} condemns their deforestation. "The black monks are a scandal to him by reason of their

---

141. For Saint Bernard's critique of the Cluniac diet in the *Apologia* (PL 182:910), see Merton, *Cistercian Fathers and Their Monastic Theology*, 148–51.

142. "They take care to cut off all that is superfluous and contrary to the integrity of the order through visitors and chapters" (*Speculum Ecclesiae* [*Giraldi Cambrensis Opera*, 8 vols. (London: Longman, Green, Longman, and Roberts, 1873), IV.102], quoted in Knowles, *Monastic Order*, 670, n. 1).

143. See 1 Kgs [3 K] 21:1-29.

inefficiency and the white by their sound business methods."[144] {See the} story of Cistercians moving boundary stones, and even a tree, in the middle of the night (Coburn Graves in *Analecta SOC*, 13 [1957], p. 47[145]). However, he still respects the Cistercians, formerly his friends, and he prays that their almsdeeds may merit for them the grace of a return to their pristine purity. In this passage (Knowles, {*Monastic Order*}, p. 672, note 1[146]), he pays tribute to the wonderful hospitality of the Cistercians. He claims the English Cistercians are not as strict as the French. (He never criticizes the Carthusians.) Gerald of Wales is a gossip, a scandal monger, easily offended, moved by hurt feelings and wounded self-interest; hence his statements are to be taken with caution, but they offer sufficiently interesting and valuable indications of the state of the Order at the end of the twelfth century. ({For a} final judgement, read Knowles, {*Monastic Order*}, p. 673.[147])

144. Knowles, *Monastic Order*, 671, which reads "inefficiency, the white."

145. Monks in the north of England desired to acquire fertile neighboring lands and when the owner refused to sell, the monks moved the boundary stones and the tree and plowed up the new land (*Giraldi Speculum Ecclesiae*, IV.225–27]); Graves calls this tale and another about monks repeatedly sowing salt in a neighbor's field until he sells the land to the monks, at which point the field recovers its fecundity ("Economic Activities," 48; [*Giraldi Speculum Ecclesiae*, IV.228–29]), "patently absurd" and "ridiculous," but adds that behind them "lies the point that the monks' hunger for land was nothing less than avid."

146. *Giraldi Speculum Ecclesiae*, IV.117.

147. "Gerald of Wales, throughout his works and in all the changes of his life, remains something of an enigma, a strange compound of prejudice and perspicacity, of superficiality and insight, of vanity and zeal, of fervent aspirations and unworthy utterances. He learnt nothing and forgot nothing, and though he was seventy or more when he revised his latest writings they are as inconsistent and irresponsible as his earliest works. It is perhaps this very characteristic of irresponsibility, joined to the vivacity which never wholly forsook him, that has caused almost all who have studied his pages to extend to him an indulgence usually accorded only to the warm and hasty aberrations of youth, and to allude to his prejudices, his obscenities and his calumnies in a tone of banter. Yet Gerald must bear the responsibility of

Walter Map, {author of} *De Nugis Curialium*,[148] {was}, like Gerald, a Welshman, {who had} studied in Paris, an archdeacon who never made it to bishop. {He was} tougher and more cynical than Gerald, a little older than he, {and a} friend of Henry II. {He was} more violent against the Cistercians. His resentment[149] was apparently due to the fact that some revenues were lost to him when some Church lands were taken over by the Cistercians of Flaxley (i.e. he probably lost the tithes on this land). {He} also resented {the} Cistercian defense of Thomas à Becket. When Map took {his} oath as a judge, he swore to be fair to everyone—except Jews and Cistercians. Once when Map was told that two Cistercians had become Jews, he rejoiced that they had changed their life for the better but regretted they had not gone all the way and become Christians. He is virulent against the Cistercian expansion—ribald, coarse even blasphemous. He "lacked both balance of mind and ethical sobriety; to the deeper aspects of the Christian life he was quite blind, and therefore failed to see any of its manifestations in those around him" (Knowles, {*Monastic Order*}, p. 676).

Nigel Wireker,[150] {author of the} *Speculum Stultorum*,[151] {was} a black Benedictine of Christ Church, Canterbury, and a noted satirist of the time. The *Speculum* is the story of an ass who wants

---

having aspersed the fair fame of a whole class of men, the majority of whom were sincerely striving to follow a high ideal, and of having done so in a way which gave those whom he attacked no means of replying, and which has poisoned the ears of countless readers in later centuries. Lightly as all profess to treat him, more than one weighty writer on monastic history has insensibly adopted Gerald's opinions and conclusions, and he has thus come to occupy among the sources of history a position of importance which is out of proportion to his worth" (*Monastic Order*, 673–74).

148. Walter Map (d. 1210), *De Nugis Curialium / Courtiers' Trifles*, ed. and trans. M. R. James, rev. C. N. L. Brooke and R. A. B. Mynors (Oxford: Clarendon Press, 1983).

149. See Graves, "Economic Activities," 48.

150. D. ca. 1207.

151. *The Anglo-Latin Satirical Poets and Epigrammatists of the Twelfth Century*, ed. T. Wright, Rolls Series 59 (London: Longman, 1872), 1.3–145.

The Cistercian Order (1153–1335)

to join a religious order, reflects on the defects of all of them, and then decides to found one of his own.[152] He is less violent than Gerald of Wales or Walter Map, but in a gentler way satirizes the same general faults in Benedictines and Cistercians. {He wrote} an epigram on {the} Cistercian paradox {of} individual poverty and communal avarice: "*Paucis contenti non cessant quaerere magna / Et cum possideant omnia, semper egent.*"[153] Note however {that} Wireker and the others agree that *all* the orders have abandoned true poverty.

Summary of these criticisms: they have a foundation in fact, but prompted by literary and political motives, based on personal spite, they are simply a rehashing of familiar satirical themes popular among the clerics of the court at the time. Yet they have had a lasting effect: (a) They helped prepare the way for the even more drastic reactions of the fourteenth and fifteenth centuries (Wycliff, etc.); (b) They have been accepted by more modern historians hostile to Catholicism and the monastic order. Much medieval history is biased by the fact that critics like these are taken as perfectly trustworthy sources in all respects, and not critically evaluated (v.g. by G. G. Coulton[154]).

---

152. See Graves, "Economic Activities," 50.

153. "Content with little, they do not cease to seek great possessions / And when they possess all, they will still be in want" (*Speculum Stultorum*, quoted in Knowles, *Monastic Order*, 678, n. 3; Graves, "Economic Activities," 50, n. 6).

154. See G. G. Coulton, *Five Centuries of Religion*, 4 vols. (Cambridge: Cambridge University Press, 1923–1950). Actually, regarding his two chapters of contemporary critique of monasticism, entitled "A Catena of Generalizations" (2.379–413; see also Appendices 34–36: "Contemporary Generalizations" 1–3 [2.504–647]), Coulton writes "that not only heretics are excluded from these chapters (xxvi and xxvii), but professional satirists also, like Nigel Wireker and Walter Map, however orthodox they may have been" (2.418)—though in citing Walter earlier he writes, "It would be unfair to emphasize unduly the evidence of professional satirists, but, on the other hand, we cannot ignore it altogether, for the satirist has, in most cases, some foundation to build upon. Those of this period spare neither the monks'

Note the *critics in the fourteenth and fifteenth centuries*: the great quarrel about religious poverty will be vastly increased in scope and violence by the coming of the mendicants. They professed an even stricter poverty than the monks, and ended in many cases by being even less faithful and even more open to the accusation of greed and avarice. Hence the vital issue {becomes the} controversy on the very possibility of poverty that is not completely separated from possessions altogether—the controversy between the *mendicants* and the *possessioners* (cf. a similar struggle in Russian monasticism of the sixteenth century[155]). The

---

morals in general, nor even those of the Cistercians" (2.98). He does include various comments of Gerald (see 2.95–98, 383, 512–14), who he claims "writes not as a satirist but as a sober historian" (2.96), though previously described as "a stylist with a strong satirical turn" (2.95).

155. Merton refers here to the conflict between those who favored a powerful monastic presence rooted in extensive landholdings and those who supported a simple, poor, more charismatic monastic presence. In his essay "Russian Mystics" he briefly describes the two groups: "Such struggles as those between St. Nilus of Sora and St. Joseph of Volokolamsk speak eloquently of the age-old conflict, within monasticism itself, between the charismatic drive to solitary contemplation plus charismatic pastoral action, and the institutional need to fit the monastic community into a structure of organized socio-religious power, as a center of liturgy and education and as a nursery of bishops" (Thomas Merton, *Mystics and Zen Masters* [New York: Farrar, Straus and Giroux, 1967], 178–79). This piece was originally written as a Preface to Sergius Bolshakoff, *Russian Mystics*, CS 26 (Kalamazoo, MI: Cistercian Publications, 1977), which was not published until after Merton's death (see pages ix–x for a slightly different version of this passage); Bolshakoff himself writes of this conflict: "St Nilus of Sora (1433–1508), who visited Mount Athos in the fifteenth century, was the first, and perhaps the greatest Russian mystic. . . . According to St Nilus the outward forms of monastic life, although important, are secondary. The chief work of the monk is spiritual: the cultivation of the Prayer of Jesus, reading the Holy Scriptures and the Fathers and keeping death in mind. Without this one cannot attain union with God. . . . St Nilus did not approve of monastic wealth and the interference of monks in the affairs of the state. He also disapproved of ritualism and formalism in religion, as well as blind attachment to conven-

heart of the controversy {was that the} *mendicants* held that the Church should not own any property. {The} *possessioners* held that only those in the state of grace were capable of valid ownership; hence those in visible union with the Church were the only ones capable of owning property, and all really belonged to them. This could be turned against the Church by kings and laypersons wanting to tax Church property. They would point to evil lives of clerics and claim that these had thus forfeited their rights to ownership. {John} *Wycliff*[156] entered the controversy in 1360. At first he was on the side of the friars and bitterly criticized the older monastic orders for their great possessions. Later he got into heresy concerning the Eucharist and was condemned in 1377. After that the friars were against him as well as the monks. He was deposed as warden of Canterbury College, Oxford, and became completely embittered. He then attacked the clergy and the monks indiscriminately, and particularly advocated the *complete suppression of the religious orders* as being made up entirely of liars, crooks and troublemakers. Their property should be confiscated, and they should be forbidden to meddle further in men's lives, corrupting the Gospel. This is substantially the position that was to be taken by the Protestant reformers. The threats were carried out to the letter.

Poem of an Anonymous Cistercian: Graves (in *ASOC* 13, p. 51) says the "most comprehensive criticism" of the Cistercians comes

---

tions and outward traditions. The supporters of the opposite view, led by St Joseph of Volokolamsk (1440–1515), entered quickly into conflict with the disciples of St Nilus. The Josephians stood for monastic estates, which they considered essential for the wellbeing of the Church, and for the strictest ritual observance. The struggle between the two parties ended in victory for the Josephians, and led to the further growth of monastic land-owning, rigid ritualism, intolerance toward all foreigners, including Orthodox, and an unreasonable worship of the past. . . . The victory of the Josephians was an unhappy event for Russia and produced in the seventeenth century the Great Russian Schism" (xxii–xxiii; see also 38, 39–40).

156. Typescript reads "*William Wycliff.*"

from an anonymous member of the Order, author of a satirical poem on the decline of the Order, *De Mutatione Mala Ordinis Cistercii*,[157] {written toward the} end of {the} thirteenth century. (1) It is particularly against the English Cistercians—the ideal is still alive in Burgundy, but it is dead in England. (2) The economy of flock-raising has led to {a} decline of labor, to living in ease and eating up the revenue that was gained by their fathers; {he} especially attacks debts and speculation on future crops, as well as carelessness and inefficiency:

Stanza 10:

> *Ampla nimis possessio*
> *et rerum delectacio*
> > *fecerunt superbire*
> > *me et plura sitire*
>
> *invaluit ambicio*
> *evanuit devocio, . . .*[158]

Stanza 11:

> *Abcessit a me sanctitas*
> *pax amor et fidelitas*
> > *et cepi transvolare*
> > *ad forum seculare*
>
> *quicquid vidi desiderans,*
> *facta domus exasperans,*
> > *cepi implacitare*
> > *vicinos et gravare,*
>
> *exosos habens pauperes*
> *et solum inter proceres*
> > *me putans sine pare.*[159]

---

157. *On the Evil Transformation of the Cistercian Order.*

158. "Ambition has become strong / Devotion has vanished / The lust for power, for property / And a delight in temporal things / Have made me proud / And made me desire more things" (Merton's translation in his oral conference presentation).

159. "Sanctity has left me / Along with peace, love and fidelity / And I have flown away to the secular market. / There desiring everything that I

Stanza 17:
> *Dum Christi patrimonium*
> *agentes mercimonium*
> *in nichil redigere,*
> *premissa patuere.*
> *et sequitur conclusio:*
> *sic periit religio*
> *res simul periere.*[160]

(quoted in Graves, *ASOC* 13, pp. 53–54). Is this critic to be taken fully seriously? This is "poetry" and "satire," hence there is bound to be some exaggeration. The fact that he is a Cistercian is not necessarily a guarantee of truth. There were possible subjective distortions and elements of bitterness in this disgruntled attacker of his own Order.

Europe in the Thirteenth Century:

To understand the history of the Cistercians after 1200, we must have some idea of the new developments in European society. This is a crucial period: {a} transition takes place *from {a} feudal, agrarian society to an urban, commercial society*, {with the} growth of the towns and of the new class of burghers, or bourgeoisie. Industry and trade begin to be more and more important. Mendicant orders—"town" orders—become more and more important. The Cistercians were of the old agrarian society. Yet their economy permitted them to enter into the new scheme of things (English wool and Flemish weavers). {The} unity of Christendom under the pope breaks down with the rise of nations

---

see, / I have become an exasperating home; / I have become a penance to my neighbors / And I have become a burden to them. / The poor do not please me / And only among men of business / Do I feel myself in my place" (Merton's translation in his oral conference presentation).

160. "While plundering the patrimony of Christ / They have reduced their possessions to nothing; / What had been concealed was exposed, / And the result follows: / Religious life has thus perished / And worldly goods have disappeared at the same time."

and the ambitions of rulers {and} struggles between emperors[161] (Frederick II), kings (Philip the Fair) and the popes. Cistercians are deeply involved and sometimes the Order is split by these struggles. Preaching becomes very important in religious life, due to new inquisitive town classes and their interest in religion and philosophy—especially the *universities*. Cistercians are called upon to preach, and hence also become involved in university life. This was also true to a lesser extent of the Benedictines. It was a normal and perhaps inevitable development. The Order simply moved with the times. However this involved a *completely new mentality*, the scholastic mentality. St. Bernard had been opposed to the forerunners of scholasticism. The first Cistercians were alien to speculative thought and to theology as a strict science. The new orders had a more centralized structure. The Cistercian constitutional set-up was modified in the thirteenth century, influenced by the mendicants—hence the foundation of a body of *definitors* and the maintenance of a *procurator* at the Court of Rome, with also a *cardinal protector*.

THE STRUGGLE OF CÎTEAUX *with the Four First Foundations*:

This is a very important problem, and a delicate question. There was a grave struggle between Cîteaux and Clairvaux in particular. Clairvaux tended to be backed by Pontigny and Morimond; La Ferté at times sided with Cîteaux. Also, the General Chapter is involved in the struggle, naturally. What is the real issue? {It} depends on {the} concept of {the} real nature of {the} Cistercian constitution. Is it *democratic*, {with the} General Chapter supreme? Or {is it} *monarchic*, {with} one abbot supreme? Actually {it is} a combination of both—a balance between {the} Abbot of Cîteaux and {the} General Chapter. But the struggle is inevitably one for monarchic power, between Cîteaux and Clairvaux, with the General Chapter trying to preserve the original structure of the Order. Is this the correct view? {What is} *certainly essen-*

---

161. Typescript reads "Europeans."

tial {is the} protection of {the} autonomy of individual houses. {The} Abbot of Cîteaux claims the right to intervene in the affairs of any monastery, not only in his own filiations, and the right to depose and punish other abbots in the Order, especially the Abbot of Clairvaux and {abbots} of the other {three of the} four first foundations. At the same time, Clairvaux considered itself almost the "head of the Order," due to the power and fame of St. Bernard, and resented interference from Cîteaux. This struggle {was} waged intermittently throughout the first half of the thirteenth century, until 1265. It threatened the unity of the Order, and caused very grave disturbances. The Holy See was from the beginning particularly anxious to see this struggle end; also, the King of France intervened with great concern to try to end the battle. The climax of the struggle came in 1264, and it was finally settled with a decision of the Holy See in the bull PARVUS FONS {of} 1265. PARVUS FONS can be regarded as the first sign of the need for reform and can be, perhaps somewhat arbitrarily, taken as the end of the Golden Age of the Order. At any rate, *Parvus Fons* is the first clear and official recognition that all is not well in the great Order of Cîteaux. But this was the result of a long struggle. The evil had already begun to appear in the middle of the twelfth century, before the death of St. Bernard.

Background: for a clear understanding of this question, one should enter into the technical and detailed studies that have been made of the *Carta Caritatis*, in its various texts and revisions. The *Summa Cartae Caritatis* (1119) is contained in the actual document presented to and approved by Callistus II in 1119.[162] (For this

---

162. "*Ad Hoc in Apostolicae*" (*Nomasticon*, 73–74) (typescript reads "Callistus IX"). For the more recent dating of the *Carta Caritatis Prior* to 1119 and the *Carta Caritatis Posterior* to 1152, with the *Summa Cartae Caritatis* being an abridgement of the *Carta Caritatis Prior*, dating from early in the abbacy of Raynald de Bar of Cîteaux (1133/34–1150), see the references to the edition of Chrysogonus Waddell on page 146, n. 22 above.

text, discovered at Trent by Dom Leclercq, see *Collectanea*, 1954, p. 97-104.[163]) Chapter 5, *De Culpis Abbatium*,[164] provides {that}:

1) An offending abbot is warned four times by his Father Immediate; {the} case is {then} to be referred to {the local} bishop. If he does not act, the offender is then deposed by the Father Immediate and two other abbots, who preside over a new election and excommunicate {the} offender if he interferes.

2) If the Abbot of Cîteaux offends, the Abbots of La Ferté, Pontigny and Clairvaux are to warn, then depose him. But they cannot excommunicate him, and the election is to be conducted by three abbots of filiations of Cîteaux.

3) La Ferté takes over when {a} vacancy is at Cîteaux.

(See also cap. 3: *De Generali Statuto inter Abbatias*,[165] restricting {the} powers of all Fathers Immediate—{they} cannot even give {the} habit to a novice or take a monk to his own house.)

The *Carta Caritatis Prior* (in the Laibach manuscript, {which} has been printed in *ASOC*, 1950[166]) made a new Preface with the following: some extracts from an original draft {of} 1114-1118 {and} extracts from the *Summa Cartae Caritatis* {of} 1119. {In} 1152, the bull *Sacrosancta* of Eugene III already indicates that the struggle has begun. This bull is the approbation of a *new text to the Carta*

---

163. Actually Dom Leclercq's discussion of the Trent manuscript of the *Exordium Cistercii*, the *Summa Cartae Caritatis*, and the *Capitula* is found in Jean Leclercq, "Une Ancienne Rédaction des Coutumes Cisterciennes," *Revue d'Histoire Ecclésiastique* 47 (1952): 172–76; J.-A. Lefèvre published his transcription of this material, from MS. 1207 of Ste. Geneviève, Paris, supplemented by the Trent MS., as an appendix (97–104) to his article "La Véritable Constitution Cistercienne de 1119," *Collectanea Ordinis Cisterciensium Reformatorum* 16, no. 2 (1954): 77–104.

164. Lefèvre, "Véritable Constitution," 100–101.

165. Lefèvre, "Véritable Constitution," 99 (typescript reads "iv").

166. Canisius Noschitzka, "Codex Manuscriptus 31 Bibliothecae Universitatis Labacensis," *Analecta Sacri Ordinis Cisterciensis* 6 (1950): 1–124; see also Josip Turk, "Charta Caritatis Prior," *Analecta Sacri Ordinis Cisterciensis* 1 (1945): 11–61, in which the text of the *Carta Caritatis Prior* from this MS. was first published (53–61).

Caritatis—i.e. the *Carta Caritatis Prior*.¹⁶⁷ It deals with the following problems:
a) What is to happen if the Abbot of Cîteaux is in some situation where correction is required? How are abuses of the Abbot of Cîteaux to be stopped? (*Read* the last two paragraphs of cap. 5 {of the} *Carta Caritatis*¹⁶⁸ as we now have it: this reflects

---

167. N.B. it was in fact the *Carta Caritatis Posterior* that was approved in *Sacrosancta*; see once again page 146, n. 22 above.

168. "*Eodem etiam modo si forte (quod absit) Abbates nostri Ordinis matrem nostram Cisterciensem ecclesiam in sancto proposito languescere, & ab observatione Regulae vel Ordinis nostri exorbitare cognoverint, Abbatem ejusdem loci, per quatuor primos Abbates, scilicet de Firmitate, de Pontiniaco, de Clara Valle & de Morimundo, sub ceterorum Abbatum nomine usque quater, ut corrigatur ipse & alios corrigere curet, admoneant; & cetera quae de aliis dicta sunt Abbatibus, si incorrigibiles apparuerint, circa eum studiose adimpleantur; excepto quod si cedere sponte noluerit, nec deponere, nec contumaci dicere anathema poterunt; donec aut in generali Capitulo, aut si illud forte jam visum fuerit exspectari non posse, in conventu alio convocatis Abbatibus qui de Cistercio exierunt, & aliquibus aliorum, virum inutilem ab officio suo deponant, & tam ipsi quam monachi Cistercienses idoneum Abbatem eligere studeant. Quod si Abbas ille & monachi Cistercienses contumaciter recalcitrare voluerint, gladio excommunicationis eos ferire minime vereantur.*

"*Postea vero si quis praevaricator tandem resipiscens, & animam suam salvare cupiens, ad quamlibet quatuor nostrarum ecclesiarum, sive ad Firmitatem, sive ad Pontiniacum, sive ad Claram Vallem, sive ad Morimundum confugerit: sicut domesticus & cohaeres ecclesiae cum regulari satisfactione recipiatur, quoadusque propriae ecclesiae, sicut justum fuerit, reconciliatiae quandoque reddatur. Interim autem annuum Abbatum capitulum non apud Cistercium, sed ubi a quatuor supra nominatis Abbatibus praevisum fuerit, celebrabitur*" (*Nomasticon*, 73) ("In the same way, also, if by chance—may it not happen—the abbots of our Order should learn that our mother church of Cîteaux is becoming slack in its sacred commitment and straying from the observance of the Rule or of our Order, let them through the four first Fathers, that is, the Abbots of La Ferté, of Pontigny, of Clairvaux and of Morimond, in the name of the rest of the abbots, admonish the abbot of that place up to four times, in order that he himself may be corrected and take care to correct the others; and let other matters be diligently taken care of, filling in for him, which have been brought up concerning other abbots, if they have appeared to be incorrigible;

the situation after *Parvus Fons*, and is far from the situation one hundred years earlier.[169])

b) How is {the} Abbot of Cîteaux able to deal with delinquent abbots and communities? Substantially the solutions to both problems involve *intervention of the bishop* in whose diocese the abbey creating the problem exists.[170] The abbots can appeal to the Bishop of Châlons to depose {the} Abbot of Cîteaux. (This was done in 1264 by {the} Abbot of Clairvaux, {as} we shall see.) The Abbot of Cîteaux can now intervene in a case of {a} delinquent abbot in *any* monastery, but requires {the local} bishop to depose such an abbot. Cîteaux {is} still not visited by anyone, but abbots of other houses must be present at {the} election of {the} Abbot of Cîteaux ({the} Abbot of La Ferté administers it when {the abbacy is} vacant.) There are still only three "First Fathers."

The Question of the Definitors: this also is important. When does it first arise? See General Chapter, 1197:57:[171] the term *defini-*

---

except that if he refuses to give way willingly, they will be able neither to depose him nor to anathematize him as a contumacious person; until, either at a General Chapter or, if it seems that perhaps the decision cannot be put off until then, at another gathering of abbots called together who have gone forth from Cîteaux, along with some others, let them depose the useless man from his office and let both the abbots themselves and the monks of Cîteaux endeavor to elect a suitable abbot. But if the abbot himself and the monks of Cîteaux contumaciously refuse to cooperate, let them not fear in the least to strike them with the sword of excommunication. But afterwards, if any prevaricator, recovering his senses at last and desiring to save his soul, should fly to any of our four churches, that is, to La Ferté, Pontigny, Clairvaux or Morimond, let him be received as a household member and a fellow heir, with the satisfaction required by the *Rule*, up to the time when he may be returned to his own church, once it has been reconciled, as would be just. Meanwhile, however, the annual chapter of abbots will be held not at Cîteaux but at a place chosen beforehand by the four abbots named above").

169. This reflects, once again, a misconception of the dating of the *Carta Caritatis Posterior*.

170. This is the case in the *Carta Caritatis Prior*, but the intervention of the bishop is eliminated in the *Carta Caritatis Posterior*.

171. Canivez, *Statuta*, 1.221.

tores is used to designate the council of the Abbot of Cîteaux, which was to decide disputes between equal parties in the Chapter. From 1223 there was apparently a regularly elected *definitorium* which acted as a commission for special business in the General Chapter (see Lekai, p. 57). This was probably due to {the} influence of the Dominican Constitution, formulated in 1220.

Outline of the Struggle:

First Period: before {the Fourth} Lateran Council (1215): {in} 1202, {a} letter of Innocent III refers to trouble in the Order. {In} 1212, Arnold I of Cîteaux apparently deposed one of the four First Fathers without consulting the others, who wanted to discuss the matter. They accused him of arbitrariness and assuming too much power to himself. The pope urged them to settle the matter honorably and quietly among themselves and sent his legate, Cardinal Ugolino, to arbitrate. {In} 1215 the conflict was only settled by the threat that it would all be aired in the Council. They agreed temporarily among themselves, but it was only a truce.

Second Period: {from the} Lateran Council to 1262. A meeting of 1222 comes to some provisional conclusions: (1) {the} Abbot of Cîteaux cannot depose one of {the} four First Fathers without consulting the others; (2) {the} Abbot of Cîteaux cannot hear confessions in monasteries not of his filiation; (3) {the} Abbot of Cîteaux has {a} right to visit only his own daughter houses; (4) the four First Fathers visit Cîteaux together and the Abbot of Cîteaux must make the corrections they impose; (5) the Abbot of Clairvaux must give up privileges which he obtained directly from {the} Holy See, contrary to the laws of the Order. This shows a tendency to restrict {the} powers of Cîteaux and {of} Clairvaux. Clairvaux is somewhat restrained from developing as an independent power by dealing direct with {the} Holy See. Cîteaux is restrained from exercising independent power over other houses of the Order, and can be checked by {the} four First Fathers. The evident aim was to prevent either Cîteaux or Clairvaux from developing a hegemony. {The} composition of this meeting {included a} First Father present—*but not Clairvaux*—other abbots {and} several bishops, {with the} papal legate (a Cistercian) presiding. The fact that Clairvaux was absent meant that this was doomed to failure. During the rest of this period, {the} statutes of 1235,[172] 1236(35),[173] 1238(6),[174] 1246(6)[175] give information. Cîteaux {was} hard hit by {an} epidemic and {a} harvest failure. But the abbot antagonizes those who try to help him. {In} 1238, {the} Abbot of Cîteaux issues {a} sentence of suspension and interdict on {the} Abbot of Chaalis, not one of his filiations. The General Chapter annuls his decision.[176]

Third Period: The Crisis (1262-1265): {in} 1262, {the} Abbot of Cîteaux, Guy de Bourgogne, is made {a} cardinal. This necessitates {the} election of a successor. To be legal, the election had to be conducted in the presence of the four First Fathers. The Prior, James, of Cîteaux, conducted the election without them, and was himself elected. In the General Chapter of 1262, James tries to run the show single-handed and to nominate all the definitors himself. The Abbots of Clairvaux, Morimond and Pontigny protest against this. {In} *1263* Urban IV intervenes and tries to stop the dispute. He names arbiters. They are not able to accomplish anything. Here a mysterious thing occurs: Pope Urban IV appoints Philip, Abbot of Clairvaux, a bishop (of St. Malo in Brittany), evidently to get him out of the way. Why {had} he attempted this expedient? He further ordered Abbot James of Cîteaux to order Abbot Philip of Clairvaux to accept {this} appointment as bishop—strange. Instead of accepting, Abbot Philip of Clairvaux hastens to Rome, to show reasons why he should not be a bishop and to expose the state of the Order to the pope. {In} *1264*, the Abbot of Cîteaux summons Philip of Clairvaux to appear before him. Philip refuses {and} sends three abbots of his filiations to say why. {On} May 1 {the} Abbot of Cîteaux comes to Clairvaux to make visitation {but} is refused admission.

172. Canivez, *Statuta*, 2.142–43 (#20).
173. Canivez, *Statuta*, 2.160.
174. Canivez, *Statuta*, 2.186.
175. Canivez, *Statuta*, 2.302–3.
176. Canivez, *Statuta*, 2.187 (#9).

He pronounces {a} sentence of excommunication on {the} Abbot of Clairvaux. {On} May 22, {the} *Paris meeting* {takes place}: St. Louis summons both parties to meet with him in Paris and settle {the} dispute. At this meeting it is once more agreed: (1) {that the} four First Fathers visit Cîteaux; (2) what is to be done when {the} abbacy of Cîteaux is vacant: {the} First Fathers must come within four days; (3) {the} Abbot of Cîteaux does not have {a} right to hear confessions, etc. and to correct faults in all the houses of the Order, only his own filiations. At this meeting all the censures were lifted, but there was still no real satisfaction. {On} June 9, {the} pope intervenes in favor of Clairvaux. {By} July 7 {there is} still no settlement; {the} pope gets {the} Bishop of Troyes to arbitrate. {In} August (?) {there is a} *meeting at Langres*, before papal representatives: Cîteaux starts fighting in opposition to the points accepted at Paris; Clairvaux, failing in pleas for peace, receives papal permission to be absent from {the} General Chapter—also houses of {the} Clairvaux filiation may absent themselves. {On} September 8, Clairvaux holds a General Chapter of its own filiations ({there is a} practical schism in {the} Order). {On} October 2, Urban IV dies {and is} succeeded by CLEMENT IV, who convokes {the} Abbot of Cîteaux and {the} four First Fathers to discuss the question. In 1265 (June) he issues {the} bull *PARVUS FONS*.

PARVUS FONS (*Nomasticon*,[177] 366ff.): this is an official interpretation of the *Carta Cartatis*, and "an organic part of Cistercian constitutional development" (Lekai[178]):

1) It confirms the basic legislation in the *Carta*, worked out 1152-1190 (the so-called *Carta Caritatis Posterior*).

2) The document is evidently due to the work of Cardinal Guy (former Abbot of Cîteaux) with other abbots of the Order and the Dominicans (Dominican influence {is} obvious).

---

177. *Nomasticon*, 366–76; also found in Canivez, *Statuta*, 3.22–30.
178. Lekai, *The White Monks*, 57.

3) This document is actually a very serious compromise, which destroys the original, traditional framework of {the} Cistercian Order: (a) it destroys the autonomy of the individual house; (b) it destroys the originality of Cistercian law in its guarantee of a balance between the Abbot of Cîteaux and the General Chapter (a parliamentary body); (c) {it} establishes the DEFINITORIUM (on {the} mendicant pattern)—this is a consultative body of twenty-five abbots, made up of {the} Abbot of Cîteaux, and {the} four First Fathers, each with four abbots from {his} own filiations (yet this had been in existence for almost a hundred years—under what form?). *Parvus Fons* comes at {the} beginning of the so-called *Libellus Antiquarum Definitionum*,[179] which was completed in 1289 and re-edited in 1316. This *Libellus* constitutes the basic legislation of the Order after the Golden Age.[180] It contains: (1) {the} *Carta Caritatis Posterior*; (2) *Parvus Fons*; (3) {the} *Bullarium* of Privileges; (4) legislation on: construction and dedication of abbeys; {the} divine office—liturgy; {the} General Chapter; punishments; visitations and elections; studies (439); leaving and entering {the} Order; regular observances—fasting, etc.; laybrothers; nuns.

Outline of *Parvus Fons*:

1) Introduction: {the} Order of Cîteaux {is} compared to the rivers of Paradise watering the whole Church.

2) The Order is founded on charity. Satan has tried to divide those who should be closely united in fraternal love—*in jucunditate unanimitatis*.[181] The Holy See will settle the discord and restore peace, so necessary to the Order.

---

179. *Nomasticon*, 366–471; *Parvus Fons* is *Distinctio* I.II of the *Libellus*.

180. See Lekai, *The White Monks*, 70–71, for the various compilations of statutes: "At the very beginning of relaxation the alert Chapter acted immediately by issuing a collection of former disciplinary regulations under the title *Institutiones Capituli Generalis* in 1240, revised in 1256. A code of similar decisions was published in 1289 and reviewed in 1316, as the *Libellus Antiquarum Definitionum* which, following the legislation of Benedict XII, was further modified and became compulsory in 1350, as the *Libellus Novellarum Definitionum*."

181. "in the enjoyment of unanimity" (*Nomasticon*, 369, which reads "*jucunditatem unanimitatis*").

3) The four First Fathers will be in charge of Cîteaux when the abbatial see is vacant, but the seal of Cîteaux will be locked up by {the} Prior of Cîteaux. In other words the seal will be in the hands of the Father Immediate during {a} vacancy.

4) {In the} *election of {the} Abbot of Cîteaux*, only the monks of Cîteaux will vote. The four First Fathers and other abbots of Cîteaux filiations will be present, but will not have {an} active vote. Clement justifies this as a *reductio ad jus commune*.[182]

5) {Regarding the} confirmation of {the} Abbot of Cîteaux, he needs no special confirmation from the Holy See. Here a Cistercian custom is maintained *against the jus commune*. This clause is considered as a confirmation of all duly elected abbots of Cîteaux.

6) The elections in ordinary abbeys follow Cistercian custom. The Cistercians are not bound by special prescriptions of {the} Fourth Lateran Council.

7) Fathers Immediate {are} not to interfere unduly in elections of {a} daughter house; {they are} not to nominate electors or influence electors nominated by {the} prior, subprior and cellarer of {a} vacant house, {are} not to remove anyone from office during {a} vacancy {and are} not to depose a rightly elected candidate.

8) {The} Definitorium {is to consist of} twenty definitors and {the} four First Fathers and {the} Abbot of Cîteaux.

ACTIVITIES OF THE CISTERCIANS {in the} Twelfth and Thirteenth Centuries:

There can be no doubt that one of the most important factors in the decline of the Cistercian Order was the great amount of activities in which its members came to be involved: first the activity connected with business of the monasteries of the Order, then affairs of the Church and public life, especially the Crusades. This must not be oversimplified. It is an immensely complex problem. However the following facts must be made clear at the outset:

1) The Cistercians considered themselves from the first *contemplatives*, in our terminology. They were monks, and the

---

182. *Nomasticon*, 370, which reads "*ad jus commune reduxerit*" ("it is rooted in the common law").

Exordium Parvum as well as the *Carta Caritatis* show distinctly that whatever may have been their concept of the contemplative life, they certainly wanted *quies monastica*[183] and sought to withdraw from the business, the litigations, the conflicts and the ambitions of "the world," not only in the sense of the profane world, but in the sense of the powerful ecclesiastical world of prelates and great abbeys. {The} *Exordium Parvum* says: *Ubi beatus Pater Benedictus docet ut monachus* a saecularibus actibus se faciat alienum *ibi liquido testatur haec non debere versari in actibus vel cordibus monachorum, qui nominis sui etymologiam haec fugiendo sectari debent.*[184]

2) Much of the activity of the Order resulted from its rapid expansion, the many foundations, the economic setup, the work involved, the building, the opening up of new land, the development of sources of income. This activity is not in itself opposed to the nature and ideal of the Order.

3) A great part of the exterior activity of the Order was carried out under obedience to the Holy See, and with repeated efforts and protests on the part of the General Chapter, striving to keep these missions and activities to a minimum. There is no question that much activity that is contrary to the spirit, even to the letter, of the *Rule*, was imposed on the Cistercians by obedience, in cases where this activity seemed to be necessary and useful to Rome.

4) In consequence of the useful activities imposed on the Order, many other less justifiable activities were also accepted

---

183. The phrase is found in the letter from Pope Paschal, the so-called "Roman Privilege" (chap. 14): "*Locum igitur illum quem inhabitandum pro quiete monastica elegistis*" ("that place in which you have chosen to dwell for monastic quiet") (*Nomasticon*, 61).

184. "When the blessed Father Benedict teaches that a monk should make himself distant from worldly activities, he testifies clearly there that these things should not be sought in the actions or in the hearts of monks, who ought to be pursuing the meaning of their name by fleeing these things" (chap. 14 [*Nomasticon*, 62]; the reference is to the Rule, chap. 4 [*The Rule of St. Benedict in Latin and English*, ed. and trans. Justin McCann (London: Burns, Oates, 1952), 26]).

and tolerated, so that the life of a Cistercian monk or brother could in fact become an extremely active one, and indeed many of these activities ruined the spirit of the Order in individuals or groups.

5) The Crusades: Cistercians since St. Bernard were involved in the preaching of crusades, and not only that, but accompanied the crusaders to the Holy Land, not only in a spiritual capacity, but even fighting and dying in battle. It is doubtful whether, for many of those who went to Palestine, there was any idea that this was not part of the vocation of a monk. Yet there were protests in the Order, and the General Chapter tried to moderate this excess of zeal.

The Order as such resisted the growth of these activities. The struggle against them was especially energetic in the twelfth century. From the mid-twelfth century on, there was a reaction against the vast expansion of the Order, new foundations were forbidden, economic expansion was discouraged, etc. But the measures taken were unavailing. The Order continued to grow, and abuses crept in on all sides. The turn of the thirteenth century can be said, in general, to mark the *general acceptance of activity* of every sort (except parish work) as normal for a Cistercian. In the second half of the twelfth century the Order then became *extremely active*; and from the thirteenth century on it was deeply involved in important and multifarious activities. There were many consequences: involvement in conflicts, litigation, business, and all the complexities of the ecclesiastical life of the Middle Ages when the Church was at the height of its power and the power was not only spiritual but *temporal*. We can briefly summarize some of the activities in which the Cistercians engaged, illustrating them by examples. The *Statuta* of the General Chapter offer much more information.

1. BUSINESS OF THE ORDER: the rich abbeys of the Order with many foundations obviously had many business ventures and problems to take up their time. For instance, the domain of Clairvaux (of course one of the largest) consisted of nearly two thousand donations made in the first century, plus many purchases,

mostly of land. The Clairvaux estate consisted of twelve granges and two "cellars" (in cities). Gifts of land sometimes brought with them churches or other ecclesiastical benefices requiring {the} service of monks—v.g. Meaux acquired with land a "chantry" requiring {the} service of seven monks.[185] {There were also} *debts*: the problem of monasteries in debt, and needing ready cash, in many cases due to overambitious building programs, come more and more to our attention. {In} 1182, in {an} effort to control this debt situation, {the} General Chapter forbids further expansion and construction to all monasteries in debt.[186] *Litigation* {was also an issue}: there were innumerable lawsuits, many of which arose from possession of illicit means of income—v.g. {the} conflict between Stanley and Salley (see Graves, *art. cit.*, p. 10[187]). The rectorship of churches also involved payment of taxes to {the} king, and complications resulted—see {the} interesting case of litigation over a debt to Aaron of Lincoln (*art. cit.*, p. 44[188]). {The} Order {was} also involved in complex cases of *others*, even marriage cases and divorces (General Chapter, 1199:4;[189] 1206:8[190]). {Note also the} *mercatores*: from the very beginning there was trouble about monks going to market. In {the} 1134 collection {of the} *Instituta* {from the} General Chapter, n. 51, {we read}: *Multa de mercationibus nostris querela est, multa confusio*.[191] Yet necessity demands that they go to fairs. They are not to sell there (only buy). Business (trading) is to be kept down; hence {they} forbid

185. See Graves, "Economic Activities," 11.
186. Canivez, *Statuta*, 1.90–91 (#9).
187. The Abbey of Stanley moves to Whalley and gains the advowson of a church there, as a result of which the Abbey of Salley loses the sum of 100 shillings per year that it formerly received.
188. A landowner in debt to Aaron gives part of his property to the Abbey of Meaux, which is thus liable for a share of the debt.
189. Canivez, *Statuta*, 1.233.
190. Canivez, *Statuta*, 1.321.
191. "There is much disagreement, much confusion about our merchants" (Canivez, *Statuta*, 1.24).

buying at {a} low price and selling at {a} high price (General Chapter, 1194:3[192]). {They are to} buy for *use*, {and are} not to accept in exchange goods that cannot be used in {the} monastery and then sell the said goods; {they} should not go to fairs more than {a} three-days' journey away {and} should not go to fairs across the sea (even {to} England).[193] Conduct of those at fairs {was} strictly regulated—only two could go at a time, {and they could} only stay three or four days.[194] This was the ideal, but in reality these rules could not be strictly kept, especially after 1153. English abbeys in {the} thirteenth century held their own fairs. Jervaulx held a weekly market and two annual fairs.[195] Houses in Boston (a wool port) were owned by Meaux, Furness, Holme Cultram,[196] Salley, Jervaulx; other abbeys had houses in York, Lincoln, etc.[197] Problems arose with transport of goods to market. {A} caravan of wagons etc. might be charged for {the} privilege of crossing private land. Monks obtained charters to evade this charge, and then abused the charters by carrying goods belonging to others. {As for} *shipping*, Beaulieu ran a ship down the French coast to Bordeaux; Quarr had one or two seagoing ships; Netley had a ship called "The Nightingale"; Furness etc. had ships.[198] {There was also} *mining*: some Cistercians in England had iron mines; Furness had forty furnaces in operation—also Rievaulx, Kirkstall, etc.[199]

{For the incident of} *the cellarer of Biddlesden*, see Knowles, *Monastic Order in England*, 665—this {is} recorded by Gerald of Wales, enemy of the Order. William, cellarer of Biddlesden, met

---

192. Canivez, *Statuta*, 1.171; see Graves, "Economic Activities," 12.
193. Canivez, *Statuta*, 1.424 (1214:36); see Graves, "Economic Activities," 11.
194. See Graves, "Economic Activities," 11.
195. See Graves, "Economic Activities," 12.
196. Typescript reads "Holucultram."
197. See Graves, "Economic Activities," 13.
198. See Graves, "Economic Activities," 16, n. 5.
199. See Graves, "Economic Activities," 17–18.

Gerald of Wales in 1192 at {the} Court of Queen Eleanor. He had recently been deposed for peculation. He was on the road, trying to get himself made bishop somewhere. {He} travelled with Gerald and they quarreled. Gerald observed his political activities, and saw that he got {the} abbacy of Bittlesden by influence. {He} reported {him} to Cîteaux and had him deposed (see *Monastic Order in England*, 667 for further details; Gerald of Wales accuses {the} Cistercians of taking his library[200]).

BUILDING: the activity connected with building one's own monastery is taken as normal and not at all opposed to {the} spirit of the Order. Monks were good architects and builders. Hence monks of one abbey could be called on to help in {the} work {of} building another one. Architects and monk-builders did in fact travel around to various building jobs. This is not in itself an abuse. However, when monks were called in to build parish churches and cathedrals, and when this became frequent, especially in Germany and East Prussia, it led to abuse. John I, Bishop of Trier, had monks of Himmerod working on his cathedral building and on other churches in the diocese. ({For} monastic building as {a} source of debt, see Graves, *art. cit.*, p. 36.)

The WOOL TRADE (England): the wool trade of the English Cistercian monasteries is an example of the business activities of the monks in {the} Middle Ages. It is thoroughly studied because there is much material on the subject. (Here we follow {the} article of Coburn Graves in *Analecta SOC*, 1957, fas. 1-2, p. 19ff.[201]) High-quality wool was the principal product of medieval England. The wool trade was {the} basis of economic and political life of England in {the} Middle Ages. Knowles even holds that Cistercians were of prime importance in developing

---

200. See Knowles, *Monastic Order*, 667: Gerald's library had been housed at the Abbey of Strata Florida in Wales, and he hoped to use it as security for a loan from the monastery to finance a trip to Rome; when one of the monks convinced the abbot that such an arrangement was inconsistent with Cistercian regulations, Gerald was forced to sell the books.

201. Chapter 2: "The Cistercians and the Wool Trade," 19–32.

the wool trade (not all agree with this last point).[202] However, it

202. See Graves, "Economic Activities," 19–20, n. 5, referring to Knowles, *Religious Orders*, 1.66, where he writes: "There is, however, little evidence of an organized trade or large-scale sheep-farming for the wool market before the arrival of the Cistercians," to which Graves responds, "he does not offer strong evidence for this position." Knowles actually presents a nuanced evaluation of the Cistercian contribution: see *Monastic Order*, 352–53: "This branch of farming, which was to become such a source of wealth to the order, became their speciality almost by accident. Wool for clothing had always been a necessity in the village economy, and in the early twelfth century religious and other landowners were already keeping large flocks on down and marshland as a commercial asset. The rising demand of the Flemish cloth industry, however, had not yet been fully met, and in the wolds and moorlands of the north the population was too scanty and conditions too unsettled for any exploitation of the grassland. But it was precisely in these desolate open spaces that the white monks first settled; wool was necessary for their habits and cowls, and it so happened that their sheep were set to graze upon the rolling pastures of Lincolnshire and Yorkshire, which ever since that time have proved among the best in the world for rearing of noble sheep and the production of the finest fleeces. Sheep farming on a large scale, which had been utterly outside the purview of the small village cultivator, fettered as he was by divided strips, fold-service and labour-dues, was eminently practicable under the grange system of the Cistercian abbeys in the valleys of Lincolnshire, Yorkshire and, later, north Wales, and before the reign of John the annual yield of wool of their fleeces had become one of the assets of the country. In the thirteenth century it developed into a great export trade to Italy and the Netherlands, and for a time the white monks were the most considerable body of producers of wool in England, till gradually the graziers and merchants of Gloucestershire, Somerset, Sussex and East Anglia become supreme." See also *Religious Orders*, 1.33: "It was doubtless this continuity of administration which gave, first to the Cistercians and later to the black monks, a leading place among the pioneers of commercial sheep and dairy-farming, as well as among the first promoters of the corn trade of England"; 1.38: "The process of commercializing the demesne was, however, a slow one, save in the matter of sheep-farming, where a boom period had begun at the middle of the twelfth century, and the simultaneous development of the Cistercian ranches and the cloth industries of the Netherlands and Lombardy had caused a rapid growth of mercantile organization"; 1.41: "The attention given to

may be true that in Yorkshire, where the Cistercian monasteries were numerous, the monks may have had a decisive influence in developing wool production to a flourishing state. {The} moors made sheep-farming {an} obvious source of income. The English Cistercians depended on wool. Matthew Paris (quoted {in} *art. cit.*, p. 20, n. 2) {said}: *Novit mundus quod in lanis eorum omnis subsistit commoditas et sustenatio.*[203] The Cistercians contributed a

---

sheep-farming perhaps deserves a separate mention, if only because the achievements of the black monks in this respect have been thrown somewhat into the shade by the more spectacular activities of the new orders. In point of fact, sheep-farming with a view to the sale of wool was the oldest of all branches of English commercial farming. . . . [T]he yield of wool of the sheep on the commons, to say nothing of districts where down- or marshland was available, must always have far exceeded domestic needs. Sheep, then, when kept in any number, were at least in part a commercial asset, and it was undoubtedly from sales of wool that the small men secured the cash which they needed to pay rent or commute labour services. As for the older religious houses, they are found possessed of large flocks before the arrival of the Cistercians"; 1.65: "Writers on monastic history have often given their readers the impression that the Cistercians both originated and monopolized the English wool trade. Such a view is incorrect, even for the twelfth and thirteenth centuries. Large flocks were being reared by the black monks and by ecclesiastical and lay landowners before the arrival of the Cistercians, and religious orders besides the white monks continued to keep large flocks for commerce throughout the middle ages. Nevertheless, it is true that the Cistercians were the first to develop sheep-farming for the export market on a really large scale, and they, together with the other new orders who imitated their economy and settled in the same districts, remained, at least until the fourteenth century, the most powerful group of wool-growers and the producers of the finest fleeces"; 1.66: "There is . . . little evidence of an organized trade or large-scale sheep-farming before the arrival of the Cistercians"; 1.70: "Although the new orders had not originated the wool trade, the excellence of their produce and the ease with which it could be viewed and collected rapidly swept them to the top of the market, and from *c.* 1170 onwards for almost a century they were undoubtedly selling the bulk of the finest wool in the country."

203. "The world came to know that all their advantage and support depends upon their wool."

year's clip of wool to contribute to {the} ransom of Richard {the} Lion-Hearted. However the part played by Cistercians in medieval wool production must not be exaggerated. They produced about one-sixth of {the} total national output in {the} thirteenth century.[204] They were important producers and exporters of wool and among religious orders they were the biggest producers. Production of wool was perfect for {the} Cistercian economy: {it could be located} in remote waste lands, moors, etc. {and} did not require too much labor—{the} grange system was ideal. {The} *effects of dependence on wool* {were}: (a) *wool* {was} *a cash crop*—hence those houses that depended on wool ceased to be economically autonomous;[205] they did not grow grain, they bought it (this made sense in Yorkshire, etc.); (b) {a} need for more and more pasture land led to much renting, to sharing pasture with seculars,[206] to eviction of villages acquired, etc.;[207] (c) {the} appearance of scab and murrain in {the} thirteenth century decimated flocks;[208] {the} Cistercians were under contract for future wool crops to Italian merchants {and} had to get special help from {the} king to acquit themselves of these obligations (*art. cit.*, p. 23); often {they} had to mortgage {the} monastery, and even disperse. *Procedures in {the} wool trade* {were developed}: (a) the wool business was in the hands of a brother called the *lanarius*, under {the} supervision of {the} cellarer; abbots signed the contracts;[209] (b) wool had to be shipped to Flanders, usually, or to English ports where Italian merchants picked it up; {it} went overland to Boston or London by wagon; {a} chain of granges belonging to {the} monastery

---

204. See Knowles, *Monastic Order*, 353, n. 1: "c. 1300 the Cistercians produced only a sixth of the national wool-crop, but in 1200 their proportional share was certainly greater"; n.b. Graves points out that the percentage is for all monastic wool, not just Cistercian (21).
 205. See Graves, "Economic Activities," 22.
 206. See Graves, "Economic Activities," 22.
 207. See Graves, "Economic Activities," 49.
 208. See Graves, "Economic Activities," 22–23.
 209. See Graves, "Economic Activities," 24.

might serve as stopover places.²¹⁰ {The} General Chapter, 1195:4,²¹¹ stipulated that abbeys marketing wine or wool should not burden other monasteries on the way to market. {An} estimate of flocks {can be made} according to woolsacks sold: Fountains must have had about 12,000 sheep, Jervaulx 15,000 in {the} thirteenth century—probably much more than this, however (*art. cit.*, p. 25). The Cistercians produced very good wool and got more than average price. It was graded—three grades: good, medium and "lock wool." {There developed a system called} *collecta*: big producers would market wool for smaller producers.²¹² Cistercian abbeys bought wool from small producers and resold it at a profit. {The} General Chapter {of} 1157 tried to prevent this (1157:19²¹³). {The} special value of this practice {was that} it not only gave a profit but it provided the Cistercian seller with {a} better basis for bargaining (bigger quantity). Henry III protested against this: it was interfering with markets at Lincoln, etc. and cutting into taxes that went to the Crown. He accused the Cistercians of violating their rules (1262).²¹⁴ This did not prevent the monasteries from continuing the practice. {In making} *contracts*, usury entered in: contracts to furnish wool for two to twenty years, for a down payment or perhaps for a lump sum, amounted to loans on {the} wool crop as security. When more security was needed, merchants demanded {a} mortgage on abbey lands and buildings (READ *art. cit.*, p. 29²¹⁵). {A} special problem {was that}

  210. See Graves, "Economic Activities," 24.
  211. Canivez, *Statuta*, 1.183.
  212. See Graves, "Economic Activities," 27–28.
  213. Canivez, *Statuta*, 1.61.
  214. See Graves, "Economic Activities," 28.
  215. "Advance selling of wool accompanied by a large prepayment seems to have been a natural, if dangerous, part of the wool trade. The earliest instance of Cistercians engaging to deliver wool is derived from the accounts of the celebrated Christian usurer, William Cade. Louth Park and Roche had received money from Cade, and they were bound to deliver wool. In the thirteenth century the length of contracts extended from two to twenty years. The chief advantage of contracts of this nature lay in the fact that the

when {a} contract demanded payment in sacks of wool, and {the} wool price went up, the monks lost. {As for the} *policy of the Order*, efforts were made by the General Chapter to curtail these practices, but the policy was inconsistent. "In the end the ideal gave way completely before the facts of trade" (*art. cit.*, p. 30). {In} 1181,[216] permission {was} granted to sell {the} wool crop one year in advance after various struggles and compromises, until 1279[217] when it was permitted to sell for any period in advance, provided {the} money was used for retiring debts. (In practice the monks had been selling as they pleased.) ({For an} example of a contract, between Pipewell and merchants of Cahors, see *art. cit.*, p. 30 bottom—a hard contract with detailed clauses covering {the} smallest eventualities.)

DEBTS AND DIFFICULTIES:[218] one might assume that such a trade would have been very profitable. Actually it was not. The houses were often in debt and the conflicts caused by this were serious. {The main} *cause* {was that} "the monks were poor managers" (*art. cit.*, p. 33). Legislation was made to prevent indebtedness:[219] {in} 1182,[220] no abbey in debt beyond fifty marks

---

merchants paid part or all of their money at the commencement of the contract. In this way the contracts came in reality to be loans with the wool serving as security. In time, however, because of the danger of total loss by murrain, the merchants came to require something other than the wool for security, and abbeys such as Pipewell, Fountains, and Darnhall actually mortgaged their lands and abbey buildings under the guise of contracts covering the sale of wool" (28–29).

216. Canivez, *Statuta*, 1.89 (#10); see Graves, "Economic Activities," 30.
217. Canivez, *Statuta*, 3.184 (#2); see Graves, "Economic Activities," 30.
218. See Graves, "Economic Activities," chapter 3: "The Financial Difficulties of the Cistercians" (32–45).
219. See Graves, "Economic Activities," 33.
220. Canivez, *Statuta*, 1.90 (1182:9); see also 1.109 (1188:10), 1.147 (1192:4), 2.334 (1249:1), 3.61 (1268:10); see Graves, "Economic Activities," 33.

could start {a} new building; {in} 1224-25,[221] no monastery with heavy debts could receive postulants. {There were} frequent instances of houses so badly in debt that they {had to} disperse. Six houses in England dispersed between 1280 and 1296.[222] Other houses were put in custody of the Crown. {For} example, *Meaux* {had} great financial difficulties, like most Yorkshire houses at {the} end of {the} thirteenth century. Causes {included}: (1) famine and flood and other natural calamities; (2) Crown exactions and money paid for privileges; (3) land hunger of the monks; (4) excessive building; (5) advance sales of wool; (6) bad management (see *art. cit.*, p. 35). Note {the} combination of causes at Meaux:[223] after Richard returned from captivity he wanted *another* year's wool crop. Meaux commuted this to a heavy fine. That year there was a poor harvest. {The} mill and grainstore burned down. {The} monks dispersed for fifteen months (119-?).[224] {The period} 1200-1210 {saw a} conflict with King John,[225] who wanted to extort heavy taxes and withdrew his protection. He seized cattle, sheep and sacred vessels of Fountains and sold them. Many ab-

---

221. Canivez, *Statuta*, 2.34 (1224:25); see Graves, "Economic Activities," 33.

222. See Graves, "Economic Activities," 36.

223. But notice that what follows refers to events a century earlier than the preceding list of causes—the end of the twelfth century (see Graves, "Economic Activities," 37–38) rather than the end of the thirteenth (see Graves, "Economic Activities," 35–36).

224. See Graves, "Economic Activities," 38; the year of the fine was 1194 (see *Monastic Order*, 353). Knowles himself does not mention this incident, referring only to two other occasions when the monks at Meaux had to disperse: first in ca. 1155, "and again as a result of John's extortions" (*Monastic Order*, 354, n. 3). On the latter occasion, after the imposition of ruinous fines on Cistercian houses in 1210, the monks of Meaux were again scattered, among houses of canons, of Black Benedictines, of Scottish Cistercians, and in "towns and castles up and down the country—for no other Cistercian abbey in England had substance enough to share with them" (*Monastic Order*, 369); "Meaux was functioning again by 1 November 1211" (*Monastic Order*, 369, n. 5).

225. See Graves, "Economic Activities," 38–39.

beys dispersed. {The} Abbot of Waverley fled by night from his bankrupt monastery. King John's precedent was followed by Henry III, etc. Henry III nominally exempted Cistercians from tax but made them pay a huge sum for privileges—including tax exemption. {The} General Chapter then penalized English abbots for not protecting {the} privileges of the Order (1233:39[226]). ({On the} struggle with Henry III, READ *art. cit.*, p. 40.[227])

226. Canivez, *Statuta*, 2.119.
227. "In 1233 the king asked from the white monks a grant equivalent to the fortieth that was being levied, but he specified that the grant was not to be called a fortieth. When the monks agreed, the general chapter enacted a penalty for the four prime abbots of England, Waverley, Furness, Rievaulx, and Fountains for consenting to infringements of the liberties of the Order which they should have been protecting. The next demand came in 1242 when Henry sent the Archbishop of York to ask the Cistercian abbots for a subsidy for his war. Although Henry wanted money, he indicated that he would be content to accept a year's supply of wool. The abbots fell back upon their traditional grounds for refusal: they could not grant the aid without the consent of the general chapter, and they could not give money for a war where blood would be shed. They did, however, promise their prayers. Totally dissatisfied with this answer Henry forbade them to go to the general chapter. The next year he relented and allowed the abbots to make their appearance at the general chapter where he petitioned to be allowed to draw money from the abbots of his realm. When he failed in his request, he reacted by forbidding the sale and shipment of Cistercian wool to transmarine parts. In 1256 Henry was granted a tenth by the pope to enable him to finance the Sicilian venture, but the Cistercians were exempted. Henry, however, alternately wooed and threatened the monks, demanding from them a free gift of not less than twenty-five thousand pounds. The abbots, fearing the loss of their liberties if this should stand as a precedent refused to make the grant. Henry called them rebels and declared that they were to be shown no favor in his courts. He then required that those abbeys which had holdings by military service were to be distrained to do the service. Two years later the monks bent before the king and granted a year's clip of wool which in some cases must have been commuted to a money payment. Byland and Rievaulx each paid four hundred marks to the crown; Kirkstead, Meaux, and Wardon paid two hundred marks apiece; and Fountains rendered five hundred marks."

Addenda: *the Cistercian house in Dijon* (see *A K*, p. 28[228]) was presented to Cîteaux in 1171 by Duchess Matilda; it came to be called *Cistercium Parvum*. Permission to say Mass in the house was granted by Urban V. It was frequently used as a refuge for the community in later years. At "Little Cîteaux" the religious of Cîteaux expelled Cardinal Richelieu (1643) {and} elected their new abbot. *The church at Scarborough* was given to pay for expenses of the *first three days* of the General Chapter. For the fourth day Alexander II of Scotland provided {the Chapter} with a gift of money. For further expenses, King Bela IV of Hungary offered four churches with their revenues (*A K*, p. 31).

2. SPECIAL BUSINESS OF THE CHURCH:

a. *Bishops*: the fact that many Cistercian bishops existed in the twelfth and thirteenth centuries is not to be considered an activity inimical to the life of the Order. Many of the bishops were saintly men; two were canonized. It can be said that in contributing bishops to the universal Church, the Order was doing the Church a signal service. The Cistercian bishops are to be taken as an evidence of the vitality of the Order—but later, they are at the same time, and perhaps more so, an evidence of its *power*. However, the General Chapter tried to limit this trend: {in} {1134}[229] {it ruled that} a Cistercian chosen as bishop cannot accept without permission of his abbot and {the} General Chapter (unless ordered by {the} pope) (cf. General Chapter, 1192[230]). They must follow {the} observances and fasts of {the} Order. They had to attend {the} General Chapter (until 1275—then {they were} relieved of this obligation[231]). Cistercian bishops naturally tended to enlist support of {the} Order for their projects.

---

228. King, *Cîteaux*.

229. Canivez, *Statuta*, 1.22 (#38); see also 1218:9 (Canivez, *Statuta*, 1.486) (text reads "1152").

230. The bishop of Brunnac, who had refused to attend the General Chapter since his elevation to the episcopacy, was summoned to the next General Chapter (Canivez, *Statuta*, 1.149 [#17]).

231. Canivez, *Statuta*, 3.140 (#6).

Note on exemption of Cistercian abbeys from episcopal power: St. Bernard inveighed against {the} desire of exemption as a manifestation of pride and disobedience in abbots of {the} Order.[232] Until the bull *Sacrosancta* (1152),[233] the bishop still intervenes in correction of abbots, according to {the} early version of *Carta Caritatis*.[234] After this, and especially under Alexander III and Lucius III (see {the} bull of 21 November 1184[235]), exemption becomes a fact. Cistercian abbots {are} on a par with bishops {and} are as active as bishops. *Note {the} Cistercian popes:*[236] two Cistercian popes are well-known—Eugene III[237] and Benedict XII. Celestine IV *may* have been a Cistercian (1241) (says AK, 37, n. l); Gregory VIII was thought to be a Cistercian by some, but was a white canon. Others have been suggested, without probability. (*Clairvaux* provided the Church with one pope, five cardinals, eleven bishops {and} seventy abbots. In St. Bernard's time it averaged two foundations a year, and two professions for the choir alone every month [more for brothers]. There were about 700 in the community at St. Bernard's death. The entire monastery was rebuilt about 1135-1149.)

b. *Monks and brothers out of the monastery with bishops or in courts of nobles*: {in} 1134,[238] Cistercian bishops were authorized to have living with them as many as two monks and three brothers as their servants and household. In the twelfth and thirteenth centuries there seem to have been about 170 Cistercian bishops

---

232. See Bernard's letter to Archbishop Henry of Sens (*De Moribus et Officio Episcoporum*), IX.33–37 (PL 182:830D–834A).

233. *Nomasticon*, 74–78.

234. *Carta Caritatis Prior*, chapter 9 (Noschitzka, 111–13; Turk, "Carta," 55–56).

235. The bull *Monasticae Sinceritas Disciplinae* (PL 201:1301B–1302B; see Mahn, *L'Ordre*, 138, 148–49).

236. See King, *Cîteaux*, 37, n. 1.

237. For a brief biographical sketch, see Merton, *Valley of Wormwood*, 250–56.

238. Canivez, *Statuta*, 1.27 (#61).

(fifteen cardinals?). If they all had companions, there were then some 300 monks and 500 brothers out of their monasteries living with bishops, not necessarily all at the same time. Yet perhaps they were replaced by others from time to time. Is it unreasonable to suppose that almost 1,000 members of the Order were absent with bishops, for a longer or shorter time, in the twelfth and thirteenth centuries? *Others than Cistercian bishops* also received permission to have monks living in their household and service (see General Chapter, 1243:41,[239] 1218:31,[240] 1202:13,[241] etc.: these statutes refer to Cistercian brothers heading, organizing or serving in private *armies* of bishops—v.g. at Milan). Brothers and monks {were found} in the household of *secular nobility and kings* (1220:3[242]). {In} 1197, statute 30[243] of {the} General Chapter summons monks and brothers in service of nobles and {the} king of England to return to their monasteries *usque ad pascalia*. 1274:48[244] comes back on this decision and allows the practice, provided the work is "fitting" for religious: *Dummodo honestis deputentur officiis*. However, {in} 1270:14[245] a final stop is put to this (successfully?). N.B. {there were} retired bishops living in monasteries. These retired bishops might or might not be Cistercians. They might be a nuisance, as for instance one who was living at Dore (England) (see General Chapter, 1239:20[246]).

239. Canivez, *Statuta*, 2.267.
240. Canivez, *Statuta*, 1.490.
241. Canivez, *Statuta*, 1.277 (typescript reads "1302").
242. Canivez, *Statuta*, 1.516–17.
243. Canivez, *Statuta*, 1.215–16, which reads "*usque ad Pascha*" ("up until Easter").
244. "*Petitio illustrissimae dominae reginae Alemanniae quae petit duos monachos vel duos conversos de Ordine, exauditur, dummodo honestis officiis deputentur*" ("A petition of the most illustrious lady the Queen of Germany, who seeks two monks or two laybrothers of the Order, is heard, provided that they are assigned to honorable duties") (Canivez, *Statuta*, 3.136 [typescript reads "1230:3"]).
245. Canivez, *Statuta*, 3.83.
246. Canivez, *Statuta*, 2.206.

c. *Cistercians in Rome*:

(1) A procuratorship for the Order in Rome was founded in 1220:49.[247] This involved the presence of at least two monks in Rome "*ad impetrandum et contradicendum*"[248] (Lekai says these were secular clerics, however[249]). This in itself was not against the spirit of the Order, and was a necessity.

(2) However there were also Cistercian brothers in Rome as *bullatores* (trustworthy keepers of seals and documents in {the} Curia); also brothers were gardeners, grooms etc. in {the} papal court.

d. *Delegation of abbots in reform measures, for other orders*: this too is a sign of the vitality of the Order and a useful service. Cistercian abbots were frequently delegated to visit abbeys of other orders and to see that decrees of reform were carried out there. When Cistercian abbots were engaged in this business of the Church, priors might replace them in visitations and other necessary business of the Order. A few examples of Cistercians intervening to effect reforms or settle disputes {include}: {in} 1185, Abbot William II of Cîteaux arbitrates in {a} dispute between monks and *conversi* at Grandmont;[250] {in} 1218,[251] {the} General Chapter delegates Conrad of Urach (Abbot of Cîteaux) with seven other abbots, to delate the papal legate in England to Honorius III for extortion[252] (Conrad is made cardinal and papal legate; he *refuses* election to {the} papacy {in} 1227[253]); {in} 1229, Walter of Ochies,[254] Abbot of Cîteaux, arbitrates between {the} Kings of France and England[255]—this was ten years after he had

---

247. Canivez, *Statuta*, 1.527.
248. "for supporting and opposing [requests]."
249. Lekai, *The White Monks*, 58.
250. See King, *Cîteaux*, 30.
251. Not included in Canivez.
252. See King, *Cîteaux*, 36.
253. See King, *Cîteaux*, 37.
254. Typescript reads "William" (here and below).
255. See King, *Cîteaux*, 38.

asked and obtained from Honorius III[256] exemption from these special delegations. However, in 1211, statute 34,[257] the Order asked the Holy See that laybrothers, priors and other monks be not sent out on active missions for the Church—only abbots. In 1219, the Abbot of Cîteaux, Walter of Ochies, asked not to be sent on any more missions by the Church; his request was favorably received, but he was still sent on diplomatic missions (see above: 1229). One of the reasons why Innocent IV supported and encouraged the College of St. Bernard was that it would make Cistercians more useful and efficient in providing such services to the Church—hence {the} emphasis on canon law. {There was} a special sense of "picked troops" of the Church!! *Note*: in 1241, several Cistercian abbots and their suite were captured and imprisoned by troops of Frederick II, who wanted to prevent them reaching the Council convoked by Gregory IX; he succeeded.[258] {In} 1260, the Holy See declared that outside prelates must not be called in to visit Cistercian monasteries. The abbots must make the visitations themselves.

e. *Cistercians employed in Civil Offices*: Cistercian laybrothers were often called upon for positions of special trust in cities, for instance as *keepers of keys for {an} arsenal*, or in charge of building and repairing fortifications, or in other positions of special importance, such as in *charge of finances*.

f. *Works of Charity*:

(1) Laybrothers were frequently in courts of ecclesiastics and secular nobles as almoners (distributors of charity) (see General Chapter, 1238,[259] 1242,[260] 1248,[261] 1254[262]).

---

256. Typescript reads "IV."
257. Canivez, *Statuta*, 1.385.
258. See King, *Cîteaux*, 40.
259. Canivez, *Statuta*, 2.188 (##17, 18, 20), 189 (#25).
260. Canivez, *Statuta*, 2.253 (#45).
261. Canivez, *Statuta*, 2.329 (#12).
262. Canivez, *Statuta*, 2.407 (#36).

The Cistercian Order (1153–1335) 209

(2) Abbots of the Order, besides taking care of nuns of the Order, also busied themselves with care of Béguines and recluses, as well as other groups of holy women. This was a laudable and fruitful work, in which the spiritual vitality of the Order allied itself with an important current of mysticism, in which direction and guidance were necessary.

(3) The Abbey of Villers was helping Béguines in several Belgian towns: Nivelles, Tirlemont, Louvain, etc. It was also taking care of a leprosarium at Ten Bank from 1240 on.

(4) {There are} numerous instances of Cistercians serving in hospitals, etc. This was a good work, and though not essential to the Order, {was} compatible with its spirit in exceptional cases.

g. *Various*: abbesses and two nuns can go out of {the} convent for business reasons (General Chapter, 1220:4[263]). Some nuns also sang in {the} choir at Savigny at {the} dedication of {the} church (1220:27[264]).

3. MILITARY OPERATIONS, CRUSADES, ETC.

{In} 1141, {the} monks of Fitero ({a} Cistercian monastery) went to fight Islam. {In} 1158, the town of Calatrava is left without a defender. Raymond, Abbot of Fitero, with some of his monks, takes over the town to defend it. A mixed army of monks and laypeople, armed, defend the town against {the} Moors. This leads to the formation of a military order—that of Calatrava.[265] After the death of St. Raymond {in} 1163, there is a schism in the Order of Calatrava: the monks (properly so-called) returned to Cistercian life; the order acquires new statutes appropriate to military life. However we are not here concerned with the military orders: only with Cistercians properly so-called, engaged in military ventures, crusades etc. {The} background {is} St. Bernard and his companions, preaching the Second Crusade.

The THIRD CRUSADE (1184-1192): this crusade was largely a Cistercian operation. It was the work of Cistercian prelates

---

263. Canivez, *Statuta*, 1.517.
264. Canivez, *Statuta*, 1.522.
265. See King, *Cîteaux*, 343–44, 347–54, 362–74.

backed by the Order, its abbots, monks and brothers. This took large numbers out of the monasteries and even into battle. Cardinal Henry de Marcy preached the crusades in France ({he was} formerly of Clairvaux).[266] Archbishop Baldwin of Canterbury (formerly Abbot of Ford) preached it in England and died in the Holy Land. The Cardinal Archbishop Gerard of Ravenna, who preached the Crusade in Italy, was killed in battle. Many abbots and monks went to the Holy Land with the Crusaders as chaplains, preachers, confessors.

The ALBIGENSIAN CRUSADE: in 1177, Count Raymond V of Toulouse wrote to {the} General Chapter for {the} help of the Order against {the} Albigensian heresy. He wanted: (a) prayers; (b) intercession for {the} help of {the} King of France; (c) *active intervention of monks themselves* in {the} fight against the heresy. Later, "Master Alan," laybrother of Cîteaux (Alan of Lille) was ordered to write against the heresy. A monk of Cîteaux, Rudolph, is mentioned in {the} (old) menology, July 9, for his labors against the heretics (AK, p. 34). But is this the notorious Rudolph who went out without mandate to preach the crusade and started a campaign of anti-Semitism? (see St. Bernard, *Ep.* 365,[267] and *Fiches*,[268] p. 186). Alexander III appointed Henry de Marcy (see above) and the Cistercian Garin, Archbishop of Bourges (formerly Abbot of Pontigny) to run this crusade.

a. The crusade began as a mission to the Albigensians: Cistercians {were} appointed as papal legates. The idea was to convert the Albigensians by *authority and power*, to summon them to return to orthodoxy and unity, or to issue condemnations if they refused. Already in 1180 military action took place. Henry de Marcy {was} at {the} head of {an} army {that} captured Lavaur.

---

266. For a description of Henry from the *Exordium Magnum*, see above, pages 77–78.

267. PL 182:570A–571C (*Letters*, 465–66 [#393]).

268. Jean de la Croix Bouton, *Histoire de l'Ordre de Cîteaux*, 3 vols. (Westmalle, Belgium: Notre Dame d'Aiguebelle, 1959, 1964, 1968) (originally issued in pamphlet form as "Fiches Cisterciennes" in 120 installments).

This tactic was ineffective. Peter of Castelnau, the legate, was discouraged and asked to return to his monastery. The pope replied, "At this hour action is better than contemplation."[269] {The} *problem* {was that} an ineffective and hopeless task, contrary to {the} spirit of {the} Order, {was} imposed on members of the Order, contrary to their own judgement and conscience. Peter of Castelnau was rewarded by martyrdom.[270] (Much could be said about this, from many points of view!) With Peter of Castelnau were other Cistercians who voiced no objections—Rainer and Guy, two Cistercian monks, Arnold, Abbot of Cîteaux, {who} heads the mission; this includes twelve other Cistercian abbots and many monks, joined by Diego of Osma and St. Dominic.

b. {In} 1208, when it is clear that the mission is not getting anywhere, and Peter of Castelnau is murdered, the venture turns into a punitive crusade. More abbots and monks from {the} Cistercian Order then join it. However, in 1211[271] the General Chapter pleads with {the} pope to spare the Order from further missions. Abbot Arnold of Cîteaux presents the plea—nothing comes of it. In 1218, the General Chapter sends three abbots on a visitation of the abbots and monks who are with the crusading armies (see General Chapter, 1218:35[272]). However the crusade had not been continuing full-force all this time. In 1212, Arnold of Cîteaux had taken off for Spain with a number of his fighting companions, went to Calatrava, joined in operations there {and} became supreme head of all the military orders, and then Archbishop of

---

269. See Lekai, *The White Monks*, 49: "The extraordinary difficulties of the undertaking among the rebellious crowds, distrustful nobility, and tepid prelates seemed to exhaust Peter's energies, and he begged the Pope to allow him to retire to the solitude of Fontfroide. The permission was not granted. 'Stay where you are,' wrote Innocent. 'At this hour, action is better than contemplation.'"

270. For a brief biography of Peter, see Merton, *Valley of Wormwood*, 85–93.

271. Canivez, *Statuta*, 1.385 (#34).

272. Canivez, *Statuta*, 1.491 (typescript reads "3").

Narbonne. He was present at {the} great defeat of the Moors at Las Navas. He died in 1225. In reality, much seems to have depended on the desires and judgements of the persons involved in pleas for exemption from active missions. Under Innocent III and Arnold of Cîteaux, the activity is unabated. But in 1219 Walter of Ochies, new Abbot of Cîteaux, obtains from Honorius III, {the} new pope, a permission granted him personally to *refuse* apostolic missions and not feel himself bound to them. Other such bulls were granted to other *individual* abbots and priors, but not to the Order at large (see *Fiches*, p. 180[273]). One of the effects of the Albigensian crusade was to show that the Cistercians had *insufficient knowledge of theology* (Mahn[274]).

The FOURTH CRUSADE: meanwhile, in 1201, Abbot Guy of Vaux de Cernay, with three other abbots and many monks, goes out to preach {the} Fourth Crusade. Ogier, writer and Abbot of Locedio,[275] preached this crusade in Italy. {This crusade resulted in} the Latin Empire of Constantinople: Cistercians {were} involved in this. Foundations {were made} in the east, Greece etc. (This needs to be studied.)

4.[276] THE PROBLEM OF STUDIES—CISTERCIAN COLLEGES: a very significant development in the thirteenth century {was the rise of} studies outside regular monasteries of the Order, in colleges. This went hand-in-hand with the activities and missions of the Order. It was evidently approved and encouraged by Rome, in view of the fact that Cistercians were relied upon to carry out special missions. The colleges then must be seen in the light of the Order's great rise to power and privilege. University studies were not required for the sake of the monastic life alone, but for the sake of the activities in which the monks and abbots were

---

273. Bouton mentions exemptions granted to the abbots and priors of the monasteries of Val-Dieu, Cambron and Ourscamp.

274. Jean-Berthold Mahn, *Le Pape Benoît XII et les Cisterciens* (Paris: Librairie Ancienne Honoré Champion, 1949), 51 (typescript reads "Malin").

275. Typescript reads "Lacedio."

276. Typescript reads "3."

engaged. The colleges are then symptomatic of a change in the spirit of the Order. They did not produce the change, though they contributed to its intensification. It is certain that the colleges must not be regarded as an unmitigated evil. They had their purpose, and the fact that Benedict XII finally regularized these institutions and gave them a permanent place in the life of the Order shows that they were necessary.[277] But by {the time of} Benedict XII a profound change had taken place in the Order, and even in the life of Christian Europe.

Background:

a. The attitude toward studies in the Order in the twelfth century {is marked by the} opposition of St. Bernard, William of St. Thierry, etc. to Abelard, Gilbert de la Porrée, the School of Chartres, and to the pre-scholastics generally. {It was an} attitude of *conservatism* and suspicion of the new developments, an intuitive resistance to new trends which threatened the old patterns with which our Fathers were familiar—a new line of thought, no longer patristic, traditionalist, {a} new emphasis on reason, on philosophy, {a} new attitude toward nature, toward secondary causes and toward rational investigation. To St. Bernard and some of his Cistercian contemporaries (not absolutely all), this sounded rash, even heretical, in its boldness. Abelard was in fact condemned for heresy. Gilbert of la Porrée was not in fact

---

277. See Merton's journal entry for June 10, 1961: "Interesting book of J. B. Mahn on Benedict XII and the Cistercians. And the question of studies (The College of St. Bernard was not a cause of the decline or even one of its symptoms). Yet one wonders at all the expense and effort put into this, and for what? Perhaps it contributed to the general stultification of the Order, or perhaps on the contrary it was necessary to hold the Order together in the lean years . . . Two aspects of inertia. From one point of view it can be regarded as stability. Yet it would perhaps be a myth to say the Order was ever really inert. There must have been also a real underlying faithfulness. . . . A Trappist formation makes it very hard to understand properly the history of the decline. Too many prejudices and myths of our own" (Thomas Merton, *Turning Toward the World: The Pivotal Years. Journals, vol. 4: 1960–1963*, ed. Victor A. Kramer [San Francisco: HarperCollins, 1996], 125–26).

condemned—on the contrary—but Cistercians never accepted his vindication by the Council of Rheims (see John of Salisbury in *Historia Pontificalis*,[278] a very objective account). Were the first Cistercians anti-intellectual? This would be a generalization, too oversimplified to be accepted. (READ St. Bernard, Sermon {on} Sts. Peter and Paul.[279]) Nevertheless the library of Clairvaux was a good one, and even had manuscripts of Roman and canon law (concerning this library, READ AK, p. 220-21[280]). The *Exordium*

---

278. Ioannis Saresberiensis, *Historia Pontificalis / John of Salisbury's Memoirs of the Papal Court*, ed. and trans. Marjorie Chibnall (New York: Thomas Nelson, 1956), 15–41 (chaps. 8–14).

279. *In Festo SS. Petri et Pauli, Sermo* 1.3 (PL 183:407AB): "*Hi sunt magistri nostri, qui a magistro omnium vias vitae plenius didicerunt, et docent nos usque in hodiernum diem. Quid ergo docuerunt vel docent nos apostoli sancti? Non piscatoriam artem, non scenofactoriam, vel quidquid huiusmodi est: non Platonem legere, non Aristotelis versutias inversare, non semper discere, et nunquam ad veritatis scientiam pervenire. Docuerunt me vivere. Putas, parva res est scire vivere? Magnum aliquid, imo maximum est. Non vivit qui superbia inflatur, qui luxuria sordidatur, qui caeteris inficitur pestibus; quoniam non est hoc vivere, sed vitam confundere, et appropinquare usque ad portas mortis. Bonam autem vitam ego puto, et mala pati, et bona facere et sic perseverare ad mortem. Dicitur vulgo, quia qui bene se pascit, bene vivit. Sed mentita es iniquitas sibi; quia non bene vivit, nisi qui bonum facit*" ("These are our masters, who learned more fully the paths of life from the Master of all, and who teach us right up to the present day. What then have the holy apostles taught us, or rather what do they teach us? Not the art of fishing, nor that of tent-making, or anything else of this sort; not to read Plato, nor to interpret the complexities of Aristotle, not to be always learning and never to reach the knowledge of the truth. They have taught me to live. Do you think it is a small thing to know how to live? It is something great, indeed the greatest of all. One is not living who is puffed up with pride, who is soiled by lust, who is infected by other plagues; because this is not living but undermining life, and drawing near to the very gates of death. I think a good life consists in enduring evil and doing good, and in this way remaining faithful even unto death. It is said by the common people that the one who feeds himself well lives well. But iniquity has deceived itself, because one does not live well unless one does good").

280. "The municipal library of Troyes has more than 50,000 volumes [*sic*] from Clairvaux, and of the 2,174 manuscripts more than half have come

Parvum[281] calls St. Alberic a man sufficiently learned in divine and human studies, implying praise for this. Yet there were in the Order of Cîteaux, after the death of St. Bernard, followers of Gilbert de la Porrée. Isaac of Stella represents perhaps a quite different tradition and attitude from that of St. Bernard—more philosophical, metaphysical. Toward the end of the twelfth century, one of the greatest doctors in the Chartres tradition, not alien to Gilbert de la Porrée, was Alan of Lille, *Doctor Universalis*, a true pre-scholastic, author of a *Summa*. He entered Cîteaux as a laybrother. Obviously he intended to give up his studies and teaching, even his writing. He did however write against the Albigenses under obedience to superiors.[282]

---

from the 'third daughter' of Cîteaux; 340 of which date from before the end of the 12th century. Of the books of the Bernardine epoch, two are outstanding; (1) a Bible in two volumes, written before 1153, which has been identified, since the 15th century, as the actual copy used by the Saint, with marginal notes in his own hand; (2) the 'Great Bible of Clairvaux,' a 12th-century work in five volumes, which appears to have been copied and illuminated at Clairvaux after the restrictive regulations of the general chapter. In the time of St Bernard, the library at Clairvaux had several manuscripts of Roman and canon law, and it was only some 30 years after the death of the Saint that the general chapter (1188) directed that books on these subjects should not be kept *in communi armario*, presumably because an excessive interest in law had arisen in Cistercian cloisters at the end of the 12th century. The library of Clairvaux thus owed its beginnings to the initiative of the 'Last of the Fathers', 'for how otherwise', says Dom Wilmart, 'can one explain the formation of an ecclesiastical library so complete and so perfectly composed'. It is little short of a caricature for Mr Colvin to suggest that the Cistercians were debarred 'from literature, learning and art' by their primitive legislation. . . . At Clairvaux, in the time of St Bernard, the books seem to have been divided between the *armarium* and the cell of the abbot's secretary, which was under the stairs leading from the cloister to the dormitory."

281. "*virum scilicet litteratum, in divinis & humanis satis gnarum*" ("a literate man, sufficiently learned in divine and human matters") (chap. 9 [*Nomasticon*, 58]).

282. See the two biographical sketches of Alan in Merton, *Valley of Wormwood*, 55–57, 277–81.

b. Legislation on studies (early) {shows a} special hostility to the *study of canon law*. They seem to have felt intuitively that this would only serve to produce disputes that would divide the Order. Yet it is not of the very nature of law to divide! On the contrary, great harm can be done in the spiritual life where, in a religious community, through ignorance of the letter and spirit of the laws, people are treated in arbitrary and unjust ways. Ignorance of law is not in itself a solution to anything. However, General Chapter, 1188:7[283] bans Gratian from the *armaria* of our monasteries. This does not mean Gratian was banned from the monasteries, but only taken out of *common use*. This {was} a wise move, if ignorant and untrained minds were apt to make a bad use of the law books, {but} superiors need to know the law! (*Today* all educated monks need to know law.) General Chapter, 1231:12 {declared that} measures of greater care {were} to be taken in receiving postulants. It is also specified that those who are received must be examined not only from the spiritual viewpoint, but also as regards their education: *tanta in litteratura . . . diligentia adhibeatur ut cedere possint ad utilitatem Ordinis et honorem.*[284]

c. The Beginning of Studies in Paris and other Universities—*background*: {there was an} insistence on clerical studies in {the} Third and Fourth Lateran Councils (1179; 1215). {The} organization of {the} Dominican *Studium Generale* in Paris {in} 1229 really started the movement for clerical studies by *religious* in residence at universities. But the Cistercians were already interested *before* this date. In 1224 (or 1227), Raoul,[285] Abbot of Clairvaux, obtains a house near Paris, on {the} left bank, for students.[286] He became {a} bishop in 1233, then Archbishop of Lyons. {In} 1234,[287] {the}

---

283. Canivez, *Statuta*, 1.108.

284. "With regard to letters, let such care be applied that they may be able to contribute to the usefulness and honor of the Order" (Canivez, *Statuta*, 2.93–94).

285. Typescript reads "Ralph."

286. See King, *Cîteaux*, 267–68.

287. Canivez, *Statuta*, 2.127 (#3).

General Chapter decrees that *abbots* must be properly educated. General Chapter, 1237:9 {declares}: *Petitio abbatis Claraevallis de clericis habendis Parisius in cappis et tunicis albis pro se et pro omnibus abbatibus aliis qui ibi eodem modo clericos habere voluerint, EXAUDITUR; abbati autem Claraevallis ut ibi monachum et duos conversos habeat, qui clericis necessaria provideat, indulgetur.*[288] This was Abbot Evrard (1235-1238).[289] The house was moved nearer the center of things, to Chardonnet.[290] Hence the idea of a house of studies in Paris is not due to Stephen of Lexington. Lekai says {the} General Chapter of 1242 protested against {the} fact that Cistercians living in Paris and studying under mendicants were transferring to mendicant orders.[291]

{The principal figure in this development was} *Stephen of Lexington*, Abbot of Clairvaux (1243-1257).[292] He had been Abbot of Stanley (England) after entering at Quarr. Previously a student under St. Edmund of Canterbury at Oxford, {he was} later Abbot of Savigny, until 1243, when {he was} elected Abbot of Clairvaux. {In} 1244, Stephen founds the College of St. Bernard, without consulting {the} General Chapter, and has it directly approved by the Holy See in {the} bull *Virtutum Intenta* (January 5, 1245), and again in *Diligentiae Studio Contemplantes* (September 4, 1245).[293] {In} 1245 {the} General Chapter (1245:4[294]) permits the foundation, but no abbot is *obliged* to send a student there. Apparently it was treated as a regular monastery {and} allowed to receive novices,

---

288. "The petition of the Abbot of Clairvaux with regard to having clerics, in capes and white tunics, in Paris, on behalf of himself and all other abbots who wished to have clerics there in the same way, is heard; so let it be permitted to the Abbot of Clairvaux to have there a monk and two laybrothers who may provide the necessities for the clerics" (Canivez, *Statuta*, 2.170) (typescript reads "*Parisiis*")
 289. See King, *Cîteaux*, 268.
 290. See King, *Cîteaux*, 270–71.
 291. Lekai, *The White Monks*, 60.
 292. See King, *Cîteaux*, 270–74.
 293. See King, *Cîteaux*, 271.
 294. Canivez, *Statuta*, 2.290.

but the superior was called provisor rather than prior. ({The} General Chapter approves treating it as a regular monastery.) Also in 1245, the General Chapter complies with {a} papal mandate to organize other houses of studies (cf. General Chapter, 1245:3[295]). {In} 1246, {the} Bishop of Langres grants forty days indulgence to benefactors who aid the foundation.[296] However, Arnulph of Louvain, Abbot of Villers, a daughter house of Clairvaux, *refused* to contribute to {the} building of {the} college, saying it was against humility.[297] Students at {the} College of St. Bernard were under {the} Abbot of Clairvaux, not under their own abbot (Mahn[298]). {In} 1247 {the} building {was} begun. It was never completely finished. {It was} partly destroyed to make way for {the} Boulevard St. Germain, but the refectory today serves as a fire station (AK 271). Other houses of studies {were} established {in} 1252 {at} Montpellier; 1280 {at} Oxford; 1281 {at} Toulouse; 1284 {at} Würzburg; 1286 {at} Estella (Pamplona).[299]

1. In résumé, behind the foundation of the College of St. Bernard is the general direction of the Church, {the} influence of two ecumenical councils, and of the newly organized *studia* of the mendicants;

2. Also {the} express wish of the popes to have Cistercians studying in the universities;

3. Above all the initiatives of Stephen of Lexington to reform and protect the Order;

---

295. Canivez, *Statuta*, 2.289–90.
296. See King, *Cîteaux*, 271.
297. See King, *Cîteaux*, 273.
298. "l'abbé de Clairvaux eut autorité sur tous les moines étudiants, sustraits ainsi à l'autorité de leurs abbés respectifs" ("the Abbot of Clairvaux held authority over all the student monks, thus withdrawn from the authority of their respective abbots") (Mahn, *Benoît XII*, 53); this ruling of 1248 altered a previous statute of 1245 that had placed the students under the supervision of their respective abbots (Mahn, *Benoît XII*, 52).
299. See King, *Cîteaux*, 272, n. 5.

4. The General Chapter on the other hand tends to oppose the development, acceding to the desires of the pope reluctantly and holding back where possible, blocking Stephen of Lexington. The pope evidently wanted all abbeys to send students to the universities, but {the} General Chapter {was} reluctant to oblige them to do this.

5. The pope wanted the houses of studies to be regular monasteries of the Order, but the General Chapter did all {that was} possible to make clear that they were unusual, exceptional, "extra-regular" communities. It also refused to take over the house for the Order, and left it in the hands of Clairvaux. Finally the conservative element in the Order persecuted the Abbot of Clairvaux.

6. What is known about the intense personal opposition met by Stephen of Lexington? This needs to be studied. Vague allusions are found here and there; nothing precise has yet been developed. "Moreover, Abbot Stephen's person became the target of bitter attacks, so finally the worthy prelate resigned his office in 1257; he died three years later" (Lekai[300]). More details are in Archdale King (*op. cit.*, p. 272f.):

a) {He} quotes Matthew Paris: *Malitiose et per invidiam machinatum est in ipsum. . . . Quod cum audisset dominus Papa, et voluisset ipsum absolutum in pristinum statum restituere, adversarii ejusdem Stephani effusa non minima pecunia in curia Romana machinati sunt, ut sententia staret quam firmaverant, de ipsius depositione*[301] (p. 272, note 2).

b) This evidently refers to a deposition. Archdale King says: "There seems little doubt that Dom Stephen was deposed by the general chapter, and the fact of deposition is confirmed by the

---

300. Lekai, *The White Monks*, 61.
301. "Plots were made against him maliciously and through envy. . . . When the Lord Pope had heard this, and had wished to restore him without reservation in his former office, adversaries of this Stephen plotted, spending no small amount of money in the Roman Curia, so that the sentence of his deposition which they had made might remain in force."

bull *Intellecto pridem* of Alexander IV (November 21, 1255), which revoked the sentence of deposition delivered by the Abbot of Cîteaux. Thomas of Luda was directed to execute the bull, to which the abbot always refused to submit" (obviously the abbot who refused to submit was the Abbot of Cîteaux who had deposed Stephen) (p. 272).

c) Dom Stephen had retired to Ourscamp, and died before a decision was reached. The pope had marked him out for preferment ({a} bishopric) in England.

Addenda to Stephen of Lexington: a manuscript of the letters of Stephen of Lexington has recently been discovered in Turin and published in *Analecta SOC* (1946; 1952)[302]—a very important historical source for the Order in the thirteenth century—not however for the college: they were written when he was Abbot of Stanley and then of Savigny. They concern visitations to the Irish monasteries {in} 1228 (very bad conditions); visitations of filiations of Savigny; nuns of the Order and various affairs of the Order; {the} reform of {the} Benedictine Abbey of Redon, carried out by Stephen in 1231.

{The} *Character of Stephen of Lexington*: this was a great man, very gifted, {an} intelligent, prudent, firm and realistic superior with a great love for the Order, but not understood by many good men in the Order. His great concern was the "lack of men" in the Cistercian Order: "*Religionis nostrae ruinam et excidium minatur, et merito,* defectus personarum."[303] Hence his idea was to form capable superiors, "*tam vita quam litteris commendabiles.*"[304]

---

302. B. Griesser, ed., "*Registrum Epistolarum Stephani de Lexinton,*" *Analecta Sacri Ordinis Cisterciensis* 2 (1946): 1–118; B. Griesser, ed., "*Registrum Epistolarum Stephani de Lexinton,*" *Analecta Sacri Ordinis Cisterciensis* 8 (1952): 181–378.

303. "The lack of men threatens the destruction and ruin of our religious life, and deservedly so" (n. 37) (Griesser, *Registrum,* 48, which reads "*nostre*").

304. "praiseworthy as much in their life as in their learning" (Griesser, *Registrum,* 48, which reads "*tam uita quam litteris digne commendabilium*").

Appendix: From {the} LETTERS OF STEPHEN OF LEXINGTON:
A. See {the} important Letters xxxi–xxxiii, on conditions in Ireland in 1228:
1) The condition was really scandalous—his first task was to absolve all generally from grave crimes and irregularities (see *ASOC* [1946], p. 35). The things he heard from visitors were less than what he saw with his eyes. He found the seal of one abbey had been pawned in a tavern for eighteen pence. Monastery property had been generally sold, and some houses even reduced to only a few acres. Many are going about begging.

2) His summary: *Nullum ibi silentium, nulla in capitulo disciplina pauci sunt habitantes in communi, sed per ternarium aut quaternarium in parvis casellis extra claustrum catervatim constituti, simbolum fatientes ad villas mercatorias mittunt et sic emunt pro facultate proprietatis suae necessaria.*[305] Chastity is not kept. There is much violence and consorting with low and criminal characters. *Interius omnia spiritualia dissoluta, exterius temporalia fere universa dilapidata . . . ibi de ordine nichil nisi habitus vestium tantum.*[306]

3) His reaction: immediate and vigorous measures of reform: *virilius et instantius—Non parcentes sumptibus aut etiam periculis carnalibus*[307]—to prevent the evil spreading to other parts of the Order. He himself was attacked and nearly killed by robbers whom he had ejected from a monastery. His life was continually in danger. ({He} had a company of soldiers with him however.)

---

305. "There is no silence there, no discipline in chapter, few are living in common but are set up in groups of threes and fours in little cottages outside the cloister; putting together their possessions they send to the shops of merchants and thus buy their necessities for the supply of their ownership" (Griesser, *"Registrum,"* 35–36).

306. "Within, all spiritual goods are dissolved; without, temporal goods are almost completely fallen apart . . . there is nothing of the Order there except merely the habit of clothing" (Griesser, *"Registrum,"* 36).

307. "more boldly and quickly, sparing no expense and even braving physical dangers" (Griesser, *"Registrum,"* 36).

4) {At a} council of abbots in Dublin (see p. 37), old abbots {were} deposed and new ones elected. N.B. he treats it as a real *schism* in the Order. He therefore applies the laws of the Order against conspirators; {he} breaks up communities, introducing small groups of regular monks from elsewhere, reconciling fugitives, apostates, etc. and dispersing them in foreign communities for life (at Mellifont he reconciled forty fugitives!). He insists that the monks be able to understand Latin and French so as to comprehend the admonitions of visitors from abroad (p. 47). *Hence monks are not to be received unless they have some education in {the} humanities.* Candidates are therefore to study humanities—even at Paris or Oxford. To implement the reform he divides up the Irish houses which were all under Mellifont, and gives them Fathers Immediate outside Ireland, who will visit them and maintain discipline (but will meet with violent opposition). *Nihil restat nisi cepta viriliter et constanter prosequi et visitatores discretos et circumspectos mittere*[308] (p. 40).

5) He gives thanks to God for the great graces that have marked the reform with conversions and general acceptance in the communities.

B. {A} letter to {the} Abbot of Pontigny (about 1233) {discusses}:

1) irregularities at Cadouin, daughterhouse of Pontigny. Here the monks are not regularly issued clothing, but each one has "his own" cattle, to provide for himself therewith.

2) What is more important is the presence of seven monks in the monastery of Cadouin openly professing heresy; also in Germany there are Cistercians infected with heresy.

3) Hence he concludes there is grave spiritual danger for the Order. Therefore the Order should be anxious for spiritual

---

308. "Nothing remains but boldly and steadfastly to pursue what has been started, and to send discreet and cautious visitors" (Griesser, *"Registrum,"* 40, which reads *"Nichil igitur . . . circumspectos anno sequenti* [the following year] *mittere"*).

reform, and not imagine that their troubles can be cured by sending prelates to Rome to obtain more privileges and defend their liberties. Stephen believed that the Order was trying to solve its problems by temporal and political means, whereas the root of the trouble was spiritual, and this in turn came from {the} lack of sound theology in the Order.

> *Pater in Christo karissime, ipsa tempora periculosa, que iam instant, nos ammonent de uigilancia et sollicitudine pro statu ordinis maxime in spiritualibus. Nam cum effectus sine causa sua stare non possit, frustra mittemus ad curias prelatorum et principum pro obseruatione bonorum temporalium uel libertatum, cum collationis et tuitionis temporalium ipsorum fructus et feruor spiritualium hucusque extiterit et adhuc causa sola existat atque precipua. Iam timendum est, ne uerbum cuiusdam de maioribus in numero predicatorum lacrimabiliter de nobis uerificetur, videlicet quod ante decennium completum oportebit ipsos regere et corrigere ordinem nostrum, eo quod a retroactis iam annis XIII^{cim} nullus famose litteratus precipue in sacra pagina ad nos se transtulerit et qui iam sunt in ordine, senescunt et tendunt ad uiam uniuerse carnis. Item ait alius: Quoniam nos erimus uel de primorum numero primi, qui recedemus a fide, eo quod propter simplicitatem et ignorantiam sacrarum litterarum, quarum limitationem non didicimus, facile seduci poterimus. Item propter silencium et solitudinem, quod instillatum fuerit per seductores, fortiter retinebimus, ita quod, ex quo prefate fraudis diabolice uenenum interiora infecerit, vix aut nunquam gladio uerbi Dei abradi poterit.*[309] (*ASOC* [1946], p. 117)

---

309. "Most dear Father in Christ, the dangerous times themselves that are now at hand warn us about vigilance and concern for the state of the Order, above all in spiritual matters. For since an effect cannot remain without its cause, we shall send in vain to the courts of prelates and princes for the sake of the preservation of temporal goods and liberties, since the sole principal cause of the situation has been up until now and is still the consequence of the collecting and defense of these very temporal goods and the eagerness to do likewise with regard to spiritual goods. It is to be feared that the word of one of the leading men among the Order of Preachers should

Note his arguments: the learned men are not coming to the Order from elsewhere any more. The members of the Order are ignorant and easily seduced by error. In silence and solitude, with no communication, the error grows unchecked.

4) For the good of the Order, the pope must urge the Abbot of Cîteaux and {the} four First Fathers to discuss means of remedying this. *This is what is behind Stephen's project to found {the} College of St. Bernard.* It is *not* merely a private operation of Clairvaux, in his intention. But since he was not supported, he went ahead on his own. He was *not yet Abbot of Clairvaux*, N.B.

Further Development of the College: {in} 1275 the college is incorporated in the University of Paris when the first Cistercian becomes {a} Master of Theology—this was John of Weerde, a monk of the Dunes. (Note: some thirty years have passed since the first students went to Paris.) John of Weerde was then appointed regent of {the} college.[310] {The} fact that {the} General Chapter allows him a position immediately after that of abbots implies a certain recognition. {In} 1281 the General Chapter (1281:9) allows any "major abbey" where there are eighty monks or more to have a *studium: Cum insipientia mentis stultitiam simul pariat et errorem et e contrario scientia ab omnibus naturaliter appetatur, concedit Cap. Gen. ut in majoribus abatiis* [i.e. philosophy and liberal arts] *et de ceteris abatiis possint illuc mittere monachi*

---

sadly be fulfilled, that is, that before ten years have passed it will be necessary that they govern and correct our Order, because during the past thirteen years no outstanding scholar, particularly in holy scripture, has joined himself to us, and those who are already in the Order are becoming old and moving along on the way of all flesh. Likewise another says: because we will be the first or among the first who drift away from the faith, due to our simplicity and our ignorance of sacred writings, of which we have not learned the basics, we will be able to be easily led astray. Likewise, due to our silence and solitude, we will strongly cling to what has been insinuated by false teachers, so that, because by that word of fraud the poison will have diabolically infected the inner substance, it will scarcely or never be able to be scraped away by the sword of the Word of God."

310. See King, *Cîteaux*, 273.

ad studendum, dum tamen pro se satisfaciant in expensis.[311] N.B.: this seems to indicate studies in the monastery itself, and that in monasteries of under eighty there would still be no studies {and} no faculty. {In} 1311 the Council of Vienne makes studies obligatory for every religious order (Lekai[312]). {In} 1321 the General Chapter (statute 9[313]) acknowledges {the} sale of the College of St. Bernard to the Order by Clairvaux and makes provision for running it in the future: *Considerans quod exinde debeat honor ordinis et profectus studii multipliciter augmentari, approbat ratificat et confirmat etc.*[314] A committee of abbots is appointed to supervise the operation, the studies etc. The definitors will see to an annual visitation, and will each year elect the provisor and the cellarer. (Clairvaux sold {the} College of St. Bernard in order to get out of debt.) {The General Chapter of} 1322[315] {has} further details on running {the} college.

C. The definitive legislation for Cistercian studies in the Middle Ages is given in the Constitution of Benedict XII, *Fulgens sicut Stella* (1335),[316] which we now consider in all its details.

Fulgens sicut Stella—The Constitution of Benedict XII:

This important reforming document marks the close of the great period of the Order. The work of the second Cistercian pope, an Avignon pope, an organizer and centralizer, it gives us a very striking picture of the Order in its "great" days of the

---

311. "Whereas foolishness of mind produces dullness and error and on the contrary knowledge is naturally sought by all, the General Chapter grants that in major abbeys [there may be a *studium*] and that from other abbeys monks can be sent there to study, provided that they take care of their own expenses" (Canivez, *Statuta*, 3.207).

312. Lekai, *The White Monks*, 61.

313. Canivez, *Statuta*, 3.353–54.

314. "Considering that the honor of the Order and progress of study should be considerably increased in this way, it approves, ratifies and confirms [this policy]" (Canivez, *Statuta*, 3.354).

315. Canivez, *Statuta*, 3.357–60 (##1–8).

316. *Nomasticon*, 473–86; also found in Canivez, *Statuta*, 3.410–36.

thirteenth and fourteenth centuries, the state of the Order as a *great active force in the Medieval Church*, and yet in decline. But this is no longer the Order of St. Stephen, or even really of St. Bernard. It is the Order that fought the Albigensians, launched the Third and Fourth Crusades, and built missionary monasteries all over Eastern Europe. Of course the differences are accidental, not essential, but they are very real and very significant.

Contrast the *Exordium Parvum* and the opening paragraph of *Fulgens sicut Stella*. The latter reads:

> Gleaming like the morning star in the midst of a clouded sky, the Sacred Cistercian Order [S.O.C.—this is the designation adopted officially by our brethren of the so-called "Common Observance"] by *its good works and edifying example shares in the combats of the Church militant*. By the sweetness of holy contemplation and the merit of a pure life it strives with Mary to ascend the mountains of God, while BY PRAISEWORTHY ACTIVITIES AND PIOUS MINISTRATION IT SEEKS TO IMITATE THE BUSY CARES OF MARTHA. [Note: this has a basis in the doctrine of St. Bernard himself,[317] though it has come to refer to external activities, not to the active life within the cloister itself as he himself intended.] Full of *zeal for the divine worship* so as to secure the salvation both of its own members and outsiders, devoted to the *study of Holy Scripture* so as to learn therefrom the science of perfection, *powerful and generous in the works of charity* so as to fulfill

---

317. See Merton's essay "Action and Contemplation in St. Bernard," in *Thomas Merton on St. Bernard*, CS 9 (Kalamazoo, MI: Cistercian Publications, 1980), 23–104, that draws particularly on Bernard's Third Sermon for the Assumption, which presents the penitential practices of Lazarus, the administrative duties of Martha, and the contemplation of Mary as a complementary threefold arrangement of the monastic household (PL 183:421C–425B). See also Thomas Merton, *"Honorable Reader": Reflections on My Work*, ed. Robert E. Daggy (New York: Crossroad, 1989), 13–22, the preface to the French translation of this essay (Thomas Merton, *Marthe, Marie et Lazare* [Paris: Desclée de Brouwer, 1956]).

the law of Christ, this Order has merited to propagate itself from one end of Europe to the other.[318]

Note here the three essential occupations of the monk: *opus Dei, lectio divina, opus manuum*[319]—but with a completely different emphasis, representing a whole new mentality. Contrast Paschal II in {the} *Exordium Parvum* (the *Privilegium Romanum*): *Meminisse debetis, quia pars vestri saeculares latitudines, pars ipsas etiam monasterii laxioris minus austeras angustias reliquistis. Ut ergo* hac semper gratia *digniores censeamini,* DEI SEMPER TIMOREM ET AMOREM IN CORDIBUS VESTRIS HABERE SATAGITE, UT QUANTO A SAECULARIBUS TUMULTIBUS ET DELICIIS LIBERIORES ESTIS, TANTO AMPLIUS PLACERE DEO TOTIS MENTIS ET ANIMAE VIRTUTIBUS ANHELETIS.[320] This too is "active life," but purely in the traditional sense of ascetic preparation for *theoria* (contemplation). Note that while religious of the active life can legitimately offer up the "cares" and "tumults" of their work in the world as a sacrifice, it is less clear whether we can do so. Strictly speaking, there is no real *contradiction* between the language of these two documents. One cannot say strictly that the kind of

---

318. "*Fulgens sicut stella matutina in medio nebulae, sacer Cisterciensis Ordo in Ecclesia militante militat operibus & exemplis: fervideque satagit per sanctae contemplationis applausum, & innocentis vitae meritum montana scandere cum Maria: seque per exercitium laudabilium actionum & pensum piorum operum curiosum Marthae satagentis officio conformare. Hic nempe Ordo in divini cultus ministerio sedulus, ut sibi & aliis proficiat ad salutem, in sacrae lectione paginae studiosus, ut ad perfectam excellentiae supernae cognitionem valeat pervenire; praestans & promptus in operibus caritatis, ut adimpleant legem Christi, a mari usque ad mare palmites suos meruit dilatare*" (*Nomasticon*, 473).

319. "the work of God" (the Divine Office), "spiritual reading," "manual labor."

320. "You should remember that one part of you left behind broad worldly ways, another part the less austere narrow ways of a more lax monastery. And so, in order always to be considered more worthy of this grace, endeavor always to have in your hearts the fear and the love of God, so that the more free you are from worldly commotions and pleasures, so much the more may you yearn to please God by all the virtues of mind and soul" (chap. 14 [*Nomasticon*, 61]).

life praised by Benedict XII lacks elements of fear and love for God, and total devotion of all the strength of one's soul to Him. Yet there are significant differences of emphasis and in fact we know that the concept of the first Fathers of Cîteaux was of a completely isolated and simple monastic life, "*a saeculi tumultibus et deliciis liberior.*" The place (Cîteaux) was chosen because it was remote and inaccessible. Urban II contrasts Cîteaux as *eremus* with Molesme as *cenobium*. {They} deliberately chose *terras ab habitatione hominum remotas* (*EP*, XV[321]) and devised an economy that would leave them as completely independent as possible from secular life. They excluded princes from their monastery (i.e., courts) and desired that there should be nothing even in liturgical matters that suggested worldly splendor. Conclusions: in effect, *Fulgens sicut Stella* is an adaptation of the Cistercian life, or rather an attempt to organize a life that has adapted itself. It is a stabilization of the life at a level which is in fact far from that of the early Cîteaux, yet not completely alien to its spirit. Nevertheless it cannot be denied that the change has been profound.

Here we may discuss the verse prologue to the *Exordium Magnum*, printed for the first time in the new edition of Griesser (1961).[322] This verse prologue is most probably by Conrad of Eberbach, where he was abbot from 1206 to 1221. Probably the prologue belongs to this period—{the} beginning of {the} thirteenth century. {It is a} *eulogy of the Cistercian Order—Cistercius Ordo*:

1) It is a renewal of ancient monasticism, a light in darkness, confounding the devil and saving countless souls.

2) {The} Order {is} characterized as one of *labor and penance* (i.e., active!): *Hoc Cistercienses excellent ordine fratres / quos labor attenuat sacer et pia poena coronat* (lines 56-57).[323] In this Order we

---

321. "lands far away from human habitation" (*Nomasticon*, 63).

322. Conrad of Eberbach, *Exordium Magnum Cisterciense*, ed. Bruno Griesser (Rome: Editiones Cistercienses, 1961), 45–47.

323. "Within this Order the Cistercian brothers stand out / Whom holy work wears out and pious penance crowns."

truly find the *sacra vestigia*[324] of ancient monachism—"*spes certa salutis*"[325] and "*Impolluta via per quam transitur ad astra*" (60).[326] He sums up, *suggesting also the apostolic fruitfulness of Cîteaux*: *Principium celebris vitae, quae gaudia caelis / Parturit et terris parat incrementa salutis* (63-64).[327]

3) {It is} important {to consider if there is here a} comparison between Cîteaux and Clairvaux? The *jam dudum sterilis*[328] of l. 66 is not a criticism of Cîteaux—the long sterile desert has now flowered. Cîteaux has spread through the world: *Cuius mellifluus mundi per climata fructus / Emissus populos pascit, recreans moribundos* etc. (67-68).[329] *Even more glorious* is the "perfect daughter of the perfect mother."[330] Clairvaux {is} like the Sun of Salvation shining over the whole world, and it is the *mystical garden* where the Spouse is united to the Bridegroom.

Benedict XII, the Avignon pope, builder of the papal palace at Avignon, is quite a different person from St. Stephen Harding. The background is altogether different. The age is different. It is two hundred years since the death of Stephen Harding. *Benedict XII*[331] (1285-1342)—Jacques Fournier—{was a} monk of Fontfroide (as {was} St. Peter of Castelnau), in the midst of Albigensian country. The heresy still smoulders. He enters Boulbonne,[332] then goes to Fontfroide, where his uncle was abbot. His life was "normal"

---

324. "sacred footsteps" (l. 58).

325. "sure hope of salvation" (l. 59).

326. "the undefiled way through which one reaches the stars!"

327. "The beginning of this auspicious life, which gives birth to joys in heaven / And prepares the seeds of salvation on earth" (typescript reads "*quandiu caelis*").

328. "long since sterile."

329. "Whose honeyed fruit, sent forth through the regions of the world, / Nourishes the peoples, reviving the dying," etc.

330. "*Perfectam sobolem docet haec te pagina matrem / Perfectam laetis generasse per omnia votis*" (ll. 70–71) ("This page teaches you that a perfect mother has borne a perfect offspring, an answer in all ways to joyous prayers").

331. See Mahn, *Benoît XII*, 8–12.

332. Typescript reads "Boulborne."

for a gifted monk of the fourteenth century. {He progressed through} the normal *cursus honorum*[333] for a young monk with promising gifts. After his one-year novitiate, he makes solemn vows, and goes to {the} College of St. Bernard (as did Benedict XII), or to some other *studium* of the Order; he takes his STB. After this the young monk would often become an abbot. But he would then be dispensed from residence in his abbey while studying for {his} doctorate. After a few years he would be {a} bishop, then even cardinal perhaps. In the case of Benedict XII, he got the STD in 1317 and succeeded his uncle as Abbot of Fontfroide when the uncle became {a} cardinal. Then {he became} Bishop of Pamiers, a diocese in Albigensian territory. He worked hard with the Inquisition, fighting heresy, using tribunals with patience and zeal to convert heretics and relapsed converts. {He} burned five recalcitrants {and} acquitted ninety-three others who had been "won over." {In} 1327, as a result of his zeal, he is elevated to the cardinalate in the court of Avignon, where he acts as a theological counselor. He was the successor to John XXII, who had made a mistake in theology, saying the saints would not have {the} beatific vision until {the} last judgement. Probably the fact that Benedict was a theologian had a lot to do with his election. On accession he straightens out the error of his predecessor. Other urgent tasks {included} reforms of the Curia {and} reform of {the} secular clergy. But he builds up {the} power of cardinals and fills {the} Sacred College with Frenchmen. We are concerned with Benedict XII and the Cistercian Order. In general, it can be said he was primarily an organizer, an administrator, "without profound sense of religious problems" (Mahn[334]). {He issued} too many

---

333. "succession of offices" (lit. "course of honors").

334. Speaking of religious orders, Mahn says that Benedict praised their merits and recognized their faults "sans découvrir les causes profondes de leur grandeur et de leur décadence, par conséquent, sans se montrer capable de promouvoir l'une ni même d'entraver l'autre" ("without discovering the profound causes of their grandeur and of their decadence, and consequently without showing himself able to promote the former or even to restrict the latter") (*Benoît XII*, 11).

minute prescriptions. In fact he was not endowed with sufficient insight to evaluate these problems really correctly, but only from the outside. He worked for reform and reorganization in almost all the existent orders, but never with complete success. The problems he faced with the Cistercian Order had, in any case, many administrative and even political aspects which were what most occupied him, rather than the inner and spiritual implications of the problems he faced. (*Note*: the greatest religious problem he faced was that of the *Fraticelli*—the "reforming" zealots in the Friars Minor. These resisted him, as did the mendicants in general, but the spirit of his legislation eventually prevailed at Trent. He wrote a tract against the Fraticelli.)

General problems of religious orders {included}: (1) great numbers of irregular or apostate monks traveling around; (2) negligence in administration, laxity of observance; (3) arbitrariness and worldliness of superiors, their misuse of power and of money; (4) heterodoxy and rebelliousness of certain groups; (5) abuses in matters of poverty, especially among {the} mendicants; (6) general moral laxity of many religious communities.

Some of the Problems Faced by Benedict XII in {the} *Cistercian Order*: we are however concerned more with the internal problems of our own Order, for which *Fulgens* was drawn up. They come under three headings: (a) the economic setup and organizational problems; (b) problems of regularity and laxity; (c) studies. Actually the third was the least urgent, and the first was the most important. Here there were very serious abuses, especially irresponsible, independent and arbitrary disposition of monastery property by abbots, or imprudent business deals, entered into independently and irresponsibly by abbots and cellarers (see General Chapter, 1318:22[335]—{the} re-sale of an abbey [Dunamunde]); {the} problem of debts (see 1322:16;[336] 1338:6;[337] 1300:3[338]); {a} case

---

335. Canivez, *Statuta*, 3.344.
336. Canivez, *Statuta*, 3.362 (text reads "1332").
337. Canivez, *Statuta*, 3.451.
338. Canivez, *Statuta*, 3.300.

of vagabond abbots (1336:9;[339] 1337:5;[340] 1338:9[341]); {the} problem of {an} abbatial "manse" (i.e., {a} mansion). The first problem then was to devise a means of control and check on the irresponsible dealing with monastic property by superiors. This was not a new problem (for this problem in primitive monasticism, see DeVogüé, *La Communauté et l'Abbé dans la Règle de Saint Benoît*, 193ff.[342]). The requirement that the community of monks should approve the official acts of the abbot in buying {and} selling etc. is already in the Code of Justinian (sixth century).[343] Also, the question of visitations was by now a serious problem; by now it is certain that visitations were not made properly. The question of attendance at {the} General Chapter was also urgent.

Problems of observance came under several headings:

1) The careless admission of candidates unfitted for the life. {It was} probably not that the Order had *become* careless, for it seems that candidates were rather freely admitted in the Golden Age; but now the screening is much more important when the general level tends to be low in the community. The problem was *general*. (Note: for mendicants, Benedict XII was {the} first to order that they have special novitiate houses, distinct from other monasteries. This they refused to do, at least the OFM—but the Dominicans adopted the measure.)

2) *Violations of poverty*: apparently there was considerable laxity in the matter of poverty—{a} tendency to permit *pecu-*

---

339. Canivez, *Statuta*, 3.443–44.

340. Canivez, *Statuta*, 3.446.

341. Canivez, *Statuta*, 3.452.

342. Adalbert DeVogüé, OSB, *La Communauté et l'Abbé dans la Règle de Saint Benoît* (Bruges: Desclée de Brouwer, 1961); *Community and Abbot in the Rule of St. Benedict*, trans. Charles Philippi, 2 vols., CS 5.1–2 (Kalamazoo, MI: Cistercian Publications, 1978), 165–67.

343. *Codex Iuris Civilis*, Lib. 1, tit. 2, #7 (see DeVogüé, 196 [*Community and Abbot*, 167, 175, nn. 20, 21]).

lium[344] in the form of supplies of food and even money given to individuals (with permission). There was a general tendency to possess private property (in small things?). Dormitories were being divided up into private cells and rooms. {There developed a} tendency to disrupt the common life, with individuals having {their} own rooms and supplies, living apart from and independent of the community. ({This was} a kind of tendency toward idiorrhythmic monachism,[345] which has been tolerated in the Orient and to some extent works there. In the West {this} has always been regarded with great suspicion, doubtless because of {the} considerable abuses which crept in.)

3) *Abstinence*: the use of meat was now becoming common, even in monastic refectories. How it crept in: (a) {through} special permissions on *journeys*: the great amount of travelling done by monks made the eating of meat on (sea) journeys, then on other journeys, familiar; (b) special permissions for retired abbots;

---

344. "a sum granted by {the} superior for spending without strings or conditions attached" (Thomas Merton, *The Life of the Vows: Initiation into the Monastic Tradition* 6, ed. Patrick F. O'Connell, MW 30 [Collegeville, MN: Cistercian Publications, 2012], 407).

345. In his essay "Mount Athos," Merton notes that "idiorrhythmic monks are peculiar to the Oriental Church, if we except those modern religious congregations in the West whose members are allowed to retain title to their property and to keep their individual earnings. The idiorrhythmic monks, whether in monasteries or out of them, retain proprietorship of what property they have, and live on the income from their labor. The monastery furnishes them with shelter and work, in a rudimentary organization which is controlled not by an abbot but by an elected committee. The monks chant the office together in choir, but work and live on their own, in or out of the monastery, cooking their own meals which can include meat on certain days. . . . It is a loose kind of life, not necessarily decadent, though it dates from a period of relaxation in the history of Athos, in the days when it was ruled by the Turks. Monasteries can choose to be either idiorrhythmic or cenobitic and some have passed back and forth from one to the other several times in the course of centuries" (Thomas Merton, *Disputed Questions* [New York: Farrar, Straus and Cudahy, 1960], 71-72).

(c) some religious, or communities (?) had special privileges from the Holy See dispensing them from abstinence; (d) special relaxations for abbots making visitations (long journeys, many houses to visit, etc.); (e) exceptional situations (v.g. famines, etc.) in which monks were permitted to have meat, and after which they were slow to return to {the} common rule (all these factors led to serious relaxation in the question of abstinence, but nevertheless there was also *real fidelity* on the part of monks and communities which resisted the trend); (f) dispensations given by {the} General Chapter tended to increase.[346]

Steps taken by Fulgens to restore discipline:[347] new monks could not be received without a vote.[348] Meat was banned from the common refectory, dispensation or privilege notwithstanding.[349] General use of individual cells {was} prohibited.[350] *Peculium,*[351] in money or supplies, {was} abolished, except in the {the} case of retired abbots. Monks may not have riding horses[352] (except cellarers and abbots). All private property {was} to be confiscated.[353] {The} community must be consulted before the abbot or cellarer makes a loan or borrows money[354] (cf. *Rule* of St. Benedict, c. 3[355]). {The} abbot may not alienate monastic property without {the} deliberative vote of {the} community and {the} consent of {the} General Chapter.[356] In the case of {the} sale of {a} whole

---

346. For an extensive discussion of the regulation of abstinence over the course of Cistercian history, see A Father of the Abbey of Gethsemani, Kentucky [Alberic Wulf, OCSO], *Compendium of the History of the Cistercian Order* (Trappist, KY: Abbey of Gethsemani, 1944), 187–205.
347. See Mahn, *Benoît XII*, 35–40.
348. N. 25.
349. Nn. 29–32.
350. N. 33.
351. N. 37.
352. N. 38.
353. N. 39
354. N. 7.
355. McCann, *The Rule*, 24.
356. N. 4.

monastery or grange, permission of the Holy See is required. The monastery funds are to be kept in a strong box with four keys, each of which is in the possession of a different officer of the community.[357] Abbot visitors should not ask a stipend for making visitation and should not burden the house visited by bringing many attendants, horses, etc.[358] Restriction {was made} of visits of monks to other monasteries (chiefly to spare {the} expense to communities giving hospitality to numerous visitors, in a continual stream): two days maximum {was} set.[359] The abbot is accountable to the *bursarius* for his expenditures.[360]

Steps taken by Fulgens to regularize studies:[361]

(*Note*: Benedict XII did a great deal for the universities in general, especially in order to ensure that ecclesiastics would be properly trained: he tightened up discipline and made the courses harder. As a *theologian* he wrote against Joachim of Flora and Meister Eckhart—these works are lost—{and composed a} commentary on part of St. Matthew. He opposed the Immaculate Conception.)

1. {It gave} confirmation of the existence of *studia generalia* for Cistercians at Paris, Oxford, Toulouse, Montpellier; {the} Spanish *studium* {was} transferred from Estella ({a} monastery in the country) to Salamanca; {a} new *studium* {was} formed at Bologna; a *studium* {was set up} at Metz for liberal arts (founded by Morimond, for its own interests).[362]

2. Every monastery of the Order having over forty monks must send two monks to study in Paris. Every monastery between thirty and forty monks must send one monk to study at Paris. All monasteries *may* send more students to Paris, or students to the *studia* in their province. Small monasteries need

357. N. 5.
358. N. 12.
359. N. 17.
360. N. 11.
361. See Mahn, *Benoît XII*, 56–59.
362. N. 42.

not send monks to Paris, but must send students to the *studia* in their province.[363]

3. The students to be sent away for studies are chosen by the abbot, together with {the} visitor and {the} *sanior pars*[364] of the community.[365]

4. Abbots who do not send students are fined double the sum that would be paid for tuition.[366]

5. Study of canon law {was} forbidden.[367]

6. Measures were taken to see that the students did not immediately avail themselves of liberties and privileges contrary to {the} spirit of the Order. The student must take an oath that he will himself spend nothing for celebration. His parents are limited in the expense to which they can go.[368]

EFFECTS OF *FULGENS SICUT STELLA*:

1. *The Order responds*: (a) by an official acknowledgement of the General Chapter[369] (1335:1 and 4[370]); (b) Cîteaux {was} in financial difficulties; {the} situation {was} regularized on appeal from Benedict XII, to which other houses responded to help Cîteaux;[371]

---

363. N. 44.

364. "the wiser portion" (see the Rule, chap. 64: "*In abbatis ordinatione illa semper consideretur ratio, ut hic constituatur quem sive omnis concors congregatio secundum timorem Dei, sive etiam pars quamvis parva congregationis saniore consilio elegerit*" ["In the appointment of the abbot let this rule always be observed, that he be made abbot who is chosen unanimously in the fear of God by the whole community, or even by a minority, however small, if its counsel be more wholesome"] [McCann, *The Rule*, 144–45]; see also *Carta Caritatis*, chap. 4: "*hi qui sanioris consilii & magis idonei aparuerint judicabunt*" ["those who have shown themselves of wiser and more suitable counsel will decide"] [*Nomasticon*, 71]).

365. N. 43.

366. N. 48.

367. N. 51.

368. N. 54.

369. See Mahn, *Benoît XII*, 41.

370. Canivez, *Statuta*, 3.436–37, 437–38.

371. See Mahn, *Benoît XII*, 46–47.

The Cistercian Order (1153–1335)

(c) Benedict XII personally watched over reform of grave abuses in individual monasteries—these cases, very serious and scandalous, show to what extent the Order had declined. For instance, {at} *Grandselve*,[372] monks were wandering around in an armed band or bands, occasionally holding up and robbing travelers. The affair was very serious and took four or five years to clear up. The offenders were imprisoned in other Cistercian monasteries. {At} *Bonnefont*,[373] a monk prisoner died of maltreatment, froze and starved to death without {the} sacraments. His body was frozen to the ground and could only be removed with shovels. {The} bishop {was} sent to prosecute {the} abbot. {At} *Marcilly*,[374] like several other abbeys (v.g. Boulbonne), some monks were practicing alchemy and also using magic to try to find a "hidden treasure"; this was set in order. {At} *Dunes*,[375] {a} fugitive monk who goes to Hungary is irregularly elected abbot, ordered to be deposed, returns to Dunes with an armed band {and} attacks and robs {the} monastery; {he} is imprisoned. {There were} countless cases of monasteries economically ruined, pillaged in war, etc. etc. {The} pope {is} concerned with all these problems and does much to get communities back in good shape.

2. *Effects of the Administrative Reform*: it seems that the response of the superiors to the reform, in so far as it affected their own policies, was not always cooperative:

a) {There was the} difficulty {of} certain abbots {being} negligent about procuring copies of the document and acquainting themselves with its contents.[376]

b) In interpreting the Bull, there was {a} danger that some would twist the meaning to favor their own policies.[377] See

---

372. See Mahn, *Benoît XII*, 43.
373. See Mahn, *Benoît XII*, 44.
374. See Mahn, *Benoît XII*, 44–45.
375. See Mahn, *Benoît XII*, 45.
376. See Mahn, *Benoît XII*, 41.
377. See Mahn, *Benoît XII*, 41–42.

General Chapter, 1337:11:[378] this statute implicitly reproves the abbots who take certain points of the papal constitution and cast doubt upon them: *"adducunt in dubium."* They therefore command all abbots who have such "doubts" to make them known before the following Easter, and they will be presented to the pope for clarification.

c) According to Mahn,[379] in practice the severer prescriptions were not applied, and in the next pontificate some abbots received privileges which enabled them to evade the strict control on finances, accountability to {the} bursar, etc.

3. *Effects of the legislation on studies*:

a) In 1336 and 1339, the pope repeated his command that all monasteries should send men to the houses of studies, according to the prescriptions of the new law.[380] Hence there was difficulty in getting abbots to comply.

b) General Chapter 1361:4[381] refers to a statute of the previous year ordering all abbots of the Order to send students to the houses of studies, according to *Fulgens*.[382] This statute is not found in 1360, which perhaps indicates that it just was not copied, in very many cases, and was practically not promulgated in many areas. The statute of 1361:4 continues: that all permissions and dispensations made by Fathers Immediate and others are null, in regard to this matter of sending students. Evidently the local superiors were getting their Fathers Immediate to say they did not have to send students.

c) The expense of sending students to Paris etc. was increasing,[383] as the cost of living rose. Hence burses and other grants

---

378. Canivez, *Statuta*, 3.448.
379. See Mahn, *Benoît XII*, 42.
380. See Mahn, *Benoît XII*, 60.
381. Canivez, *Statuta*, 3.538.
382. See Mahn, *Benoît XII*, 60.
383. See Mahn, *Benoît XII*, 60–61.

were increased in 1342,[384] 1343,[385] 1348[386] (of course the local abbots had to pay these).

d) There was intervention in favor of abbots who had been elected while still studying and who wished to stay away from their monastery until completing studies for the doctorate.[387]

e) *Fruits*: the whole study program of the Cistercians was not very fruitful in producing theologians. A few solid theologians existed:[388] William of Curti (later a cardinal), Jean of Cercamp, William of Poblet. Two Cistercians defended the Immaculate Conception: John de Nova Villa {and} James of Eltvill. Two others were somewhat prominent as adversaries of Wycliff: William Remington and Henry Crumpe. Others were notoriously off in their theology, including Jean de Mirecourt,[389] a nominalist who was censured in 1347 for teaching God is the cause of sin as sin; another, Richard of Lincoln,[390] was forbidden to teach the *Sentences "propter suas opiniones phantasticas."*[391] In the *Dictionnaire de Théologie Catholique*,[392] though relatively much space is given to the Fathers and spiritual writers of the early centuries, including Caesar of Heisterbach and a minor hagiographer of the late thirteenth century, Engelhard of Lanckheim, there is little about professional theologians, especially in the fourteenth century, the time that interests us most. The only "professional theologians" listed in the Middle Ages—and these are the ones presumably who would show us the trend at the College of St. Bernard and elsewhere, about the time of *Fulgens* and after—

---

384. Canivez, *Statuta*, 3.471 (#5).
385. Canivez, *Statuta*, 3.472–73 (#1).
386. Canivez, *Statuta*, 3.513 (#15).
387. See Mahn, *Benoît XII*, 63–64.
388. See Mahn, *Benoît XII*, 67–68.
389. See Mahn, *Benoît XII*, 67.
390. See Mahn, *Benoît XII*, 62–63.
391. "on account of his outlandish opinions."
392. J. Besse, "Cisterciens, vii: Écrivains," *Dictionnaire de Théologie Catholique*, 15 vols. (Paris: Letouzey et Ané, 1923–1950), 2:2538–50.

are the following: Jacques de Termes, Abbot of Pontigny, defender of privileges and exemptions of regulars against {the} Bishop of Bourges; Adam of Rewley, adversary of Wycliff {and} author of *De Cavendo ab Haeresi, De Ordine Monastico, Dialogus Rationis et Animae*; Henry Crumpe is mentioned as also {a} controversialist against {the} mendicants and author of *Determinationes Scholasticae* (what these were is not said); Henry Collingham, obviously an Englishman, but in France, {wrote a} *Commentarius Sorbonicus de Eucharistia*. In the fifteenth century, Giles of the Dunes wrote *De Regimine Monialium* and *Regula Confessoris Monialium*, as well as a dialogue between the soul and a religious man. A certain Robert de Caremadio left what was obviously a work of edification rather than of theology, *Cato Moralisatus*. This is about all we find;[393] in other words there is no serious theology written, and apparently what was taught was very conventional and perhaps tending in the direction of the times, towards the decadence of scholasticism. What is written is concerned with practical organizational problems, if not legal questions. *After the Reformation*, we find some Cistercians commenting on Scripture (nothing of this {is} registered in {the} Middle Ages after the Golden Age), others writing works of edification, such as a commentary on the words of the Blessed Virgin. In the sixteenth century a cellarer of the College of St. Bernard brought out editions of some of the Fathers—Hilary, Ambrose, Gregory the Great, Bernard. In 1612 we find a Spanish Cistercian, Luis de Mendoza, producing a *Summa Totius Theologiae Moralis*. But generally we still find the Cistercians producing either collections of sermons or works of edification (not many), or treatises on immunities and privileges. In the seventeenth century, we begin to see Cistercians doing serious work in {the} history of the Order, etc., but this has not necessarily anything to do with the colleges as such. (In history etc. {we find} such names as Julien Paris, editor of first *Nomasticon*; Charles de Visch, {producer of} historical work and editions

---

393. Col. 2540.

of Cistercian Fathers; Ughelli, {author of} *Italia Sacra*; Manrique, {author of} *Annales Cistercienses*.)

A note on *Caramuel*:[394] a rare Cistercian "theologian" who is sometimes referred to in manuals is Caramuel, the "prince of laxists."[395] Caramuel y Lobkovitz {was} born {in} Madrid {in} 1606. {A} monk of Espina, {he} studied at Salamanca {and} taught in {the} Cistercian College at Alcalá; {he} went to Dunes, took {his} doctorate at Louvain, became Abbot of Melrose {and} Vicar General for Great Britain and Ireland, {then a} bishop in Germany. {He} was in Prague and defended {the} city with other ecclesiastics by arms against {the} Swedes, {became a} bishop in Italy, then {in} Spain, where he died {in} 1682.[396] {He led a} very active life all over Europe. {He} wrote on {the} *Rule* of St. Benedict, St. Bernard's *De Praecepto et Dispensatione*, St. Bernard's controversy with Abelard and Gilbert, the Medal of St. Benedict, fundamental theology, moral {theology}, some apologetics, controversy with Protestants, etc. {He} held very lax opinions about confession, which would permit confessions that did not reveal certain species of sins—i.e., permitted confession of some sins in vague and general terms, including some opinions that have arisen today in discussions raised by certain psychotherapists in regard to some sins *contra sextum*[397] (see for instance Denzinger, 1198 and 1199:[398] propositions commonly attributed to Caramuel). Caramuel must

---

394. V. Oblet, "Caramuel y Lobkovitz, Jean," *DTC* 2:1709–12.

395. This was the title given to him by Saint Alphonsus Liguori (col. 1711).

396. Typescript reads "1637."

397. "against the sixth [commandment]."

398. *Enchiridion Symbolorum Definitionum et Declarationum de Rebus Fidei et Morum*, 11th ed., ed. Heinrich Denzinger and Clement Bannwart, SJ (Freiburg: B. Herder, 1911), 353; in these *"Errores Varii de Rebus Moralibus"* ("Various Errors concerning Moral Matters") condemned by Pope Innocent XI in 1679, the first (#48) claims that fornication in itself does not entail intrinsic evil (*"malitiam"*) and is evil only because it has been forbidden, the contrary position seeming to be completely incompatible with reason, while the second (#49) claims that unmanly behavior (*"mollities"*—i.e. masturbation)

not simply be derided—he was a brilliant mind and an energetic worker for the good of the Order and the Church.

4. *Abuses in the Colleges*:

a) It seems that there was trouble with monks who were not students and were simply in Paris (or other centers) on business or for some other reason, {who} were making use of the colleges as residences and availing themselves of the privileges reserved for students.³⁹⁹

b) Abbots also made use of their students in Paris to carry out certain errands and business deals for them.⁴⁰⁰ General Chapter, 1338, n. 1 is a long statute regarding the College of St. Bernard. One of the provisions is: *"Ne praesumat aliquis abbas monachum proprium scolarem procuratorem constituere de cetero quovismodo, cum ob huiusmodi procurationes possint ad loca inhonesta in Ordinis scandalum declinare."*⁴⁰¹

c) Irregularities crept into the life of the students.⁴⁰² First, such matters as being absent from meals (see 1338:1):⁴⁰³ {this is} important in {the} setup of the medieval university, because—v.g. at Cambridge—presence "in hall" is {an} indication that one is present at the university. {The} statute provides that those who miss meals shall not be given any responsibility in the (student) community. General Chapter 1339:6⁴⁰⁴ laments the irregularity of students, out at night with arms, in secular clothes, arrested, jailed, etc. Such are to be sent to {their} home monastery at once.

---

is not prohibited according to natural law and that if God had not forbidden it, it would often be good and sometimes obligatory.

399. See Mahn, *Benoît XII*, 61.

400. See Mahn, *Benoît XII*, 61.

401. "Let not any abbot presume to appoint his own student monk as an agent concerning any other matter whatsoever, since on account of commissions of this sort they could stray off to dishonorable places, bringing scandal on the Order" (Canivez, *Statuta*, 3.449–50).

402. See Mahn, *Benoît XII*, 61–62.

403. Canivez, *Statuta*, 3.450.

404. Canivez, *Statuta*, 3.456–57.

1339:7 {notes that} the students of the different "nations" are introducing the custom of worldly celebrations, *in commessationibus, in ludis, ineptisque conventiculis*,[405] on certain feasts; *idem*, 8[406] {adds that} furthermore, they are dancing around the garden and in the streets playing musical instruments, and they are wearing masks; they are gambling in the cells, they are raising cain in the dormitory, they have servants, and so on. 1341:3[407] {points out that} the previous statutes have not been obeyed, the parties and dances have continued, and furthermore there has been a riot with a murder and many have been wounded; also there have been apostasies. {The} Abbots of Clairvaux and Pontigny {were} appointed to look into the matter and depose or otherwise punish those responsible, including the superiors of the college. 1343:1[408] {states that} to try to bring a little order and discipline into the college, the cellarer is forbidden to provide the students with food to eat in their rooms. If they want meat "they must go and buy it themselves"[409]—the cellarer must not provide it. Anyway the ordinary undergraduates should not have rooms at all; such rooms as there are, are for those with degrees and for the sick, etc. Without prolonging this painful list of abuses, it may be mentioned that all along these statutes are filled at the same time with details about the payment of bills, the burses and so on. In estimating all these facts at their value, one sees that it was a situation in which everyone was to some extent at fault, and there were many explanations possible. From the moment every abbey had to send students, it is possible that a great number who were neither worthy nor fit to study at the university, were sent there. The atmosphere of the university was not conducive to regular life or to monastic discipline. The students, feeling themselves

---

405. "in banqueting, in games and unsuitable gatherings" (Canivez, *Statuta*, 3.457, which reads "*commessationibus, ludis*").
406. Canivez, *Statuta*, 3.457–58.
407. Canivez, *Statuta*, 3.466–67.
408. Canivez, *Statuta*, 3.472–73.
409. "*de bursa emat propria.*"

important and believing, not without reason, that their abbots somehow would back them up, were bold and irregular. Abbots were not beyond getting the students mixed up in worldly affairs for the sake of expediency. It is hard to see how the men who studied in the College of St. Bernard would make really good superiors who would maintain the monastic spirit in the Order.

Conclusions: the Order under Benedict XII begins to fall into {the} background.

a) Cistercian activity under Benedict XII:[410] actually, the activity of Cistercians dropped off under Benedict XII. He called on them for active missions less than his predecessors had done. In his own conflict with Louis of Bavaria, they did not play a large part; this was interpreted in some quarters as {a} lack of zeal. It would be instructive to study the reasons for the diminution of Cistercian activities under Benedict XII. A few Cistercian abbots of course were still chosen to investigate abuses, reconcile litigants, reform monasteries, etc., but in general these missions were more and more confided to the mendicants.

b) Summary of the effect of Benedict's reforms:

1) There was not perfect cooperation in {the} Order with the administrative reforms. Nevertheless strong intervention by the Holy See did clear up some flagrant abuses.

2) The severe measures of Benedict XII did not really halt the decline. They were not generally effective. For what reasons? This remains to be studied. Probably it can be said that the decline of the Order had already gone too far.

3) The nature of the reform itself was insufficient. Benedict, an administrator, lacked the deep religious insight and creative fervor that would have been necessary for a genuine and deep reform. Nor is it reasonable to expect these qualities in him. He was a theology professor and a lawyer. He did not have the monastic spirit of the first age of the Order.

---

410. See Mahn, *Benoît XII*, 76–80.

4) In any case, the aim of his reform was simply to stabilize the Order at the more or less mediocre level of the thirteenth century, and to prevent grave abuses and further decline. In an age like the fourteenth century, with the whole edifice of medieval religious society falling apart, this was insufficient. The final collapse was then inevitable.

5) Nevertheless, Benedict was a practical and conscientious man, and his work was not totally in vain. The Cistercian Order was not completely corrupted or destroyed. Even in the worst days, there were good communities and good individuals in them. There were still saintly men in the Order. *The Imitation of Christ*, at the very worst period of the decline, could point to the Cistercians, along with the Carthusians, as models worthy of imitation, for their zeal for prayer and the work of God, as well as for their generally strict life.[411]

6) In particular, {regarding} the *College of St. Bernard*:

(a) This contributed little or nothing to the reform of the Order, {and} probably it contributed to the decline, *per accidens*.

(b) The plan of Stephen of Lexington had been good in its basic concept of the need for well-formed and well-educated men in the Order.

(c) Naturally, in order to have access to professors, students had to be sent to universities. Perhaps the danger involved in this was not fully realized at the time. Stephen of Lexington developed his plan when the universities were still new (but the example of the rather wild life at cathedral schools of earlier days might have been instructive).

(d) If the studies could have been carried out in regular monasteries of the Order, the program might have been of much greater value.

(e) Benedict's insistence on better organization in studies was simply the fruit of his own character and background—an alumnus of the College, a theology professor, a curial official,

---

411. See above, page 151, n. 45.

he naturally thought in these terms. But this was of no real help to the Order, at least as a *monastic* order. We must not, however, exaggerate the limitations or defects of the College of St. Bernard, and above all must not go to the other extreme and say it proves the "danger of studies."

Omissions: in these too brief notes, many important items have been completely omitted or referred to only in passing. They must at least be mentioned here, because of their great importance in the history of the Order at this period:

1. The monastic mission in Eastern Europe {was} a great civilizing force, with a character and energy of its own and a history of great complexity and interest. History {was} made by "fighting" Cistercian bishops (Berthold of Loccum, Dietrich of Dunamunde). The Cistercians {were an important presence} in Poland—{cf.} St. Hedwig (d. 1278).[412] Here too, however, the unfinished "mission" work of the Cistercians was taken over by Dominicans.

2. The nuns of the Order, {including} the mystics and saints among the Cistercian nuns; the "problems" presented by the multiplication of convents of the Order; the refusal of the Order to accept many convents of contemplatives (v.g. Helfta); the great movement of Cistercian mysticism in the Low Countries, and its influence on the whole mystical development of the Rhineland and Netherlands in the fourteenth century. The powerful spiritual life of the Order flowed into this channel above all in the period we have discussed. Here is where we must look for the greatest Cistercian saints of the period. Here too we must look for a real and vitally important development in the spirituality of the Order.

3. The crisis in the laybrotherhood of the Order:

A. In the twelfth century, the great flood of vocations to the laybrothers was of vital importance; {it} aided the economic development of the Order. In {the} twelfth century the brothers tended to outnumber the monks in many monasteries. It can be said that an influx of vocations to the brothers is a sign of real

---

412. For a brief character sketch, see Merton, *Valley of Wormwood*, 357–62.

fervor in a monastery or in the Order. But the influx brought many problems with it. In the beginning there was no special legislation for the brothers, hence there was no real protection for them. Often they were "used" rather than really developed. Their spiritual life tended to be regarded as secondary to their work, not in the sense that there was any misconception, in the early Order, about a supposed opposition between "work" and "prayer" (as if one could not pray until work was over), but in another sense—that as long as the brothers turned out the required (high) quota of work, nobody cared too much about what happened to them. Hence there was sometimes a serious relaxation of discipline, and in any case formation was poor or perhaps in some cases non-existent (?).

B. In the fourteenth century the laybrothers had almost died out. There were only a few in each monastery. In 1381, Rievaulx, which had had 600 laybrothers in the time of St. Ailred, had only two; at Jervaulx there were six (a large number); Roche had one. By 1400 there were practically no brothers in any of the English monasteries. The laybrotherhood had died out.

C. The crucial period for the brothers was the end of the twelfth century, and the decline went on throughout the thirteenth century. There was a big flare-up, a crisis, in which it was decided by most abbots, apparently, that the laybrothers constituted too much of a problem. After that, serious steps to preserve the brothers as an institution were not taken, and it seems that they were willingly permitted to die out. It was felt to be more convenient and expedient to replace laybrothers with hired secular help. At the same time, it came to be easier and more profitable to let out the land rather than have it worked by brothers, {and} collect rent instead.

D. What was the crisis in the laybrotherhood? It seems to have taken the form of violence and disobedience, often breaking out into open rebellion[413]—due to {the} fact that these were in the

---

413. See Donnelly, *Decline*, chap. 3: "Violations of Discipline and Their Effects" (22–37) and "Appendix: List of 123 Revolts in the Period 1168–1308" (71–80).

first place uneducated men from rugged country populations, especially backwoods types, as in Wales. {The} first recorded rebellion of laybrothers {arose} concerning the boots—a rather comical incident (see *Exordium Magnum*[414]) {in} 1168. In England and Wales {there were} difficulties concerning legislation that prohibits giving brothers beer at the granges. {The} background {was that} brothers {were} often alone at granges, without a grangemaster or superior of any kind, {and were} probably not too well-formed in any case. When they were also primitive people, as in Wales, this led to abuses. Around 1190, the problem centers around the prohibition of beer at granges. {The} General Chapter wants to prohibit beer. Abbots tend to allow beer in order to keep peace. {The} brothers {are} ready to riot if refused beer. {In} 1192,[415] {the} General Chapter gets tough {and} forbids English houses to receive brother novices as long as beer is allowed at granges. There had already been considerable trouble on this {point} at {the} Abbey of Margam in Wales. {In} 1206 {there is a} big revolt of {the} brothers at Margam, {who} chase the abbot fifteen miles, barricade themselves in {the} brothers' dormitory, and refuse to work. {In} 1237,[416] {the} General Chapter begins to relax legislation on beer etc. at granges, but at {the} same time discourages further reception of brothers, tightening up requirements. There were about 123 serious disturbances in Cistercian monasteries caused by *group* violence (not just individual flare-ups) between 1190 and 1308. Brothers were involved in *most* of

---

414. At the monastery of Schönau in Germany, when the abbot stopped the custom of giving the laybrothers new boots each year, they conspired to enter the choir monks' dormitory during the work period on Christmas Eve and cut up the monks' boots in reprisal, but the ringleader suddenly died in agony on his way to carry out the plot, an event predicted by the abbot; in response to the pleas of the other brothers, the abbot agreed to bury the dead man according to the usual customs, and they in turn renounced all their rebellious ways (bk. 5, chap. 10 [Griesser, ed., *Exordium Magnum*, 292–98]).

415. Canivez, *Statuta*, 1.149 (#16).

416. Canivez, *Statuta*, 2.169 (#6).

these disturbances, but not all. Note: as the end drew near, the brothers became aware of the fact that they were being allowed to die out, and even believed rumors that they were to be abolished outright in certain communities. This caused special difficulties.

E. Real Reasons for Decline of the Laybrotherhood: (1) first, too many brothers had been taken in, *en masse*—they were not properly formed {and} they were too quickly sent off to isolated places that presupposed a sense of responsibility and solid formation; (2) they were often overworked, regularity was not observed and relaxations were granted as {a} reward for hard work, hence {there was a} rapid decline of spirit; (3) the quality of vocations declined; (4) it became harder and harder for brothers to carry on at granges etc., {leading to an} increase of discontent and confusion; (5) {an} ever greater separation {developed} between {the} brothers and {the} choir; (6) with the decline in fervor of the whole Order, the choir monks and abbots tend to evade the whole issue of the brothers by just easing them out, renting out land, hiring labor, etc. In any case, it is evident that the crisis in the laybrotherhood played a very important part in the decline of the whole Order: (a) it came precisely at the most critical period, the turning point—1200; (b) it was closely connected with the economic revolution in the Order; (c) it was the spiritually weak spot in the Order, where the weakness of the rest showed up—i.e., the activism and mushrooming of the Order.

EPILOGUE—After *Fulgens*:

1. The Black Death (1347-1351): bubonic plague, from the Near East, swept Europe; {it} wiped out half or one-third of {the} population of England in one year. It came in repeated waves (1361, 1362, 1368-1369). It was especially dangerous in communities and is said to have swept away three-fifths of the Cistercians in Northern Europe. (This figure {is} perhaps too high.) Knowles says[417] that in the Abbey of Meaux, with a community

---

417. Knowles actually writes, "at Meaux in Yorkshire, only ten monks survived from a community of forty-two monks and seven converses" (*Religious Orders*, 2.10–11); it is Wulf who writes, "in the Abbey of Meaux out of

of fifty monks and ten novices, forty monks and all ten novices died in the plague. In Eastertide of 1349, at the Abbey of St. Albans (OSB), the prior, abbot, subprior and forty-six monks died within a few days.[418] {At} Newenham (Cistercian), only the abbot and two monks were left.[419] Among the canons of Bodwin, says Knowles, "The Prior and all but two of the canons went, leaving only an invalid and a simpleton to look after each other."[420] Some communities were entirely wiped out: v.g. all the Dominicans at Norwich.[421] However Knowles[422] disputed the arguments of some earlier historians, such as Gasquet, who attributed all the decline, evils etc. of the monastic Middle Ages on the Black Death. Conclusions: the Black Death did not ruin the Order; there was a revival after it.

2. {In} 1337, the Hundred Years' War begins. This of course made it exceptionally difficult for houses to get back on their feet and perhaps had a great deal of influence in slowing down the effect of *Fulgens*. Monasteries were regularly sacked and burned; Pontigny was destroyed in 1360; Cîteaux frequently took refuge in Dijon. Visitations became impossible. When monastery property was abandoned for long periods, nobles took it over.

---

fifty monks and ten novices, forty monks and all the novices died" (*Compendium*, 174); he is quoting F. A. Gasquet, *Henry VIII and the English Monasteries* (London: John C. Nimmo, 1899), 4; Knowles' slightly different count is also found in Cardinal Gasquet—in this case F. A. Gasquet, *The Black Death of 1348 and 1349* (London: G. Bell, 1908), 178, translating from *The Chronicle of Meaux* itself: "besides himself [the abbot] had in the convent 42 monks and seven lay brethren. . . . [W]hen the plague ceased, out of the said 50 monks and lay brethren, only ten monks with no lay brethren were left"; apparently Gasquet makes no distinction in the earlier text between monks and laybrothers—the total of fifty includes the abbot, whom Knowles does not take into account in his enumeration.

418. See Knowles, *Religious Orders*, 2.10.
419. See Knowles, *Religious Orders*, 2.10.
420. Knowles, *Religious Orders*, 2.11.
421. See Knowles, *Religious Orders*, 2.11.
422. See Knowles, *Religious Orders*, 2.8–9.

3. The Great Schism (1378-1409): Knowles says the Cistercians were hardest hit of all by this, because of the split in the Order it involved.[423] Cîteaux, with {the} Avignon popes, united French abbots in a General Chapter. Other parts of Europe, under Rome, had {a} General Chapter at Rome. {The} Abbot of Cîteaux {was} suspended by Urban VI, who appointed a vicar general. He released English abbots from obedience to Cîteaux and told them to hold their own General Chapter. This finally undermined the authority of the central governing body of the Order, and was disastrous. When the Order got together again, after 1417, it obtained {an} indult allowing {the} General Chapter to suppress any monastery that could not maintain itself properly. After the Great Schism, Cistercians were commonly out in parish work. It also became easy for monks to obtain special exemptions from Rome. Many privileges and exemptions {ensued}, such as that of holding a benefice[424] or of becoming irremovable in office[425] ({N.B. the} effect on regularity!).

4. The *Commendam*:[426] commendatory abbots, a fifteenth-century phenomenon, certainly gave the death blow to the monastic spirit. The commendatory abbot was an absentee abbot, not a member of the Order, interested only in collecting revenues and without concern for the community. In some cases he was just a child. (Yet note that it was a commendatory abbot, de Rancé, who became the reformer of La Trappe when he embraced the regular life himself with fervor.) The Order tried to protect itself against this abuse, but under Antipope Felix V it crept in. In 1515, Francis I got {the} power to appoint abbots in France in {a} concordat.

5. *Attempts at Reform*: efforts of {the} General Chapter to preserve vestiges of regularity {included an} insistence on attendance in choir, including getting up at 2 {a.m.}; in order to make choir "interesting," addition {was made} of other little

---

423. Knowles, *Religious Orders*, 2.168–69.
424. See Knowles, *Religious Orders*, 2.172.
425. See Knowles, *Religious Orders*, 2.173.
426. See Lekai, *The White Monks*, 75–78; Wulf, *Compendium*, 178–81.

offices, devotions etc.; PONTIFICALIA[427] come in at this period of decadence, to make {the} liturgy more "attractive." But the General Chapter has declined in authority. Spanish abbots have ceased attending {and} run their own affairs. {An} attempted reform of Martin de Vargas[428] (Spain) {was} without {any} basis in {the} traditions of {the} Order—priors (first superiors) {were} elected triennially. {This} reform {was} squashed by {the} General Chapter {in} 1445[429] (Martin de Vargas dies in prison). {In} 1438, 8000 unpaid mercenary soldiers ravage Cîteaux. {By} 1475, {the} state of {the} Order {was} critical. Jean de Cirey and other French abbots at {the} end of {the} fifteenth century try to stabilize {the} Order; printing of {the} first breviaries and missals helps. Protestants, Hussites, etc. etc. in Germany and Central Europe bring further crushing blows. This is an important period and should be studied. It is difficult to see how the Order survived at all. Fortunately the Council of Trent, with its emphasis on renewal and reform in the Church, started a movement which also led to a renewal of life in the Cistercian Order.

427. I.e, the ceremonial ornaments of a bishop (pectoral cross, ring, miter and crosier).
428. See Lekai, *The White Monks*, 82–83.
429. Canivez, *Statuta*, 4.564 (#13).

APPENDIX A

Textual Notes

Additions and Alterations

3	monks (?)] (?) *interlined*
4	Cluniac influence] *interlined and marked with arrow for insertion*
8	other *lectio*] *preceded by cancelled* Lectio after Prime not [ ]
9	ringing . . . 30] *interlined*
	1a) . . . nocturns] *interlined and marked with arrow for insertion*
11–12	and again . . . nocturns] *added in right margin*
18	other days] *followed by cancelled* all
	read also . . . poor] *added in right margin*
20	Worcester] *interlined above cancelled* Winchester
21	in] *preceded by cancelled etiam*
	etiam] *interlined with a caret*
23	*St. Mayeul . . . Venerable*] *added in right margin*
24	monastery . . . at Cluny] *added in left margin*
25	Heaven will . . . *mystery of charity*] *added in left margin*
27	organizers . . . builders] *added in upper margin*
	read H. . . . 50] *interlined*
29	*Bl.*] *interlined above cancelled* St.
	of Volpiano] *interlined with a caret*
30	bottom 91] *interlined*
32	prior] *interlined above cancelled* abbot
41	read . . . 29] *interlined and marked for insertion*
47	gifts . . . houses] *interlined*
	By 1098 . . . nunneries] *added in right margin*

	COURT . . . monastery] *added in left margin*
	1090 . . . Aulps] *added in left margin*
	cf. Subiaco] *added in left margin and marked for insertion*
	foundation . . . one abbey] *added in right margin and marked for insertion*
	Alberic {is} imprisoned (?)] *added in right margin and marked for insertion*
48	see the next page] *added in right margin*
	character . . . center] *opposite page*
	n. b. . . . Jully] *interlined*
50	21 . . . monastery] *added in left margin*
51	letter of two] *letter altered from letters*
52	make] *preceded by cancelled* renew
56	approbatus] *altered from probatus*
57	eligendo] *followed by cancelled sibi*
58	imprisoned (DHGE)] (DHGE) *added in left margin*
59	study . . . 13] *added in right margin*
59–61	Exordium . . . anheletis.] *opposite page*
59	(?)] *interlined*
60	sacratiorem; secretiorem] *added in right margin and marked for insertion*
	animarum salutem] salutem animarum *marked for transposition*
66	text approved] *preceded by cancelled* original
66–67	A. . . . 1119] *follows* B. . . . corrections. *in text*
67	of direct filiations] *interlined with a caret*
	B. . . . Laibach] *added in left margin*
	(cc. 4–7)] 4 *written over* 3 *and* 7 *added on line following cancelled* 8
	The three-fold . . . text.] *follows* A. . . . 1119 *in text*
	C. . . . Posterior] *added in left margin*
	this . . . Nomasticon] *added in left margin*
68	N.B. . . . Chapter.] *opposite page*
70	fidelissimus] *altered from fidelissimusque*
71	can] *interlined above cancelled* to
	who] *preceded by cancelled* which
	this . . . 10] *interlined and marked for insertion*

Appendix A

74	Cap. 2 . . . precedence] *following* impoverished abbeys *and marked for transposition*
76	begun to decline] *interlined below cancelled* decline
	Distinctio I covers . . . Germany.] *opposite page*
	ending with . . . "the Great"] *added in upper margin and marked for insertion*
	Bl. Goswin] *added on line and marked for insertion*
	commanded . . . regularity] *added in right margin and marked for insertion*
	Bl. Lambert . . . 12] *added on line*
	extraordinary . . . Germany] *added on line*
77	St. Bernard . . . 1186] *opposite page*
	Bl. Gerard (+1175)] *added on line*
	read—character] *added on line*
79	including laybrothers] *added on line*
80	St. Stephen . . . *animo* . . . Malmesbury] *opposite page*
	cf. . . . Bernard] *added in left margin and marked for insertion*
81	love of . . . IV.1] *opposite page*
	encouraged . . . visions] *added on line*
83	*Ut inter*] *preceded by cancelled* Ut ab omnibus
	LI: *De Nundinis*] *added on line*
86	commemoration . . . XCI] *added on line*
87	last psalm of] *interlined above cancelled* end of
	vigils] *preceded by cancelled* night
88	novice . . . here] *added in left margin below cancelled* Nov. habit given here
89	*enim*] *preceded by cancelled omnia*
90	adversary . . . worship.] *opposite page*
91	cf. . . . Griffiths] *added in lower margin*
93	cf. . . . 106] *added in right margin*
	Garnier . . . Jew!!] *opposite page*
	Septuagesima] *preceded by cancelled* Easter to Pentecost
	Laetare Sunday] *interlined above cancelled* Easter
96–97	Note: for . . . n. 4] *opposite page*
99	set as . . . to] *interlined above cancelled* offer present
100	n.b. exemption?] *added in left margin*

	crusade . . . 1218] added in right margin
	crusades . . . 931] interlined and marked for insertion
101–101	*abbots . . . 933] added in left margin*
102	*read . . . 637] added in left margin*
102–103	In *Religious . . . was this?] opposite page*
103	*However . . . 1196.] added on line following cancelled* until 14th 15th centuries
104	*what really] preceded by illegible cancellation*
104–105	*Thirteenth . . . sanctions them.] opposite page*
106	*read ROE p. 66] added in left margin*
	ROE p. 67] added in left margin
107	*multiplication . . . granges] added on line*
	p. 68] added in left margin
109	*II] preceded by cancelled* III
	wanted . . . influence] added in left margin
	recognition] preceded by cancelled resulting from
109–10	*See. Exemption . . . 1132 . . . 1184] opposite page*
110–11	*tithes first . . . 1182.] opposite page*
110	*Innocent II . . . 1132] interlined with a caret*
112	*and support] interlined with a caret*
113	*1474 . . . ab homine] added in lower margin*
115	*Peter {the} Venerable {is} more . . . ideal.] opposite page*
117	*The true . . . Dispensatione] added in left margin*
119	*1189] altered from* 1188
120	*wanted] preceded by cancelled* did
	Meissen . . . Saint Benedict] added in left margin
	difference in . . . Eucharistic] added in left margin and marked for insertion
121	*transfretavit (Archdale King)]* Archdale King *added in upper margin*
122	*1113 . . . La Ferté] added in left margin*
	Carta . . . 1954 #1] added in left margin
	Bouton . . . 180] added in left margin
129	*facta sunt"] followed by cancelled* In his
130	*a sweetness . . . sufferings] added in right margin and marked for insertion*

131	Here . . . sermon?] *added in left margin and cancelled but followed by uncancelled* no Abraham *added on line*
132	*Paschal] interlined above cancelled Easter celeb*
134	the devil . . . sin] *interlined below cancelled* Death + Hell.
136	*reaedificabo] followed by cancelled vestrum*
138	*gratiam] interlined below cancelled vitam*

APPENDIX B

Table of Correspondences

Medieval Cistercian History—Lectures and Taped Conferences

Date	Page #	Opening Words	TMC CD #	Published Tape Title & #
9/7/62	--	--	21.2	Medieval Monastic Movements 1
9/14/62	--	--	22.1	Medieval Monastic Movements 2
9/21/62	1	Early Monasticism	25.1	Medieval Monastic Movements 3
9/28/62	8	Sources	26.4	Medieval Monastic Movements 4
10/5/62	21	Cluny	27.4	Medieval Monastic Movements 5
10/12/62	27	Norman Monasticism	28.4	Medieval Monastic Movements 6
11/2/62	33	New Orders	29.4	Introduction to Cistercian Order 1
11/9/62	38	Cistercian History	31.3	Introduction to Cistercian Order 2
11/16/62	46	St. Robert	32.2	Introduction to Cistercian Order 3
11/23/62	58	St. Alberic	33.2	Introduction to Cistercian Order 4
11/30/62	62	{The} *Instituta* (study)	34.2	
12/7/62	63	St. Stephen Harding	37.3	Introduction to Cistercian Order 5

12/14/62	64	*Doctrine*	34.4	Introduction to Cistercian Order 6	
12/21/62	68	*The Spirituality*	35.3	Monastic Spirituality: Cîteaux (2083) Introduction to Cistercian Order 7	
10/21/62	139	Introduction	36.2		
	182	THE STRUGGLE			
10/28/62	142	4. One thing	36.3		
	193	1. BUSINESS			
	158	{As for} *serfs*,			
11/4/62	201	DEBTS AND DIFFICULTIES	36.4		
	171	5) *Criticisms*			
11/11/62	204	2. SPECIAL BUSINESS	39.1		
11/18/62	212	4. PROBLEM OF STUDIES	39.2		
11/25/62	225	FULGENS SICUT STELLA	39.3		
12/2/62	220	*Addenda to Stephen*	39.4		
	234	*Steps taken by Fulgens*			
12/9/62	244	b) Summary	40.1		

- Written text corresponding to first two conferences not extant
- Published recordings available from Now You Know Media; #35.3 also published previously by Credence Communications

APPENDIX C

For Further Reading

A. Other Writings by Merton on Topics Treated in *Medieval Cistercian History*

Charter, Customs, and Constitutions of the Cistercians: Initiation into the Monastic Tradition 7. Ed. Patrick F. O'Connell. Monastic Wisdom [MW] vol. 41. Collegeville, MN: Cistercian Publications, 2015.

Cistercian Fathers and Forefathers: Essays and Conferences. Ed. Patrick F. O'Connell. Hyde Park, NY: New City Press, 2018.

The Cistercian Fathers and Their Monastic Theology: Initiation into the Monastic Tradition 8. Ed. Patrick F. O'Connell. MW 42. Collegeville, MN: Cistercian Publications, 2016.

In the Valley of Wormwood: Cistercian Blessed and Saints of the Golden Age. Ed. with an Introduction by Patrick Hart, OCSO; foreword by Brian Patrick McGuire. Cistercian Studies [CS] vol. 233. Collegeville, MN: Cistercian Publications, 2013.

The Silent Life. New York: Farrar, Straus & Cudahy, 1957.

The Waters of Siloe. New York: Harcourt, Brace, 1949.

B. Significant Writings by Other Authors on Topics Treated in *Medieval Cistercian History*

Berman, Constance H. *The Cistercian Evolution: The Invention of a Religious Order in Twelfth-Century Europe*. Philadelphia: University of Pennsylvania Press, 2000.

Bruun, Mette Birkedal, ed. *The Cambridge Companion to the Cistercian Order*. Cambridge, UK: Cambridge University Press, 2013.

Burton, Janet, and Julie Kerr. *The Cistercians in the Middle Ages*. Woodbridge, UK: Boydell & Brewer, 2011.

Elder, E. Rozanne, ed. *The New Monastery: Texts and Studies on the Earliest Cistercians*. Cistercian Fathers Series, vol. 60. Kalamazoo, MI: Cistercian Publications, 1998.

Jamroziak, Emilia. *The Cistercian Order in Medieval Europe, 1090–1500*. New York: Routledge, 2013.

Kinder, Terryl. *Cistercian Europe: Architecture of Contemplation*. Grand Rapids MI: Eerdmans, 2002.

Lekai, Louis J. *The Cistercians: Ideals and Reality*. Kent, OH: Kent State University Press, 1977.

Newman, Martha G. *The Boundaries of Charity: Cistercian Culture and Ecclesiastical Reform, 1098–1180*. Stanford, CA: Stanford University Press, 1996.

van Damme, Jean Baptiste. *The Three Founders of Cîteaux: Robert of Molesme, Alberic, Stephen Harding*. Trans. Nicholas Groves and Christian Carr. CS 176. Kalamazoo, MI: Cistercian Publications, 1998.

Williams, David H. *The Cistercians in the Early Middle Ages*. Leominster, UK: Gracewing, 1998.

INDEX

Aaron of Lincoln: 108, 171, 194
abandonment, by God: 135
abbesses, Cistercian: 209; French: 119; general chapters of: 119–20, 145; of Castile and Leon: 119, 145; traveling with: 120
abbeys, autonomy of: 183; Cistercian: 205; construction of: 190; daughter: 103; dedication of: 190; English: 146, 195; great: lx, 192; impoverished: 75; incorporation of: 152; major: 224–25; rich: 193; Welsh: 106
Abbo, Abbot: 4
abbot(s): xlix, lix, lxvi, 3, 7, 15, 18, 46, 54, 56, 67, 100–101, 111, 113, 117, 166, 199, 212, 224, 234–36, 238, 242, 244, 249–50; absentee: 251; abuses of: 231; acts of: 232; as arbitrators: lxii, 207; as builders: 32; as feudal lord: liv, 104, 150; as mediators: lxii, 207; as reformers: lxii, 32; as taking place of Christ: 13; authority of: 218; Benedictine: lviii, 172; cell of: 124; chapter of: 46; Cistercian: xxxvii–xxxviii, 46, 76, 85, 119, 145, 150, 164, 185, 189, 205, 207–10, 230; commendatory: lxviii–lxix, 251; committee of: 225; correction of: 205; council of: 222; death of: 18, 250; defaulting: 104; delinquent: xlix, 186; deposition of: 73, 102–103, 109–10, 183, 186, 222; educated: 217; election(s) of: 7, 73, 110, 144, 184, 191, 222, 239; English: 103, 143, 164, 251; excommunication of: 184, 186, 189; French: 251–52; gathering of: 3, 186; illiterate: 21; interdict of: 188; Irish: 103, 222; lay: 22; local: 75, 239; major: 104; negligent: 237; neighboring: 84; Norman: 32; offending: 184; permission of: 204; policies of: 237; power(s) of: 104, 187; prestige of: 104; proclamation of: 75; punishment of: 183; resignation of: 73, 103; retired: 233–34; Scottish: 103; Spanish: 120, 252; suitable: 186; suspension of: 188; Syrian: 104; unworthy: xlix; vagabond: 232; visiting: 86, 102
Abbott, Walter M.: lxxv
Abelard, Peter: ix, xxxix, lxiv, 116, 160, 213, 241
Abingdon, Abbey of: 4, 6, 8; abbot of: 20
Abraham: 26, 131; guests of: 131; meal of: 131
abstinence: lxvi, 61, 233–34; regulation of: 234
abundance: 133
abuse(s): 158, 193, 196, 231, 233, 244; flagrant: lxvii, 244; grave: 237, 245; of abbot of Cîteaux: 185
Achard of Clairvaux: 78
acquisition(s): 111, 165, 169–70; of buildings: 171; of lands: 171; of villages: 171
action: lxv, 151; charismatic: 178; dynamism of: 99; pastoral: 178; preferable to contemplation: 211; voluntary: 165

263

activities: 193; acceptance of: 193; building: 192, 196; Cistercian: lxi–lxii, lxvii, lxx, 191–220, 244; ecclesial: lx, lxii, 193–204; economic: lx–lxi, lv, 204–209; exterior: 192; external: 226; growth of: 193; historical: 89; intellectual: lx, 23; justifiable: 192; military: lx, lxii–lxiii, 209–12; political: lx, 196; praiseworthy: 226; resistance to: 193; theological: 99; useful: 192; worldly: 192
Acts of the Apostles: 75
Adam of Rewley: 240
Adam Scot: 94
Adams, Henry: xxvi, xlvii, 27–29
administration: 173; Cistercian: 109; negligence in: 231; simplified: 106
admiration: 135
admonitions: 128; of visitors: 222
adolescentia: 93
adoration, of cross: 16; spirit of: 25
Adrian, IV, Pope: 122, 144, 163
adultery, woman taken in: 134
adversaries, struggle with: 94
advowson: 158, 194
Aelfheah (Alfeth), Bp.: 2, 20–21
Aelfric of Eynsham, Abbot: 4
Aelred (Ailred) of Rievaulx, St.: xli–xliii, 102, 125–28, 140, 153, 247; as seneschal: 126; charity of: xli, 128; death of: 146–47; entrance to Rievaulx of: 126–27; *Life* of: xli–xlii, 125–28; personality of: 125–26; sermons of: xlii–xliii, 129–34; simplicity of: xli, 128; tears of: 127–28; tenderness of: xli, 126; vocation of: 125–28; writings of: xli, 128
affairs, secular: 104; worldly: 244
affection(s), fraternal: 115; pious: 127
affectivity: 120
affluence: lxi
Africa: lxxii

age(s): 82; of Father: 97; of history: xxxvi, 89, 91–94; of Holy Spirit: xxxv, 97–98; of Son: 97; of world: 96
agriculture: lxi
Aidan, St.: 1
Aix, Synod of: xxi
Alan of Lille: 210, 215
Alberic, St.: xxvii, xxix, xxxi, xlviii, 41–45, 49–50, 58–62, 64, 70, 76; administration of: 45; as founder of Cîteaux: 41–42; as prior of Molesme: 42–43, 58–59; character of: xxix, 59; death of: 62; imprisonment of: xlviii, 44, 47; *Instituta* of: xxix, lvi–lvii, 45, 62, 84, 114, 148, 152, 154, 157–58, 170; learning of: 215; sainthood of: xxix, 62–63; tomb of: 62
Albigensians: 100, 145, 151, 210, 215, 226, 229
Alcalá: 241
alchemy: 237
Aleth (Aleyde) of Scharbeek, Bl.: 120
Alexander of Cîteaux, Bl.: 76
Alexander II, King: 204
Alexander II, Pope: 36–38
Alexander III, Pope: xxxviii, liii, lvii–lviii, 99, 110–11, 122, 144–47, 163, 171, 205, 210; criticisms by: lvii–lviii, 164, 168–69, 171–72; letters of: 168–69, 171–72; love for Cistercians of: 171
Alexander IV, Pope: 113, 220
Alfonso VIII, King: 119
Alfred, King: 2, 6
All Saints, Feast of: 87
All Souls, Feast of: 23
almoners, laybrothers as: 208
alms: 118
almsdeeds: 175
Alps: 39, 58
Alquirinus, Bl.: 81
altar(s): 15–16; living from: 90; of Clairvaux: 123
Amadée of Aulps: 47

ambition(s): lviii, 180; of rulers: 182; of world: lx, 192
Ambrose, St.: 8, 29, 240
America: 96
Amiens, cathedral of: 27
Anacletus II, Antipope: 110
Anastasius IV, Pope: 122, 144
Andrew, brother of St. Bernard: 123
angel(s): 10, 81, 131; rejoicing: 56; union with: 26
Aniane, constitutions of: 23; customs of: 23
animal(s): 106, 156; friendship with: 26; ownership of: 83; useless: 83
Anjou: 118; counts of: 22
anomalies, liturgical: 116
Anselm of Canterbury, St.: xxvi, 30, 32–34
Anselm of Havelberg: 89–90, 94
Anthony of Egypt, St.: 40
anti-intellectualism, Cistercian: 214
antiphoner: 14; Cistercian: 64; Roman: 9; Vatican: 4
antipope(s): 97, 145–46
anti-Semitism: 210
apocalypse, of Spirit: 95
apologetics: 241
apostasy, monastic: 57, 81, 243
apostates: 222
apostle(s): 26, 133; holy: 214
apostolate: 95
apparition(s), Easter: 132; of Mary: xxix, 46–47, 61; of monk: 122
Aquitaine: 22, 27; dukes of: 21–22
arable: 105
arbitrariness: 187; of superiors: 231
archdeacon: 176
archimandrites: 96
architects, monks as: 196
architecture, Gothic: xlvii; Romanesque: xlvii, 23
Aristotle: 214
ark of the covenant: 129

armaria: 216
armies, Christian: 97; crusading: 211; mixed: 209
arms: 22, 242
Arnold I of Cîteaux, Abbot: 145, 187, 211–12
Arnold of Morimond, Abbot: 55, 124
Arnulf of Louvain, Abbot: 218
Arnulf of Villers: lxxiii
arrests, of students: 242
arsenals, doorkeepers of: lxx; keys to: lxxiii, 208
art(s), Gothic: 29; liberal: 224, 235; liturgical: 25; monastic centers of: 4; of fishing: 214; of tent-making: 214
Arthur, King: xlv
Ascension, Feast of: 87
asceticism: 227; bibliographical: 123
Ash Wednesday: 14, 87
ashes: 131
aspects, administrative: 231; political: 231
ass, story of: 176–77
asset, commercial: 198
Assumption, Feast of: 87
Athos, Mount: 233
attitude, metaphysical: 215; philosophical: 215
attractiveness: 5
auditorium: 17
Augustine of Canterbury, St.: xxi, 6
Augustine of Hippo, St.: xxxv, 82, 89, 99
Aulps, Abbey of: 39, 47, 58
Aumône, Abbey of: 148
austerity: xlv, 30, 41, 45, 105, 151, 174; communal: lvi; personal: lvi
Austria, Cistercian monasteries of: 148
authorities, Cistercian: lxvii; political: lxviii; religious: lxviii
authority: 136, 210; communal: lix; decline in: 252; Roman: xxxviii
autonomy, monastic: 45; of Cistercian houses: 190

Aux (Auch), hermitage of: 44, 47, 58
Auxerre: 123
avarice: lvii, 170, 172, 174, 178; communal: 177
Avignon, court of: 230; papacy: lxviii, 225, 229, 251

Babylon: 91
bad: 28
bakehouse, duties of: 19
bakeries, manorial: lvi–lvii, 154
baking: 8
balance, Benedictine: 60; Cistercian: 45; monastic: lvi, 47
Baldwin of Canterbury, Abp.: 210
Baltasar, King: 91
Baltic region: 147
bands, armed: 237
Bannwart, Clement, sj: 241
banqueting: 243
baptism: 137; grace of: 138
Bartholomew, brother of St. Bernard: 123
Basil, St.: xxv
Bath, Abbey of: 6, 19
bathing: 17
battle: 193, 210
Baudrillart, Alfred: xxxvii, 58
bear(s): 83, 91
beast(s): 91–92; rearing: 155
Beaulieu, Abbey of: 105, 151, 195
beauty, interior: 26
Bec, Abbey of: xxvi, 30–32, 160
Becket, St. Thomas: liii, 98, 146, 176
Bede, St.: 1–3
beds: 124
Beeforth: 108
beer: xlvii, 124, 248
Béguines: 98, 151, 153, 209
behavior, unmanly: 241; worldly: 31
Bela IV, King: 204
Belfays, Abbey of: 119
Belgium: lxxii, 125, 209; Cistercian monasteries of: 148

Belial, son of: 78
bell(s): 88
Bellarmine University: xviii, lxxviii
Bellevaux, Abbey of: 157–58, 167
bell-ringing: xlv, 3, 9, 17
Belmont, Abbey of: 119
Benedict Biscop, St.: 2
Benedict, Card.: 51, 60
Benedict, St.: xi, xx–xxii, xlvi, 8, 17, 21, 47, 56, 114, 123, 192; as *caritatis notarius*: 25; influence of: 1; life of: xx–xxi; medal of: 241; Order of: 115, 120; relics of: 21
Benedict of Aniane, St.: xxi, 9
Benedict XII, Pope: xi, li–lii, lxiv–lxvii, lxx, lxxvi, 190, 205, 213, 225, 228, 235–36, 244; activist mentality of: lxv; as administrator: lxv, 230; as centralizer: 225; as curial official: 245; as lawyer: 244; as organizer: lxv, 225, 230; as reformer: lxv, 231; as theologian: 230, 235, 244–45; life of: 229–31; reforms of: xi, xxxiv, lxv–lxvi, lxxi, 225–39, 244–46
benediction, episcopal: 111
benefactor(s): xxi, 52, 154, 161, 218
benefice(s): 168, 251; ecclesiastical: 194; investiture of: 59
Berengarius of Tours: 32
Bernard of Clairvaux, St.: viii–ix, xvi, xviii, xxvii, xxxi–xxxii, xxxviii–xl, liv, lix, lxxv–lxxvi, 25, 29, 34, 39, 41, 48–49, 62, 65, 70, 76–77, 79–80, 102, 109–10, 118, 122–24, 140, 142–43, 149–50, 153, 160, 163, 174, 193, 205, 209–10, 214, 226, 240–41; *Apologia* of: 123, 174; attitude toward studies of: lxiv, 182, 213–14; brothers of: 123; canonization of: liii, 147, 171; companions of: 123; death of: xi, xxxiv, li, liii–liv, 101, 143, 145, 183, 215; *De Praecepto* of: 117, 241; fame of: 183; life of: xv, 160; Mass of: 112;

Index

relations with Cluny of: 115–18; personality of: xxxix, 115; power of: 183; successors of: 104; work of: xv
Bernard of Tiron, Abbot: 36
Berno, St.: 22
Berthold of Loccum, Bp.: 147, 246
Besse, J.: 239
biberes: xlvii, 9
Bible: 89; Douay-Rheims: lxxvii; Vulgate: 123
Biddlesden, abbacy of: 196; cellarer of: 195–96
bills, payment of: 243
birds: 108
birth, carnal: xliii, 137; immortal: xliii, 137; spiritual: xliii, 137
bishop(s): xxxviii, xlix, lxii, 3, 23, 110–11, 144, 146, 162, 176, 196, 205, 237; censures by: 113; Cistercian: liv, lxii, lxx, 147, 150, 204–206, 230, 246; conflict with: 74; fighting: 246; intervention of: 186; local: xlix, 184; monastic: 3; ornaments of: 252; retired: 206; visitations by: 110
Bithaine, abbot of: 100
bitterness: 130, 133, 181; of life: 130
Black Death: lxviii, lxxiii, 249–50
Blanchette, Gaetan, ocso: lxxviii
blessing: xliv, 10
blood: 203
Bobbio, Abbey of: xxii
Bochen, Christine M.: xxv
Bodwin: 250
body, health of: 12; lightsome: 117; resurrection of: 137
Bois-Grolland, Abbey of: 105
Bologna: 235
Bolshakoff, Sergius: 178
bond(s), between man and wife: xliii, 134; between mother and child: xliii, 134; of love: 135; of person with self: xliii, 135; uniting man and God: 134

Boniface, St.: xxii, 26
Bonnefont, Abbey of: 237
Bonnes, Jean-Paul: 30
book(s): 17, 88; clasps for: 85; new: 86; unity in: 83
boots: 88, 248
Bordeaux: 195
Boso of Clairvaux: 78
Boston: 195, 199
Boulbonne, Abbey of: 229, 237
Boulogne, church of: 104, 160
Bourg Dieu, Abbey of: 164
bourgeoisie: 181
Bourges, bishop of: 240
Bouton, Jean de la Croix: xl, 49, 51, 116, 118–20, 122, 210, 212
bowing: xliv
Brabant, duke of: 100
bread, daily: 13, 85; leavened: 116–17; unleavened: 116–17; white: 85
breviary, of St. Stephen: 123; printing of: 252
brigands: 79
British Isles: 102
Brittany: lx, 36, 188
Brogne, Abbey of: 29
Brooke, C. N. L.: 176
brothers: xiv; merger with choir: xiv; change in canonical status of: xlviii
Brown, Raphael: 75
Brunnac, bishop of: 204
Bruno, St.: xxvii, 37–38, 47
Brussels: 153
builders, laybrothers as: 208; monks as: lxi, 196
building(s), abbey: 200–201; acquisition of: 171; excessive: 202; farm(s): xliv, 108; larger: liv, 149; monastic: 149; new: 202; of villages: 158; simplicity in: 169
bullatores, laybrothers as: 207
Bunyan, John: xlv

burden, to neighbors: 181
burghers: 181
Burgos: 119, 145
Burgundy: xxvi, 36–38, 180; Duke of: xlv, 40, 44–45; hermitage of: 152
burial privileges: lvi–lvii, 154
Burns, Flavian, ocso: xii
bursar(s): 155, 235, 238
burses: 238, 243
Burton, Janet: lxxiv
business: 104, 107, 126, 193–94, 242; earthly: xlix; ecclesial: lxii, 101; in history: 89; journeys for: 155; men of: 173, 181; methods of: 175; of Church: 204–209; of Cistercian Order: lxi–lxii, lxx, 100, 191, 193–203, 207; of world: lx, 192
butter: 132
buying: 171; large-scale: 107
Byland, Abbey of: 158–60, 203
Byrhtferth: 4

Cade, William: 200
Cadouin, Abbey of: lxiv, 157, 222
Caedmon: 1
Caen: 32
Caesar of Heisterbach: 239
Cahors, merchants of: 201
cake, hearth: 131
calamities, natural: 202
Calatrava, defense of: lxii, 209, 211; Order of: liii, 145, 209; Rule of: 145
calefactory: 14
California: lxxii
Callistus II, Pope: xxx, 65–68, 122, 146, 183
Camaldolese: 33, 142
Cambridge, University of: lxxii–lxxiii, 242
Cambron, Abbey of: 212
candidates, admission of: lxvi, 232; for office: 191
candle(s): 14–15; paschal: 17

Canivez, J.-M.: xxxvi–xxxviii, lv, 49, 58, 63–64, 67, 100–101, 103–105, 107–13, 119–20, 143–44, 149, 152–53, 158, 160–62, 165–70, 186, 188–89, 194–95, 200–209, 211, 216–18, 225, 231–32, 236, 238–39, 242–43, 248, 252
canonization, formal: 62; local: 62; *per modum favoris*: 62–63
canons: 9, 105, 107, 152, 157, 174, 202, 205, 250; Austin: 125
Canossa: 35
Canterbury, Abbey of: 2, 6, 176; abbot of: 2; archbishop(s) of: xxvi, xxxviii, 3, 5–6, 32–33
Canterbury College: 179
cantor: 7
capes: 217
capitalism, western: 95
capitalists, monks as: lvi, 156
Capitula: xxx, 67–68, 184
captives, deliverance of: 26
Caramuel y Lobkowicz, Juan: lxvi, lxxi, 241–42
Cardigan: 106
cardinal(s), Cistercian: 109, 152, 188, 205–207, 230; French: 230; power of: 230
care(s): 227; of dying: xxiv, 19; of poor: xxiv, 18; of sick: xxiv, 19
carelessness: 180
Caremadio, Robert de: 240
Carmarthen: 106
Carmelites: 31, 151
Carnarvon: 106
carols, Christmas: xliv
Carta Caritatis: xvii–xviii, xxix, xxxi, xxxiii, xlviii, liii, lix, lxii, 45, 65–67, 70–75, 82, 101–102, 106, 108–109, 122, 140, 144, 183–85, 189, 192, 205, 236
Carta Caritatis Posterior: xxx–xxxi, xlviii–xlix, liii, lix–lx, 45, 66–67, 70–72, 146, 183, 185–86, 189–90

Carta Caritatis Prior: xxx–xxxi, xlviii–xlix, liii, lix, 45, 65–67, 70–73, 144, 146, 183–86, 205
Carthusian(s): 80, 142, 151, 153, 175, 245
cash, need for: 107
Cassian, John: 10–11
Castile, kings of: 145
castles: 202
Cathars: lxiii, 98, 100
cathedrals: 32; building of: 196
Catholicism, hostility to: 177
Catholics: 114
cattle: 202, 222
causality, historical: 89
causes, secondary: 213
Cavallera, F.: 63
celebrations, worldly: 243
Celestine IV, Pope: 205
celibacy, clerical: 35
cell(s): 47; abbot's: 124; individual: 234; isolated: 174; private: 233
cellarer(s): liv, lvi, lxvi, 7, 101, 106, 150, 155, 191, 199, 225, 234, 243; abuses of: 231
cellaria: 148
Celle, Abbey of: 38
cenobites: 38
cenobium: 26
censure(s): 113, 189; *ab homine*: 113; episcopal: 23, 113
centaur: 117
Cenwald, Bishop: 19
ceremonial, monastic: 3
ceremonies, Holy Week: xxiv, 14–17
Chaalis, abbot of: 188
chalice, new: 129; old: 129–30
Chalivois, abbot of: 100
Châlons, 52; bishop of: 52, 144, 186; Diocese of: 40
Champagne: 38
change: 141; ecclesiastical: 102; political: 102

chant, Gregorian: 4; monastic: 4; plain: 4; reform of: 45, 64
chantry: 194
chapel, of Clairvaux: 123
chaplains, Cistercian: 210
chapter, daily: xliv, 7, 13, 17, 122; hall: 123; monastic: 88, 221; of faults: 13, 67, 85, 88
chapter room: xlviii
characters, criminal: 221; low: 221
Chardonnet: 217
charity: xli, 25, 74–75, 117, 190; distributors of: 208; mystery of: xxv, 25; recorder of: 25; school of: viii, 25; sincere: xxxix, 117; works of: lxii, lxv, 173, 208–209, 226
Charlemagne: xxi, 96; canonization of: 97
charters: 195
Chartres, cathedral of: 27; counts of: 22; school of: 98, 213; tradition of: 215
chastity: xlix, 221
châtelet: 29
Cheddar Gorge: 3
cheese: xliv
cheese-making: 106, 157
Chenu, Marie-Dominique, OP: xxxiv–xxxvi, 89–91, 93–99
Chibnall, Marjorie: 214
child, bond of mother with: xliii, 134
children: 132; in monasteries: 4, 7, 12, 14–15, 17, 47; of God: xxv
China: xliv
choir: 87, 233; attendance in: 251
Christ Church, Abbey of: 176
Christ, Jesus: 78, 133, 137–38; abbot as taking place of: 13; arms of: 129; as Bridegroom: 229; as Divine Word: 24; as Good Shepherd: 56; as King: 97; as Savior: 16; as Son: 97; as Word: 136; binding of: 134; blessing of: 11; blood of: 129; body of: 10, 16–17, 24, 129, 136; breast of: 129; burial of: 131;

Cistercian community as: 80; compassion of: 135; contemplation of: 131; cross of: xlii, 130–31, 134; crucified: 81, 130; death of: 15, 134–35, 137; desire for: xlii, 133; devotion to: 35; disciples of: xlii, 130–31, 134; divinity of: xlii, 131, 136; enemies of: 135; essence of: ix; following: 40; glorification of: 24, 133; glorified: xxxv; goodness of: x; heart of: ix; home in: 127; humanity of: 136; humiliation of: 130; humility of: 118, 130; immolation of: 133; Incarnation of: 135; infant: 80–81; judgment seat of: 13; law of: 227; life in: 69, 136; life of: x; life with: 138; love for: 127; love of: 132; mercy of: x, 130; mysteries of: 35; obedience of: 15, 136; passion of: xlii, 15, 58, 129–31, 133, 135; patrimony of: 181; poor of: 60; prayer of: 178; promises of: 61; real presence of: 32; reception of: xlii; resurrected body of: 24; resurrection of: xlii–xliii, 17, 130–34, 137; return of: 24; revelation of: 133; rising with: 138; sacramental presence of: xxxii; Sacred Heart of: 120; service of: 151; soldiers of: 69; soul of: 135–36; suffering with: 138; sufferings of: xlii, 130; sweetness of: xlii, 129; temptations of: 134; tomb of: 131, 137; union with: ix, 26; vision(s) of: 79, 81; will of: 136; words of: x

Christendom: 25, 95

Christian of l'Aumone: 76, 81

Christianity, Orthodox: 96

Christians: 176; Byzantine: 145; Eastern: 145

Christmas: 3, 87–88, 117; Eve: 248; octave of: 9

Christoffersen, Hans: lxxviii

Church: xxv, 62, 96–97, 142, 150, 190, 218; affairs of: 191; ages of: 94; at low ebb: xxiv, 21; business of: 204–209; critics of: lviii, 177; diversity in: 116; doctor of: 34; doctrines of: 99; evolution within: 89; good of: 242; hierarchy of: lxv; holy: 94; institutional: 99; local: xxxviii; medieval: 226; militant: 226; missions of: 208; mystery of: xxv, 24–25; of perfect: 24; oriental: 233; power of: 193; progress within: 89; reform of: 252; renewal of: lxix, 252; struggles of: liv, 150; treasures of: 23; true: 96; union with: 179; universal: 204; well-being of: 179

church(es), abbey: xlvii, 12; as source of income: lvi–lvii, 40, 47, 104, 152, 154, 157, 160–62, 168; as source of political patronage: 160–61; building of: 196; destruction of: 158; English: xlv; gifts of: 194; monastic: xlvii, 3; ownership of: lxx, 158, 171; parish: 154, 157–58, 160–61, 164, 167–68, 196; property of: 179; rectorship of: 194; rental of: 160; revenues of: 160–61; town: 3; upkeep of: 162

circa (circator): 7, 17

Cistercian Order: xii, xxvi, lxvi, 30, 36, 39, 41, 45–46, 58, 110–11, 120, 152, 157, 190, 230–31, 245; abbots of: xxxvii–xxxviii, 46, 76, 85, 119, 145, 150, 164, 185, 189, 205, 207–210, 230; activities of: lxi–lxiv, lxvii, lxx, 191–220, 244; actual: 140; affiliation to: 172; affiliation with Order of Calatrava of: 145; affluence of: lxi; as active force: liv, lxv, 147; as ahead of its time: lii, lxx, 142; as capitalist: 156; as contemplative: liv, 147, 150, 191; as evangelists: 101; as judges: 101; as Order of St. Bernard: 150; as progressive: 142; as regressive: lii, lxx, 142; as representative of its

Index

time: lii, lxx, 142; attacks on: 174, 181; avarice of: lvii; Benedictine criticisms of: xl, 116–18; bishops of: liv, lxii, lxx, 147, 150, 204–206, 230, 246; business of: lxi–lxii, lxx, 100, 191, 193–203, 207; cardinals of: 109, 152, 188, 205–207, 230; centralization of: li, 109, 139; charism of: lxxv; collapse of: 245; college(s) of: xxxvii, lxiv, lxvi, lxx–lxxi, 101, 112, 142–43, 208, 212–20, 224–25, 230, 239–40, 242–46; condition of: 151; conflicts of: xii, 100; constitution(s) of: 102, 182; controversy of with Cluny: xxxviii–xl, xlvii, 110, 114–18; criticism(s) of: lvi–lviii, lxx, 110–11, 116–18, 154, 167, 171–81; critics of: lvii–lviii, lxx, 116, 171–81; customs of: lv, 151, 191; daughter houses of: 74, 144; decadence of: li, 139, 252; decline of: xiii, xxxvi–xxxviii, li–lii, lxviii, lxxiv, 99–109, 139, 141–43, 151, 180, 191, 213, 226, 244–45, 249; definitors of: 182, 186–87, 191, 225; *definitorium* of: lx, 109, 187, 190–91; difficulties of: 142, 201–203; diplomacy of: xlix, 207–208, 212; discord in: 190; early documents of: xi, xvii–xviii, xx, xxix–xxxi, xlvii–xlix, lii–liii, lxv, 65–75, 82–88; economic situation of: liv–lvii, lxi, lxx, 154–62, 181, 192, 246, 249; enemies of: 163; entering: 190; eulogy of: 228; evangelists of: 140; evolution of: lxx; example of: 226; exemptions of: xxxviii, liii, lvii, 100, 109–12, 147, 203, 205, 251; expansion of: liv, lxx, 56, 102, 142, 144, 147–49, 152–53, 176, 192–93; fervor of: 142, 246–47; First Fathers of: lix–lx, 71, 100, 108–109, 113, 146, 185–87, 189–91, 224, 228; first foundations of: 108, 182–83; formation of: li, lxxvi, 139; formative period of: lii; foundational period of: xix, lxx; foundations of: liv, 45, 85, 122–25, 144, 149, 153–54, 172, 192–93; founders of: lxxv, 41, 154; framework of: 190; friends of: 171; General Chapter(s) of: xiii–xiv, xxx, xxxiii, xxxvii, liii–liv, lvi, lix–lxii, lxiv, 45–46, 48, 53, 57, 63–64, 67–68, 72, 75, 82, 84–86, 100–101, 103–105, 107, 109, 111, 113, 119, 122, 143–47, 149, 152–54, 160–61, 164, 166–71, 182, 186–90, 192–95, 200–201, 203–204, 206, 208–11, 215–19, 224–25, 231–32, 234, 236, 238, 242–43, 248, 251–52; Golden Age of: xii–xiii, lxx, 147, 183, 232, 240; good of: 242; greatness of: 147; growth of: li–lii, 139, 152–53; history of: vii, xi–xii, xv–xvi, xxii–xxiii, xliii, lii, lxix–lxx, lxxiv–lxxv, 139, 141, 143, 240; honor of: 216, 225; humility of: 115; ideal(s) of: lii, 140, 192; immunities of: 240; influence of: liv; integrity of: lviii; irregularities in: 157–62; labors of: 110; law(s) of: 187, 190, 222; leaving: 190; legislation of: lv, 140, 149, 190, 201–202, 225–28; liberties of: 203; love for: 171; martyrs of: 147; maturity of: li–lii, lxxvi, 139–40; military operations of: lxi–lxiii, 209–12; missionary activity of: xxxvii, liii, lxvii, 100, 147, 152, 192, 212, 226, 244, 246; mother houses of: 74; mystics of: xl, 246; nature of: 192; nuns of: xl–xli, lv, lxvii, lxxii, 63, 118–21, 145, 151, 153, 209, 220, 246; observances of: xl, 116, 119, 159; of Common Observance: lxx, 141, 226; of Strict Observance; lxx–lxxi, lxxvi; originality of: 142; origins of: xix, xxvii; peace in: 190; policy of: 201; popes of: lii–liii, lxii, lxiv, 205, 225; position of: 150;

power of: liv, lxii, 147, 212; prayers of: 153; preaching in: 147, 210; prelates of: 209–10; principles of: lx–lxi; privilege(s) of: xxxviii, 109–13, 166, 203, 212, 240, 251; problems of: xii, 231–34; procurator general of: 109; prosperity of: 140, 154; proto-abbots of: 108–109; reform of: xii, li, lxix, 67, 113, 139, 183, 222, 244–45, 251–52; relations with bishops of: 146–47; renewal of: xii, lxix, lxxiv, 252; reputation of: lviii; respect for: lvi; revival of: 250; rights of: 111; rise of: xiii, xxiii, xxxvi; rivalry in: 108–109, 182–91; saints of: xl, 246; schism(s) in: 189, 222; size of: 142; spirit of: lxiii, 74, 150, 193, 196, 207, 209, 211, 213, 236, 244; spirituality of: xv, xl, xlix, 246; stabilization of: 228, 245; state of: 223, 226; strength of: 142; studies and: xxxvii, lxiii–lxiv, 212–20, 225; stultification of: 213; success of: xii, 118; superiors in: 113; theologians of: 239–41; tithes and: lvi–lvii, lxxi, 40, 100, 104–105, 110–11, 115, 154, 157, 161–68, 171; unchecked growth of: liv; unity of: 183; *Usages* of: xi; usefulness of: 216; vision of: xlix; visitations in: xxxiii, xxxvii, 45, 74–75, 86, 101–103, 109, 144, 211, 220–22, 250; vitality of: lxii, 142, 204, 207; wealth of: 142, 154, 197; work(s) of: 192, 226

Cistercium Parvum: 204

Cîteaux, Abbey of: viii, xxvi, xxxi, xlv, lxii, lxv, lxxiii, 31, 36, 49, 55, 57, 63, 73, 77, 81, 102–103, 120, 122, 160–61, 167, 182, 185, 191, 196, 204, 210, 215, 228, 250; abbatial depositions at: 146, 185–86; abbatial elections at: 146, 189, 191; abbot(s) of: xxxvii, xlix, lix–lx, 48, 73–76, 84, 100, 108–109, 113, 121, 144, 146, 161, 164, 182–91, 208, 212, 215, 220, 224, 251; chapel at: 51; comparison with Clairvaux: 229; consecration of: 50; controversies of: lix; daughter houses of: xxxi, xxxvii, xli, lix, 63, 71–72, 123–24, 148, 187, 215; decline of: 76; early: 228; early constitution of: 50; early fathers of: 80; epidemic at: 188; filiations of: 123–24, 148, 183–84, 187, 189; financial difficulties of: 236; foundation of: xi, xxii–xxiv, xxx, liv, 38–52, 76, 113–14; founders of: viii, xxvi, xxxviii, xlix, 58, 68–69, 74; harvest failure at: 188; location of: xxxi, 40, 51, 69, 228; monks of: 53, 67, 167, 186; observance of: 51; origins of: viii, 38–64; patrons of: 44; persecution of: 51; poverty of: 121; power of: 204; prior of: 191; ravaging of: 252; refectory of: 85; relations with Molesme of: 70; seal of: 191; spirit of: 228; struggle with first foundations: lix, 182–91; survival of: 140; vacancy at: 184, 191; visitation(s) of: 71, 108–109, 144, 146, 149

citizenship, in heaven: 137

city: 95, 97; of God: xxxv, 96; of man: xxxv; of the world: 96; temporal: 97; terrestrial: 97

Clairvaux, Abbey of: xxxii, lix–lx, 71, 79, 102, 104, 124, 143, 160, 182–83, 186, 188, 205, 210, 214–15, 219, 225; abbot(s) of: xxxvii, lx, lxiv, 48, 76–79, 113, 144, 146, 183–89, 217, 219, 243; abbots from: 205; Bibles of: 215; bishops from: 205; brothers of: 205; cardinals from: 205; cellars of: 194; comparison with Cîteaux of: 229; dependent monasteries of: 147–48, 218; distinguished monks of: 78; domaine of: 193–94; estate of: 194; filiation(s) of: 113, 125, 148, 189;

Index

foundations by: 205; granges of: 79, 194; library of: 214–15; location of: 124; love for community of: 81; monks of: 205; obscure monks of: 79; original buildings of: 123–24; pope from: 205; professions at: 205; refectory of: 123–24; size of: 153, 205; struggle with Cîteaux of: lix–lx, 182–91

class(es), lower: 97; of burghers: 181; town: 182

Cleeve, Abbey of: 160

clemency: 127

Clement of Rome, St.: xliv

Clement IV, Pope: lx, 109, 139, 189, 191

Clement XI, Pope: 63

clerics: lviii, 3, 177, 217; decadence of: 90; rootless: 173; secular: 207; talented: 173

clergy, as levitical army: 35; attack on: 179; local: 162; reform of: 35; secular: 162, 230

clerks, secular: 4

cloister(s): 3, 17, 221; burial in: 161

clothing: 17, 23, 40, 117, 197, 222; of laybrothers: xxxiv, 88; of novices: 184; secular: 242

clouds, of heaven: 92

Cluny, Abbey of: viii, xxiv, xxvi, xxxix, xlvii, 21–26, 29–31, 93, 110, 120; abbots of: xxiv, 23–24; as center of fervor: 23; as nursery of bishops: 24; as nursery of saints: 23; as second capital of Christendom: 25; church of: 23, 25; complaints of: xxxviii; conflict of with Cîteaux: xxxviii–xl, xlvii, 110, 114–18; esteem for: 76; Golden Age of: xxiv, 24; influence of: 4; life at: 23–24; location of: xlvii; spirit of: xvii, xxiv, 24–25

Cnut (Canute), King: 4–5

cock, as symbol of vigilance: 27

coercion: 95

Colan, hermitage of: xxvii, 36–37, 43–44, 47, 58

Colbaz, Abbey of: 147, 167

collecta: 200

college(s): lxvi; abuses in: lxxi, 242–44; as residences: 242; Cistercian: xxxvii, lxiv, lxvi, lxx–lxxi, 101, 112, 142–43, 208, 212–20, 224–25, 230, 239–40, 242–46; discipline at: 243; food at: 243; order at: 243; superiors of: 243

Collingham, Henry: 240

Cologne, archbishop of: 36

Columba, St.: xxii, 1

Columban, St.: xxii

Colvin, H. M.: 215

commendam: 251

commerce: 198; atmosphere of: 159

commitment, religious: 60, 69

commotions, worldly: 227

communion, daily: xxiv, 3, 7, 9, 13; general: 17; holy: 87

community, as presence of Christ: xxxii; Christian: 90; Cistercian: 80; consultation of: 232, 234; delinquent: 186; foreign: 222; good: 245; monastic: xxi, xlii, 86, 232; religious: 216, 231; solitude in: l

complaint(s): 170; legitimate: 164

compline: 9, 13, 17, 87

compromise(s): 150, 201; ethos of: lxxv

compunction: 11, 15

concern(s): 223; heavenly: xlix, 68; worldly: liv

condemnations: 210

conditions, scandalous: 221

conferences, novitiate: vii–ix, xi–xvii; appendices to: xvi, xviii; audience for: xi–xiii, lxxi, lxxiv; manuscripts of: xvi–xvii, xx, xxii–xxiii, xlvii, l; on art and poetry: xvi; on Church Fathers: xvi; on monastic spirituality: xvi; on *The Ways to God*: xvi; oral

presentation of: xxxii, xliii–l, lxix–lxxiv, 180–81; organization of: li; recordings of: xii, xliii; structure of: xix–xx, li; texts of: xv–xvii, l–li, lxxvi–lxxvii
confession(s): 8, 241; of sin: xlvi; power to hear: 187, 189; sincere: 13
confessors, Cistercian: 113, 210
conflicts: 193; Cistercian: xii, 100; economic: xxxix, 115; of Cîteaux and Cluny: xxxviii–xl, xlvii, 110, 114–18; of world: lx, 192; political: xxxix, 114–15
congregation, angelic: 81
conquest: 94; Danish: 5
Conrad of Eberbach: xxviii, xxxi–xxxii, 49, 53, 55, 75, 228
Conrad of Urach, Abbot: 207
conscience: lxiii, 111, 211; historical: 91
conservatism: 213
consolation: 15
conspiracy, danger of: 79
conspirators, laws against: 222
Constable, Giles: 116
Constantine, Emperor: 95
Constantinople: 153; conquest of: lxiii; fall of: 96; Latin Empire of: 212
constitution, Cistercian: 182; democratic: 182; Dominican: 187; monarchic: 182
Consuetudines: xvii–xviii, xxxiii, 74, 82–88, 122
contemplation: lxv, 129, 151, 226–27; haven of: 151; holy: 226; of Jesus: 131; solitary: 178; sweetness of: 226; vs. action: 211
contemplative(s): 150; Cistercians as: liv, 147, 191
contracts: 199–201
control, episcopal: liii, 109, 146–47
controversies, Eucharistic: 32; resolution of: 75
conventions: 178–79

convents: 120, 153
conversi: 34, 207
conversions: 222
converts, relapsed: 230
cooking: 8, 14
Copernicus, Nicholas: xlv; uncle of: xlv–xlvi
Corbie, Abbey of: xxii, 6, 20
cord, three-fold: 134
corn: 154
corruption, of gospel: 179
costs, overhead: 106
Coulton, G. G.: 177–78
council(s), ecumenical: 218; of abbots: 222
Counter-Reformation: 36
countryfolk: 154
court(s), ecclesiastical: 101, 208; of nobility: 208; of prelates: 223; of princes: 223, 228; papal: lxii, 207
Cousin, Patrice, OSB: 23
Cowdrey, H. E. J.: 35
cow(s): xlvi, 79, 197
cowl: 81; dying in: 79
cranes: 83
creation: xxv; days of: xxxvi, 91, 93; new: 91; unity with: lxxv
credit: 156
Crediton, Abbey of: 6
creditors: lxxiii
crimes, grave: 221
criticism: 141
Croo: 108
crooks, monastic: 179
crop(s), speculation on: 180; wool: 199, 201
crosier: 252
cross: 10, 12–13, 15; adoration of: 16; of Christ: xlii, 130–31, 134; painted: 85–86; pectoral: 252; sign of: 11; sign on: 93; veneration of: 16
crown, custody of: 202
crumbs: 133

Crumpe, Henry: 239–40
crusade(s): xxxv, 24, 91, 100, 153, 191, 193, 209–12; Albigensian: lxiii, lxxii, 100, 210–12, 226; Cistercians as participants in: lxx, 193, 209–12; Cistercians as preachers of: lxx, 193, 209–12; Fourth: lxiii, 100, 153, 212, 226; of St. Louis: 100; punitive: 211; Second: 145, 209; Third: lxii, 209–10, 226
crusaders: 193, 210
cult: xxxvi, 96; ideal of: 24; of Our Lady: 23; of saints: 23
cultivation: 103, 107, 154, 156–57; open-field strip: 106; system of: 106
cup, Eucharistic: xlii, 130
cupidity: 134, 165, 169
curia, papal: 35, 207; reforms of: 230; Roman: 219
cursus honorum: 230
customary, Cistercian: 65, 67
customs, Anglo-Saxon: 9; Benedictine: 9; Cluniac: 14; diversity of: 116–18; liturgical: xxiv, 11–16; monastic: 2, 42–43, 60, 74; of laybrothers: 87–88; Roman: 2; unity in: 83
custos: 7
Cuthbert, St.: 1

Daggy, Robert E.: lxxviii
Dalgairns, John B.: xxx, 37–38, 46
dancing: 243
Danes: xxii, 2
danger(s): 27; of studies: lxvii, 246; pagan: 27; physical: 221
Daniel: 91–92; prophecies of: 96
Daniel, Walter: xlii, 128
Dardenne, Myriam, ocso: lxxii
Dargun, Abbey of: 147
darkness: 37; light in: 228
Darnhall, Abbey of: 201
David, King: 129
David of Scotland, King: 125–27

day(s), of creation: 91, 93; of the Lord: 94; of week: 93
deacons: 16
dead, care of: xxiv, 19; office of: 7; prayers for: 3; visions of: 80–81
deals, business: lxvi, 231, 242
dean: 7, 17
death: 28, 135, 214; by starvation: 237; gates of: 214; mindfulness of: 178; of sin: 136; of soul: 135; shameful: 135; to flesh: 137; to sin: 137; to world: 137; wretched: 82
debt(s): lxi–lxii, 108, 149, 172, 180, 194, 201–204; building as source of: 196; danger of: 170–71; problem of: 231
debtors: 171
decadence, Cistercian: li, 139, 252; of clerics: 90; of religious orders: 230
decline: 141, 142; Cistercian: xiii, xxxvi–xxxviii, li–lii, lxviii, lxxiv, 99–109, 139, 141–43, 151, 180, 191, 213, 226, 244–45, 249; intellectual: 99; monastic: 99, 141; notable: 105; of laybrothers: xxxvii, 108, 247–49; spiritual: 99
decrepitude: 93
deer: 83
definitor(s): 182, 186–87, 190–91, 225
definitorium: lx, 109, 187, 190–91
deforestation: 174
degrees, academic: 243
delight, in righteousness: 136
De Lubac, Henri, sj: 93
demesne, commercializing: 197
demons, visions of: 82
Denmark: 125; Cistercian monasteries of: 148
Denzinger, Heinrich: 241
deprivation: 138
desert: 34; sterile: 229
desire(s): 69, 82, 133, 180, 212; ardent: 82; for heaven: 132; religious: 150; to build: 107

desolation: 57
despair: 31, 80
destiny, of empire: 97; of man: 97
destruction, of monastic communities: xxi–xxii
devil(s): xlvi, 26–27, 37–38, 134, 228
de Visch, Charles: 240–41
DeVogüé, Adalbert, OSB: 232
devotion(s): lxix, 15, 78, 180, 252; community: 86; new: 6; ointments of: 131; to Blessed Mother: xxxii, 35; to Christ: 35; to God: 228; to Sacred Heart: 120
diaconate: 113
Dialogus inter Cluniacensem Monachum et Cisterciensem: xxxviii–xxxix, 113–14
Diego of Osma, Bp.: 100, 211
diet: 173–74
Dietrich of Dunamunde, Bp.: 246
difficulties, economic: xxxvii, 104; financial: 201–204
dignity: 78; of toil: lvii, 156
Dijon: 29–31, 122; Cistercian house in: lxxiii, 204, 250
directive, spiritual: xliv
disasters, natural: lxii
discernment: 70
disciples, of Christ: xlii, 130–31, 134
discipleship, Christian: lxxv
discipline: 102, 150, 159; at college: 243; Church: 125; claustral: 7; ecclesiastical: 102; lack of: 221; maintaining: 102, 222; monastic: lxvi, 243; of Rule: 70; painful: 38; religious: 106; restoring: 102, 234–35; rigor of: 78
discontents: 249; current: lii, 141
dishes: 174
disobedience: 55, 135, 205; evil of: 135
dispensations: 102–103, 234
disputes: 187; religious: lxii; secular: lxii
dissension: 116; cause of: 118; diabolical: 116; of laybrothers: xxxvii; spirit of: xxxvii, 104

distortions, subjective: 181
disturbances: 249; grave: 183
divorces: 194
docility: 86
doctorate: 230, 239
doctrine(s): 25, 99; holy: 151; laxity in: lxvi
documents, papal: 58
dogs: xlvi, 22, 133
Dominic, St.: 100, 211
Dominicans: lx, 100, 109, 161, 189, 216, 223–24, 232, 246, 250
donations: lvii, lxi, 148; of land: 111, 148, 154, 193
Donnelly, James S.: lv, 139, 171–72, 247
donors: 162
doorkeepers, Cistercian: lxx
Dore, Abbey of: 206
dormitory, monastic: xlviii, 14, 233; of Clairvaux: 123; of students: 243
downs: 197–98
dowries: 118
drama, medieval: xlvi
dream: 95
Dublin: 222
Duchesne, A.: 168
Ducourneau, Othon: 43–44, 49, 53–54, 59
dullness: 225
Dunamunde, Abbey of: 231
Dundrennan, Abbey of: 102
Dunes, Abbey of: 224, 237, 241
Dunstan, St.: xxii–xxiii, xlv, 2, 5–7, 13, 19–21; as abbot of Glastonbury: 20; as archbishop of Canterbury: 6; as bishop of Worcester: 6; attractiveness of: 5; death of: 5–7; exile of: 20; sanctity of: 5; statesmanship of: 5; wisdom of: 5
Durand, Ursinus: 113
Durham: 2
duties, administrative: 226; of bakehouse: 19; of kitchen: 19; religious: 82

Dutton, Marsha: lxxviii
dwellings, town: 83
dying: 229; care of: 19

Eadmer: 26
eagle: 91, 94
Earll, Mary Beth: lxxix
earth: 27, 132, 229
east: 89
East Anglia: 106, 197
Easter: 9, 16–17, 87–88, 122, 132, 206, 238, 250; apparitions of: 132; Cistercian sermons on: xix, xxxvi, xlii–xliii, 93, 129–38; dating of: 1; food of: 132; grace of 132; services of: 8–9
Eberbach, Abbey of: xxxii
Ecclesiastica Officia: xviii, xxxiii, 74, 82
ecclesiastics, training of: 235
Eckhart, Meister: 235
economies, Cistercian: lv–lvii, lxi, 154–62; problems of: lxvi
economy, agrarian: 105–108; Cistercian: 198–99, 228; of flock-raising: 180; village: 197
Edgar, King: 2, 5
edification, works of: 240
Edinburgh: 125
Edmund, King: 3, 6
education: 178, 216; formal: lxiii–lxiv; in humanities: 222; inadequate: lxiv; necessity of: 6; patterns of: lii
Edward the Confessor, St.: 5
Edward the Elder, King: 6
efficiency, of Cistercian economic system: lvi, 106, 154
eggs: 14, 161
Egypt: 75, 133
Eilaf: 125
Einsiedeln, Abbey of: 19
Eldena, Abbey of: 147
Elder, E. Rozanne: xxxi, xlviii, 64
Eleanor of Aquitaine, Queen: 196

election(s), candidates for: 191; episcopal: 115; legislation on abbatial: 190–91; of abbots: 7, 73, 110, 144, 184, 191, 239
electors, abbatial: 191
elite: 150
Elizabeth of Jully: 118
Elizabeth, St.: 81
Ely, Abbey of: 4, 7
ember days: 87
emperor(s): 182; as Catholic: 97; Byzantine: 96; Holy Roman: xxxv, 172
empire, Carolingian: 21; destiny of: 97; Frankish: 22; Holy Roman: xxxv, 23, 95–97, 99; Latin: 153, 212; transference of: 96
employment, types of: lxi
England: xxvi, 30, 44, 63, 102–103, 108, 121, 125–26, 159–60, 172, 195–97, 210, 220, 248–49; Cistercian influence in: 118; Cistercian life in: 155, 180; Cistercian monasteries of: 148, 206; economic life in: 196; king(s) of: 206–207; monastic life in: vii, 1–21; monastic origins in: xvii, xxi, 1–2; Norman Conquest of: xxii, xxvi, xlvi, 30, 32; northern: 156; political life in: 196; shrines of: 105
Englehard of Lanckheim: 239
Enlightenment: 141
entertainments: 22
enterprise, productive: 155
Ephrem, St.: xxv
episcopacy: 174
episticula: 19
Ermengarde: 46–47
error: 224–25; seduction by: 224; theological: 230
eschatology, Trinitarian: xxxv
Eskil of Clairvaux: 78
Espec, Walter: 126–27
Espina, Abbey of: 241
estates, monastic: 179

Estella, Abbey of: 218, 235
Ethelwald (Aethelwald), St.: xxiii, 3, 5–7, 20; as abbot of Abingdon: 5–6, 20; as bishop of Worcester: 5
Eucharist: xlii, 129–30, 133, 138, 179, 240; controversy on: 32; eschatological conception of: 25; institution of: 129; type of: 131
Eudes II, Abbot: 48
Eugene III, Pope: xxx, liii, 66–67, 109, 115, 122, 143–46, 158, 164, 184, 205
Europe: xxi, 227, 241, 249, 251; central: 252; Christian: 213; continental: 107; eastern: lxvii, 152, 167, 226, 246; northern: 101, 249; southern: 156; thirteenth-century: lix, 181–82
events, sporting: 22
Everyman: xlvi
evil(s): 11, 213; endurance of: 214; intrinsic: 241; of disobedience: 135; prevention of: 221
Evrard of Clairvaux, Abbot: 217
Evrard of Molesme, Abbot: 48
ewes: 106, 157
exactions, royal: lxii, 202
exaggeration: 35
examination, episcopal: 112
excess: 63
excommunication: 81, 110; exemption from: 110–11; immunity from: 112; of abbots: 184, 186, 189
exemption(s), Cistercian: xxxviii, liii, lvii, 100, 109–12, 147, 203, 205, 251; from delegations: 208; from episcopal control: 109–10, 112, 205; from excommunication: 110–11; from missions: 212; from secular control: 45; from taxes: 203; of regulars: 240
exile: xxv, 25–26; of monastic communities: xxi
Exodus, Book of: xlii

Exordium Cistercii: xvii, xxx–xxxi, xlix, 43, 65, 67–70, 184; spirituality of: xxxi, 68–70
Exordium Magnum: xxviii, xxxi, xli, 49, 53–58, 122, 210, 248; as testimony: xxxii, 75; defense of Order in: xxxii, 55–56; prologue of: lxv, 228–29; sections of: xxxii; spirituality of: xxxi–xxxii, 75–82
Exordium Parvum: xxviii–xxx, xxxiii, xxxix, xlvii–xlviii, liii, lvi–lvii, lxv, lxx, 41, 45, 47–51, 55–57, 59–60, 62–63, 65, 73, 80, 84, 110, 114, 122, 140, 148, 154, 167, 170, 192, 214–15, 228; compared with *Fulgens sicut Stella*: lxv, 226–27
expansion, Cistercian: liv, lxx, 56, 102, 142, 144, 147–49, 152–53, 176, 192–93; economic: 159, 193; missionary: xxxv, 91; of possessions: 169
expediency: 244
experiments, monastic: xlv
export: 106, 157
exporters: 107, 157
eye(s): 91; bodily: 129; inner: 130; of flesh: 131; of heart: 129; single: 117

fabric: 105, 152
facts, historical: 141
fairs: lxi, 83, 86; annual: 195; attendance at: 170, 194–95
faith: 78, 98, 116–17, 135, 224; authentic: xxxix; growth in: 132; orthodox: lxiii
faithfulness: 213–14
familiars, Cistercian: 110
famine(s): 202, 234
farm, work on: 155
farmers: 154; order of: 97
farming, commercial: 106; dairy: 197; sheep: 106–107, 197–98
fasting: xxiv, 61, 88, 117; days of: 87; legislation on: 190; monastic: 8, 14; necessity of: 47

Fastrad of Cîteaux, Bl.: 76–77, 80–82
Father(s) Immediate: 144, 184, 191, 222, 238
fatherhood: 78
fatherland, heavenly: 132
Fathers, Church: xvi, 178; Cistercian: xliii, 155, 213, 239, 241; footsteps of: 40; monastic: 40
faults, chapter of: 13, 67, 85, 88; correction of: 75, 86, 189
fear: 15, 133; of God: 227–28
feast(s): 88; major: 87; of sermon: 88, 123; of twelve lessons: 8, 123; of two Masses: 87, 123; simple: 123; with octave: 123
Fécamp, Abbey of: 29–30, 33
fees, burial: lvii, lxx, 161–62
Felix V, Antipope: 251
ferment, intellectual: xxxvi
fervor: 23, 90, 99, 105, 251; contemplative: lv, 105, 151; creative: lxvii, 244; decline in: 249; diminishment of: lii; lack of: 47; monastic: 102; spiritual: xxxvii, lxvii–lxviii
fidelity: 80, 180, 234; to Benedictine Rule: lvi, 47, 69
fiefs: 22
field(s): 106, 155, 165, 175; fecundity of: 175; neighbor's: lviii, 175; work in: 155
finances, control of: 208, 238
finery, ecclesial: xliv; liturgical: xliv
fines: 236
Fioretti: xxxii, 75
fire: 3, 91–92; new: 17; station: 218
fish: 80, 161; two: 130
fisheries: 166
fishing, art of: 214
Fitero, Abbey of: 145, 209
Flanders: 3, 20, 120, 199; counts of: 22
Flaxley, Abbey of: 176
flea: 133
fleeces: 197–98; quality of: 107, 157

flesh: 78, 91, 138; death to: 137; eyes of: 131; heart of: 127; vice of: 112; way of all: 224
fleshpots: 133
Fleury, Abbey of: 3–4, 6, 9, 19–21
flocks: 105, 152, 172, 197–98; decimated: 199; size of: 200
flood: 202
flowers, desert: 56
fold-service: 197
font, baptismal: 137
Fontanelle, Abbey of: xxii
Fonte Avellana, Abbey of: 34
Fontevrault, Abbey of: 118
Fontfroide, Abbey of: 211, 229; abbot of: 229–30
Fontguilhem, Abbey of: 157
food: xxiv, 7, 15, 17, 23, 40, 87, 132, 138; amount of: 83; at college: 243; Easter: 132; gift of: 80; God as: 138; material: xliii, 138; new: 138; supplies of: 233; sweetest: 129; unity in: 83
foolishness, of mind: 225
footsteps, sacred: 229
footwashing: 7, 18, 130
forage: 166
force, civilizing: 246
Ford, abbot of: 210
foreigners: 179
forest(s): 154, 173; work in: 155
forgiveness: 13, 34
formalism, religious: 178
formation, program of monastic: xiv, xliii; Trappist: 213
fornication: 241
fortifications: 208
fortitude: 134
Fossanova, Abbey of: 160
Fountains, Abbey of: 105, 107, 152–53, 159, 200–203; foundation of: 159; original fathers of: 159
Fournier, P.: 58, 62

fowl: 91
Fox, Peggy: lxxviii
frailty: 60
France: xl, 124, 172, 210, 240; king(s) of: 183, 207, 210
Francis I, King: 251
Francis of Assisi, St.: 75, 98–99
Franciscans: 161, 231–32; early: 80; spiritual: 98
Fraticelli: 231
fraud: 224
Frederick Barbarossa, Emperor: 95–97
Frederick II, Emperor: 182, 208
freedom, of sons of God: xxv, 26
French, understanding of: 222
friars: 150, 161, 179; fervor of: 99; poverty of: 99
friends, faithful: 12
friendship, with animals: 26
fruit, honeyed: 229
Frutuaria, Abbey of: 33
fugitives: 84, 117, 222
Fulda, Abbey of: xxii
fulfillment, eschatological: xliii, 137
Fulgens sicut Stella: li–lii, lxiv–lxvi, lxx–lxxi, 225–28, 250; compared with *Exordium Parvum*: lxv, 226–27; effects of: 236–41
funds, monastery: 235
funerals: 87
furnaces: 195
Furness, Abbey of: 154, 168, 195, 203; abbot of: 143
furs: 40, 88, 117
fury: 133

gall: 129
gambling: 243
games: 243
garden(s): 166; mystical: 229
gardeners, laybrothers as: 207
Gardiner, Harold, sj: 151
Garin of Bourges, Abp.: 210

Garnier de Rochefort, Bp.: xxxvi, 93
Gasquet, F. A.: 250
gatherings, unsuitable: 243
Gaucher of Molesme, Abbot: 48
Gaudry, uncle of St. Bernard: 123
Gaul: 2
gems: 84
generation: 137
Geneva, Diocese of: 39
gentleness: 26
Geoffrey de la Roche: 104, 115, 123, 160
Geoffrey of Auxerre, Abbot: 77, 160
Geoffrey of Molesme, Abbot: 52
Gerald of Wales: lviii, 173–78, 195–96; activity of: 173; aspirations of: 175; calumnies of: 175; character of: 175–76; charm of: 173; conclusions of: 176; disappointments of: 173; frustration of: 173; insight of: 175; library of: 196; obscenities of: 175; opinions of: 176; perspicacity of: 175; prejudice of: 175; resentment of: 173; superficiality of: 175; talent of: 173; utterances of: 175; vanity of: 175; waste of: 173; writings of: 173–75; zeal of: 175
Gerard, Bl., brother of St. Bernard: 78, 123
Gerard of Brogne, Abbot: 6, 9, 19–20
Gerard of Clairvaux, Abbot: 77
Gerard of Ravenna, Card.: 210
Germany: xxii, xxxii, 55, 75–76, 124, 140, 196, 222, 241, 252; Cistercian monasteries of: 148; queen of: 206
Gertrude of Hackborn, St.: 120
Gertrude the Great, St.: 120
Gethsemani, Abbey of: vii, xi–xiii, lxxviii–lxxix, 33, 62; centenary celebration of: xlv
Ghent, Abbey of: 3, 6, 9, 29
gifts: 161; acceptance of: 159; of churches: 47; of land: 106, 194; of tithes: 47; refusal of: 158–59

Gigny, Abbey of: 115, 164
Gilbert de la Porrée: 213–15, 241
Gilbert of Brionne, Count: 31
Gilbert of Cîteaux, Bl.: 76
Gilbert of Sempringham, St.: 118, 144
Giles of the Dunes: 240
Gilson, Étienne: ix, lxxii
Gimont, Abbey of: 167
Giraut of Molesme, Abbot: 48
Glastonbury: 6; Abbey of: xxii, xlv, 2–3, 20–21
glory: 92, 118; heavenly: xxv, 25
Gloucestershire: 197
God: x, 89, 134–35, 242; abandonment by: 135; as Ancient of Days: 91–92; as cause of sin: 239; as Father: 15, 97, 133; as food: 138; as inner judge: 78; as nourishment: 138; children of: xxv; city of: xxxv, 95–96; commandments of: 32; devotion to: 228; fear of: 227–28; glorification of: xxxvi, 96; grace of: 114, 169; house of: 63; Kingdom of: xxxvi, 93, 95; living: 56; love for: 61, 78, 227–28; mercy of: 80, 127, 169; mountains of: 226; obedience to: 15, 135; pleasing: 97, 227; salvific plan of: 89; service of: 5; sons of: xxv, 26; submission to: 135; thanks to: 222; trust in: xxxii; union with: xlviii, lxxv, 136, 178; word of: 94, 127, 224; work of: 56, 70, 227, 245
gold: 84
good: 28; doing of: 214; greater: 57; lesser: 57
Good Friday: 16–17, 33
goods, exchange of: 195; spiritual: 221, 223; temporal: 221, 223; transport of: 195; worldly: 181
Gorze, Abbey of: 29
gospel: 75; corruption of: 179; spread of: 97; universality of: 96
Goswin of Cîteaux, Bl.: 76, 149
governor, of Kentucky: xlv

grace(s): xlv, 19, 56, 222, 227; evangelical: 90; of baptism: 138; of Easter: 132; of God: 114, 169; of Holy Spirit: 18, 40; of prayer: 56; state of: 179; time of: 94
gradual, Vatican: 4
Grail, Holy: xlv
grain: 199
grainstore: 202
Grande Chartreuse: xxvii
grandeur, of religious orders: 230
Grandmont, Abbey of: 207
Grandselve, Abbey of: 237
grange(s): 47, 52, 83, 84, 87–88, 106, 108, 158, 199, 248–49; as agricultural unit: 106; distant: 107; isolated: lxviii; location of: 155; of Clairvaux: 79, 148; sale of: 234–35; system: lvi, lxi, 197, 199
grange masters: 155, 248
grapes, bunch of: 131
grassland: 197
Gratian: 97, 216
gratitude: 41
Graves, Coburn V.: lv, lxii, 158, 160, 162, 164, 171–73, 175–77, 179–81, 194–203
graziers: 197
Great Britain, vicar general of: 241
Greece, Cistercian foundations in: lxiii, 153, 212
greed: 178; for land: lvi
Greek(s): xxxvi, 93; language: xxxvi, 93
Gregory of Einsiedeln, Abbot: 19–20
Gregory of Nyssa, St.: xviii
Gregory the Great, St.: xx–xxi, xlvi, 9, 25, 240
Gregory VII (Hildebrand), St.: 34–36
Gregory VIII, Pope: 205
Gregory IX, Pope: 208
Griesser, Bruno: xxxi, 49, 53, 55–57, 75–82, 122, 220–24, 228–29, 248
Griffith, Sidney H.: vii
Griffiths, Bede: 91

Grimes, William R.: vii–x, lxxviii
grooms, laybrothers as: 207
Grosbois, Abbey of: 157
Grosseteste, Bp. Robert: 112
Grottaferrata, Abbey of: 34
Guerric of Igny, Bl.: 78, 93, 140, 147
guests: 17; of Abraham: 131; poor: 7; reception of: 117; room for: 124
guesthouse: 18
Guignard, Philippe: 122
Gunnar of Clairvaux: 78
Guy, brother of St. Bernard: 118, 123
Guy, companion of Peter of Castelnau: 211
Guy de Bourgogne, Card.: 188–89
Guy de Chastel-Censoir, Abbot: 48
Guy of Aulps: 47
Guy of Cîteaux, Abbot: 76
Guy of Vaux de Cernay, Abbot: 212

habit, as humble: 118; as penitential: 118; Benedictine: 61, 117–18; Cistercian: xxix, 61, 117–18, 120, 197, 221; color of: 61, 116–18; monastic: 6; of novice: 184; religious: 84
Habitantes in Domo Dei: 110, 162
habitation, human: 228
hagiographer: 239
hagiography: 25; themes of: 25–26
Hampshire: 105, 151
happiness: 133
harlot: 133
harshness: 35
Hart, Patrick, OCSO: ix, lxxii–lxxiii, lxxviii, 39, 125, 143
harvest: 116; poor: 202
Hautecombe, Abbey of: 160
Hayles, Abbey of: 105, 151
Hazeka, Bl.: 153
health, of body: 12; of mind: 12
heart(s): 98, 130, 227; eyes of: 129; intentions of: 78; of flesh: 127; of man: 91; of monks: 192; thoughts of: 78

heaven(s): 18, 27, 91, 133, 137; citizenship in: 137; clouds of: 92; desire for: 132; joys of: 229; kingdom of: xxv, 24–25; rest in: 137; vision of: 82
hebdomadary: 14
Hebrew: xxxvi, 93
Hedwig, St.: 121, 246
hegemony: 187
Helfta, convent of: 120, 246; saints of: 120, 246
hell, vision of: 82
Helmsley: 126–27
Heloise: ix
help, secular: 247
Henry de Marcy, Card.: lxxii, 77–78, 81, 210; character of: 77–78
Henry, Duke of Burgundy: 40
Henry of Sens, Abp.: 205
Henry IV, Emperor: 35
Henry V, Emperor: 59
Henry I, King: 126
Henry II, King: liii, 146, 176
Henry III, King: lxxiii, 200, 203
herbs, bitter: 133
heresy: lxiv, 222, 230; Albigensian: 151, 210, 229; Eucharistic: 179
heretics: 177, 230
heritage, monastic: xx
Herluin of Bec, Abbot: xxvi, 30–32
hermit(s): 36, 38, 44, 47, 58
hermitage: 26
heroism: 43
heterodoxy: 231
Hexham: 125
Hibernia: 121
hierarchy: 109
Hilary of Poitiers, St.: 240
Hilda of Whitby, St.: 1
Himmerod, Abbey of: 196
historians, anti-Catholic: lviii; Cistercian: xxxv, 168, 240–41; medieval: xvi, 89–99; modern: lviii, 177; monastic: 198; progressive: xxxv

historiography: xxxv–xxxvi
history: 25; ages of: xxxvi, 89, 91–94; awareness of: 89; business in: 89; Christian: 93; Christian conception of: 93, 98; Church: 93; Communist: 141; honest: xii; intelligibility of: 89; medieval: 177; medieval Cistercian: vii, xi–xii, xv–xvi, xxii–xxiii, xliii, lii, lxix–lxx, lxxiv–lxxv, 139, 141, 143, 240; monastic: xv, xxi, xxvi, 75, 150, 176, 198; movement of: 89; of salvation: xxxv, 24, 89; periods of: xxxvi, 89, 91–94; person in: 89; place in: 89; progressive view of: 98–99; sacred: xxxv, 89; time in: 89; Trinity and: 97–98; universal: 89
holiness: 38
Holme Cultram, Abbey of: 195
Holy Innocents, Feast of: 9
Holy Land: 100, 193, 210; Cistercian foundations in: 153
Holy Saturday: 17
Holy See: lxiv, 23, 25, 45, 74, 109, 114, 183, 187, 190–91, 208, 217, 234–35, 244; obedience to: 192
Holy Spirit: xlv, 18, 31, 40, 56, 95, 127; Age of: xxxv, 97–98; apocalypse of: 95; impetus of: 142; work of: 95
Holy Thursday: 13
Holy Week, liturgy of: xlvi; rites of: 9, 14–17; services of: xxiv, 8
home-farm: 106
Honorius III, Pope: 112, 166, 207–208, 212
hope: 29; of salvation: 229
horarium, monastic: 23
horns: 91–92
horse(s): 80, 127; of visitors: 235; riding: 234
horseback-riding: 22
hospitality: 160, 175, 235; ordinary: 112
hospitals: 209
hostility: 163

hours, canonical: 9; day: 87
household(s), monastic: 226; of kings: lxii; of nobles: lxii
Huelgas, Abbey of Las: 119–20, 145
Huerta, Abbey of: 119
Hugh of Amiens: xxxix, 116
Hugh of Cluny, St.: 23
Hugh of Lyons, Abp.: xxviii, 44, 47–48, 50–52, 54–57, 59, 69; letter of: 47, 50–51, 60, 69
Hugh of Mâcon, Abbot: 123
Hugh of Molesme, Prior: 58
Hugh of St. Victor: 89
human being: 135
humanism, Benedictine: 116
humanities, education in: lxiv, 222
Humbeline: xl, 48, 119
Humber River: 106
Humbert of Igny, Bl.: 78, 81
humility: xxxix, xliv, 78, 130, 218; Cistercian: 115; of Christ: 118, 130
Hümpfner, Tiburtius: 53
Hundred Years War: lxviii, 161, 250
Hungarians: xxii
Hungary: 237; Cistercian monasteries of: 148, 166; king of: 100
hunger, for land: lviii, 175, 202; for righteousness: 132
Huntingdonshire: 6
husbandry: 106; Cistercian: 106; English: 106, 156
Hussites: 252
hymnal, Cistercian: 64–65
hymns, Ambrosian: 116

Ida of Leeuwen, Bl.: 120
Ida of Louvain, Bl.: 120
Ida of Nivelles, Bl.: 120
ideal, Benedictine: xxxvi; Cistercian: 192
idols: 134
Idung of Prüfening: 114
ignorance, of law: 216; of sacred writings: 224

Igny, Abbey of: 160
Ilbodus of Cîteaux: 51, 59
illness, mental: 150
Imitation of Christ: 151, 245
Immaculate Conception, doctrine of: 235, 239; Feast of: xv
immortality: xlii, 133, 137
immunities, from suspension: xx, 11; treatises on: 240;
implements: 106
implications, inner: 231; spiritual: 231
income, outside: 84; sources of: lvi, 84, 152, 154–55, 158, 168, 192, 198
incontinence: 174
India: xliv
individuals, good: 245
indolence: 103
indulgences: 218
indult: 251
industry: 156, 181; cloth: 197; fishing: 161; Flemish: 197
inefficiency: 175, 180
inertia: 213
infantia: 93
influence, Cluniac: 4
iniquity: 133, 136, 214
innocence: 78
Innocent II, Pope: 110, 162
Innocent III, Pope: lix, 100–101, 109, 112, 147, 151, 166, 187, 212
Innocent IV, Pope: 112, 166, 208
Innocent VIII, Pope: 113
Innocent IX, Pope: 241
Inquisition: 230
insight: 231; religious: lxvii, 244
inspiration: 142
instability: 26
Instituta Generalis Capituli: xvii–xviii, xxxii–xxxiv, 73, 82–86, 109, 190, 194
Instituta of St. Alberic: xxix, lvi–lvii, 45, 62, 84, 114, 148, 152, 154, 157–58, 170
instruments, musical: 243
intention, pure: xxxix, 117

interdict, general: 111; immunity against: 111–12; local: 111
interest, lack of: 103
intervention, episcopal: 73
intolerance: 179
invasions, Danish: 2
investigation, rational: 213
investiture, of benefices: 59
Iona, Abbey of: xxii, 1
Ireland: 63, 121, 221–22; Cistercians in: lxiv, 148, 221–22; vicar general of: 241
Irish: 3
irregularities, monastic: lvii, 157–62, 221
Isaac of Stella, Abbot: xlii–xliii, 134–38, 147, 215
Isaias (Isaiah): 129
Islam: 209
isolation: lxiv
Israel: 93
issues, institutional: lxvii; structural: lxvii
Italy: xxii, 33, 99, 124–25, 197, 210, 212, 241; Cistercian monasteries of: 148
Ivan III, Grand Duke: 96
Ivanhoe: xlvi

jails, monastic: xlviii; students in: 242
James, Bruno Scott: 39, 55, 115, 124, 160
James, M. R.: 176
James of Eltvill: 239
James II of Cîteaux, Abbot: 109, 188
Jamroziak, Emilia: lxxiv
Janauschek, Leopold: 125
Jarrow, Abbey of: 2
jealousy: 22, 118; local: 115
Jean de Cirey, Abbot: 61, 252
Jean de Mirecourt: 239
Jean of Cercamp: 239
Jerome, St.: 35, 99
Jerusalem, New: 24; outposts of: 105, 152

Jervaulx, Abbey of: 195, 200, 247
Jew(s): xxxvi, xlii, 35, 93, 129–30, 133, 171, 176; as chattels of king: 171; dialogue with: 25
Joachim of Flora: xxxv, 95, 98, 235
John, Card.: 51, 60
John de Nova Villa: 239
John, Eric: 21
John Gualbert, St.: 33–34
John, King: 108, 159, 197, 202–203
John of Cîteaux: 50–51, 59
John of Fécamp, Abbot: xvii, xxvi, 29–30, 33
John of Salisbury: xxxv, 98–99, 214
John of Toledo, Card.: 113
John of Weerde: 224
John the Archcantor: 2
John the Baptist, St.: xviii
John I of Trier, Bp.: 196
John XXII, Pope: 230
John XXIII, Pope: lxxii
Jordan of Mont-Saint-Michel, Abbot: 28
Joseph of Arimathaea, St.: xlv
Joseph of Volokolamsk, St.: 178–79
journeys: 233–34; business: 155; sea: 233
joy(s): 61; heavenly: 229
Judas: 129
judges, order of: 97
judgment(s): lxiii, 91–92, 159, 211–12; divine: 56; human: 55; just: 82; last: 230; wiser: 73
Julian of Norwich: xviii
Jully, convent of: xl, 48, 118–19
Jumièges, Abbey of: xxii, 27, 29
jurisdiction, episcopal: 59, 112
justification: 135
Justinian, Code of: 232
juventus: 93

Kaul, B.: 64
Kelty, Matthew, OCSO: xii
Kentucky, governor of: xlv
Kerr, Julie: lxxiv
keys: 235; to arsenals: lxxiii, 208
kindness: 127
King, Archdale: xli, 44–45, 61–62, 67, 76, 93, 95, 110–13, 119, 121–25, 160, 204–205, 207–209, 214–20, 224
king(s): lix, 18, 92, 171, 179, 182, 194, 199; households of: lxii; representatives of: 161
kingdom(s): 92; four: 92; heavenly: xxv, 24–25; of God: xxxvi, 93, 95; pagan: 93
Kirkstall, Abbey of: 158, 195
Kirkstead, Abbey of: 203
kitchen, duties of: 19; of Clairvaux: 123
knighthood, order of: 97
knowledge: 225; of truth: 214
Knowles, David: xxiii, xxvi, xxxvii, lv–lvii, 2–4, 27, 29–36, 102–103, 105–108, 118, 151–52, 154–59, 171, 173–77, 195–99, 202, 249–51
Kramer, Victor A.: xii–xiii, 95, 213
Kritzeck, James: 116

labor(s): 81, 133, 155, 162, 199, 228, 233; Cistercian: 110; decline of: 180; dignity of: lvii; dues: 197; economized: 106; forces of: 156; hard: 61, 78; hired: 249; lowly: 78; manual: xxi, xxxii, lvi, lxv, 8, 47, 60, 78, 81, 83, 90, 117, 227; of nuns: 118; penitential: 61; psalmody at: 9
laborers, hired: lvi, 158
Lackner, Bede K.: 36, 42, 47
Laetare Sunday: 93
La Ferté, Abbey of: lix, 71, 122–23, 182, 186; abbot(s) of: 113, 144, 146, 184–85; filiations of: 113, 124, 148; location of: 124
Laibach (Ljubljana) codex: xxx, xlviii, 60, 63, 66–67, 70–74, 184
laity, vocation of: xxxvi

lamb(s): 166; immolation of: 133; paschal: 129–30, 133;
Lambert of Cîteaux, Bl.: 76
lanarius: 199
land(s), abbey: 200; acquisition of: liv, 149, 158, 164–66, 169, 171–72; agricultural: 156; alienated: 169; convenient: 165; cultivated: 164, 166; cultivation of: lvi, 163–64; donations of: 111, 148, 154, 193–94; exemptions on: lvii; farm: 106; gifts of: 106, 156, 171, 194; good: 165; greed for: lvi; hunger for: lviii, 175, 202; lease of: 107; monastic: 228; mortgaged: 108, 201; new: lvi, 111, 163, 165, 172, 192; of living: 82; ownership of: 83; pasture: 165, 199; private: 195; purchases of: 106, 111, 148, 193–94; rental of: 108, 154, 166, 169, 199, 247, 249; revenues from: 108; tithes on: 111, 154, 163; waste: 199
landholdings: 178
landowners: 197; ecclesiastical: 198; lay: 198
land-owning, monastic: 179
Lanfranc: xxvi, 30, 32
Langres: 189; bishop(s) of: 52, 54–55, 58, 93, 115, 160, 218; Diocese of: 37, 58
language(s), Greek: xxxvi, 93; Hebrew: xxxvi, 93; Latin: xxxvi, 6, 93, 222
Las Navas, Battle of: 212
Lateran Council, Third: 164, 216
Lateran Council, Fourth: lix, 46, 103, 111, 166, 187, 191, 216
latifundia: lvii, 156
Latin: xxvi, 6, 93; understanding of: 222
La Trappe, Abbey of: lxxi, lxxiv, 143, 251
lauds: 7, 12, 87; of all saints: 12; of dead: 12
Laughlin, James: ix

Laurent, Jacques: 54
Lavaur: lxxii, 210
law(s), canon: 208, 214–16, 236; Church: xxviii; Cistercian: 187, 190, 222; code of canon: 113; common: 191; ignorance of: 216; letter of: 216; natural: 242; nature of: 216; of Christ: 227; old: 129; Roman: 214–15; spirit of: 216; spiritual understanding of: 129; time before: 94; time under: 94; violations of: 158
Lawrence of Clairvaux, Br.: 79
Lawrence, St.: 124
lawsuits: 194
lawyers, order of: 97
laxists, prince of: 241
laxity: 174, 231–32; in doctrine: lxvi; in morals: lxvi, 231; in observance: lxvi, 231–32
laybrother(s): lxii, lxxiii, 45, 79, 84–85, 87–88, 139, 100, 208, 215, 217; as almoners: 208; as builders: 208; as *bullatores*: 207; as gardeners: 207; as grooms: 207; as keepers of documents: 207; as keepers of seals: 207; as liability: lxviii; as officials: lxii; as workers: lxii; chapter of: 88; clothing of: xxxiv, 88; crisis of: lxvii, 100, 246–49; customs of: 87–88; daily schedule of: xxxiv, 87–88; decline of: xxxvii, 108, 247–49; discontent of: 249; disobedience of: 247; dissension among: xxxvii; economic benefits of: lxvii; employment of: 155; exploitation of: lxviii; food of: xxxiv; forbidden to learn to read: lxxi, 88; formation of: lxviii, 247, 249; in armies: 206, 210; in courts of nobles: 205–206; in royal households: 206; institution of: xxix, xlviii, lvi, 62; isolation of: 249; leading role of: lvi; legislation on: 190, 247; novices: xiv, 88, 248; numbers of: lxviii, 153–54,

Index

249; office of: 87; participation in chapter of: xxxiv, 88; problem of: 87, 154, 247; profession of: 88; protection for: 247; rebellion of: 247–48; relaxed discipline for: lxviii, 247, 249; rite of profession of: xxxiv, 88; separation of: 249; spiritual life of: 247; treatment of: xxxiv, 87; usages of: xviii, xxxiv, 87–88; violence of: 247–48; vocations of: xlviii, 108, 154–55, 246–47, 249; with bishops: 205–206; work of: xxxiv, lxviii, 87–88, 154–55, 208, 247, 249
laymen: 21, 99, 145
laypeople: 179, 209; order of: 97
Lazarus: 130, 226
learning, love for: 32
Leclercq, Jean, osb: xxiv–xxv, xlvi, lv, 24–26, 30, 33, 99, 115, 168–70, 184
lectio divina: xxxii, lxv, 7–8, 60, 82, 227
lees: 130
Lefèvre, J.-A.: xxx–xxxi, liii, 65–69, 122, 140, 144, 146, 184
legacy, spiritual: 33
legate(s), papal: xxviii, lxiii, 47, 50, 52, 59, 112, 187–88, 207, 210
legend, satirical: 173
legislation, Cistercian: lv, 140, 149, 190, 201–202, 225–28; liturgical: 190; on nuns: 190; on punishments: 190; on studies: 190, 216
Lekai, Louis: xxxvii, lxix, 41–42, 46, 50–51, 59, 104, 108–109, 118, 123, 148, 150, 166, 187, 189–90, 207, 211, 217, 219, 225, 251–52
Le Miroir, Abbey of: 115, 164
Lennsen, Séraphin: xxvii, 41, 45, 48, 54, 58
Lent: 8, 14
Leo IX, Pope: 35
leopard: 91
leprosarium: 209
leprosy: 120

Lérins, Abbey of: 2
lessons: 17
letters: 86, 216; ignorance of: 32; sacred: 82
lettuce: 130, 133
Leubus, Abbey of: 152
levity, vice of: 83
liars, monastic: 179
Libellus Antiquarum Definitionum: 109, 190
Libellus Novellarum Definitionum: 190
liberties: 236; Cistercian: 203; defense of: 223; temporal: 223
library, ecclesiastical: 215; of Clairvaux: 214–15
lie, shameless: 55
life: 28; active: 226–27; agrarian: 106; apostolic: xxxvi, 90, 97, 99; ascetic: 26; auspicious: 229; austere: 60, 151; Benedictine: viii, xxi, xxiv, lxv, lxxv, 7, 21; bitterness of: 130; business: liv; canonical: 93, 99; carnal: xliii, 138; cenobitic: xx; Christian: ix, 176; Cistercian: xxix, xlix, li, lv, lix, 45, 209, 228; claustral: 22; common: 35, 78, 81, 90, 99, 233; contemplative: lx, 192; deprivation of: 138; ecclesiastical: lxi, 193; economic: lxi, 196; evil: 150; fraternal: 90; hermit: xx; holier: 60; in monastery: 147; isolated: 228; itinerant: 99; laxer: 56; liturgical: 4; mendicant: 93; military: 209; mode of: 90; monastic: vii–ix, xx–xxi, xxiii–xxiv, xxvii, xlix, lxix, 7, 22, 34–35, 47, 90, 150–51, 155, 178, 212, 228; mystical: lv, 151; nearness to: 135; new: 137; newness of: 137; of poverty: xxix; of righteousness: 136; of simplicity: xxix; of world: lvi–lvii, 156; penitential: 73; political: 196; preaching: 99; priestly: 90; public: 150, 191; pure: 226; regular: lv, 7–8, 150, 251;

religious: lxi, lxvi, lxxiv, 44, 60, 70, 181–82, 220; restoration to: 135; risen: 136, 138; sanctity of: 30; scandalous: 150; secular: lxi, 228; simple: 155, 228; solitary: 33; spiritual: ix, xliii, xlv, 43, 138, 216, 246–47; state(s) of: 90, 93, 97; strict: 150, 245; university: 182; with Christ: 138; word of: 136
light, eternal: 12; in darkness: 228; ray of: 28
Liguori, St. Alphonsus: 241
Lincoln: 195, 200
Lincolnshire: 197
Lindisfarne, Abbey of: xxii, 1–2
linens: 40
lioness: 91
lips: xxxvi, 93
Litald of Cîteaux: 50
litanies: 7, 13, 17
literalism: 130
literature, hagiographical: xxv; satirical: 173–77, 179–81
litigants: 244
litigation(s): lxi, 168, 193–94; atmosphere of: 159; of world: lx, 192
Little, Lester K.: xxxv, 89–91, 93–94, 96–99
liturgy: xxi, xxiv–xxv, lxv, 45, 178, 252; Holy Week: xlvi; legislation on: 190; long: 23; monastic: 3–4, 82; reform of: 45; Roman: 2; simplicity of: xxxiii, 86, 169
living, land of: 82; luxurious: 173
Livonia: 147
loan(s): 107, 200–201, 234
loaves, five: 130
Locedio, abbot of: 212
Locus Sancti Bernardi, abbot of: 153
Lombardy: xxii, 30, 34, 197
London: 199
Longpont, Abbey of: 148; abbot of: 172
lords, secular: 162, 168; temporal: 23

Lorraine: 9, 29, 33, 124
Louis of Bavaria, Emperor: 244
Louis the Pious, King: xxi
Louis IX, St.: lx, 100, 109, 148, 189
Louis XI, King: 27
Louth Park, Abbey of: 154, 200
Louvain: 209, 241
love: 74, 94, 180; bond of: 135; for Cistercians: 171; for God: 61, 78, 227–28; fraternal: 190; of poor: xxxii, 81; wandering: 136
Low Countries: 140, 151, 246
Lucius III, Pope: liii, 111, 147, 205
lust: 214
Lutgarde of Aywières, St.: 120
Luxeuil, Abbey of: xx, xxii
Lyons: 50; archbishop of: 216; First Council of: 112; Poor Men of: 99

Macarius, St.: 40
machinery, steam-driven: 155
Madrid: 241
Mafalda, St.: 121
magic: 237
magnificence: 25
Mahn, Jean-Berthold: lv, lxv, 54, 59, 104–105, 110–13, 147, 158, 162–64, 166–67, 205, 212–13, 218, 229–30, 234–39, 242, 244
Maine: xxvi, 36
malice: 134
Malines: 153
Malquet, convent of: 120
maltreatment: 237
Mammon: 38
man, ages of: 93; as a unity: 89; city of: xxxv, 95–97; destiny of: 97; eyes of: 91; feet of: 91; heart of: 91; motives of: 89; son of: 92
management, bad: 202; slipshod: lxii
mandatum (maundy), daily: 7, 17–18; of brethren: 18; of monks: 7; of poor: 7; of Holy Thursday: 15; Saturday: 7

manna: 133
manor(s): 106–107, 157; normal: 106
Manrique, Angel: 44–46, 59, 62, 64, 119, 241
manse, abbatial: 232
manuscript(s): 53, 86, 214–15; copying of: 8, 23; Laibach: xxx, xlviii, 60, 63, 66–67, 70–74, 184; Trent: 183–84; Vauclair: 168–69
Maoris: lxxii
Map, Walter: lviii, 176–77
Marcilly, Abbey of: 237
Margam, Abbey of: 248; abbot of: 248
Marienstatt, Abbey of: 153
market(s): lxi, 194–95, 200; export: 198; secular: 180; weekly: 195; wool: 197
marriage, cases of: 194
marsh(es): 107, 154, 157, 197–98
Martène, Edmond: 113
Martha, St.: 226
martyrdom: 26, 211
Mary, Blessed Virgin: 12, 25, 27, 38, 62, 123, 137; apparition(s) of: xxix, 46–47, 61; as model of monasticism: 25; as protectress of monasticism: 25; commemoration of: 86–87; dedication of monasteries to: 85; devotion to: xxxii, 35; vision of: 80–81; votive Mass of: 13; words of: 240
Mary Magdalene, St.: 81
Mary of Bethany, St.: 226
masks: 243
Mass(es) : 3–4, 7, 9, 12, 14, 17, 80, 87, 204; conventual: 7, 23, 87; daily: 116; major: 7, 13; matutinal: 7, 88; minor: 14; morrow: 7, 14; of Holy Cross: 13; of Blessed Virgin Mary: 13; private: 7; stipends: lvi–lvii, 154
masturbation: 241
material, raw: 156
Matilda, Duchess: 204

matins: 7
matters, divine: 83, 215; earthly: 68; human: 83, 215; liturgical: 228; spiritual: 119, 223
maturity, political: 98
Mayeul, St.: 23
McCann, Justin, OSB: 14, 17–19, 117–18, 192, 234, 236
McCormick, Anne: lxxviii
McGinn, Bernard: 146
Meade, Mark C.: lxxviii
meal(s): 8, 233; absence from: 242; Passover: xlii
means, political: 223; temporal: 223
meat: 8, 61, 233–34, 243
Meaux, Abbey of: 108, 158, 160, 162, 194–95, 202–203, 249–50
Mechtilde of Hackborn, St.: 120
Mechtilde of Magdeburg, St.: 120
mediocrity, ethos of: lxxv
Meissen, convent of: 120
Mellifont, Abbey of: 222
Melrose, Abbey of: 102; abbot of: 241
memories, of resurrection: 132; strong: 32
men, lack of: 220; learned: 224; monasteries of: 144; saintly: 245; uneducated: 248
mendicant(s): lxvii, 113, 161, 178–79, 182, 190, 217, 231, 244; novitiates of: 232; opponent of: 240; rise of: xii, xxxvi; *studia* of: 218
Mendoza, Luis de: 240
mentality, new: 182; scholastic: 182
mention, nominal: 112
merchant(s): 79, 97, 170, 194, 197, 200–201; exporting: 157; foreign: 107; Italian: 108, 199; of Cahors: 201; shops of: 221; wool: 107, 157
mercy: 127; divine: 135; of Christ: x, 130; of God: 80, 127, 169
Merioneth: 106
merit: 134

Merton, Thomas, and peacemakers retreat: 33–34; anecdotes of: xlv, xlviii, lxxii–lxxiii; as community member: xii; as contemplative: xliv; as friend: viii; as guide: lxxv; as instructor: lxxv; as intellect: vii; as leader: viii; as master of novices: vii, xi, xix, li, lxxi–lxxii; as master of students: xvi; as mentor: viii; as monk: xliv; as mystic: vii; as poet: vii; as spiritual director: vii; as spiritual guide: viii, lxxviii; as teacher: vii, xii, lxxviii; as writer: vii, xii; hermitage of: lxxvi; humor of: viii–ix, xxxvi, xlvi–xlix, lxxii–lxxiv; identified as Jesuit: lxxiii; pedagogy of: xxii; reminiscences of: xlv, lxxii–lxxiii; WORKS: *Asian Journal*: ix; *Entering the Silence*: 101; *Cassian and the Fathers*: 11; *Charter, Customs, Constitutions of the Cistercians*: xviii, 66, 74, 82, 120; *Cistercian Fathers and Forefathers*: 33–34, 93, 125–26, 140, 147; *Cistercian Fathers and Their Monastic Theology*: viii–ix, xii, xv, xviii, xl, 115–17, 123, 128, 140, 147, 174; *Conjectures of a Guilty Bystander*: 98; *Disputed Questions*: 233; "History of the Cistercian Order": xvi; "Honorable Reader": 226; *In the Valley of Wormwood*: lxxiii, 39, 46–48, 58, 61–63, 81, 119–21, 143, 145, 205, 211, 215, 246; *Introduction to Christian Mysticism*: 98; *Life of the Vows*: 233; *Marthe, Marie et Lazare*: 226; *Monastic Observances*: 7, 161; *Mystics and Zen Masters*: xxv, 178; *Other Side of the Mountain*: lxxii; *Pre-Benedictine Monasticism*: vii, xiv–xv, xxv; *Rule of Saint Benedict*: xxi, 47; *Sign of Jonas*: 101; *Thomas Merton on St. Bernard*: 226; *Turning Toward the World*: xiii–xvi, xxv, xxxiv, xlvi–xlvii, lxxii–lxxiii, 95–96, 98, 213; *Waters of Siloe*: lxxvi, 101; *What Are These Wounds?*: 120; *Zen and the Birds of Appetite*: xxv

Merveille: 28
Metz: 29, 235
Meursault: 52
Michael the Archangel, St.: 27–28; as conqueror of Satan: 27; Order of: 27
Middle Ages, late: 141
Migne, J.-P.: 11, 162
Milan: 206
Miles of Bar: 118
milk: 14, 106, 131–32, 157, 166; rational: xlii, 129
mill(s): lvi–lvii, 154–55, 161–62, 166, 169–70, 202
Milton Abbas, Abbey of: 6
mind(s), foolishness of: 225; health of: 12; keen: 32; virtues of: 227
mines: lxi, 105; iron: 195
ministration, pious: 226
miracles: 40, 56, 76
misery: 133
missals, printing of: 252
missile crisis, Cuban: xliv
mission(s), active: 208, 212; apostolic: 212; Cistercian: xxxvii, liii, lxvii, 100, 147, 152, 192, 212, 226, 244, 246; diplomatic: lxii, lxvii, 208; for Church: 208; monastic: 246; of reform: lxvii
missionaries: xxxv, 4; monks as: xxi–xxii, 26
mistake, theological: 230
miter: 252
mixt: 88
Mobray, Roger de: 158
moderation: 172
Mohammedanism: 152
Mohammedans, dialogue with: 25
Molesme, Abbey of: viii, xxvi–xxviii, xxx–xxxi, xl, xlviii, 30, 36–39, 48–53,

56–58, 63, 114, 118, 121, 228; abbot of: 48, 118; as conventional: 39; comforts of: 58; decadence of: 48; departure from: xxviii, 44, 68–69, 159; development of: 47; dissatisfaction at: 47; divisions at: 47; foundation of: xxvii, 37, 47; monks of: 55; relations with Cîteaux of: 70

monarchs: 27

monasteries: 90, 155; Anglo-Saxon: 2; as anticipation of kingdom of heaven: xxv; as city of God: 96; as true Church: xxv, 25, 96; attack on: 237; attitudes toward: lviii; average: 151; bankrupt: 203; Basilian: 34; Benedictine: 30, 43, 155; building of: lx, 196; children in: 4, 7, 12, 14–15, 17, 47; Cistercian: lv, 100, 108, 141, 151, 198, 237; critics of: lviii; double: 118, 144; English: 4, 151, 159, 161, 247; founders of: 161; founding of: lx; functioning of: lx; German: 19; growth of: lx; home: 242; in Greece: lxiii; influence of: lviii; Irish: lxiv, 220–22; lax: 227; location of: 83; lay founders of: xxi; missionary: 226; mortgaging: 199; of men: 144; of women: 144; poor: 170; power of: lviii; prosperous: 151; quiet: 151; reform of: 244; regular: 218, 245; relations between: 84; sale of: 234–35; size of: 153–54; small: 170; typical: lv; well-ordered: 151

monasticism: viii; ancient: 228; as nursery of bishops: 178; austere: 35; Benedictine: xxii, 2, 35; Celtic: 2; cenobitic: 233; charismatic: 178–79; Cistercian: viii; clerical: xxxvi; Cluniac: xxiv–xxv, 30; continental: 20; critics of: lvii–lviii; decline of: lii; early: viii; eastern Christian: xv; English: xxii–xxiv, 1–21; eremitical: xxvi, 35; European: xi; idiorrhythmic: 233; institutional: 178–79; Irish: xxii; missionary dimension of: xxi–xxii, 26, 246; Norman: xxii, xxvi, xlvii, 27–33; Oriental: 233; patrons of: xxi; power of: 150; pre-Benedictine: xv; primitive: 232; Russian: 178–79; social: 30; solitary: 30; tenth-century: 7; troubled: lxvi; wealth of: 150; Western: 233

money: 80, 233–34; borrowing: 170–71; misuse of: 231

monk(s): xxxviii, 12, 18, 90, 97, 145, 151, 178, 208; actions of: 192; apostate: 231; apparition of: 122; as angelic men: 126; as architects: 196; as builders: 8, 196; as capitalists: lvi, 156; as genuine Christian: 96; as missionaries: 26; as models: 245; as poor managers: 201; as preachers: 182; as robbers: 237; as soldiers: 209–10; attack on: 179; Benedictine (black): viii, xxxii, xxxix, 46, 51, 55, 61, 105–107, 117, 151–52, 155, 157, 162, 164, 173–77, 182, 197–98, 202; Celtic: 1; choir: xiv, lxviii, 205, 249; Cistercian (white): viii–ix, xxxix, 74, 85, 98, 100, 107, 117, 125, 155–57, 159, 164, 168–69, 172–75, 177, 180, 182, 197, 202–203, 245; clerical: 23–24; Cluniac: 23, 174; educated: 216; English: 32, 105, 159, 168, 172, 180, 175; fervor of: 154; French: 175; fugitive: 237; German: xxxii, 55; hearts of: 192; idiorrhythmic: 233; ignorant: 224; intervention of: 210; Irish: xx; irregular: 231; Norman: 32; ordination of: 112; prisoner: 237; professed: 86; prophetic mission of: 98; regular: 222; Roman: 1; Scottish: 202; service of: 194; student: 218, 242; typical: lv; with bishops: 205–206; work of: 106, 154; visits of: 235; vocation of: 193; voices of: 4

monster: 117
Mont-Saint-Michel, Abbey of: xxvi, xlvii, 27–29; architect of: 28; church of: 28; cloisters of: 28; refectory of: 28
Montclos, Jean de: 32
Monte Cassino, Abbey of: xxi, 2, 47
Montfort, Simon de: 100
Montpellier: 218, 235
moor(s): 107, 157, 197–99
Moors: lxii, 145, 209, 212
morals, laxity in: lxvi, 231
Morey, Lawrence, ocso: lxxviii
Morimond, Abbey of: lix, 55, 71, 95, 124, 182, 186, 235; abbot(s) of: 55, 113, 146, 185, 188; filiations of: 113, 119, 125, 148; location of: 124; refectory of: 124
mortality: xlii, 133
mortgage(s): 107–108, 200–201
Moscow: 95
Moses: 94
mother, bond with child of: xliii, 134; perfect: 229
motives, human: 89
Mount Athos: 178
mountain(s): 94, 107, 157; of God: 226
mouth: 91–92
Moutier la Celle, Abbey of: 44, 46
movement(s), mendicant: 99; new: 99
Müller, Gregor: xxvii, lxix, 41–43, 143
munditiae: 18
Murdac, Abp. Henry: 158
murder: 243
murmuring: 117
murrain: 199, 201
music, organ: 4
Mynors, R. A. B.: 176
mystery, of charity: xxv, 25; of Church: xxv, 24–25
mysticism: 209; Cistercian: 140, 246; medieval: 98, 120
mystics, Cistercian: xl, 246; Rhenish: 98, 151; Russian: 178; women: xl, 120

Naboth: 174
Namur: 29
Narbonne, archbishop of: 145, 211–12
nationalism: lix
nations, rise of: 181
nature, attitude toward: 213
Near East: 249
needs, domestic:198; institutional: 178; new: 97; religious: 150
negligence(s): 13, 76; in administration: 231
neighbors, burden to: 181; enmity of: lvi–lvii, 156; penance to: 181
Netherlands: 197, 246
Netley, Abbey of: 195
New Zealand: lxxii
Newenham, Abbey of: 250
newness, of life: 137
Nilus of Rossano, St.: 33–34
Nilus of Sora, St.: 178–79
Nivard, brother of St. Bernard: 123
Nivelles: 153, 209
nobles: 27, 250; courts of: 47, 205–206; households of: lxii
nobility, courts of: 208; distrustful: 211; secular: 206
nocturns: 9, 12, 17, 87
Noirlac, Abbey of: 164; abbot of: 100
nominalism: 239
none: 7–9, 14, 17
Normandy: xxvi, 27–28, 31, 33; duke of: 30
Normans: 21, 27, 35; as builders: 27; as organizers: 27; as pagans: 27
North Africa: 100
Northumbria: xxii, 1
Norway, Cistercian monasteries of: 148
Norwich: 250
Noschitzka, Canisius: 60, 63, 70–74, 184, 205
Nostel: 125
nourishment, carnal: xliii, 138; in resurrection: xliii, 138; spiritual: xliii, 138

novice(s): 86, 217; clothing of: 184; Gethsemani: vii, xi, xiii, xix–xx, xxix, xliii–xliv, xlvii, lxxi–lxxii; master of: xlvii
novitiate(s): 140, 230; length of: 117; merger of: xiv, xliii; of mendicants: 232
nun(s): xlvi, 47, 151, 153, 240; care for: 209; Cistercian: xl–xli, lv, lxvii, lxxii, 63, 118–21, 145, 151, 153, 209, 220, 246; contemplative: 118; foundations of: 119–20; general chapters of: xl, 119–20; legislation on: 190
nunneries: 47

oath: 236
Obazine, Order of: liii, 143
obedience: xlix, 19, 79, 86, 135; heroic: 54; to God: 135; to pope: lxi, 46, 192; to superiors: 215
obedientiaries: 107, 157
oblates: 12
Oblet, V.: 241
obligation, feudal: 52
oblivion, curse of: 82
observance(s), accidentals of: xxxix, 116; changes in: 75; Cistercian: xl, 116, 119, 159; Cluniac: 47, 116; disagreement over: xxxix, 114–18; divergence of: 114–18; diversities of: 116; essentials of: xxxix, 116; laxity in: lxvi, 231–32; legislation on: 190; monastic: xxxix, 6, 8, 20, 43; problems of: 232–34; regular: 190; religious: 41, 68; ritual: 179
Ocampo, Victoria: lxxiii
O'Connell, Patrick F.: vii–viii, xii, xiv, xviii, xxi, xxv, 7, 11, 33, 47, 66, 98, 115, 140, 161, 233
Oda, Bishop: 19
Odilo, St.: 23
Odo (Eudes), Duke of Burgundy: 40, 44–45, 52, 69

Odo of Cîteaux: 50
Odo of Cluny, St.: 9, 19, 21, 23–24
offense, egregious: 112
offerings: 40
office: 233; canonical: 7; celebration of: 111; Cistercian: 64; divine: xxiv, xlvii, 4, 51, 79, 190, 227; legislation on: 190; little: 7, 251–52; long: 23; night: 14; of all saints: 7, 9; of the dead: 7, 9, 19; shortening of: 47; simplification of: 45
office(s), civil: lxii, 208; financial: lxii; irremovability in: 251; military: lxii; succession of: 230
officials, laybrothers as: lxii; local: xxxviii
offspring, perfect: 229
Ogier of Locedio, Abbot: 212
ointments, of devotion: 131
Oliva, Abbey of: 147
olive: 156
openness: 79
opinions, lax: 241
opposition, violent: 222
opus Dei: 227
opus manuum: 227
orations: 12
Orbestier, Abbey of: 105
orchards: 166
ordeal, trial by: 97
order(s), active: lxv; Benedictine: 34; eremitical: 142; mendicant: 181, 217; military: 209, 211; monastic: 34, 93, 103, 141, 177, 179, 246; new: xxvi, 33–34, 182, 198; of farmers: 97; of judges: 97; of knighthood: 97; of lawyers: 97; of laypeople: 97; religious: lxvi, 177, 179, 198–99, 230–31; town: 181
orders, sacred: 79, 155; major: 113; minor: 113
Ordericus Vitalis: xxvii, xxxv, 39–41, 49, 98

ordinaries, local: 112
ordination, of monks: 112; priestly: xiv, 112; simoniacal: 34
ordo, monastic: 76
Ordo Qualiter: 8
Ordo Romanus: 8
organ: 4
organization, mercantile: 197; of studies: 245
orientation, active: liv
ornaments, ceremonial: 252
Orthodox: 179
orthodoxy: 210
Orwell, George: lxxiv
Oswald, St.: xxiii, 5–7, 19–20; as abbot of Ramsey: 5; as archbishop of York: 5–6; as bishop of Worcester: 5–6, 20; *Life* of: 4, 8
Ottaviani, Card. Alfredo: xlvii
Otto of Freising, Bp.: xxxv–xxxvi, 89, 94–97
Ourscamp, Abbey of: 167, 212, 220
Oursel, Charles: 64
oversight, episcopal: lxii
ownership: 179; of animals: 83; of land: 83; of serfs: 158; valid: 179
oxen: 79
Oxford: 218, 222, 235; University: lxiv, 179, 217
Oyer, Gordon: 34

Pachomius, St.: xx, xxv, 40
Paderborn: 120
pagans: 152
palace, papal: 229
Palestine: 104, 193
Palm Sunday: 7
Pamiers, bishop of: 230
Pamplona: 218
papacy, Avignon: lxviii, 225, 229, 251; power of: 35
paradise: 24–26; return to: xxv; rivers of: 190

Paris: xxxvii, lxiii, lxvi, 98, 101, 176, 189, 217, 222, 224, 235–36, 238, 242; University of: lxiv, lxvi, lxxii, 216, 224
Paris, Julien: 45, 139, 240
Paris, Matthew: 198, 219
parties: 243
Parvus Fons: xxxvii, li, lix–lx, lxix–lxx, 109, 113, 139, 183, 186, 189–91
Paschal II, Pope: lxv, 50–51, 59, 192, 227
Passover, of perfected: 133; of saints: 133
past, worship of: 179
pastor, appointment of: 158
pasture: 105, 199
patience: 230
patrimony, of Christ: 181
patrons, burials of: lvii, 161–62
Paul, St.: 19, 25, 40, 137, 214
paupers: 173
Pax Romana: 95
payment: 108; of tithes: 162, 166–67
peace: 2, 28, 74–75, 94, 115, 180, 190; imposed: 97; mutual: 70, 74; vision of: 105, 152
Pearson, Paul M.: lxxviii
peasants: 107, 154
peculation: 196
peculium: 232–34
pedagogy, divine: 89; of states: 93
penance(s): 24, 61, 73, 75, 102–103, 120, 228; humble: 13; necessity of: 47; pious: 228; to neighbors: 181
Pennington, M. Basil, ocso: 65
Pentecost, Feast of: 80, 87–88, 121; octave of: 7
people(s): 92; common: 214
Percy, Lady: 160
perfect, church of: 24
Perfectae Caritatis: lxxv
perfected, Passover of: 133
perfection, apostolic: 90; science of: lxv, 226; standard of: 141
perjury: 114

person, in history: 89; just: 135
perspectives, pagan: 93
Peter Damian, St.: 34–36
Peter de Roya: 124
Peter Monoculus, St.: 75, 77–78, 81
Peter of Castelnau, Bl.: lxiii, 100, 211, 229
Peter of Celles: 132–33
Peter of Cîteaux: 50
Peter of Molesme: 47, 80
Peter of Tarantaise, St.: 146
Peter, St.: 25, 214
Peter the Venerable, Abbot: xxxix–xl, 23–25, 115–18; letter of: 116–18; personality of: 115
Peterborough, Abbey of: 4–5
Pharisee(s): 133–34
Philip of Clairvaux, Abbot: 109, 188
Philip I, King: 40
Philip II (Augustus), King: 28
Philip IV (the Fair), King: 182
Philistines: 134
philosophy: 224; Christian: 56; emphasis on: 213; interest in: 182
pictures: 86
Piedmont: 99
Pierce (Pron) of Molesme: 118
Pierre le Roy, Abbot: 29
piety, Eucharistic: 120; filial: 41
pig: xlvi
pilgrimage: 26–27, 63
pilgrims: 17–18
Pipewell, Abbey of: 160, 201
pittances: 85, 161
Pius XI, Pope: xvi
Pius XII, Pope: xvi
place(s), dishonorable: 242; in history: 89
plague(s): 214; bubonic: 249–50
Plato: 214
pleasure(s): 76, 134; worldly: 227
poet: 29, anonymous Cistercian: lviii, 179–81; vernacular: 1

Poitiers: 36
Poland: 124, 147, 152; Cistercian monasteries of: 148, 246
politician: 29
politics: 99
polyphony: 4
pontificalia: 252
Pontigny, Abbey of: liii, lix, 67, 71, 123, 146, 182, 186, 188; abbot(s) of: lxiv, 113, 144, 146, 184–85, 210, 222, 240, 243; destruction of: 250; filiations of: 113, 124, 148, 222; location of: 123–24
Pontius of Clairvaux, Abbot: 77
poor: 15, 17–18, 110, 132, 162, 164, 173–74, 181; care of: xxiv, 7; love of: xxxii, 81; *mandatum* of: 7; of Christ: 60
pope(s): lix, 38, 52, 101, 110, 112, 115, 147, 150, 164, 181–82, 187–89, 203–204, 211, 218, 224, 237; Avignon: lxiv, 225, 229, 251; Cistercian: lii–liii, lxii, lxiv, 205, 225; desires of: 218–19; obedience to: lxi, 46, 192
Port Anselle, Synod of: xxviii, 52
Portugal: 121, 152; Cistercian monasteries of: 148
positions, ecclesiastical: lxx; temporal: lxx
possession, demonic: xlvi
possessioners: 178–79
possessions: 178–79, 181; exemptions of: 170; expansion of: 169, 172; material: 68
postulant(s): xii, xvi, 149, 202, 216; stealing: 84
poverty: xxxii–xxxiii, xliii, xlix–l, lxvi, 24, 45, 53, 63, 68, 70, 80–81, 84, 90, 99, 121, 231; abandonment of: 177; commitment to: xxxvii; compromise of: 104; corruption of: 63; decline of: 104; holy: 40, 80; individual: 177; life of: xxix; necessity of: 47; of

soil: 105; religious: 178; solitary: 53, 57; true: 177; violations of: 232–33; voluntary: 38
power(s): 91–92, 180, 210; Cistercian: liv, lxii, 147, 212; episcopal: 205; established: 142; independent: 187; misuse of: 231; monarchic: 182; of abbots: 104, 187; of Church: 193; of papacy: 35; rivalry for: 109; secular: 35; socio-religious: 178; spiritual: 193; temporal: 193
Powicke, F. M.: xlii, 128
practice(s), Benedictine: xxvii; exterior: lxv; monastic: xxiii; penitential: 226; transformative: xliv
Prague: 241
praise: 25
prayer(s): lxxv, 11, 29, 31, 60, 86, 100, 155, 210, 247; extra: 8; for dead: 3; for king: 8, 11–12, 203; for royal house: 9, 11–12; graces of: 56; intercessory: xxi, 100; interior: liv; Jesus: 178; joyous: 229; life of: 151; long: 151; private: 14; promise of: 203; spirit of: 25; zeal for: 245
preachers, Cistercian: lxiii, 210; monks as: 182
preaching: 96, 147, 151, 182; apostolic: 15; itinerant: xxxvi
precedence: 75
prelates: lx, 192, 223; Cistercian: 209–10; courts of: 223
pre-scholastics: 213
prescriptions, minute: 231; severer: 238
prestige, of General Chapter: 109
price, high: 195; low: 195
pride: 63, 180, 205, 214
priest(s): 28, 38, 111; appointment of: 171; as chaplains: 118; multiplication of: 96; parish: 167
priesthood: 26
prime: 7, 9, 12–13
primitivism: 33

princes, courts of: 223, 228
principles, Cistercian: lx–lxi
prior(s): 7, 101, 191, 207–208, 212, 250; claustral: 118; election of: 252
prioress: 118
priories, dependent: 47
privileges: lxxiii–lxxiv, 166, 223, 234, 236, 238; *bullarium* of: 190; burial: 154; Cistercian: xxxviii, liii, 109–13, 166, 203, 212, 240, 251; legitimate: 167; monastic: 71, 86; of regulars: 240; of students: 242; papal: xxxviii, lx, 60, 74, 195; payment for: lxxiii, 195, 202–203; royal: lxxiii; treatises on: 240
Privilegium Romanum: xxix, lxv, 45, 50–51, 59–61, 110, 192, 227
problem(s), economic: xxxvii, lxvi, 231; internal: 231; of Cistercian Order: xii, 231–34; of regularity: lxvi, 231; of religious orders: 231; of observance: 232–34; of studies: lxvi, lxx, 212–20, 231; of tithes: 162–68; organizational: lxvi, 231, 240; practical: 240; religious: lxv, 230
Pro Civitate Christiana: 95
procession(s): 3; daily: 23; penitential: 100
proctor: 161
procurator, Cistercian: 173, 182, 207
produce: 106; tithes on: 154
producers, wool: lxi, 106
production, wool: 106, 198
profession, monastic: xxxix, 116; solemn: 114
professors: 245
program(s), building: 149, 192, 194; of studies: lxvii
progress, of studies: 225; spiritual: 137
progressivism, false: 98
property: 152, 180; acquisition of: liv, 111, 149, 154, 170; adjacent: lviii; Church: 179; confiscation of: 179;

disposition of: 231; inherited: 22; management of: 167; monastic: lvii, lxi, lxvi, 154, 221, 231–32, 250; moveable: 170; ownership of: 179; private: 233–34; purchase of: 232; rental of: lxviii; retention of: 233; sale of: 232; tithed: 162
proprietor, monastic: 22
proprietorship: 233; evil of: 79
prosperity: 23, 105; Cistercian: 140, 154; economic: lvi, 154; material: 140; present: lii, 141; spiritual: 140
protection, apostolic: 59; papal: 59; royal: 202
protector, cardinal: 182
Protestants: lxxii, 114, 252; controversy with: 241
protests: 193
proud: 78
Providence: 95; divine: 58; trust in: 80
Provins: 44
provisor: 218, 225
provost: 7
prudence: 117
Prussia: 147; East: 196
psalm(s): 7, 11–12, 86; extra: 13, 23; gradual: 7, 9, 12; penitential: 7, 16, 81
psalmody: 9
psalter: 31
psychotherapists: 241
publicans: 132
pueritia: 93
punishment(s): 84–85, 146; legislation on: 190
puppies: 133
purgation, spiritual: 13
purgatory: 99
purity: 78, 175; monastic: 43, 159

Quarr, Abbey of: 195, 217
quarrels: 22, 84
Quem Quaeritis trope: xlvi, 9–10, 17

questions, disputed: 117; legal: lxvi, 240; liturgical: 116
Quierry, capitulary of: 22
quiet: 14; monastic: 60, 192
Quincy, Abbey of: 104, 160

rabbits: 88
race, German: 96; human: 95
raids, Danish: 6; Viking: xxiii, 2, 6
Raine, James: 8
Rainer, companion of Peter of Castelnau: 211
Ramsey, Abbey of: 4–6; as center of reform: 6
Rancé, Abbot Armand de: lxx–lxxi, lxxiv, 251
ranches, Cistercian: 156, 197
Raoul of Clairvaux, Abbot: 216
Ravenna: 33
Raymond of Fitero, St.: 145, 209
Raymond V of Toulouse, Count: 210
Raynald de Bar, Abbot: 65–66, 72, 76, 81, 149, 183
Raynald of Clairvaux: 81
reading, Lenten: xvii; of Rule: 155; reflective: lxxv; spiritual: 82, 227
real estate: 165
realm, Carolingian: xxi
reason: 241; emphasis on: 213
rebelliousness: 231
recalcitrants: 230
receptivity: 86
recluses: 153, 209
recreation: 8
redemption: 134
Redon, Abbey of: 220
Redwoods, Monastery of: lxxii
refectory: 15, 85, 161; common: 234; monastic: 233; of Clairvaux: 123–24; of College of St. Bernard: 218
reform(s): 207; administrative: 237–38, 244; Benedictine: 19; Cluniac: xxiv, 9; decrees of: 207; efforts at: 251–52;

English: 19; Gregorian: 90; insufficiency of: 244; liturgical: 45; Lorraine: 9, 29; Lotharingian: 28–29; measures of: 221; monastic: xxiv, xxvi, 6; need for: 183; of Benedict of Aniane: 9; of Benedict XII: xi, xxxiv, lxv–lxvi, lxxi, 225–39, 244–46; of Church: 252; of Cistercian Order: xii, li, lxix, 64, 113, 139, 183, 222, 244–45, 251–52; of clergy: 35; of religious orders: 231; of studies: 238–41; organizational: lxxi; spiritual: 222–23; superficial: lxix; Trappist: lii, lxx, lxxvi, 140
Reformation, Protestant: lii, lviii, lxix, lxxvi, 99, 141, 161, 173, 240
reformers, Protestant: 179
refuge: 204
regalia, liturgical: lxix
regeneration: 137–38
Regularis Concordia: xvii, xxiii–xxiv, xliv–xlvi, 3, 5–20; sources of: 8–9
regularity, monastic: xxxvii, lxxiii, 76, 151, 174, 249, 251
regulation(s), monastic: xxiii, lxvi; of abstinence: 234
relaxation(s): 190, 234, 247, 249; questionable: lxviii
relevance, spiritual: xliv
relic: 151
religion: 29; interest in: 182; wars of: 29
religious, active: 227; privileges of: 234; regular: 113
reliquaries: 23
Remington, William: 239
Renaissance: 23
renewal: 141; of Church: lxix, 252; of Cistercian Order: xii, lxix, lxxiv, 252; of monastic life: viii–ix
rents: 152, 173, 198
renunciation: 84; of tithes: 162
reorganization, of religious orders: 231
repentance: xlvi
representatives, papal: 189
repression: 95
reprimands: 103
reputation: 70
research, nature of historical: xx
resentment: 176
resources, exploitation of: lvi, 156
responsibility: 78, 95; for nuns: 153; sacred: 97; sense of: 249
rest: 133; in heaven: 137
resurrection: 135, 137–38; first: 135; memory of: 132; nourishment in: xliii, 138; of body: 137; of Christ: xlii–xliii, 17, 130–34, 137; second: 135; sweetness of: 131
revelation, of children of God: xxv
revenue(s): 90, 158, 161, 173, 176, 180, 251; from land: 108; of church: 160–61, 167
reverence: 14
Revesby, Abbey of: 102
revival, Benedictine: 5; monastic: xxiii–xxiv, 2, 6
Revolution, French: 141
Rheims, archbishop of: 172; Council of: 214
Rhineland: 246
rich: 18
Rich, St. Edmund: xliv, 217
Richard of Canterbury, Abp.: 110–11, 164, 171
Richard of Fountains, Abbot: 159
Richard of Lincoln: 239
Richard I, Duke of Normandy: 27
Richard I, King: lvii–lviii, 104, 160–61, 167, 172; ransom of: 172, 199, 202
Richelieu, Card. Armand: 204
riches: 18
Rie River: 126
Rievaulx, Abbey of: xli–xlii, 102, 105, 108, 126–28, 152, 158–59, 171, 195, 203, 247; abbot of: 161; gatekeeper of: 127–28; guestmaster of: 127–28; prior of: 127–28; size of: 153

righteousness: 78; delight in: 136; hunger and thirst for: 132; life of: 136; way of: 82
rigidity: 142
ring, episcopal: 252
riot: 243
Ripon, Abbey of: 1
rite(s), Holy Week: 9; Roman: 9, 17
ritual, Cistercian: 16
ritualism, religious: xxi, 178–79
rivalry, for power: 109
robbers, monks as: 237
Robert of Arbrissel, Bl.: 118
Robert of Bruges, Bl.: 77
Robert of Châtillon: 115
Robert of Langres, Bp.: 52, 54–55, 58
Robert of Molesme, St.: xxvii–xxviii, xxxi, xlviii, 37–58, 62, 64, 76, 80, 118; as abbot of St. Michel de Tonnerre: 47; as first abbot of Cîteaux: 48–49; as founder of Cîteaux: 39–40, 58; as founder of Molesme: 38, 40, 47; character of: 48; controversy about: xxviii, 39–46, 53–54; *Life* of: 49, 58; instability of: 57; return to Molesme of: xxviii, 45, 52–54, 57–58, 69–70
Roche, Abbey of: 200, 247
Roger of Byland, Abbot: 159
roles, military: lxi
Rome: xxi, 1–2, 35, 38, 47, 51, 63, 79–80, 109, 112, 121, 188, 192, 196, 212, 223, 251; Cistercians in: 207; court of: 182; General Chapter in: 251; loyalty to: lxviii; Third: 96; vocation of: 95–96
Romuald, St.: 33–35
rooks: 108
Rossi, Giovanni: 95
Rouen, Abbey of: xxii
routine, liturgical: xxi, xxiv
Rudolph of Cîteaux: 210
Ruffini, Card. Ernesto: xlvii
Rufford, Abbey of: 102
rugby: lxxii

ruin, economic: 237
Rule of St. Benedict: viii, xxi, xxviii, lxii, 1–2, 14, 17–22, 35, 38, 40, 42–43, 50, 56, 60, 93, 114, 117, 186, 232, 241; adaptation of: 150; as directory: 2; as inspiration: 2; authority of: 17; commands of: 117; discipline of: 70; essentials of: 117; fidelity to: lvi, 47, 69; interpretation(s) of: 74, 83, 117; letter of: 192; lover of: 59, 80; observance of: 85, 185; purity of: 43, 56; reading of: 13, 155; simplicity of: 56; spirit of: 192; violation of: 47, 114; vision of: lvi; c. 3: 234; c. 4: 192; c. 35: 18–19; c. 41: 14, 117; c. 53: 17, 117; c. 55: 118; c. 64: 236
rule(s), apostolic: 90; Cistercian: 74, 109, 143, 153, 195, 200; common: 234; monastic: xxi, 90; rigid: lxviii
rulers, ambitions of: 182
Rupert of Deutz: xxxix, 90, 93, 96–98, 116
Russia, as Third Rome: 96; Holy: 96

Sacerdos, St. (Martin Mãnoz y Finajosa): 119
sacrament(s): xliii, 96, 138, 237
sacramentaries, Gelasian: 12; Gregorian: 12; Leofric: 12
sacrifice(s): 159, 227; spirit of: 25
sacristan: 7, 14
Sacrosancta: liii, 144, 146, 184, 205
sadness: 80
safety: 133
St. Aigulphus (Ayoul), Abbey of: 38, 44, 47
St. Albans, Abbey of: 250
St. Antonin: lxxii
St. Augustine, Abbey of: 6
St. Benignus (Benigne), Abbey of: 29, 33
St. Bernard, College of: xxxvii, lxiv, lxx, 101, 112, 142, 208, 217–18, 224–25, 230, 239–40, 242–46
St. Bertin, Abbey of: 19

St. Cyprian, Abbey of: 36
St. David, Diocese of: 174
St. Gall, Abbey of: xxii, 19
St. Germain, Boulevard: 218
St. Malo, Diocese of: 188
St. Mary's Abbey, York: 159
St. Michael, Feast of: 119
St. Michel de Tonnerre, Abbey of: 37–38, 44
St. Ouen, Abbey of: 28–29
St. Peter's Basilica: 2, 23, 25
St. Peter's, Ghent, Abbey of: 20
St. Wandrille, Abbey of: 27
saints: 23, 92, 230; Cistercian: xl, 246; cult of: 23; lives of: 25; of Helfta: 120, 246; Passover of: 133; Saxon: 125; women: xl, 120–21, 246
Salamanca: 235, 241
Salley, Abbey of: 160, 194–95
salt: 175
salt flats: 166
salt-pits: 105
salvation: xlii, 11, 15, 129, 132, 226; history of: xxxv, 24, 89; hope of: 229; of souls: 60, 72, 75, 117; seeds of: 229; sun of: 229; word of: 94
Sambucina, abbot of: 100
Samson: 134
Sancha, St.: 121
Sancho I, King: 121
sanctity: lxxv, 5, 30, 180
sane laborum: lvii, 162–63, 166
sane novalium: lvii, 163–64
Saracens: xx–xxii, 21
Satan: 27, 37, 134, 190
satire: lviii, 173–81
satirists: lxx; professional: 177
Saulieu: 122
Savage, Paul: 53
Savigny, Abbey of: xxvi, 143, 209; abbot of: 217, 220; filiations of: 220; Order of: liii, lvii, 30, 36, 143, 147, 157, 167–69

Saxony: 147
scab: 199
scale, economies of: lvi
scandal(s): 54, 165, 169, 237, 242
Scandinavia, missions to: 4
Scarborough, church of: lv, 104, 160–61, 167–68, 204
schism(s): 70; Cistercian: 189, 222; Cologne: 36; Great: lxviii, lxxiii, 251; Great Russian: 179; in Order of Calatrava: 209; monastic: 114; papal: liii, 147, 168
Schmitt, F. S.: 33
Schmitz, Philibert, OSB: 21–22
scholar: 224
scholasticism, decadence of: lxvi, 240; early: lxiv; forerunners of: 182
Schönau, Abbey of: 248; abbot of: 248
school(s): 99; cathedral: 245; of charity: viii, 25; of Chartres: 98, 213
Schroeder, H. J., OP: 103, 112, 166
science, of perfection: 226
Scotia: 63, 121
Scotland: 1, 63, 103, 121; Cistercian monasteries of: 148; king of: 125, 127
Scott, Sir Walter: xlvi
scriptoria: 86
scripture(s): 26, 178, 224; anagogical sense of: xliii; commentaries on: 240; historical sense of: 89; literal sense of: 131; spiritual meaning of: 131; spiritual sense(s) of: xlii–xliii, 89, 129; study of: 226; translation of: 45; tropological sense of: xlii–xliii; typological sense of: xlii
sculpture(s): 85; Romanesque: 23
sea: 91
seal, abbatial: 221
secession: 159
seculars: 199
security, on loans: 200–201
seeds, of salvation: 229

Séjalon, Hugo: 45, 139
self-justification: 141
seminarians, Episcopal, xliii
senectus: 93
Septuagesima: 93
sepulcher, holy: 24
sequence, narrative: 89
serf(s): lvi–lvii, lxx, 37, 51, 104, 154, 158; ownership of: 158; purchase of: 158
Serlo of Fountains: 159
Serlo of Savigny, Abbot: 143
sermons, collections of: 240
servants, female: 83; of students: 243
service, liturgical: 90; military: 30, 203; of God: 5, 23; of monks: 194
sext: 7
shadow: 28
shame: 11
Shannon, William H.: xxv
sharecroppers: 152, 154, 168
shaving: 17
sheep: 156–57, 172, 197–98, 202; pasturing of: 106, 156; wandering: 56
sheepskins: 88
sheep-walks: 107, 157
shelter: 3
shepherd: 78
Sherborne, Abbey of: 37, 63–64, 121
shipping: 195; overseas: 170
ships: lxi
shocks: 91
shrines: 151
Sichem, abbot of: 153
Sicily: 203; king of: 79
sick: 243; care of: xxiv, 7, 19
sight, to blind: 130
Siguenza: 119
silence: lxiv, 8, 17, 86, 88, 224; at work: 88; great: 8, 17; lack of: 221; on feast days: 9; regulations on: xxxiv, 88; strict: 17
Silesia: 121
silk: 84
silver: 84
simony: 35
simplicity: xli, xlv, lvi, 30, 33, 63, 74, 84, 224; life of: xxix; liturgical: xxxiii, 86, 169; in buildings: 169
sin(s): 24, 59, 135; confession of: xlvi, 241; death of: 136; death to: 137; God as cause of: 239; original: 134; species of: 241
singing: 15, 86
sinner(s): 29, 132
Sion (Sitten), Diocese of: 39
sisters, lay: 118–19
situation(s), economic: 169; exceptional: 234; peaceful: 151; regular: 151
slave: 135
society: 150; agrarian: 181; Christian: lii, 141; commercial: 181; European: 181; feudal: xxxv, lvii, 90, 97, 156, 181; lay: xxi; medieval: lxvii, 95, 245; religious: lxvii, 245; stable: 97; urban: 181
soldier(s): 27, 29, 145, 221; mercenary: 252; monks as: 209–10; of Christ: 69
solitude: xxv, lxiv, 1, 30, 33, 37, 41, 45, 57, 114, 224; in community: l; vast: 69
Somerset: 2, 197
Somerville, Mary: lxxviii
soul(s): 35, 80, 138, 186, 228; death of: 135; dialogue of: 240; good of: 74; salvation of: 60, 72, 75, 117; strength of: 228; uneasiness of: 90; virtues of: 227
Spain: xl, 125, 211, 241; Cistercian monasteries of: 148
Spaniard: 96
speculation, economic: 180; historical: 91; Patristic: 91
spheres, divine: 74; human: 74
spirit: 135; Christian: 95; Cistercian: lxiii, 74, 150, 193, 196, 207, 209, 211,

213, 236, 244; Cluniac: xvii, xxiv, 24–25; human: 74; monastic: 244, 251; of adoration: 25; of dissension: xxxvii, 104; of laws: 216; of prayer: 25; of sacrifice: 25; unity in: 74
spirituality, Cistercian: xv, xlix, 246; monastic: xiv, xvi, xxiv, xlix, 10–19; triumphalist: xxv
splendor, liturgical: xxv, 23; of worship: 25, 90; worldly: 228
spouse, mystical: 229
stability: 60, 213; monastic: 52, 74
stabilization: 228, 245
Standaert, Maur: xxx, 63
standard, of perfection: 141
Stanley, Abbey of: 160, 194; abbot of: 217, 220
star(s): 229; morning: 226
starvation, death by: 237
state, affairs of: 178
statesmanship: 5
Statuta: 170, 193
statutes, exceptions to: 170; reservations to: 170
Stephen Harding, St.: xxvii, xxix–xxxiii, xlv, xlviii, 37–38, 41–47, 49–50, 58, 62–76, 80, 82, 121–23, 226, 229; administration of: 45–46; as author of *Carta Caritatis*: 45, 66–67, 70–73; as founder of Cîteaux: 43–44; as founder of Tart: xl, 119; as glory of England: 44; breviary of: 123; death of: 63, 142, 229; doctrine of: 64; Feast of: 63–64, 123; letter of: 64; life of: xli, 37–38, 63, 121–23; trial of: 70, 80, 121–22; writings of: xxx–xxxi, 64–75, 121–22
Stephen Obazine, St.: 143
Stephen of Lexington, Abbot: lxiv, lxxi, 217–24, 245; as founder of College of St. Bernard: lxiv, 217–19; attack on: 221; character of: 220; deposition of: lxiv, 219–20; letters of: l, lxiv, lxxi, 221–24; persecution of: 219; plots against: 219
Stephen of St. Geneviève, Abbot: 172
Stiller, Colleen: lxxviii
stipends, Mass: lvi–lvii, 154
stock: 106
stone(s), boundary: 175; literal sense as: 131
Stone, Naomi Burton: ix
strangers: 18
Strata Florida, Abbey of: 196
strength, of soul: 228
strictness, apologia for: 75
structures, institutional: lxv
struggle(s): 201; between Cîteaux and first foundations: lix, 182–91; of Church: 150; over tithes: 110–11; physical: 163; political: 182; power: xxxvii; with adversaries: 94
students: 12, 86, 235–36; arrests of: 242; bold: 244; dormitory of: 243; irregular: 244; irregularities of: 242–44; parents of: 236; privileges of: 242; servants of: 243
studia generalia: 225, 230, 235–36
studies: lxiv, 32, 215, 225; at monasteries: 225; beginning of: 216–20; clerical: 216; danger of: lxvii, 246; divine: 215; houses of: 101, 217–19, 238; human: 215; legislation on: 190, 216; liberal: 82; of scripture: 226; organization of: 245; problem of: lxvi, lxx, 212–20, 231; program of: lxvii; progress of: 225; reform of: 238–41; regularizing of: 235–36
subdiaconate: 113
Subiaco: xx, 47
submission, mutual: xliv; to God: 135
subprior(s): 7, 101, 191, 250
suffering(s): 130; cosmic: xxv, 26; of Christ: xlii, 130
Summa Carta Caritatis: xxx, xlviii–xlix, 65, 67–68, 70, 72, 146, 183–84

sun, of salvation: 229
sunset: 89
superior(s): 216, 248; arbitrariness of: 231; capable: 220; Cistercian: 113; ecclesiastical: 113; good: 244; irresponsible: 232; local: 238; misuse of money by: 231; misuse of power by: 231; monastic: 86; obedience to: 215; of college: 243; worldliness of: 231
supper, paschal: xlii, 132
supplies: 80, 234
suppression, of religious orders: 179
surrender, of will: 136
suspension, immunity from: 112
suspicion: 233
Sussex: 197
Sweden: 125
Swedes: 241
sweetness: 130, 134; of Christ: xlii, 129; of contemplation: 226; of resurrection: 129
Swineshead, Abbey of: 168
Switzerland, Cistercian monasteries of: 148
Symons, Thomas, OSB: xvii, xxiii, 5, 7–8, 19–21
Syria: 104; Cistercian foundations in: 153
system, economic: 154; feudal: 22; grange: 197, 199

tabernacle: 24, 93
table: 133; abbot's: 117; heavenly: 132
tailors: 88
Talbot, C. H.: lv, 64, 104, 116, 128, 132, 160–61
Tart, Abbey of: xl, 63, 119
tavern: 221
taxes: 200, 202–203; exemption from: 100; payment of: 194
Taylor, Jerome: xxxv, 89–91, 93–94, 96–99
teachers, false: 224

teaching: 215; pastoral: xliii; spiritual: xliii
tears: 127–28
teeth: 91
Templars: 145
temple: 24; bodily: 136; destruction of: 136
temptation(s): xlv, 37, 95; of Christ: 134; wealth as: liv
Ten Bank: 209
tenderness: xli, 126
tent-making, art of: 214
tepidity: 57
Ter Doest, Abbey of: 167
Termes, Jacques de, Abbot: 240
Tescelin, father of St. Bernard: 123
thanksgiving: 19; to God: 222
Theodoret of Cyrrhus: xxv
theologian(s): 116; Cistercian: 239–41; professional: 239; solid: 239
theology: 99; as science: 182; fundamental: 241; knowledge of: lxiii, 212; monastic: xiv, xxv; moral: xxxii, 79, 241; serious: lxvi, 240; sound: lxvi, 223
Theresa of Portugal, St.: 121
things, divine: 137; heavenly: 137; spiritual: 23, 127, 137; temporal: 23, 180; true: 137
thirst, for righteousness: 132
Thomas à Kempis: 151
Thomas Aquinas, St.: xvi, 94
Thomas Merton Center: xviii–xix, lxxviii
Thomas of Luda: 220
thought, patristic: 213; speculative: 182; traditionalist: 213
throat: xxxvi, 93
thrones: 91
Thurston, Herbert, SJ: 46
tierce: 7, 9
time, before law: 94; in history: 89; increment of: 94; of grace: 94; of law: 94

Tirlemont: 153, 209
Tiron, Abbey of: xxvi, 30–31, 36
tithes: lvi, lxxi, 40, 47, 104–105, 154, 157, 161–68, 171–72; as source of conflict: 166–67; as source of income: 167–68; collection of: lvii, 165, 167–68; controversy over: 115; exemptions from: lvii, 110–11, 162–64, 166–67; freedom from: 162; from villages: 167; gifts of: 167; legislation on: 166; levying: 105; new: 163; on land: 154, 163; on new lands: 111; on others' work: 154; payment of: 162, 166–67; problem of: 162–68; refusal to pay: 111; renunciation of: 162; retention of: 165
toil, dignity of: 156
tombs, as source of income: 161
tongues: 92
topos: 21
Toulouse: lxxii, 218, 235; siege of: 100
tourists: 27
tournament: 37
towns: 83, 97, 202; growth of: 181
trade: lxi, 156, 181, 194; corn: 197; export: 197; facts of: lxii, 201; organized: 106, 157, 197–98; wool: xxxvii, lxi, lxx, 196–201
tradition(s), metaphysical: 215; monastic: xxi, 43; of Chartres: 215; outward: 179; philosophical: 215
tranquility: 60
transactions, honest: 170
Transfiguration, Feast of: 24
transgressions: 112
transitus: xlii
transubstantiation: 99
travelers: 84–85, 88, 173; robbery of by monks: 237
treatise(s), on immunities and privileges: 240; on moral theology: xxxii, 79
Trebnitz, Abbey of: 121

tree(s): lviii, 56, 108, 175
trends, new: 97
Trent, Council of: xlvii, lxix, lxxii, 231, 252; manuscript: 183–84
trial, by ordeal: 97
tribes: 92; Germanic: xxi
tricenary: 19
trina oratio: 7, 9, 11–12, 14, 16
Trinity, Blessed: 9, 14; and history: 97–98
triumphalism: lxxii
trope, Easter: 9–10, 17
tropers: 4
troublemakers, monastic: 179
Troyes: 38; bishop of: 189; library of: 214–15
trust, in God: xxxii; in providence: 80
truth: 181; highest: 98; knowledge of: 214
tuition: 236
tumults: 227
tunics, white: 217
Turin: 220
Turk, Josip (Ioseph): xxxi, 54–55, 65–67, 70–71, 73, 184, 205
Turks, Ottoman: 96, 233

Ughelli, Ferdinando: 241
Ugolino de Segni, Card.: 187
Umbald: 115
unanimity, enjoyment of: 190
undergarments: 40
understanding, spiritual: 129
uneasiness, of soul: 90
union, contemplative: lxxv; divine: 134; perfect: 136; personal: 136; visible: 179; with angels: 26; with Christ: ix, 26; with Church: 179; with God: xlviii, lxxv, 136, 178
unit, economic: 156
unity, among abbeys: 83; ecclesial: 210; in books: 83; in customs: 83; in food: 83; in spirit: 74; loss of: 29; man as:

Index 305

89; of all people: ix; of Christendom: 181; of Cistercian Order: 183; original: ix; with all humanity: lxxv; with creation: lxxv
universe, sacralized: 97
universities: lxiii, 142, 182, 216–19, 235, 242, 245; atmosphere of: lxvi, 243; rise of: lix
Urban II, Pope: xxviii, 48, 50–51, 57, 60, 69, 228
Urban IV, Pope: 109, 188–89
Urban V, Pope: 204
Urban VI, Pope: 251
usages, Cistercian: 65, 67, 120; monastic: 40, 42; of laybrothers: xxxiv, 87–88
usury: 200
Usus Conversorum: xviii, xxxii–xxxiv, 74, 82, 87–88, 145

Val de Choux, Priory of: 152–53
Val-Dieu, Abbey of: 212
Vallombrosans: 34
Van Engen, John: 90, 116
vanity: 76, 134; Cistercian: 118
Vargas, Martin de: 252
Vatican Council, Second: xliv, lxxii, lxxv
Vauclair, manuscript of: 168–69
vegetables: 124
ventures, business: 193; military: 209
Vergil: 98
vespers: 7–9, 14, 17
vessels, sacred: 23, 202
vicar: 161
vice(s): xxxii, 79; of flesh: 112; punishment of: xxxii, 79
Victor IV, Antipope: 145, 168
victory, Christian: xxxvi, 96
Vienne, bishop of: 122; Council of: 113, 225
views, progressive: 98
vigilance: 223

vigils: 23; choir: 87
Vikings: xxi, xxiii
village(s): 83, 106–107, 157, 162, 168–69; acquisition of: 171; as source of income: lvi–lvii, 104, 152, 154, 158, 167; buildings of: 158; eviction of: 199; inhabitants of: 158
villein: 108
Villers, Abbey of: 209; abbot of: 100, 153, 218
vine(s): 94, 156
vineyard(s): 52, 148, 165–66
Vinicus, hermitage of: 49, 58
violations, of letter: 158; of poverty: 152, 232–33; of regulation: 161–62; of spirit: 158
violence: 40, 172, 221; group: 248; of laybrothers: 247–48
virtue(s): xxxii, 40, 56, 68, 77; guardian of: 63; lovers of: 68; of mind: 227; of soul: 227
vision(s): 120; beatific: 94, 230; Benedictine: xxvii; blessed: 94; Cistercian: xlix, 41; eschatological: xxv; of angels: 81; of Christ: 79–81; of Daniel: 91–92; of dead: 80–81; of demons; 82; of heaven: 82; of hell: 82; of Mary: 80–81; of Mary Magdalene: 81–82; of peace: 105, 152; of St. Augustine: 82; of St. Elizabeth: 81
visits: 235
visitations: xxxiii, 45, 174, 232, 234–35; annual: 225; Cistercian: xxxiii, xxxvii, 45, 74–75, 86, 101–103, 211, 220, 250; episcopal: 110; legislation on: 190; process of: xxxvii, 86; regular: lxviii, 101, 103; special: 103; stipends for: 235
visitor(s): 86, 128, 221, 236; abbot: 235; admonitions of: 222; attendants of: 235; Cistercian: 120, 222; hospitality to: 235; rights of: 109
Vitalis of Savigny, St.: 36

vitality: 99; Cistercian: lxii, 142, 209; spiritual: 142, 209
vocation(s): ix, 150; contemplative: 150; lay: 99; mendicant: 150; monastic: lxi, 80; of laity: xxxvi; of laybrothers: 108, 154–55, 246–47; of monks: 193; of Rome: 95–96; prophecy of: 122; religious: lxxv
voices, falsetto: 86
vote: 113, 234
vows: 56, 69, 150; conferences on: xliv; private: 3; solemn: 230

Waddell, Chrysogonus, OCSO: xxx, xlviii–xlix, 51, 55, 64–68, 71, 140, 146, 183
wagon(s): 80, 195, 199
wakefulness: 79
Waldef, St.: 125–26
Waldensians: 99
Waldo, Peter: 99
Wales: 102, 156, 196, 248; north: 197
Walter of Châlons, Bp.: 44, 51–52
Walter of Ochies, Abbot: 207–208, 212
war(s): 28, 203; India-China: xliv; of religion: 29; pillaging of monasteries in: 237
Wardon, Abbey of: 160, 203
warehouses, urban: lxi
Warnefrid, Paul: 10–11
Warren (Guarinus, Guerin), St.: 38–39, 47, 58
water: 124; holy: 96
Waverly, Abbey of: 108, 203; abbot of: lxxiii, 203; size of: 153
way, of righteousness: 82; undefiled: 229
wealth, as temptation: liv; Cistercian: 142, 154, 197; monastic: 178
Wearmouth, Abbey of: 2
weavers, Flemish: 181
Wessex: 2
west: 89

Westbury, Abbey of: 8, 20
Whalley, Abbey of: 194
wheels: 91
whelps: 132
Whitby, Abbey of: 1; Synod of: 1
wickedness: 38
wife, bond with: xliii, 134
wilderness: 57, 156, 173; lover of: 80
Wilfrid, St.: 1–2; *Life* of: 26
will, disposition of: 136; divine: 136; of Christ: 136; surrender of: 136
Willems, Eugène: lxix, 42–43, 143–47
William, Duke of Aquitaine: 21–22
William of Biddleston: 195–96
William of Clairvaux: 78
William of Curti: 239
William of Malmesbury: xxvii–xxviii, 20, 41, 43–44, 46, 49, 53–54, 63–64, 80, 121
William of Poblet: 239
William of St.-Thierry: 140, 147, 213
William of Volpiano, Bl.: 29, 33
William the Conqueror, King: 32
William II of Cîteaux, Abbot: 207
Williams, Watkin: xxxii, 75–76, 79, 114
Willibald, Abbot: 2
Wilmart, André, OSB: 29, 116, 215
Winchester: 2; Abbey of: 4, 6; bishop of: 20; Council of: 3–4, 6, 8, 19–20
wind(s), four: 91
windows: 86
wine: 129–31, 161, 166, 200; bitter: xlii, 131
wine cellar: 134
Wireker, Nigel: lviii, 176–77
wisdom: xxxi, 5, 24, 70, 78, 82, 134
withdrawal: 31
Woburn, Abbey of: 102, 160
wold(s): 107, 157, 197
women: 83–84; at tomb: 131; holy: 131, 209; monasteries of: 144; mystics: xl, 120; role of: xlii, 132; saints: xl, 120–21, 246

Index 307

wool: 106, 157, 166, 197–201, 203; as cash crop: 199; as material of habit: 61; clip of: 203; crop of: 107, 157, 172, 200; dependence on: 199; English: 106, 157, 181, 197–201; for export: 106, 157; for resale: 107; graded: 157, 200; growers: 198; hair as: 91; lock: 200; market for: 157, 197; monastic: 199; price of: 201; producers of: lxi, 106; production: 198–99; sacks of: 107, 157, 200–201; sales of: 198, 202; surplus: 107, 157; trade: xxxvii, lxi, lxx, 106, 157, 196–201; unbleached: 61
woolmonger: 107, 157
Worcester, Abbey of: 3, 6; bishop of: 3
word, of God: 94, 127, 224; of life: 136; of salvation: 94; written: 88
work(s): lxxv, 7–8, 227; agricultural: 155; artistic: 23; Cistercian: 192, 226; farm: 155; field: 155; forest: 155; good: 209, 226; holy: 228; intellectual: 8; manual: 23, 40; necessary: 8; of brothers: xxxiv, lxviii, 87–88, 154–55, 208, 247, 249; of charity: lxii, lxv, 173, 208–209, 226; of edification: 240; of God: 56, 70, 227, 245; of Holy Spirit: 95; of monks: 154; parish: lxi, 193, 251; productive: 155; tithes on others': 154; transforming: 95; zealous: 155
workers, female: 83; laybrothers as: lxii, 207–208; secular: lxviii
world: xxv; ages of: 96; ambitions of: lx, 192; beyond monastery: xliv;

business: 150; business of: lx, 192; Cistercian involvement in: lx; closed: 91; conflicts of: lx, 192; confrontation of: 97; contemporary: xliv; death to: 137; decline of: 94; ecclesiastical: lx, 192; life of: lvi–lvii; litigations of: lx, 192; modern: lii; politico-religious: 95; profane: lx, 192; regions of: 229; remoteness from: l; Roman: 95–97; work in: 227
worldliness, of superiors: 231
worship: 25; divine: 226; of past: 179; splendor of: 25, 90; unreasonable: 179
Wright, T.: 176
writer(s), clerical: 173–77; spiritual: 29, 239
writing(s): 215; sacred: 224
Wulf, Alberic, ocso: xxxvii, 62–63, 67, 101–104, 125, 234, 249–51
Würzburg: 218
Wycliff, John: l, 177, 179, 239–40

York: 126, 195; archbishop of: 1, 5–6, 126, 161, 203
Yorkshire: lxi, 105, 125, 158, 160, 167, 197–99, 202; abbeys of: xli, 152, 159; Church in: 125

zeal: 18–19, 35, 226, 230; burning: 115; exaggerated: 81; excess of: 193; for prayer: 245

CORRIGENDA FOR VOLUME 8

Cistercian Fathers and Their Monastic Theology

Page 123, n. 470
FOR: Philibert Schmitz READ: F. S. Schmitt
FOR: Schmitz, 1:1 20 READ: Schmitt, 1:120

Page 448
FOR: 1/5/63 21 READ: 1/5/63 48
FOR: 1/19/63 24 READ: 1/19/63 54
FOR: 2/2/63 26 READ: 2/2/63 58
FOR: 2/9/63 31 READ: 2/9/63 68
FOR: 2/16/63 33 READ: 2/16/63 72
FOR: 2/23/63 33 READ: 2/23/63 74
FOR: 3/2/63 38 READ: 3/2/63 81
FOR: 3/9/63 38 READ: 3/9/63 82
FOR: 3/23/63 41 READ: 3/23/63 88
FOR: 3/30/63 43 READ: 3/30/63 92
FOR: 4/20/63 45 READ: 4/20/63 96
FOR: 4/27/63 38 READ: 4/27/63 81
FOR: 5/11/63 48 READ: 5/11/63 102
FOR: 5/18/63 49 READ: 5/18/63 103
FOR: 5/25/63 51 READ: 5/25/63 107
FOR: 6/15/63 51 READ: 6/15/63 108
FOR: 6/22/63 52 READ: 6/22/63 110
FOR: 7/13/63 55 READ: 7/13/63 117

Page 449
FOR: 7/20/63 55 READ: 7/20/63 117
FOR: 8/17/63 56 READ: 8/17/63 118
FOR: 8/31/63 57 READ: 8/31/63 121
FOR: 9/28/63 59 READ: 9/28/63 125

FOR: 10/5/63 60   READ: 10/5/63 127
FOR: 10/12/63 62   READ: 10/12/63 130
FOR: 10/19/63 64   READ: 10/19/63 136
FOR: 10/26/63 66   READ: 10/26/63 139
FOR: 11/9/63 66   READ: 11/9/63 139
FOR: 11/23/63 70   READ: 11/23/63 148
FOR: 1/11/64 77   READ: 1/11/64 160
FOR: 1/18/64 80   READ: 1/18/64 166
FOR: 2/8/64 84   READ: 2/8/64 175
FOR: 2/22/64 83   READ: 2/22/64 172
FOR: 2/29/64 84   READ: 2/29/64 176
FOR: 3/7/64 86   READ: 3/7/64 180
FOR: 3/14/64 87   READ: 3/14/64 180
FOR: 4/4/64 90   READ: 4/4/64 186
FOR: 4/11/64 90   READ: 4/11/64 187
FOR: 4/18/64 91   READ: 4/18/64 188
FOR: 5/2/64 92   READ: 5/2/64 181
FOR: 5/9/64 93   READ: 5/9/64 193
FOR: 5/16/64 95   READ: 5/16/64 197
FOR: 5/23/64 97   READ: 5/23/64 200
FOR: 5/30/64 100   READ: 5/30/64 206
FOR: 6/13/64 101   READ: 6/13/64 209
FOR: 6/20/64 8   READ: 6/20/64 15

Page 449
FOR: 6/27/64 10   READ: 6/27/64 19
FOR: 7/18/64 13   READ: 7/18/64 26
FOR: 8/8/64 110   READ: 8/8/64 224

www.ingramcontent.com/pod-product-compliance
Lightning Source LLC
Chambersburg PA
CBHW020637300426
44112CB00007B/145